Understanding **Child Language Acquisition**

Taking an accessible and cross-linguistic approach, *Understanding Child Language Acquisition* introduces readers to the most important research on child language acquisition over the last fifty years, as well as to some of the most influential theories in the field. Rather than just describing what children can do at different ages, Rowland explains why these research findings are important and what they tell us about how children acquire language.

Key features include:

- Cross-linguistic analysis of how language acquisition differs between languages
- A chapter on how multilingual children acquire several languages at once
- Exercises to test comprehension
- Chapters organised around key questions that discuss the critical issues posed by researchers in the field, with summaries at the end
- Further reading suggestions to broaden understanding of the subject

With its particular focus on outlining key similarities and differences across languages and what this cross-linguistic variation means for our ideas about language acquisition, *Understanding Child Language Acquisition* forms a comprehensive introduction to the subject for students of linguistics, psychology, and speech and language pathology.

Students and instructors will benefit from the comprehensive companion website (www.routledge.com/cw/rowland) that includes a students' section featuring interactive comprehension exercises, extension activities, chapter recaps and answers to the exercises within the book. Material for instructors includes sample essay questions, answers to the extension activities for students and PowerPoint slides including all the figures from the book.

Caroline Rowland is Professor of Developmental Psychology at the University of Liverpool. Her research focuses on how children acquire language, with a particular interest in grammar and in assessing how the child's environment promotes and shapes language growth. She is a series editor for the Trends in Language Acquisition (TiLAR) book series and an associate editor for the *Journal of Child Language*.

Understanding Language series

Series editors:

Bernard Comrie, Max Planck Institute for Evolutionary Anthropology, Leipzig, Germany
Greville Corbett, Surrey Morphology Group, University of Surrey, UK

The Understanding Language series provides approachable, yet authoritative, introductions to major topics in linguistics. Ideal for students with little or no prior knowledge of linguistics, each book carefully explains the basics, emphasising understanding of the essential notions rather than arguing for a particular theoretical position.

Other titles in the series:

Understanding Language Testing
Dan Douglas

Understanding Morphology, Second Edition
Martin Haspelmath
Andrea D. Sims

Understanding Phonetics
Patricia Ashby

Understanding Phonology, Third Edition
Carlos Gussenhoven
Haike Jacobs

Understanding Pragmatics
Jef Verschueren

Understanding Second Language Learning
Lourdes Ortega

Understanding Syntax, Third Edition
Maggie Tallerman

Understanding Semantics, Second Edition
Sebastian Löbner

For more information on any of these titles, or to order, go to www.routledge.com/linguistics

Understanding

Child Language Acquisition

Caroline Rowland

Routledge
Taylor & Francis Group

LONDON AND NEW YORK

First published 2014
by Routledge
2 Park Square, Milton Park, Abingdon, Oxon OX14 4RN

Simultaneously published in the USA and Canada
by Routledge
711 Third Avenue, New York, NY 10017

Routledge is an imprint of the Taylor & Francis Group, an informa business

British Library Cataloguing in Publication Data
A catalogue record for this book is available from the British Library

Library of Congress Cataloging in Publication Data
Rowland, Caroline, 1971-
    Understanding child language acquisition / Caroline Rowland.
        pages cm. -- (Understanding Language Series)
    Includes bibliographical references and index.
    1. Language acquisition. 2. Language awareness in children. I. Title.
    P118.R69 2013
    401'.93--dc23
    2013008620

ISBN: 978-0-415-82713-3 (hbk)
ISBN: 978-1-4441-5265-4 (pbk)
ISBN: 978-0-203-77602-5 (ebk)

Typeset in 11 on 12pt Minion by Phoenix Photosetting, Chatham, Kent

Printed and bound in Great Britain by
CPI Group (UK) Ltd, Croydon, CR0 4YY

For George, Lauren and Amy

Contents

Figures and tables

FIGURES

TABLES

Acknowledgements

The author and publishers would like to thank the following copyright holders for permission to reproduce the following material:

Figure 1.1, "Proposed relations between brain regions and symptoms of aphasia". Reproduced from Figure 19.13, p. 506 of Chapter 18, 'Memory' in Kolb, B. & Whishaw, I. Q. (2003). *Fundamentals of Human NeuroPsychology*. New York: Worth Publishers.

Figure 2.2, "Bimodal vs. unimodal distributions of [da]–[ta] stimuli during familiarisation". Reproduced from Figure 1, p. B104, Maye, J., Werker, J. F. & Gerken, L. (2002). Infant sensitivity to distributional information can affect phonetic perception. *Cognition, 82*, B101–B111.

Figure 3.1, "Categorisation of some object placements in English and Korean". Reprinted with the permission of Cambridge University Press from Figure 16.1, p. 482, of Bowerman, M. & Choi, S. (2001). Shaping meanings for language: Universal and language-specific in the acquisition of semantic categories. In M. Bowerman & S. C. Levinson (Eds), *Language acquisition and conceptual development*. Cambridge: Cambridge University Press.

Figure 5.4, "The basic structure of the single route model". Reprinted with permission from Figure 1, p. 222, Rumelhart, D. E. & McClelland, J. L. (1986). On learning the past tenses of English verbs. In J. L. McClelland, D. E. Rumelhart & the PDP Research Group (Eds), *Parallel Distributed Processing: Vol 2* (pp. 216–227). Cambridge, MA: MIT Press.

Figure 6.1, "Diagnostic criteria for autistic disorder". Reprinted with permission from *Diagnostic and Statistical Manual of Mental Disorders* (4th ed, Text Revision) Copyright ©2000. American Psychiatric Association.

Figure 7.1, "English vocabulary scores for monolingually developing children together with a) English and Spanish vocabulary scores for bilingually developing children and b) total vocabulary scores (English+Spanish) for bilingually developing children at 1;10, 2;1 and 2;6". Reproduced with permission from Figure 1 (p. 7) and Figure 2 (p. 8) in Hoff, E., Core, C., Place, S., Rumiche, R., Señor, M. & Parra, M. (2011). Dual language exposure and early bilingual development. *Journal of Child Language, 39*(1), 1–27.

Figure 9.1, "The Nicaraguan Sign Language signs (a) 'see' and (b) 'pay' produced in a neutral direction and spatially modulated to the signer's left". Reproduced with permission from Figure 1, p. 324, of Senghas, A. & Coppola, M. (2001). Children creating language: How Nicaraguan Sign Language acquired a spatial grammar. *Psychological Sciences, 12*(4), 323–328.

While the publishers have made every effort to contact copyright holders of material used in this volume, they would be grateful to hear from any that were unavailable.

Preface

The goal of this book is to introduce the reader to child language acquisition. Here, the reader will find a discussion of the most exciting findings to emerge over the last 50 years or so, as well as some of the most influential theories of language acquisition. Rather than just describing what children can do at different ages, the aim is to explain why the research findings are important and what they tell us about how children acquire language. There is a particular emphasis on outlining key similarities and differences across languages and what this cross-linguistic variation means for our ideas about language acquisition.

The chapters are organised around key questions that summarise the critical issues posed by researchers in the field. Each chapter begins with a section that explains what the issues are, followed by a discussion of the theories and research evidence relevant to each key question. Each chapter closes with a summary that reviews the current 'state of play' in regard to each key question and makes suggestions for further reading.

Readers will not need a background in linguistics or psychology or, indeed, any prior knowledge of research in language acquisition. However, the book is also suitable as a first-base textbook for more advanced readers looking for a summary of the debates and evidence in the field. For these readers, the textbook can be used in conjunction with the discussion articles available online and the suggestions for further reading given at the end of each chapter.

Online resources for teachers and students accompany this book on the companion website, www.routledge.com/cw/rowland. These include PowerPoint slides of the illustrations, summaries of each chapter, a list of key articles together with questions to stimulate discussion, practical exercises that provide the reader with first-hand experience of analysing data, and suggested essay titles. These activities can be completed independently or used as discussion points for small group debates. They could also be used as the basis for verbal presentations if required.

Many people have given up their time to help with the writing of this book. Grateful thanks are due to Anna Theakston, Ben Ambridge, Eileen Graf, Elena Lieven, Evan Kidd, Julian Pine, Ludovica Serratrice, Marilyn Vihman, Nameera Akhtar and Tamar Keren-Portnoy who gave invaluable comments, corrected mistakes, suggested additional references and, generally, checked that I had not misinterpreted their work or that of their colleagues. Extremely grateful thanks go to the series editors, Greville Corbett and Bernard Comrie, as well as John Hadwin and Mildred Hadwin, who read and commented on every single chapter. This book would never have been written without the help of these lovely people.

Introduction to child language acquisition

1.1 THE ISSUE

In the first volume of his autobiography, *My Family and other Animals*, the naturalist Gerald Durrell tells of his idyllic childhood in Corfu and how it inspired his love of the natural world. In his book, Durrell applies his gentle, good-humoured observational power to both the people of the island and its wildlife. The behaviour of the people around him is discussed in the same affectionate but dispassionate terms as the hunting behaviour of a spider or the maternal instincts of an earwig. The humour in the book comes, of course, from the incongruity of applying the same narrative formula to humans and to other animals. The people of Corfu are very different from its wildlife, not least because they are capable of reading, and presumably protesting against, Durrell's descriptions of them. In essence, humans have language and other animals do not.

Researchers have spent many years arguing about how to characterise the differences between human and animal communication. However, all agree that human language is more complex, more sophisticated and more powerful than any other animal communication system. Not even dolphins or chimpanzees come close. Yet human children seem to acquire this system without any apparent effort. It has become a trite phrase, but it is no less true for that: human children acquire the most complex communication system known to man before they learn to tie their shoelaces.

How do children do this? How do children acquire language? The short answer is we do not know. We are not even close to an answer. So the aim of this book is not to answer this question for you but to try to convince you that the journey of discovery itself is a fascinating one. Here you will find the big questions that intrigue those of us who listen to children talk and marvel at their achievements. We will cover as many of the great debates as we can. How do children learn to produce the sounds of their language? How do they learn to associate words with meanings? How do they acquire the rules of grammar? Why do children differ in the speed of their language acquisition? Is there a critical period for language acquisition? What innate knowledge do children bring to the task? How do children fare who acquire two languages at once? For each of the big questions we will discover the theories that have been devised and we will debate the evidence that supports or discredits them. By the end of this book, you will not have an indisputable answer to the question of how children acquire language, I'm afraid. However, you should have a better understanding of the possibilities and, hopefully, will have developed some theories and solutions of your own.

1.2   WHAT IS LANGUAGE?

The phrase 'acquiring a language' implies that language is a unitary thing. The implication is that we simply have to master one thing – language – and we are done. However, this trivialises the task. In fact, language has many facets, so when we talk about acquiring a language we are actually talking about learning a whole range of different skills and acquiring many different types of knowledge. Thus, in order to understand what it means to 'acquire a language', the first key question we must consider is this:

Key question: what skills and knowledge do children have to master in order to acquire a language?

The short answer is that a number of skills and abilities are required. First children have to learn to distinguish speech sounds from other noises so that they know which sounds to pay attention to. So they need to distinguish, for example, between human speech and birdsong and between human speech and other human sounds such as whistling or humming. Then, once they have learnt to recognise these speech sounds, they have to learn to produce them by manipulating the passage of air through their vocal tract and mouth using precise sequences of lips, tongue and vocal cord movements.

That is just the start of the process though. Children then have to learn how to combine speech sounds into meaningful words. This is trickier than you might think. When a child hears her mother cry *look, rabbit!* how does the child know what her mother is referring to? She may be referring to the animal she just saw scurrying by, but the word could equally as easily mean *animal, mammal, grass, beautiful sunset* or even *dinner*. So matching words to referents is not an easy matter and takes children quite a while.

However, even that is not the end of the process. Once children have discovered the meaning of words, they need to work out how words fit together into sentences. They have to learn that changes in meaning may be signalled by sequencing words in different ways: *man bites dog* is newsworthy, *dog bites man* is not. They have to learn that adding certain endings to words changes their meaning in precise but subtle ways; for example, by turning *kick* into *kicked* we indicate that the kicking action took place in the past. They also have to learn how to express and understand the hidden meaning behind words and sentences. They have to learn, for example, that the expression *can you pass the salt?* does not simply require the answer *yes* but is an implicit request to carry out the action. Finally, children have to learn to string their thoughts together in a coherent way in order to hold a conversation and to respond appropriately to the sentences of others.

1.2.1 Language or languages?

All the skills described in the previous paragraph must be mastered in order to acquire a language. However, strictly speaking we should be talking about acquiring languages, rather than acquiring a language, because there are thousands of different languages, each with very different characteristics. The most obvious difference is in our vocabulary. A rose by any other name must smell as sweet, since a rose really does have many other names. The Spanish call it *una rosa*, to Arabic speakers it is *warda* and in Japanese it is *bara*. However, vocabulary differences are just the beginning. There are differences on all levels; in the sounds of the language, in the way in which words are combined and in the way in which language is used. For example, Zulu learners have to learn to produce click consonants that sound, to English speakers, just like a bottle top popping off a bottle.

To illustrate, here is a comparison of two languages, English and Turkish (based on descriptions in the chapters by de Villiers and de Villiers and Aksu-Koç and Slobin in Slobin, 1985). English is described as a word order language, because the order of words in a sentence is the primary determinant of the meaning of the sentence. Thus, the simple sentence *the man bites the dog* has a very different meaning from the sentence *the dog bites the man* because the basic word order of English is SUBJECT-VERB-OBJECT (SVO), as in *the man* (SUBJECT) *bites* (VERB) *the dog* (OBJECT). Because English is a word order language, words can be re-ordered in systematic ways to convey different meanings. For example, English also has passives (*the man was bitten by the dog*), wh-questions (*who did the dog bite?*), negatives (*the dog didn't bite the man*) and imperatives (*bite the man!*) as well as many other structures. English also has an inflectional system, in which markers (suffixes) are added to the ends of words to modify their meanings (e.g. *kick* becomes *kicked* to signify that the action took place in the past). However, the inflectional system of English is very simple. Nouns are marked only for plurality and possession, allowing us to say *the dogs* (plural) and *the dog's bite* (possessive). Verbs too have very little inflectional marking, which means that verb conjugation tables look very simple in English compared to those of most other languages. For example:

I bite

You bite

He/she/it bite<u>s</u>

We bite

You (pl) bite

They bite

Turkish also has a default word order, which is SUBJECT-OBJECT-VERB (SOV). However, unlike in English, in Turkish, changing the word order does not necessarily change the meaning of the sentence, although it does allow speakers to highlight different parts of the sentence. So to a Turkish speaker, *man bites dog, dog bites man* and even *man dog bites* could all refer to an incident in which a man bites a dog. This is possible because Turkish has a very sophisticated inflectional system in which different endings added to nouns and verbs convey who did what to whom. The example below, taken from Aksu-Koç and Slobin (1985), shows how a number of different inflectional markers can be added to the noun *hand* (*el*). These markers are always added in a particular order, so that the original noun (the stem) becomes longer as more are added.

El	'hand'
El-ler	'hands'
El-ler-im	'my hands'
El-ler-de	'in hands'
El-ler-im-de	'in my hands'

Because nouns and verbs contain all this information within their suffixes, it is possible to re-order the words of a sentence and still convey the sentence's meaning.

Not surprisingly, English and Turkish children show different patterns of language acquisition. For example, English children's early sentences tend to be combinations of bare stem forms without inflection markers (see de Villiers & de Villiers, 1985). So a two-year-old will produce something like *Daddy book* instead of *Daddy's book* or *two chair* instead of *two chairs* (see Brown, 1973 for more examples). English children's early speech also lacks the 'little words' of the language; words like *a, the, of, in, is, are* (determiners, prepositions, auxiliaries). So *sit chair* will be produced instead of *sit in the chair*, or *this telephone* instead of *this is my telephone*.

Brown (1973) called this early speech 'Stage 1' speech and observed that it is not until 'Stage 2', a few months later, that the markers and 'little words' start to appear in children's speech. Stage 2 speech is still short and simple, but sounds more adultlike because of the presence of these morphemes. In Brown's words, all the morphemes "like an intricate sort of ivy, begin to grow up between and upon the major construction blocks, the nouns and verbs, to which Stage I is largely limited" (Brown, 1973, p. 289).

In Turkish, by contrast, the markers and 'little words' appear much earlier (see Aksu-Koç & Slobin, 1985). Noun and verb inflections are common in the very earliest stages of development, even before the children are putting words together into sentences. In fact, Aksu-Koç and Slobin suggest that children as young as 15 months show some understanding of how to use inflections. Thus, although young children's utterances are short and relatively simple, they "do not have the familiar 'child language' look evidenced in most other languages" (Aksu-Koç & Slobin, 1985, p. 845).

It is also important to note that differences across languages are not the only differences between children. There are also individual differences between children acquiring the same language; some children are faster and others are slower, and some children are born with cognitive impairments that prevent them from acquiring language without a lot of specialist help. We also must not forget that in much of the world, children acquire two or more languages simultaneously. So we need to consider how learning two languages at once differs from learning one language at a time.

That said, no one would dispute that English, Turkish and all the other thousands of languages in the world can all be described as languages. So what do all these languages have in common that allows us to call them languages? What makes a language a language?

1.2.2 What makes a language?

In the 1960s, Charles Hockett set out to define the characteristics of language. He initially proposed 13 *design features* of language, but these were later extended to 16. He argued that "there is solid empirical justification for the belief that all the languages of the world share every one of them" (Hockett, 1982, p. 6) Although some of these design features are shared by other animal communication systems, only human languages are said to have all the features.

Table 1.1
Hockett's design features of language (Hockett, 1963; Hockett & Altmann, 1968)

Feature	Description
Vocal-auditory channel (Manual-visual channel added in 1968 to incorporate sign languages)	Language is composed of spoken sounds that are transmitted to the ears and auditory channels.
Broadcast transmission and directional reception	Speech sounds radiate in all directions so that they can be perceived by any listener. However, the listener can determine the direction from which the sound comes (and thus can determine the identity of the speaker).
Rapid fading	Speech sounds are transitory; they do not last very long.
Interchangeability	Any human can reproduce any aspect of language they hear, regardless of age and gender. This is quite unusual in nature (e.g. female birds do not reproduce the mating calls of male birds).
Complete feedback	Speakers can monitor their own speech at every level, allowing them to make minute adjustments to ensure clarity and to catch and correct speech errors.
Specialisation	The organs used for producing speech are specially adapted for language (lips, tongue, vocal tract) and the ear and auditory tract are specially sensitive to speech sounds.
Semanticity	Language carries meaning. In particular, words carry a particular fixed meaning that is shared among communities. For example, the word *salt* means salt and only salt. It cannot be used to refer to sugar or pepper.

Feature	Description
Arbitrariness	Although words carry fixed meaning, there is no intrinsic reason why any word is linked to a particular meaning. Although some words sound like their meanings (*crack, hiss*), most words do not. This is why different languages can use different words to refer to the same object (e.g. *dog/ chien/Hund*).
Discreteness	Language is made up of a string of discrete sounds chained together. Each of these sounds varies only minimally from others, but we perceive them as very different.
Displacement	We can talk about things that are remote in time and space (e.g. the past, the future, things that are not physically present).
Productivity	We can create and understand words and sentences that have never before been uttered. We create new sentences by combining words in new ways and we create novel uses for familiar words (e.g. *text* was originally a noun but is now used as a verb, e.g. *text me*).
Traditional transmission	Language is transmitted from one generation to the next in the traditional way, by learning and teaching.
Duality of patterning	Language exists on two levels. On one level are words, which carry meaning. On the other level, these words are made up of speech sounds (phonemes) which carry no meaning.
Prevarication (added by Hockett & Altmann, 1968)	Language can convey imaginary information (e.g. lies, stories, hypothetical entities).
Reflexiveness (added by Hockett & Altmann, 1968)	Language can be used to talk about language itself (metalinguistic ability).
Learnability (added by Hockett & Altmann, 1968)	Humans, at least when they are young, have the ability to learn any new languages, not just the language of their biological parents.

Hockett's design features are summarised in table 1.1 but it is worth looking at four of them in more detail. The first is *semanticity*. By this Hockett was referring to the idea that languages contain symbols (words) that carry a fixed meaning that is shared among members of a community. Thus, although different languages have different words to refer to a *rose*, all speakers of the same language must use the same word. Otherwise, successful communication cannot take place. It is important, too, that words do not refer to specific objects but to a whole category of objects. Thus the word *rose* can be used to refer to any rose in the world, not just a particular rose in my garden. This is crucial because a language that required us to dream up a different word for every single object in the world (every leaf, every flower, every tree) would simply be unlearnable.

A second important design feature is *arbitrariness*. Most words have no intrinsic relationship at all with the objects they represent. For example, there is no particular reason why the word *rose* should be the one we use to refer to that particular flower.

In fact, in other languages, a different word is chosen. The word *rose* carries its meaning simply because we – the community of English speakers – have decided that it is so. If we wanted, we could unanimously decide to swap the words *rose* and *daffodil* around so that the word *rose* was used to describe a daffodil and vice versa. The only consequence would be the expense of re-setting and re-publishing dictionaries and gardening books. As long as everyone agreed to the change, we would still be able to communicate successfully about flowers.

A third design feature is *productivity*. Humans are immensely creative with their language, inventing new words all the time, keeping dictionary compilers on their toes. Eighty-six new words were added to the Collins Online English Dictionary in 2012, including *floordrobe* (a pile of clothes left on the floor of a room), *hangry* (the irritability that results from the feeling of hunger) and *amazeballs* (an exclamation expressing enthusiastic approval; see http://www.collinsdictionary.com/). However, creativity is not restricted to new words. There is another type of creative ability that humans use every day in their language, instinctively. This is the ability to produce completely new sentences at will, and to comprehend novel sentences produced by others. For example, in 1957, Chomsky created the sentence *colourless green ideas sleep furiously* in order to demonstrate that sentences can be both grammatically correct and meaningless at the same time (Chomsky, 1957). Chomsky's sentence is now legendary, but any speaker can create a whole raft of similar sentences just as quickly and easily as Chomsky: *colourless green ideas slept furiously yesterday*, *who knows why colourless ideas sleep furiously*, *did colourless green ideas sleep furiously or gently?* All languages carry this creative power.

A fourth important design feature is *displacement*. This refers to the fact that humans can talk about events that are remote in time and space. With language, we can talk about events in the past or in the future as easily as we talk about events in the present. This means that I can invite you to a party next week as easily as I can thank you for attending my party last night. We can also talk about events that are remote in space; events that occur in far off places like the moon or on Mars. We can even talk about concepts that do not actually exist in any physical sense, such as truth, justice and the American way. In other words, all languages allow us to discuss events that are displaced from our immediate context.

Hockett's design features neatly and effectively capture the characteristic features of human languages. Let us suppose that next week, an intrepid adventurer happens upon a new isolated tribe in the remote Amazonian jungle. It is highly probable that this tribe's system of communication will contain all of Hockett's design features. In fact, most linguists would probably be willing to bet money on it.

However, although Hockett's design features may be universal across all human languages, they may not be unique to human languages. Honey bees, for example, use a complex system of dance moves and tail waggles to communicate the direction and distance of new sources of nectar from the hive (von Frisch, 1954). Bee communications, then, clearly demonstrate the feature of displacement, communicating information about a distant location. Perhaps, then, language is not unique to humans.

1.3 HUMANS AND OTHER ANIMALS

(Bark bark.) What's that, Lassie? You say Timmy fell down the well? Lassie was the canine star of a twentieth century TV series and was famously capable of communicating complex messages with just a single bark. Real life animals are less stylish communicators. However, that is not the same as saying they have limited communicative abilities. Many animal communication systems are very sophisticated indeed. Is it appropriate, then, to describe the communication systems of other animals as languages? And could animals learn human language given the right circumstances? In other words:

Key question: are humans the only animals that can acquire a language?

1.3.1 Can we teach language to animals?

Over the decades, researchers have tried to teach language to apes, parrots and dogs. Initial attempts focussed on teaching apes to speak, but these were frustrated by the fact that the structure of the ape vocal tract prevents them producing many speech sounds. More successful attempts have come from programmes using sign languages or lexigrams, which are visual symbols representing words (see, for example, Gardner, Gardner & Van Cantfort, 1989; Savage-Rumbaugh et al., 1993).

The most successful attempts come when very young apes are exposed to language in much the same manner as human infants. For example, Savage-Rumbaugh's star bonobo – Kanzi – was not taught language explicitly but was exposed to it in naturalistic surroundings "to determine what he could learn on his own" (Savage-Rumbaugh et al., 1993, p. 45). In fact, Kanzi's first exposure to language came about by accident. Savage-Rumbaugh and her team were trying to teach Kanzi's mother to comprehend spoken English and to reproduce English words using a lexigram board (a board showing visual symbols representing words). So Kanzi was exposed to language from about six months of age simply because he accompanied his mother to these sessions. By two years of age he began to show evidence of understanding speech, and by two and a half he was spontaneously using the lexigram board to communicate with humans himself.

The researchers decided not to train Kanzi explicitly but to talk to and communicate with him naturally, much as one would with a human child. Every day during the summer, human caregivers would accompany Kanzi into the 50 acre forest that surrounded the laboratory. In the winter, Kanzi would play indoors; painting, helping to cook, watching television and playing with other apes. All of these everyday activities were accompanied by caretakers who talked to him in "any way that seemed natural to the caretakers" (Savage-Rumbaugh et al., 1993, p. 46). They talked to him about topics that he found interesting and about everyday tasks like finding food. They carried the lexigram board at all times so that they could point to the relevant symbols on the board as they talked and so that Kanzi could use the board to respond. By the age of five this technique had paid off. Kanzi could use over 100 symbols on his lexigram keyboard. He could learn new words relatively quickly and could even combine words into simple two and three word utterances to convey very specific meanings:

> When Kanzi says 'peanut hide' and looks at your pocket, he is asking you if you have peanuts. If he says 'peanut hide' and drops some peanuts on the ground into a clump of grass, he is talking about what he is doing – hiding peanuts. And if he says 'peanut hide' and takes you to the staff office and points to the cabinets, he is trying to tell you that he wants some of the peanuts that are kept there.
>
> (Savage-Rumbaugh, 1999, p. 139)

Kanzi also has a preferred word order, which tells us that he is not simply combining words randomly. For example, he is much more likely to produce an ACTOR+ACTION pattern (e.g. *Kanzi eat*) than an ACTION+ACTOR pattern (*eat Kanzi*; see Greenfield & Savage-Rumbaugh, 1990). He also tends to produce action words in the order in which he wants the actions to be carried out, so *chase tickle* means that he wants to be chased and then tickled (Savage-Rumbaugh et al., 1993).

There is very little dispute about what apes like Kanzi can do. They can understand and use many different words. They can combine words into simple sentences and they can respond to simple sentences appropriately. The disputes come when we consider whether these abilities stem from the same underlying language learning mechanism as the abilities of children. Can we conclude from these studies that apes and humans share similar language learning abilities? Or do the abilities of apes stem from different mechanisms? The debate has been heated at times. Personal insults have been known to fly. In fact, the debate has been termed 'the chimp wars' by many commentators.

One important question concerns the underlying relationship between a word and the object it represents. Critics claim that it is possible to train an ape to associate a word with an object in the same way it is possible to train a rat to associate pressing a lever with obtaining food. However, this is an associative relationship between a word and an object. In human languages, words are not simply associated with objects, they actually symbolise the object itself. Because words are symbols, we can use them flexibly to talk about objects in a variety of situations. We can not only request objects (*banana please*) but we can also comment on objects' existence (*there's a banana*), their location (*the banana is here*), their attributes (*this banana is black*) or even offer the object to another (*would you like my banana?*). The critics claim that apes are not using the word to symbolise the object. They have merely learnt to associate the word with the object, which allows them to use the word to obtain the object in the same way that a rat can learn to press a lever to obtain food (see for example Seidenberg & Petitto, 1987).

This criticism is more obviously valid in some cases than others. For example, it may apply to attempts to teach language to dogs. Kaminski and colleagues have tested the vocabulary of a dog called Rico, and have reported that he understands over 200 words (Kaminski, Call & Fischer, 2004). However, Rico's understanding was only tested in the context of fetching the objects from a different room and it is not at all clear whether he can generalise this knowledge to other contexts. For example, Bloom asks "can Rico follow an instruction *not* to fetch an item, just as one can tell a child not to touch something?" (P. Bloom, 2004, p. 1606). The validity of the criticism is harder to judge in other cases. Kanzi the bonobo uses his words more flexibly than Rico. For example, Savage-Rumbaugh reports that he uses the lexigram for *strawberry* in a variety of different contexts. He can use it to ask to go to the place where strawberries grow and to label a picture of strawberries. The latter is particularly important because Kanzi is not using the word as a means to get what he wants in this case. He is simply using it to name a familiar object in a picture, which seems more like the symbolic relationship we see between words and objects in human language (Savage-Rumbaugh, MacDonald, Sevcik, Hopkins & Rubert, 1986).

Another criticism of the ape language studies focusses on the complexity of the sentences produced by apes. This criticism is also clearly valid in the sense that apes cannot produce grammatical sentences of the same complexity as children. Even young children can produce some quite complex grammatical sentences. However, ape sentences simply become more repetitive as they get longer (e.g. *me Nim eat me, drink eat me Nim, eat grape eat Nim*; Terrace, 1979). Apes and humans clearly differ in their ability to string words together into meaningful sentences.

However, the situation is less clear when it comes to comprehending sentences. Savage-Rumbaugh compared Kanzi's comprehension abilities with those of a two-year-old girl called Alia and concluded that "both ... comprehended novel requests and simple syntactic devices" to an equivalent degree (Savage-Rumbaugh et al., 1993, p. v). In this study, both Kanzi and Alia were presented with the same sentence types, both were tested in familiar surroundings by familiar adults, and the responses of both were coded using the same robust coding scheme. Under these strictly controlled conditions, the researchers reported similar comprehension abilities for both species and even, sometimes, better abilities in the ape than in the child. For example, Kanzi was very good at interpreting reversed sentence pairs in which the same objects and locations were mentioned but the action required the objects to be acted upon in reverse order. For example, the command *take the potato outdoors* required that Kanzi first pick up the potato and then take it outside. The command *go outdoors and get the potato* required that Kanzi first go outside and then find a potato to bring indoors. Kanzi responded to these commands correctly about 74 per cent of the time. Interestingly, Alia only responded correctly 38 per cent of the time, showing that Kanzi's ability to understand these sentences was better than Alia's.

It could be argued that Kanzi does not need to understand English grammar to respond to the commands in this study. After all, if you were given a dog and a snake and then asked to *make the dog bite the snake* you might guess what to do even if the only word you understood was *bite*. So the critics suggest that Kanzi was simply guessing what he was expected to do. Savage-Rumbaugh has argued vehemently that this alone cannot explain Kanzi's performance, particularly his success with the reversible sentences above or with unusual sentences such as *feed your ball some tomato* (Savage-Rumbaugh, Rumbaugh & Fields, 2009). However, the critics are not yet convinced.

In addition, although Kanzi's abilities are impressive, it must not be forgotten that he was eight years old at the time of testing whereas Alia was only two years old. Alia's development was undoubtedly much faster and I have no doubt that her abilities as an adult now far outstrip those of Kanzi. It is important to remember that the debate concerns which aspects of the potential for language acquisition are shared across species not whether animals can develop the same sophisticated linguistic abilities as humans. No one, as far as I am aware, has ever suggested that animals can develop a communication system as powerful as human language as quickly and as easily as humans can.

1.3.2   Animal communication systems

The chimp wars continue to produce very interesting data but this is not the only strand of relevant comparative research. Other work focusses on whether animal communication systems share some of the features of human languages. Many animals communicate with each other. Dogs bark to warn others of the presence of an intruder. Cats hiss and arch their backs to ward off threats. Lambs bleat in order to call to their mothers. These are very simple forms of communication, but there are also some quite complex communication systems in the animal kingdom, some of which contain some of Hockett's design features. Would it be legitimate to call these languages?

For example, dolphins use physical contact, gestures and vocal sounds for communication (Dudzinski, Thomas & Gregg, 2008). They nuzzle each other, administer playful or aggressive bites, pet each other with their pectoral fins and even smack each other on the head. Frustration or anger can be communicated with a bobbing of the head or an opening of the mouth. Dolphins also use vocal sounds such as whistles, screams, squawks and chirps to communicate emotional states and information about their age, gender or reproductive state to other dolphins. In fact, in Laguna in Brazil, dolphins and humans communicate to catch fish, coordinating their hunting efforts. The dolphins herd shoals of fish towards the shallow water where the fishermen stand with their nets and then jump out of the water to signal to the fishermen that the fish are close.

Most highly social animals have communication systems. Bees dance to communicate the direction and distance of food from the hive (von Frisch, 1954). Vervet monkeys have distinct alarm calls to signal the presence of different predators (leopards, eagles, pythons and baboons; Seyfarth, Cheney & Marler, 1980). Gibbon mated pairs sing duets in the early morning to strengthen their pair bond (Geissmann & Orgeldinger, 2000). Chimpanzees use over a hundred hand gestures to communicate concepts to do with feeding, nursing, fighting and reproduction (Call & Tomasello, 2007). Bengalese finches produce songs made up of strings of syllable-like motifs that have been compared to human grammars (Abe & Watanabe, 2011). Many of these communication systems illustrate aspects of Hockett's design features. The bee dance communicates the location of food sources distant from the hive, illustrating *displacement*. Vervet monkey alarm calls demonstrate *arbitrariness* as there is no intrinsic relationship between the sound of the call and the predator it represents. Bengalese finch songs are made up of strings of discrete sounds chained together, thus illustrating *discreteness*.

However, unlike human languages, no animal communication system demonstrates all of Hockett's design features. For example, vervet monkeys do not invent new calls for new predators or string calls together to convey different meanings (*productivity*) or use their calls to reflect on and talk about the calls themselves (*reflexiveness*). Animal communication systems also differ in scope from human languages. Chimpanzees have hundreds of gestures but human languages have tens of thousands of words. Bees can combine the features of their dances and tail waggles in different ways to convey different information but they cannot invent a new type of tail waggle in the same way that we invent new words. Unfortunately, dogs like Lassie, whose barks were miraculously interpreted by her owners despite the complexity of the message, do not exist. Thus, there are few who would argue that animal communication systems are the same as human languages.

1.3.3 Shared aspects of language

We have one final issue to address in our discussion of the differences between humans and animals: whether some of the mechanisms and abilities required for language acquisition also occur in other species. The simple answer to this question is this: some of these mechanisms and abilities occur in other species. However, that is not a very informative answer. We really need to know which aspects of our abilities are shared with other animals. This is where the difficulties lie. This debate will be covered in more depth in other chapters, but it is worth mentioning briefly here.

Some of our language learning abilities are clearly shared by other species in the animal world. For example, an important feature of the human language system is categorical perception. This refers to humans' ability to register some differences in speech sounds and ignore others. For example, English speakers will always register the difference between /p/ and /b/.[1] This allows us to distinguish between words that contain /p/ and those that contain /b/, such as *pat* and *bat*. However, our auditory system filters out any acoustic differences in the signal caused by the same speech sound (e.g. /p/) being produced by different speakers or different rates of speech. This means that no matter who produces the word *pat*, we will still hear it as *pat*. This ability is called categorical perception.

Categorical perception is centrally important in language acquisition but it is also shared by other animals. For example, chinchillas (small furry rodents) were trained by Kuhl and Miller to respond categorically to stimuli ranging across a continuum from [da] at one end to [ta] at the other (Kuhl & Miller, 1975). The chinchillas responded in much the same way as English speakers, suggesting that they too were capable of categorical perception.

However, it is not clear how similar human and animal abilities are in this respect. Chinchillas need to be exposed to thousands of training trials before they learn to perceive phonemes categorically whereas human infants do it with very little

---

1   When we want to refer to discrete speech sounds (phonemes), we sandwich the letter between two slash signs (/). So /p/ refers to the phoneme *p* as in *pat*.

training. There is also the fact that many speech sounds are perceived differently by humans and non-human animals (see Sinnott, 1998). So it is not the case that animals respond in exactly the same way as humans to speech sounds. In other words, other species may share some aspects of the human language learning mechanisms, but this does not mean that they have the same underlying abilities or utilise the mechanisms in the same way.

In sum, our foray into the animal world has been revealing but has not changed the underlying message with which we began: human language is more complex, more sophisticated and more powerful than other animal communication systems. Yet human children seem to acquire this system without any apparent effort. The next question we must consider, then, concerns why this is the case. What is it that allows humans to acquire a language?

1.4 GETTING THE CONDITIONS RIGHT

Animals find it difficult to learn human languages even with extensive training. Children find it easy. Why is this? What do children possess that allow them to acquire language? In other words:

Key question: what is required in order for children to acquire a language?

This question is central to the nature–nurture debate, the debate over the relative contribution of genes and the environment to development. On one level the answer is very simple: both nature and nurture contribute to language acquisition. In Karmiloff-Smith's words: "All scientists … from the staunchest Chomskian nativist to the most domain-general empiricist … agree that development involves contributions from both genes and environment" (Karmiloff-Smith, 1998, p. 389). However, questions about how nature and nurture contribute and how these contributions interact throughout development are still hotly debated. Many of these debates will be discussed in more detail later in this book. In what follows we will simply summarise some of the ideas from the literature about what may need to be built into our genes (nature) and what we may need from our environment (nurture) in order to acquire language.

1.4.1 The language centres of the brain

The first thing required to acquire a language is a human brain. There is no doubt that human language would not be possible if the human brain was wired up in a different way.

Interestingly, there is robust evidence that the brain processes language in a very similar way no matter what the language is. We now have evidence from a range of European and Asian languages, including English, French, Italian, German, Finnish, Mandarin Chinese and Japanese. In all of these languages, the same 'language areas' of the brain seem to respond in similar ways to language tasks (Cabeza & Nyberg,

Figure 1.1
Proposed relations between brain regions and symptoms of aphasia. Note these relations are different from those originally proposed by Broca and Wernicke. Reproduced from Kolb and Whishaw (2003, p. 506, Figure 19.13).

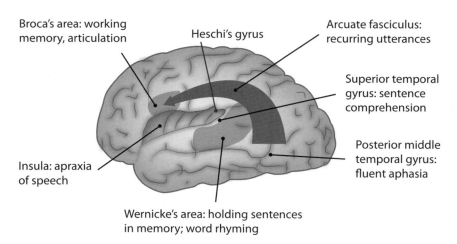

Broca's area: working memory, articulation

Heschi's gyrus

Arcuate fasciculus: recurring utterances

Superior temporal gyrus: sentence comprehension

Insula: apraxia of speech

Posterior middle temporal gyrus: fluent aphasia

Wernicke's area: holding sentences in memory; word rhyming

2000; Chee et al., 2000; Crozier et al., 1999; Friederici, Ruschemeyer, Hahner & Fiebach, 2003; Homae, Hashimoto, Nakajima, Miyashita & Sakai, 2002; Indefrey, Hagoort, Herzog, Seitz & Brown, 2001; Laine, Rinne, Krause, Tereas & Sipilea, 1999; Moro et al., 2001).

First, it is clear that the brain tends to be *lateralised* for language. This means that the left hemisphere does most of the work processing language. Thus, damage to certain areas in the left hemisphere often results in the patient being diagnosed with aphasia (a language disorder resulting from brain damage). Damage to the corresponding areas in the right hemisphere is less likely to result in aphasic symptoms. Second, the brain tends to be *localised* for language. Within the left and right hemispheres, some regions are much more active when people use language than others. One very important area is in the left inferior frontal gyrus. This is commonly known as *Broca's area*, after Paul Pierre Broca, the nineteenth-century French anatomist who first discovered its role in language processing. Another important part is the superior temporal gyrus, particularly the posterior part, which is known as *Wernicke's area*, after Carl Wernicke, the nineteenth-century German neurologist. Since Broca's and Wernicke's original publications, other areas have been found to be involved in language processing as well (see figure 1.1).

Interestingly, the same brain regions are implicated in sign language as in spoken language. This is perhaps an unexpected finding because visual and auditory information are usually processed in different regions of the brain. Thus, we might expect sign language, which relies on processing visual information such as hand shape and motion, to involve different brain regions from spoken language. However, the findings do not support this prediction. Aphasia studies show that damage to left hemisphere 'language areas' produces the same aphasias in sign language users as in spoken language users (see Poizner, Klima & Bellugi, 1987).[2]

It is important to note, however, that the brain does not start off with these clear divisions. Localisation and lateralisation are not present from birth but develop gradually as the child ages. The infant brain has the property of *plasticity*, which means that it has the ability to develop, re-organise and become specialised through experience and development. For example, Mills and colleagues tracked developmental changes in language-related brain activity in infants aged between six and 42 months of age (Mills, Coffey-Corina & Neville, 1997). They measured the ERPs (*event related potentials*) in the brains of infants as the infants listened to familiar words, unfamiliar words and backwards words. ERPs are the changes in electrical potential that occur in neurons as the brain processes information, so they tell us which areas of the brain are active when learners listen or produce language. Between 13 and 17 months of age, familiar and unfamiliar words elicited ERPs, which suggests that the infants recognised the familiar words. However, these response differences were distributed over frontal, temporal parietal and occipital lobes in both hemispheres, suggesting a broad distribution of language-related brain activity. By 20 months, however, the response differences had localised. They were now much more focussed in the temporal and parietal lobes in the left hemisphere only. By the way, this sequence of increasing specialisation with development also means that the consequences of brain injuries tend to be less severe for children than adults. Intact regions of children's brains more easily take over the language processing tasks because they have not yet become specialised for other functions (Bates et al., 1997).

1.4.2   What else might be built into the human brain?

All agree that we need a brain that is configured in a certain way in order to acquire language. But what else might we need? This is where the arguments start. One influential debate revolves around what language-specific knowledge needs to be encoded in our genes. One view is that we are born with a specialised *linguistic toolkit* (Jackendoff, 2002) containing innate knowledge of the principles of language. An alternative, opposing view is that more general-purpose cognitive skills and abilities are sufficient to acquire language. On this latter view, what makes humans uniquely capable of language acquisition is not the existence of a linguistic toolkit but the sophisticated way in which a set of general-purpose cognitive abilities interact (Christiansen & Chater, 2008; Tomasello, 2003).

A neat way of characterising the difference between these two viewpoints is by considering what different types of information might be encoded in our genes. Elman and colleagues have described three different types of innate constraint

---

2   Be careful not to assume that these so-called language areas are solely dedicated to language processing, since they also have other functions. Broca's area, for example, is involved in recognising and imitating motor actions like hand gestures (see e.g. Grèzes, Costes & Decety, 1998). In fact, Rizzolatti and Arbib (1998) have argued that Broca's area's involvement in language processing stems from its role in the mirror neurone system, which is central to our ability to imitate the actions and gestures of others (though others, such as Grodinsky, 2000, disagree).

that might be part of our genetic inheritance (Elman et al., 1996). The first are *representational constraints*. This is the idea that knowledge about the properties of language is encoded in our genes. For example, Pinker has suggested that children are born with the knowledge that human languages contain nouns and verbs (Pinker, 1994). The implication of this statement is that this knowledge is pre-encoded in our genes and has a direct effect on how the brain is built and wired up while the foetus is in the womb. Representational nativism is proposed by nativist theorists such as Pinker and Chomsky, whose theories we will discuss in more detail later in the book. Many nativist theories also promote the idea that language is processed in an innate language *module*, a closed subsystem in the brain that processes one type of information exclusively, in this case, language information (Fodor, 1983).

Alternatively, *architectural constraints* might be built into the brain. This is the idea that genes specify a set of blueprints for building a language acquisition mechanism. In other words, architectural constraints allow our genes to structure the infant brain in such a way that infants can learn the properties of language from the input they hear. For example, Tomasello, among others, has proposed that in order to acquire grammar, human infants need to be able to recognise recurring patterns in speech and link words together into categories based on these recurring patterns (Tomasello, 2003). Our genes must then contain the information to build this pattern-recognition mechanism into our brains. Architectural constraints are proposed by constructivist theorists such as Tomasello and Elman, whose ideas we will also discuss in more detail later in this book.

Third, we have *chronotopic constraints*. These constrain the timing of development, ensuring that certain mechanisms are available at the right point in development. Importantly, if aspects of language development are governed by chronotopic constraints, the timing of exposure to critical events in the environment is crucial. For example, there is evidence that the age at which a child is first exposed to a language affects how the brain processes that language. Weber-Fox & Neville (1996) measured the ERPs of Chinese–English bilingual speakers, some of whom had started learning English in early childhood and some of whom only started to learn English after the age of 16 years. The researchers reported that the early and late learning bilinguals showed very different ERP responses to violations of English syntactic rules (e.g. *the scientist criticized Max's of proof the theorem*). The researchers concluded that whether the learners were exposed to English in childhood or adulthood had a direct effect on how English was processed in the brain. These types of chronotopic constraints are espoused by both nativist and constructivist theories of language development.

1.4.3 The right environment

The second pre-requisite we need to acquire language is an environment in which we are exposed to a language. A very famous case that demonstrates the importance of exposure is that of Genie (Curtiss, 1977). From about 20 months of age, Genie was maltreated by her father. By day she was strapped to a potty and at night she was transferred into a restrictive sleeping bag. She was kept in a bare room with very little to stimulate her senses and she was raised in virtual silence. In fact her father would beat her if she attempted to produce sounds. When discovered at the age of 13 years, Genie understood only a very few words (*mother, walk, go, red, blue, green*) and could produce only two phrases (*stop it* and *no more*). Because she had not been exposed to human speech in childhood, she had not learnt to talk. In fact, even children with loving parents will not acquire language unless they are exposed to it. Deaf children do not acquire a language unless they have intensive training or are exposed to sign language from early on (in which case, they acquire it as easily as hearing children acquire spoken languages; Woolfe, Herman, Roy & Woll, 2010).

Although cases such as Genie's show that exposure to language is clearly necessary, there are debates about what type of environment is necessary and about why the environment is necessary. It is indisputable that the amount of speech that children hear can speed up or slow down the language acquisition process. Parents who use more words and who use a greater variety of different words tend to have children whose vocabulary develops more quickly (Hart & Risley, 1995). However, it is not clear whether the way in which we speak to children has an effect over and above this. For example although many parents use a distinctive speech style when talking with their children, we do not know whether this has an effect on how easily children learn (see Snow & Ferguson, 1977). It is certainly not essential to adopt this speech style in order to help children acquire language. For example, Ochs & Schieffelin (1984) reported that the Kaluli of Papua New Guinea believe that children are helpless and have little or no understanding of the world around them. As a result, they rarely engage young children in conversations at all, yet Kaluli children acquire language perfectly well.

There are also debates about the precise role of the input. In some theories, the role of the input is simply to trigger the innate knowledge that is encoded in the genes and to allow the child to map this innate knowledge onto the language that she is hearing (e.g. Hyams, 1986). In others, the input is given a more substantial role. For example, in constructivist theories of syntax development, the child's task is to learn how different words behave in sentences, and to categorise together words that behave in similar ways (see e.g. Tomasello, 2003). Thus, the amount and type of input that the child hears has a crucial role to play in her ability to build the syntax of her language.

1.5 CHAPTER SUMMARY

The aim of this introductory chapter was to introduce readers to what we mean when we talk about acquiring a 'language'. We began by discussing what languages are, addressing the key question:

What skills and knowledge do children have to master in order to acquire a language?

We discovered that language is multi-faceted, requiring the child to master a whole range of different skills and many different types of knowledge. The kind of knowledge that children have to learn also depends on which one of the thousands of the world's languages the child is exposed to. However, there are some common design features that must occur for a language to be termed a language (e.g. semanticity, arbitrariness, productivity and displacement).

In the second subsection we explored some of the differences between human languages and other animal communication systems, focussing on the key question:

Are humans the only animals that can acquire a language?

Attempts to teach language to apes have been successful in some respects but apes' abilities never mirror those of human children, even after years of exposure. Animals' own communication systems show surprising sophistication, but none of them have the complexity and sophistication of human languages. Animals also share some of our language learning abilities, such as categorical perception, but these abilities rarely manifest themselves in exactly the same way in animals and humans.

In the third subsection we touched on the nature–nurture debate, in response to the key question:

What is required in order for children to acquire a language?

The human brain is clearly configured for language. Although language processing is not localised in any particular part of an infant's brain, both lateralisation and localisation occur as the infant develops. However, we do not know what else needs to be built into the human brain: representational constraints, architectural constraints or chronotopic constraints. We also know that children must be exposed to a language in order to acquire it, but we do not know what types of environment are optimal for language acquisition, nor do we know precisely what role the input plays. These are all questions that we will return to throughout the course of this book.

1.6 SUGGESTED READING

Saxton, M. (2010). *Child language: Acquisition and development*. London: Sage. Saxton presents a more detailed review of the chimp wars debate as well as other attempts to teach animals to talk.

Savage-Rumbaugh, E. S. (1996). *Kanzi. The ape at the brink of the human mind*. New York: Wiley. Learn more about Kanzi the bonobo.

1.7 SUGGESTED READING (ADVANCED LEVEL)

Elman, J. L., Bates, E., Johnson, M. H., Karmiloff-Smith, A., Parisi, D. & Plunkett, K. (1996). *Rethinking innateness: A connectionist perspective on development*.

Cambridge, MA: MIT Press. The famous thesis of some very influential constructivists.

Hockett, C. F. (1963). The problem of universals in language. In J. H. Greenberg (Ed.), *Universals of language* (pp. 1–29). Cambridge, MA: MIT Press. The paper in which Hockett outlines the first 13 of his design features.

Kuhl, P. & Rivera-Gaxiola, M. (2008). Neural substrates of language acquisition. *Annual Review of Neuroscience, 31*, 511–534. A detailed look at the neural basis of language development.

Pepperberg, I. M. (1991) *The Alex Studies: Cognitive and communicative abilities of grey parrots.* Cambridge, MA: Harvard University Press. Reports on a 30-year programme to teach Alex the parrot to talk.

1.8 USEFUL WEBSITES

- http://www.dolphincommunicationproject.org/: More extraordinary information about the communicative abilities of dolphins.

- http://kanzi.bvu.edu/: Video footage of the ape language work including testing and training videos as well as details of daily life.

1.9 COMPREHENSION CHECK

1. Explain in your own words what is meant by:
   a. Semanticity
   b. Arbitrariness
   c. Productivity
   d. Displacement

2. Why don't we refer to the communications systems of other animals as languages?

3. Kanzi learnt to produce and understand words and produce and understand simple sentences. Why do some critics argue that, despite this, animals cannot learn human language?

4. What is the evidence that adult brains are lateralised and localised for language?

5. What evidence do we have that babies' brains are not lateralised or localised for language?

6. It is indisputable that both genes and environment are needed in order to acquire a language. But what aspects of the nature–nurture debate are still being discussed today?

The sounds of language

2.1 THE ISSUE

When did you learn to talk? Put this question to your parents and they will likely assume that you are referring to your first word. Unless you were an exceptionally early or late talker, the answer will probably be somewhere between 10 and 18 months of age.

However, to get to this stage, the 'baby you' had already put in a lot of ground work. Try to imagine what is like for a newborn baby. After nine months of a warm, safe environment she is catapulted into a world full of sensations; experiences to touch, taste, hear, see and smell. One of these sensations is a stream of sound. This sound is never the same from one moment to the next. Sometimes it is low pitched, sometimes high pitched, sometimes it comes in short bursts, sometimes long streams, sometimes it is loud, sometimes soft. In order to even begin the process of producing words, the baby first has to decipher this stream of sound.

By her first birthday, the baby will have learnt a number of things about this stream of sound. She will have learnt that it is composed of small sets of repeated sound segments – like *ma*, *ga* and *da*. She will have learnt that these sound segments can be combined to make up little chunks of sound – like *mama* and *dada* – which carry meaning; they map onto different objects and events in the world. In fact, there is even a sound that refers to the baby herself. Finally, she will have learnt how to imitate these sounds themselves by moving mouth, tongue and vocal cords in a complex but precise pattern of movement.

How do infants achieve all this within the first 12 months? This is the question we will address in this chapter. We will discuss, in turn, three tasks that face infants during the first year or so of life. The first is learning to identify the meaningful sounds of their own language. The second is working out how the speech stream maps onto meaningful units; in other words, how to segment what is a continuous stream of speech into individual words. And the third is learning how to match these speech sounds and produce them for themselves.

2.2 SPEECH PERCEPTION: IDENTIFYING THE MEANINGFUL SOUNDS OF OUR LANGUAGE

William James famously once suggested that "The baby, assailed by eyes, ears, nose, skin, and entrails at once, feels it all as one great blooming, buzzing confusion" (James, 1890, p. 462). However, nowadays we know that infants do not perceive the world as a "blooming, buzzing confusion". In fact, they start to make sense of their world, even their language, even before they are born. We know this from a seminal experiment by DeCasper and Spence (1986), which discovered that infants in the womb are already paying attention to certain characteristics of speech. De Casper and Spence asked pregnant women to read *The Cat in the Hat* (a famous and fabulous book by Dr. Seuss) to their unborn children, twice a day for the last two and a half months of their pregnancy. Three days after birth, the researchers played tape recordings of the story to the infants, together with two similar, but unfamiliar, stories. Infant interest was measured by testing how hard the infants sucked on an artificial teat. The infants sucked significantly harder when listening to *The Cat in the Hat*, showing a distinct preference for the story they had heard before birth. De Casper and Spence surmised that the babies had tuned into the acoustic properties of the story while in the womb (e.g. the stress pattern, the rhythm of the syllables, the order of sounds etc.). In addition, subsequent studies have shown that newborn infants prefer to listen to their own mother's speech over that of a stranger and to their native language over languages that have different acoustic properties (Moon, Cooper & Fifer, 1993; Nazzi, Bertoncini & Mehler, 1998; Spence & Freeman, 1996). So, even before birth, infants are starting to show distinct preferences for familiar speech.

Unfortunately, paying attention to the acoustic properties of speech is just the beginning. Speech is not just a continuous stream of sound but is made up of hundreds of distinct individual units of sound, which can be combined in many ways to make up syllables and words. For example, English contains the speech sounds /b/, /m/, /p/ and /t/, which can be combined into syllables (/ba/, /ma/, /pa/ and /at/) and ultimately into words (*bat, mat, pat*). It is these speech sounds – phonemes – that children have to learn.[1]

Phonemes are the smallest units of sound that have contrastive meaning in a language. Thus, /b/ and /m/ are defined as phonemes because replacing one with another creates a word with a different meaning (e.g. *bat* becomes *mat*). However, learning phonemes is complicated by two major problems. First is the lack of acoustic invariance. This refers to the fact that each time we hear a phoneme it probably sounds a little bit different from the last time we heard it. For example, men tend to have lower voices than women, so the phonemes /a/, /i/ and /u/ produced by a man will sound different to those produced by a woman (Hillenbrand, Getty, Clark & Wheeler, 1995). Even when the same speaker produces the same phoneme twice, the

---

1 Phonemes are usually written in the International Phonetic Alphabet, which allows us to represent the sounds of language more accurately than standard letters. See http://www.langsci.ucl.ac.uk/ipa/ipachart.html for details.

sound will often differ across different instances. For example, a phoneme produced in fast speech has different acoustic properties from the same phoneme produced in slow speech.

In fact, the sound of a phoneme can even differ from one word to the next in the same stream of speech, depending on its position within a word. So the /p/ in *pet* is pronounced slightly differently to the /p/ in *map*. We call these different instances of the phoneme *allophones*. Also, neighbouring phonemes are affected by each other in fluent speech; this is called *co-articulation*. So the /p/ in *pet* may be pronounced slightly differently if embedded in a phrase such as *Sooty is my pet rabbit*. Co-articulation is a very useful skill for speakers because the ability to modify how we pronounce speech sounds in this way allows us to speak faster and more fluently. However, it means that the listener has to ignore what are sometimes very large differences between two pronunciations of the same phoneme, but pay attention to (often small) differences that change the sound from one phoneme to another (e.g. /p/ to /b/). In fact, computer software companies have spent millions of dollars over decades trying to get speech recognition software to compensate for co-articulation.

How do adults deal with this problem? The adult auditory system is set up very cleverly so that it registers differences that change one phoneme into another (differences that cross a phoneme boundary) more easily than other differences (differences within a phoneme boundary). This means that every time English listeners hear the speech sound /p/, we hear it simply as /p/ despite acoustic differences caused by different speakers, co-articulation or speech rate. It also means that we will always register the difference between /p/ and /b/, because this change in acoustic properties crosses a phoneme boundary. This allows us to distinguish, for example, between *pat* and *bat* (an important skill if your mother has just told you to *pat the dog*). In other words, adults have a speech perception system that is tuned to the important phoneme differences in their language. We call this ability *categorical perception* because it allows us to focus on differences between categories of speech sounds. It is fundamental to our ability to use language. Without it we would be lost in a sea of meaningless sound.

The second problem the learner faces results from cross-linguistic differences. Ladefoged has hazarded a guess that there are about 600 different consonants and about 200 different vowels used across the world's languages (it is difficult to know for sure; Ladefoged, 2004, p. 179). However, each individual language will only use a subset of these, and each subset will be different. Thus, the infant has to learn which set of phonemes is important for her language and which phonemes are unimportant.

For example, in English, we have the consonants /r/ and /l/. These are both liquid consonants with one simple difference. To produce /l/ the tongue has to touch the upper alveolar ridge of the mouth, just behind the upper front teeth. To produce /r/ the tongue is further back, usually not quite touching the roof of the mouth or curled back slightly in the centre of the roof of the mouth. English speakers can easily hear the difference between these phonemes, which is important because we use them to pronounce different words (compare *rap* and *lap*). Japanese, however, does not contrast /r/ and /l/. Japanese speakers use these consonants as free variants (or at least as allophones of the same phoneme; Ladefoged & Maddieson, 1996). Because they do not have the /r/ vs. /l/ contrast in their language, Japanese adults have great difficulty distinguishing between English /r/ and /l/. English speakers will, similarly, have problems with unfamiliar aspects of the Japanese sound system. In other words, children learning different languages will have to learn to carve up the sound system in a different way.

The key question then, is this: given that adults hear and interpret phonemes so effortlessly, and given that the important differences between phonemes differ from language to language, how do infants learn the sound system of their language? In other words:

Key question: how do we learn the phonemes of our language?

In the remainder of this section we discuss a number of possible answers to this question, starting with some of the oldest theories and finishing with some of the most recent. As we will see, later theories often build on earlier theories, incorporating modifications to explain the data that are incompatible with the earlier theories.

2.2.1 The motor theory of speech perception

One possible explanation for how we learn speech sounds is that we get a helping hand from innate knowledge. If we are born sensitive to all the possible sounds of all possible languages, the task of learning becomes a little simpler. We just have to figure out which of these sound contrasts are meaningful in our own language. One such explanation is provided by the *motor theory of speech perception* (Liberman, Harris, Hoffman & Griffith, 1957). This suggests that we are born with a universal inventory of distinctive articulatory *feature detectors* that map the speech sounds we hear onto the *articulatory gestures (features)* we use to produce them (i.e. movements of the mouth, tongue etc.). In other words, we are born with an innate speech motor system that both produces speech sounds and detects them.

Support for innate knowledge of this kind was provided by Eimas and colleagues, who discovered that one- and four-month-old infants could rival adults in categorical perception tasks (Eimas, Siqueland, Jusczyk & Vigorito, 1971). This finding was seen as evidence that humans possess an innate system for perceiving speech sounds categorically, just as Liberman suggested. In the study, Eimas and colleagues tested one- and four-month-old infants' ability to discriminate between different phonemes using a high amplitude sucking technique. This technique capitalises on the fact that babies tend to suck harder on an artificial teat if they hear a novel or interesting stimulus. By measuring how hard the infants suck on the teat in response to different sounds, we can test whether they discriminate between them.

The researchers created six artificial speech sounds that differed only in Voice Onset Time (VOT). Voice Onset Time refers to the length of time that passes between the lips opening and the vocal cords vibrating and it varies according to the consonant produced (e.g. /p/ and /b/ differ in VOT, as do /d/ and /t/, and /k/ and /g/, see figure

Figure 2.1

The difference between [ba] and [pa] is Voice Onset Time. In [ba] the vocal cords start to vibrate very soon after the lips start to open (VOT is less than 25 msecs in English). In [pa], the vocal cords start to vibrate a little later (VOT is more than 25 msecs in English).

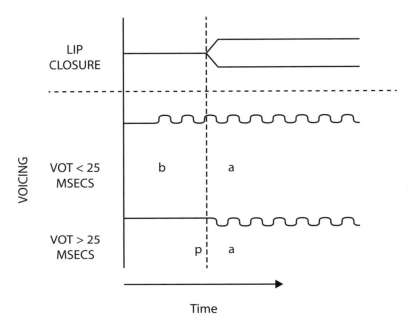

2.1). In this experiment, the VOT of each sound differed by only 20 milliseconds (msecs) from its neighbour, so the sounds had VOTs of 80, 60, 40, 20, 0 and -20 msecs respectively. However, crucially, the difference between only two of these sounds crossed a phoneme boundary (between 40 and 20 msecs).

Because of our categorical perception abilities, adult English speakers hear the three sounds with VOTs of 40 msecs and above as [pa].[2] Similarly, the three sounds with VOTs of 20 msecs or below are perceived as [ba]. The question Eimas and colleagues asked was: will infants hear the sounds in the same categorical way as adults? The answer was a categorical yes. None of the infants reacted to changes within a phoneme boundary (e.g. a change from 0 msecs to 20 msecs). However, they did react, with increased rates of sucking, to changes that crossed a boundary (from 20 msecs to 40 msecs). Eimas concluded that "infants are able to sort acoustic variations of adult phonemes into categories with relatively little exposure to speech,

---

2   When we want to refer to variants of phonemes, we use the symbols [ ]. So [*pa*] refers to the sound we make when we say *pa*, as in *pat*. We also use this to distinguish easily between phonemes and variants within a phonemic category. For example, when we write /p/ we are referring to the phoneme, which incorporates all the variants of /p/. However, when we write [p] we are referring to a particular variant of the phoneme /p/.

as well as virtually no experience in producing these same sounds" (Eimas et al., 1971, p. 306). These findings have been replicated since with a range of different phonemes (e.g. /b/ and /d/, /r/ and /l/, /m/ and /n/; Eimas, 1974, 1975; Eimas & Miller, 1980). In other words, categorical perception does seem to be an innate, not learnt, ability.

More surprisingly perhaps, young infants can perceive the difference between phonemes that do not even exist in their native language. For example, Trehub (1976) found that Canadian one- and four-month-old infants responded to the difference between a vowel contrast found in Polish and French ([pa] vs. [pā]) and between one found in Czech ([řa] vs. [za]), despite the fact that neither occurred in the English they were hearing every day. These findings also provide support for the idea that we are born with an innate set of feature detectors, capable of distinguishing between all the possible sounds of all the world's languages.

However, there is one major problem with the motor theory of speech perception. The theory claims that the feature detectors responsible for categorical perception are dedicated solely to the perception of speech. This is not the case. For example, Pisoni (1977) demonstrated that human adults show categorical perception of musical tones, suggesting that categorical perception is not speech-specific but is a more general property of our auditory system. Perhaps more surprisingly, a number of studies have shown that non-human mammals can also respond categorically to speech stimuli, suggesting that categorical perception is not specific to humans either. For example, as mentioned above, Kuhl & Miller (1975) trained chinchillas to respond differently to [da] and [ta] and then played them a range of sounds along the [da]–[ta] continuum. The chinchillas switched responses at a change-over point that closely resembled the boundary used by English speakers, suggesting that they shared the human capacity for categorical perception. Later, Kuhl and Padden (1982, 1983) extended the finding to macaque monkeys and to a range of different speech sounds. In each case, the monkeys' ability to discriminate between phonemes was eerily similar to those of humans.

One caveat is needed before we get too excited about these findings. These animals needed thousands of training trials before they would respond categorically, whereas human infants seem to do it without thinking. There are also many phonemes that are perceived differently by humans and non-human animals, as well as those that are perceived in a similar manner (see Sinnott, 1998). However, even with these reservations, the findings do suggest that categorical perception – the building block of speech perception – is neither human nor speech-specific, contrary to the prediction of the motor theory of speech perception.

2.2.2 The universal theory (maintenance and loss)

In 1980, Aslin and Pisoni outlined possible alternative theories to the motor theory, one of which – *universal theory* – has attracted a lot of attention in the literature (Aslin & Pisoni, 1980; Aslin, Werker & Morgan, 2002). According to the universal theory, infants initially perceive speech sounds using general auditory mechanisms that are "categorical in nature and independent of experience with any native language"

(Aslin et al., 2002, p. 1257). On this view, as in the motor theory, our ability to perceive differences between speech sounds is innate (i.e. not dependent on experience with the language). However, unlike in the motor theory, this innate ability derives from general all-purpose perceptual mechanisms that we share with other animals.

On this view, the infant is initially capable of discriminating between the phonemes of all languages (the *universal set*). Throughout the first year of life, she gradually becomes tuned to the phonemes of her own native language, so that contrasts that are present in the ambient language are maintained and those that are not present are lost. For example, English infants will maintain the ability to distinguish between /r/ and /l/ because it is meaningful in English (compare *rap* with *lap*), whereas Japanese speakers will lose this ability because the distinction is meaningless in Japanese.

The universal theory predicts that categorical perception will be an innate, universal ability that is not dependent on the language to which children are exposed. This prediction seems to be upheld by experiments like those of Eimas and Trehub described above (Eimas et al., 1971; Trehub, 1976). However, there is also evidence for the universal theory's idea that children's abilities change as they experience more of their language, so that phoneme contrasts that are relevant to the language are maintained and those that are not used are lost. One very famous experiment that demonstrated maintenance/loss was published by Werker and Tees (1984).

Werker and Tees (1984) tested whether English infants could distinguish between two contrasts that are not phonemic (i.e. meaningful) in English but are phonemic in Hindi and in Thompson Salish. Hindi is a language spoken in south Asian countries such as India and Thompson Salish is a native American language spoken in central British Columbia (it is now more commonly referred to by its indigenous name Ntlakapamux). The two Hindi sounds they used were [ṭa] and [ta] and the two Thompson Salish sounds were [k'i] and [q'i]. English adults do not distinguish between [ṭa] and [ta] or between [k'i] and [q'i]. However, Werker and Tees showed that eight- to 10-month-old, but not 10- to 12-month-old, English infants could.

The method used was the *conditioned head turn paradigm*. In this method, infants are trained to turn their heads away from the experimenter and towards a loudspeaker and a reinforcer (an electronically activated toy) only when they hear a change in the sound coming out of the loudspeaker. Infants who respond to the change with a head turn are said to be able to discriminate the sound change (e.g. from [k'i] to [q'i]). The experimenters, thus, kept a record of each time an infant turned her head correctly, each time she did not turn her head during a change trial (i.e. misses) and each time she turned her head during a no-change trial (false positives). The infants were considered to have discriminated the difference between the sounds if they had 8 out of 10 correct responses to change trials, with no more than two errors (either misses or false positives).

The results showed that the eight- to 10-month-old English infants could distinguish between the two Hindi contrasts and between the two Thompson contrasts. However, the 10- to 12-month-old infants could not. In other words, the younger infants were sensitive to sound contrasts that were not present in their native language (English) but the older infants had lost this ability. Interestingly, a control group of Hindi and Thompson learning infants did not show the same decline with age; even older infants were capable of distinguishing the relevant contrasts. The authors concluded that unless infants have experience of a particular sound contrast in their language, they lose the ability to discriminate the contrast within the first year of life. This finding can be seen as support for the idea of maintenance/loss suggested by the universal theory.

The experiment by Werker and Tees is as important for its methodological innovation as its interesting results. To get the speech sounds necessary for the study, the researchers recorded several native speakers and used multiple examples of each sound in the discrimination. This was so they could check that the infants were capable of ignoring speaker differences, just as we have to do in natural language processing. They also included controls such as tests of English native contrasts ([ba] and [da]) and tests of native Thompson Salish and Hindi infants to ensure that failures to discriminate were not due to confounding variables such as the infants' lack of attention. They even adapted the procedure to control for baseline infant biases (e.g. preferring to turn the head to one side rather than the other). Many of the experiments we do today are based on their methodological innovations.

However, although the study remains influential today, the universal theory has run into problems (in fact, it is important to note that Werker & Tees themselves favoured a different theory). Two sets of findings are particularly problematic for the universal theory. First are findings that show that we do not lose the ability to distinguish non-native contrasts completely. Second are findings that suggest that infants are not born with the ability to distinguish all the contrasts of all languages after all.

The first problem concerns the idea of maintenance/loss because it turns out that not all non-native sound contrasts are lost. For example, Best and colleagues tested whether English infants and adults could discriminate a click contrast that occurs in Zulu but not English (Best, McRoberts & Sithole, 1988). Zulu, like many African languages, contains click consonants that sound extremely strange to English listeners. These click consonants are sometimes described as equivalent to the sound of a bottle top popping off or to the clicking noise horse-riders make to encourage a horse to walk-on. A number of different contrastive click types occur in Zulu; so just like moving from /r/ to /l/ can change the meaning of English words (e.g. *rip/lip*), changing from one click to another can change the meaning of Zulu words. Best and her colleagues reported that all their English infants (6–14 months of age) discriminated between the different types of clicks, with no loss of discrimination as they got older. In fact, even English adults could tell the difference between the different types of click. The authors concluded that there was no evidence of a decline in sensitivity to this non-native contrast, which clearly contradicts the prediction of the universal theory.

In fact, there is quite a lot of evidence that our sensitivity to non-native sound contrasts is not irretrievably lost. For example, Japanese adults can teach themselves to recognise the difference between /r/ and /l/ (Flege, Takagi & Mann, 1995). More surprisingly perhaps, even when infants and adults are unable to detect a sound difference, the brain still registers this difference. Rivera-Gaxiola, Silva-Pereyra &

Kuhl (2005) measured how infants' brains reacted to different sound contrasts by testing their brain waves with EEGs (*electroencephalograms*). EEGs allow us to collect data about how electrical energy flows through the brain by recording *event related potentials* (ERPs). In this way we can measure how the brain responds to stimuli. Rivera-Gaxiola and colleagues found that although the 11-month-old English infants did not behave as if they had registered the difference between two Spanish native sound contrasts, the pattern of ERPs indicated that their brains did respond to the change in signal. Thus, the infant auditory system retained at least some ability to discriminate between the two speech sounds. This is not compatible with the idea that we lose all sensitivity to those speech sounds we do not hear in our native language.

The second problem with the universal theory is that infants are not born sensitive to all the possible contrasts of all languages. This is problematic for the claim that the infant is capable of discriminating between the phonemes of all languages (the universal set). For example, Lasky and colleagues reported that Guatemalan Spanish learning infants (between four and six and a half months of age) could not distinguish between the Spanish phonemes /ba/ (with VOT of −20 msec) and /pa/ (VOT +20 msec) despite the fact that this sound contrast is meaningful in the Spanish language (Lasky, Syrdal-Lasky & Klein, 1975). This ability develops as the children age. There are also conflicting reports about whether young infants are capable of discriminating between different fricatives. Fricatives are phonemes like /s/, /f/, /z/ and /θ/ (as in s̲ail, f̲ail, z̲ebra, t̲h̲ink). Eilers and colleagues found that six- to eight-month-olds could not distinguish between [f] and [θ], which contradicts the universal theory's claims about the universal set. However, Holmberg and colleagues found that six-month-olds could distinguish between [fa] and [θa], which supports it (see Eilers, Wilson & Moore, 1979; Holmberg, Morgan & Kuhl, 1977). Whatever the eventual outcome of the research, it seems likely that some sounds are more easily discriminated by infants than others, which does not fit with the idea that infants are born sensitive to all possible speech sounds. Instead, it seems more plausible to suggest that we are born with sensitivity to certain differences but that others have to be created or fine-tuned from our exposure to our native language. This idea, which Aslin and Pisoni (1980) called attunement, forms the basis of many current theories of speech perception.

2.2.3   Attunement theory: native language magnet theory-expanded (NLM-e)

Attunement theories are based on two premises. The first is that infants begin life with the ability to partition sounds into categories (categorical perception) but that these "basic cuts" only "roughly partition sounds" (Kuhl, 2004, p. 832). This is not at all the same thing as saying that the newborn can distinguish all the sounds of all languages. The second premise is that experience with the language tunes those basic perceptual abilities. An infant's experience with language makes her focus on the contrasts that play a role in distinguishing words. Importantly, this is not the same as maintenance/loss. Instead, exposure to a language leads to a type of "perceptual reorganisation" (Werker & Tees, 1984, p. 121), where the infants' innate perceptual abilities are tuned, modified and, ultimately, reorganised by exposure to a particular language.

A number of attunement theories have been proposed. These include theories by Best (Perceptual Assimilation Model, see Best, 1994, 1995), Werker (PRIMIR, Werker & Curtin, 2005) and Jusczyk (2000). We will focus here on one theory only, in order to illustrate the issues: Kuhl's native language magnet theory-expanded (NLM-e, see Kuhl et al., 2008).

Like other attunement theorists, Kuhl suggests that infants begin life with the ability to partition sounds roughly into categories (categorical perception). She also suggests that language experience is necessary to tune infants' ability to perceive the sounds of their own language. The focus of much of Kuhl's work is on how the infant goes about this tuning process. She proposes that exposure to a language changes the way in which the neural pathways in the brain are wired up (i.e. how the neurons in the brain connect to each other). Through experience with language, the neural pathways become committed to a particular configuration (*native language neural commitment*). So ultimately "language learning produces dedicated neural networks that code the patterns of native-language speech" (Kuhl, 2004, p. 838).

One of the consequences of this neural commitment is what Kuhl calls a *perceptual magnet effect*. This arises because the brain stores representations of highly frequent speech sounds as prototypes, which then act as *perceptual magnets* for other members of that phoneme category. The effect of this is to make phonemes that are similar to the prototype sound as if they were identical to the prototype. This decreases our ability to tell the difference between members of the same phonemic category, which means that different variants of a phoneme start to sound the same (e.g. different variants of /a/ sounds start to sound like a prototypical /a/).

This distortion in how we perceive speech sounds results in us becoming less sensitive to within-category differences in our own language and more sensitive to between-category differences. It also makes us less sensitive to between-category differences in other languages, because we have not experienced these differences in our language. This explains why we develop a diminished sensitivity to non-native contrasts as we accrue more experience of our language. Interestingly, there is evidence that the perceptual magnet effect may be human/language specific, unlike the more general broad categorical perceptual abilities that we are born with. Kuhl (1991) demonstrated that human infants and adults showed a perceptual magnet effect for different variants of the vowel /i/ (as in *peep*) but monkeys did not (the article is unambiguously titled 'Human adults and human infants show a "perceptual magnet effect" for the prototypes of speech categories, monkeys do not', which pretty much tells you all you need to know).

Another nice feature of this theory is that it provides an explanation for how exposure to language tunes our perceptual system. Remember that each time we hear phonemes such as /r/ and /l/, each instance will actually sound a little bit different from the last. As a result both Japanese and English infants, for example, are likely to hear a whole range of different sounds on the [l]–[r] spectrum; some will sound more like a [r] sound, some like a [l] sound and others will be somewhere in the middle. How do English, but not Japanese, children learn to put a category boundary in the middle of this spectrum, so that they can discriminate between /r/ and /l/? Kuhl's solution is to propose that there are different distributional properties in the speech signal of different languages, and these cause language-specific prototypes to develop. So, for example, Japanese and English infants will hear a different distribution of [l] and [r] sounds along the [l]–[r] spectrum, which leads English children to develop two prototypes (one for [l] sounds and one for [r] sounds) and Japanese children to develop only one intermediate prototype.

Figure 2.2
Bimodal vs. unimodal distributions of [da]–[ta] stimuli during familiarisation. Presentation frequency for infants in the bimodal groups is shown by the dotted line, and for the unimodal group by the solid line. Reproduced from Maye et al. (2002, p. B104, Figure 1).

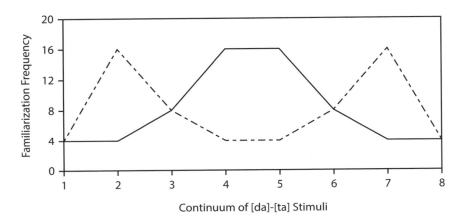

Support for this idea was provided by a study by Maye and her colleagues (2002). They managed to induce six- and eight-month-old infants to learn different patterns of categorical perception in the lab by varying the distribution of sounds that the infants heard. They created eight artificial syllables that varied along a continuum from [ta] to [da]. Half the infants then heard these syllables with a bimodal distribution (see figure 2.2), which means that the syllables near the ends of the continuum were presented more frequently than those in the centre. The other group of infants heard the syllables with a unimodal distribution, which means that the syllables from the centre of the continuum occurred more frequently. In the subsequent test trials, the infants heard either alternating syllables (da-ta-da-ta-da-ta) or non-alternating syllables (da-da-da or ta-ta-ta). The infants in the bimodal group listened for significantly longer to non-alternating trials than alternating trials, a difference which indicated they could distinguish between the syllables. The unimodal group did not show this effect, which indicated that they were treating both [da] and [ta] as if they were the same syllable. In other words, simply by varying the frequency with which the infants had heard different variants on the [ta]–[da] spectrum the researchers had induced the infants to create different category boundaries. They concluded that "infants are able to use distributional information in input speech to detect phonetic category structure" (Maye et al., 2002, p. B109), just as Kuhl predicted.

There are, however, critics both of Kuhl's theory in particular and attunement theories in general. Many of the criticisms have focussed on the idea that we are born with innate categorical perception abilities. For example, Nittrouer has suggested that researchers have over-estimated the perceptual abilities of infants (Nittrouer, 2001). She tested whether six- to 14-month-old English infants and two- to three-year-old English children could discriminate a range of contrasts. These were a vowel contrast ([sa] compared to [su]), a VOT contrast ([ta] compared to [da]) and two fricative contrasts (e.g. [sa] compared to [ʃa] and [su] compared to [ʃu]).[3] She reported very mixed results. For example, only 65 per cent of the infants tested with the vowel contrast successfully discriminated the contrast and only 35 per cent of the infants tested on the VOT contrast were successful. Even the three-year-olds did not perform very well, for example, only 56 per cent were successful with the vowel contrast. Nittrouer's results led her to the conclusion that "the data do not support the proposition that infants have clearly established phonetic categories, separated by well-defined boundaries" (Nittrouer, 2001, p. 1603). She also suggested that the difference between her results and those of previous studies could be attributed to the fact that the previous studies had excluded a substantial proportion of infants due to fussiness. Fussiness is a catch-all term that researchers use to exclude infants who fall asleep, cry, wriggle or otherwise fail to pay attention during experiments. In essence, Nittrouer was suggesting that if the researchers had not excluded all the children who did not pay attention, they would have concluded that many infants cannot distinguish between phonemes (though see Aslin et al., 2002 for a robust reply).

Pierrehumbert (2003) similarly has challenged the idea that the speech perception system originates in an innate ability to categorise sounds. She has argued that all the evidence for innate categorical perception comes from experiments in which infants simply hear two contrasts presented repeatedly (e.g. [ba]–[da]), which is very different to the task that faces the infant when listening to normal speech. In normal speech, each time the child hears the phonemes /p/ and /d/ they will sound slightly different depending on speaker identity, speaker emotional state, the number and type of neighbouring phonemes and so on. Thus, even if very young infants can discriminate between these phonemes in the lab, this is no guarantee that they can do so in the speech they actually hear. In fact, Pierrehumbert has suggested that there is no need to posit innate knowledge at all. Instead, infants could be building the sound system of their language from the bottom up, via the type of distributional analysis that Maye and colleagues showed infants are perfectly capable of performing. Research investigating this idea that infants do not come equipped with innate categorical perception is still in its infancy so there are very few detailed studies that test the relevant predictions (though see Pierrehumbert, 2003 for some preliminary ideas and de Boer, 2000; Steels & de Boer, 2007, for some computer modelling work). Nevertheless, it is an intriguing idea that should generate interesting studies in future.

---

3 ʃ is pronounced '*sh*' as in *sheep*.

2.3 HOW DO WE LEARN TO SEGMENT THE SPEECH STREAM?

Once an infant has started to learn the sound system of her language, what happens next? It is all very well knowing that your language distinguishes between /p/ and /d/ but this is not much help given that your ultimate aim is to learn to produce meaningful words. The next problem facing the infant, then, is working out how to segment the stream of sounds into meaningful words and phrases. We call this the segmentation problem.

Segmenting the speech stream is difficult because all we actually hear is a continuous stream of speech, with very few gaps or pauses between words. As adults we can easily experience the infants' problem by listening to conversations in foreign languages. Tune into any foreign radio station and attempt to work out where the different words begin and end. Eventually you may pick up a few isolated words but you will find it virtually impossible to segment the sentences you hear into separate words. Brent and Siskind explained the problem very succinctly. They wrote "Fluent speech contains no known acoustic analogue of the blank spaces between printed words" (Brent & Siskind, 2001, p. B33).

Nevertheless, although there are no blank spaces between words in speech, there are other cues that we can use to segment the speech stream. For example, to learn where words begin and end, we might be able to use consistent stress patterns. Given this, the key question is thus:

Key question: what cues might infants use to segment the speech stream?

Below we consider some of the possibilities.

2.3.1 Prosodic cues

Prosodic cues relate to the rhythm, stress pattern and intonation of speech. Given that many languages tend to have quite distinctive rhythms and stress patterns, it is logical to suggest that these cues could help infants segment words from the speech stream. For example, English has a trochaic stress pattern, which means that most words have a strong–weak stress pattern (e.g. *DOCtor*, *HEADache*; Cutler & Carter, 1987). The alternative, iambic, weak–strong pattern is far less frequent (e.g. *gi-RAFFE*, *tra-PEZE*). Thus "a listener encountering a strong syllable in spontaneous English conversation would seem to have about a three to one chance of finding that strong syllable to be the onset of a new lexical word" (Cutler, 1994, p. 90). In other words, if English-learning infants assumed that sequences of speech with a strong–weak stress pattern were words, they would end up with a relatively accurate segmentation strategy. This is known as the *Metrical Segmentation Strategy* (MSS, see e.g. Cutler & Norris, 1988).

There is quite a lot of evidence for this idea, but the most famous comes from an impressive sequence of 15 experiments by Juszyk and colleagues (Jusczyk, Houston & Newsome, 1999). These demonstrated quite conclusively that English-learning infants are sensitive to strong–weak stress patterns and can use these to segment words out of the speech stream. For example, in the second experiment in the paper, seven-and-a-half-month-old infants were familiarised to (i.e. heard repeatedly) passages of text containing words with trochaic stress (e.g. *doctor, hamlet*). Then, in the test phase, the infants heard both the familiar words (*doctor, hamlet*) and unfamiliar words in isolation. The infants listened significantly longer to the familiar than the unfamiliar words, showing that they had managed to segment these words out of the speech stream in the familiarisation phase. Interestingly, the infants did not show the same preferences when familiarised to monosyllabic words (e.g. *king, ham*) and then tested on the disyllabic words which contained these monosyllables (*kingdom, hamlet*; experiment 3). In this case, they did not prefer to listen to the words *kingdom* and *hamlet*. This indicates that the infants were not simply responding to the sound of the strong syllable (*king, ham*) but were segmenting the speech stream according to the dominant strong–weak trochaic stress pattern of English.

It is important to note that paying attention to stress cues would not work for all languages. For example, stress patterns do not provide a reliable cue to word boundaries in Inuktitut (a language from the Eskimo-Aleut family), because a complex interaction of factors determines where stress falls in a word (e.g. number of syllables and syllable length). In fact, there are a number of languages that do not have the type of word-initial or word-final stress patterns that would be needed to segment words in this way. Cutler has recognised this point, suggesting that children learning other languages may use different strategies. However, what these strategies are has not yet been determined. One possibility, for example, is that infants learning languages like French, which do not have a regular stress pattern, may use a syllable-based strategy. However, it seems that French infants are not sensitive to these cues until well after the onset of word learning (16 months; see Nazzi, Iakimova, Bertoncini, Frédonie & Alcantara, 2006; though see Polka, Sundara & Blue, 2002 for contradictory evidence). More work on the role of stress- and syllable-based strategies in other languages is required.

2.3.2   Phonotactic regularities

Information about how to segment words might also come from phonotactic regularities. Phonotactic regularities occur because there are restrictions on which sounds can co-occur in words in a language. For example, there are no English words that begin with the sound [vzg],̓ because this is not a permissible word-initial combination in English. It is, however, permissible in Russian (e.g. *vzglyad* 'glance'). Similarly, [br] is a sound that occurs at the beginning of words in English much more often than at the end, whereas [nt] is more likely at the end. If infants are sensitive to which sound combinations can occur at the beginning and ends of words, they could use this information to segment words out of the speech stream.

Many studies have demonstrated that infants are, indeed, sensitive to these restrictions. For example, Mattys and colleagues tested whether infants were sensitive to phonotactic regularities by presenting infants with syllable sequences that varied in their probability of occurrence within words (Mattys, Jusczyk, Luce & Morgan, 1999). To do this, they created some two-syllable nonsense words such as *nongkuth* and *nongtuth*. For half of these words, the medial consonant cluster was one that occurs frequently within English words but infrequently between words. For example, take *nongkuth*. This word contains the consonant cluster *ngk* in the middle, which is relatively frequent at syllable boundaries within words but it is not very frequent across word boundaries in English. So, if we hear two syllables with the sound *ngk* in the middle (e.g. *nong-kuth*), it would be best to assume that the two syllables make up one word (*nongkuth*). The other half of the words contained medial consonant clusters that occur more frequently between than within words. For example, the cluster *ngt* is infrequent within words but frequent across word boundaries. Thus, if we hear two syllables with the sound combination *ngt* in the middle (e.g. *nong-tuth*), it would be safest to assume that these two syllables are part of two separate words (*nong* and *tuth*). Mattys and colleagues found that even infants as young as nine months were sensitive to this difference; they listened longer to the nonsense words made up of consonant clusters that were frequent within words (i.e. those that were more likely to be words according to the phonotactic regularities of English). Thus, they concluded that infants could use phonotactic regularities to learn word boundaries from nine months of age.

2.3.3   Allophonic variation

We have already been introduced to the idea of allophonic variation in section 2.2 above. Allophonic variation results because a single phoneme (e.g. /p/) can be pronounced in very different ways depending on its position within a word. This is also information that infants could potentially use to identify word boundaries. For example, at the beginning of words, the phoneme /t/ is often pronounced with a little burst of air (we say it is aspirated; e.g. *tab*). At the end of words (e.g. *bat*) the little burst of air is missing (unaspirated). If infants are sensitive to the correspondence between a phoneme's position in the word and its pronunciation, they could use this information to find word boundaries.

On the surface, it seems unlikely that infants could pick up on these extremely subtle correspondences. But, unlikely or not, infants are indeed sensitive to this information, as Jusczyk and his colleagues discovered (Jusczyk, Hohne & Bauman, 1999). Jusczyk had previously reported that two-month-olds could discriminate between aspirated and unaspirated /t/ (Hohne & Jusczyk, 1994). So in this study, he and his colleagues set out to discover whether infants could use this information to locate word boundaries. They used a *conditioned headturn procedure*, in which the speech sounds are played only when the infant's head is turned towards a flashing red light positioned above the speaker. They first familiarised infants either to the word *nitrates* or to the two word phrase *night rates*, by playing them the word or phrase repeatedly, interspersed with a control word (either *doctor* or *hamlet*). Importantly, the two stimuli (*nitrates* and *night rates*) contain the same phonemes but these phonemes are pronounced differently because of the presence/absence of the word boundary. For example, the duration of the [a] vowel in *night rates* is significantly longer than in *nitrates*, and the initial /t/ is aspirated in *nitrates* but unaspirated in *night rates*. The key question was this: would the infants, familiarised to one of these stimuli, be able to use these subtle differences to distinguish between the familiar stimuli and the novel one in a test phase?

During the test phase, the infants heard multiple examples of *night rates* and *nitrates* embedded in passages of text. For example the infants heard "*Night rates can help us to save some money. Businesses try to use night rates to send their packages*" and "*Nitrates are something that everyone needs. My teacher told me all about nitrates*" and so on. Clearly the infants were not expected to understand what the passages meant. However, if they had detected the allophonic differences between *night rates* and *nitrates*, we would expect them to respond differently to the two passages. This is what the researchers found: 10-and-a-half-month-old infants (experiment 4) though not nine-month-olds (experiment 1) detected the difference. In other words, the 10-and-a-half-month-old infants who had heard *night rates* in the familiarisation stage listened longer to the passage containing the phrase *night rates*. Those who had heard *nitrates* in the familiarisation phase listened longer to the passage containing the word *nitrates*. The researchers concluded that sensitivity to the allophonic cues of a language develops between nine and 10 and half months of age. This ability develops slightly later than infants' ability to use other cues but this is not really surprising given how subtle a cue it is. In fact, one could argue that it is surprising that infants can do this at all.

Overall, then, there is an impressive body of evidence that infants are sensitive to prosodic cues and to phonotactic regularities by nine months and to allophonic cues by 10 and a half months of age. However, showing that infants are sensitive to these cues is not the same as showing that these cues lead to accurate segmentation. There are two problems. First, in all cases an over-reliance on these cues would lead to mis-segmentation. For example, as well as showing that infants can use stress patterns to segment trochaic strong–weak words correctly (e.g. *DOCtor*; see section 2.3.1 above), Jusczyk also showed that the strategy led infants to mis-segment words with iambic weak–strong stress patterns (e.g. *guiTAR*; Jusczyk et al., 1999). Similarly, a reliance on allophonic variation could be misleading. For example, although aspirated /t/ often occurs at the beginning of words, there are cases where it occurs word internally (e.g. *atomic*). Over-reliance on this cue would lead to mis-segmentation into two words (*a* and *tomic*). These examples illustrate the problem that a cue's usefulness relies on how often it occurs in the wrong place as much as the right place (a problem pointed out by Fernald & McRoberts, 1996). Thus although infants may be sensitive to these cues, we have yet to establish how important they are as solutions to the segmentation problem in real speech.

A second problem is that all these cues pattern differently across different languages. This means that infants have to first identify which pattern is relevant for their language, before they can use it to segment words. This introduces a catch-22 type dilemma. In order to identify which cues indicate word boundaries in their language, infants must first learn some words. But if they need to first segment the speech stream in order to learn words, how can they learn the words that will teach them what cues to use? For example, in order to use trochaic word-based stress patterns to segment the speech stream, English infants need to have learnt that English words have a trochaic stress pattern. But to identify that English words have this pattern, they need to have already segmented and learnt some English words. The problem here is that the infants need some other way to get an initial hold on their language. How do they solve this initial problem?

One possibility is that infants begin by using different cues, which help them learn the first few words. Once they have a few words in their vocabulary, they can learn language-specific cues such as stress patterns, which they then use to segment other words. If this is how children do it, we need to consider what cues they might use at the start. There are a number of possibilities, which we will discuss below.

2.3.4 Isolated words

Until now, we have assumed that infants hear a continuous stream of speech, from which they have to segment words. However, perhaps they begin by learning words that occur in isolation. Brent and Siskind explored this idea by studying what young English-learning infants actually hear (Brent & Siskind, 2001). They analysed transcripts of mothers talking to infants and calculated how many isolated words these mothers produced. Isolated words were defined as words that were separated from other words in the speech stream by a pause of no less than 300 msecs. For example, if a mother said "*that's it ... mummy ... mummy hen*", *mummy* would be counted as an isolated word only if the pauses before and after lasted for 300 msecs or more. The researchers reported that 9 per cent of the words that children hear occur in isolation. Thus, there was plenty of evidence that infants do hear some words in isolation, from which they could learn segmentation cues. Even more interestingly, these isolated words tended to be the ones that infants learnt first. In fact, whether a child could produce a word at 12 months of age was predicted by the frequency with which she heard that word produced by her mother in isolation (and not by the frequency with which she heard the word overall). They concluded that it is perfectly possible that infants begin by learning those words that occur in isolation in their input. Their knowledge of these words would then help them to segment the rest of the speech stream.

However, although this is a plausible strategy, it is unlikely to be the whole solution. Brent and Cartwright (1996) have identified some problems with this strategy, one of which seems particularly difficult to solve. The problem is that it is difficult to see how the infant could distinguish isolated words from isolated phrases. For example, how does the infant tell that the word *mummy* is a word but the phrase *mummy hen* is not? Without this ability, infants are likely to learn quite a lot of phrases as if they are words. This is not necessarily a problem for Brent and Siskind's claim that children can learn words in this way, because there is evidence that infants do treat some frequent phrases as if they were isolated words (e.g. *what's that?*, see Pine & Lieven, 1993). However, if infants are trying to learn segmentation strategies such as stress cues from these phrases, they will not provide the infants with accurate word stress information.

2.3.5 Transitional probabilities

Another possibility is that infants are clever statisticians, who keep track of the probability with which sounds co-occur (*transitional probabilities*) and use these probabilities to make intelligent guesses about where words begin and end. To understand what is meant by transitional probabilities it is best to start with an example. Assume that you hear the syllable *pre* (pronounced pri: /prɪ/). What is the probability that the next syllable will be *ty* (i.e. what is the transitional probability that *pre* will transition into *ty*)? Well, the probability is quite high because the word *pretty* (*pre-ty*) is relatively common in the English language. However, the probability of *ty* being followed by *bab* is much lower, because there is no word *tybab* in the English language. This means that we will only hear *tybab* when a word like *pretty* is immediately followed by a word like *baby*. In other words, because the transition between *ty* to *bab* only occurs between words not within a word, it is less likely to occur. In sum, transitional probabilities refer to the likelihood of one syllable being followed by another, and tend to be higher between syllables within words than between syllables in different words.

If infants are capable of keeping track of transitional probabilities they could use this information to work out where words begin and end. For example, syllable strings with high transitional probabilities (e.g. *pre-ty*) are likely to be words. Syllable strings with low transitional probabilities (*ty-bab*) are unlikely to be words. Paying attention to this will allow infants to segment phrases like *pretty baby* into two words correctly.

On the surface, this would seem like a very difficult task but in fact eight-month-old infants can do it. Saffran, Aslin and Newport demonstrated this very neatly (Saffran et al., 1996). They showed that eight-month-old English infants can identify the transitional probabilities between syllables in a continuous speech stream of nonsense syllables (e.g. *bidakupadotigolabubidaku …*) and can use these transitional probabilities to segment 'words'.

How did they show this? Well, the speech stream of nonsense syllables they used was actually made up of four three-syllable nonsense words: *bidaku*, *padoti*, *golabu* and *tupiro*. Because of this, the transitional probabilities between syllables within a word were 1 (or 100 per cent). In other words, the syllable [bi] was always followed by the syllable [da] (because it occurred in the word *bidaku*). Transitional probabilities between words were always 0.33 (or 33 per cent). This is because the final syllable of a word (e.g. the [ku] in *bidaku*) could be followed by the initial syllable of any of the other three words ([pa], [go] or [tu]).

During the familiarisation phase of the experiment, the infants heard the continuous speech stream for two minutes, with no pauses, no intonational patterns and no other potential cues (the speech was actually generated by a speech synthesiser). The infants were then tested, in a test phase, with the 'words' that made up the speech stream (e.g. *bidaku*, *padoti*), non-words (with the same syllables in a different order) or part-words (made up of the final syllable of one 'word' and the beginning of another; e.g. *kupado* or *tigola*). They found that, surprisingly, the infants listened significantly longer to the non-words and part-words than the familiar 'words'. This preference for unfamiliar words (called a novelty preference) indicates that the infants were capable of distinguishing between the familiar words and the new/part words. To do this the infants must have been paying attention to the transitional probabilities between syllables during the familiarisation phase and using these to segment out 'words'. This is powerful evidence that eight-month-old infants are sensitive to transitional probabilities between syllables.

However, once again, discovering that infants can do this in the lab is different from showing that infants can use these cues to segment real speech. One big difference between Saffran's artificial language and real speech is that real speech is made up of words of different lengths. There are monosyllabic words (e.g. *cat*), disyllabic words (*giraffe*) as well as trisyllabic words (*elephant*). Using transitional probabilities to segment speech made up of words of different lengths is likely to be a much harder task, as Gambell and Yang have demonstrated (Gambell & Yang, 2003; Yang, 2002). They used a computer model to test whether transitional probabilities (what they called 'TP local minima') could be used to segment words from real speech to children. They reported quite disappointing results. Only about 41 per cent of the 'words' that their model learner identified using transitional probabilities were real English words. The rest were nonsense words. In addition, the model failed to identify about 77 per cent of the real words in the corpus. The root of the problem was the number of monosyllabic words in real speech to children (85 per cent of the input given to the model). The authors explained why their results were so disappointing; "in order for SL (statistical learning) to be effective, a TP [transitional probability] at an actual word boundary must be lower than its neighbors. Obviously this condition cannot be met if the input is a sequence of monosyllabic words" (Gambell & Yang, 2004, p. 50). If Gambell and Yang are right then transitional probabilities on their own will not be enough to segment real corpora (though to be fair, Saffran and colleagues never claimed it would be sufficient on its own). Models that make use of multiple sources of statistical information do better but even these are not completely accurate (Brent & Cartwright, 1996; Swingley, 2005).

2.3.6 A multiple cues approach

From the discussion above it seems unlikely that any of the cues could do the segmentation job on their own. So perhaps what is important is the integration of different cues. This has been suggested by Ambridge and Lieven in their review of the literature (2011). They have argued that the solution may be in multiple cues, together with some developing understanding that the intention behind speech is to convey meaning. For example, it is possible that when infants hear a sound pattern consistently paired with an object or person they know well (e.g. *Mummy*), they assume that it is a word, even if it occurs in a stream of speech. "Thus, meaning fixes the initial words as words and then allows the infant to identify the typical patterns of word stress (and also allophonic and phonotactic constraints) in the language" (Ambridge & Lieven, 2011, p. 37). It is also possible that infants use different combinations of cues in different ways. For example, there is evidence that seven-month-old infants give more weight to transitional probabilities but nine-month-old infants prioritise stress cues (Thiessen & Saffran, 2003). The challenge for integration theories, however, is to investigate which cues children are sensitive to, what children do when cues conflict (as they sometimes do) and how children's responses to segmentation cues change with development.

2.4 SPEECH PRODUCTION: LEARNING TO PRODUCE THE MEANINGFUL SOUNDS OF OUR LANGUAGE

If you are alone when you are reading this, try saying the syllable [ba] (you can do it in a public place if you want, but you may get some funny looks). Now say [pa]. How did you produce these two sounds? What did you do to change the [ba] into a [pa]?

You did it by a clever combination of different articulatory gestures. The sounds [p] and [b] are both what we call plosive consonants that are produced with the lips pressed together. The closure of the lips causes an obstruction that blocks the air in the mouth cavity for a short time. Then the lips are opened quickly and the air passes through with an (ex)plosion. The difference between [p] and [b] comes from the vocal cords. When we produce [b] the air from our lungs sets our vocal cords vibrating soon after we open our lips. When we produce [p], the air passes freely between the vocal cords for longer, so they do not vibrate until a little later.

Not surprisingly, it takes children quite a long time to learn how to reproduce speech sounds accurately. In fact, the newborn could not produce these sounds even if she wanted to because her vocal tract is the wrong shape. A newborn baby has a much shorter vocal tract than an adult because her larynx is placed higher up than that of an adult. This means it is impossible for her to produce the range of sounds necessary for speech until her larynx starts to descend in the first year. In addition, her tongue is very large, filling up much of her mouth, and she has under-developed tongue muscles, meaning that she cannot produce the complex tongue movements required for many speech sounds.

However, the infant is capable of vocalising, even if she is not capable of producing speech sounds. There seems to be a distinct sequence of sound development over the first year of life, which culminates in infants producing their first words. Cross-linguistic comparisons show that the sequence of development is broadly comparable across languages, although there are some subtle differences that we will discuss later on. For example, Vihman (1996) compared studies of English, Dutch and Swedish infants and suggested a number of commonalities in the sounds infants produce in the first year. Her findings are summarised in table 2.1.

This sequence of prelinguistic vocal development culminates in the infant producing her first words. However, even after that, it takes her a while to get the speech sounds right. The transition from babbling to words is far from easy, so infants' first words and sentences often sound very odd. Lust (2006) has identified four different types of pronunciation "deformations" in young children's speech (Lust, 2006, p. 157). First, sounds are often omitted (so *broke* becomes *bok* and *that* becomes *da*). Second, sounds can also be substituted for each other (so *rabbit* becomes *wabbit*). Third, sounds within a word can be assimilated to each other,

Table 2.1
Stages of vocal sound acquisition, summarised from Vihman (1996)

Stage	Type of sound	Approximate age	Description
1	Reflexive vocalisation	0–2 months	Sounds expressive of discomfort, crying and fussing Vegetative sounds (coughing, swallowing, burping etc.) Sounds that result from physical activity (grunts, sighs) Occasional rare and limited use of speech-like sounds (e.g. /ŋ/, which is pronounced as in *sing*)
2	Cooing and laughter	2–4 months	The first comfort sounds (typically in response to another's smiling or talking) Frequency of crying and primitive vegetative sounds starts to decline Sustained laughter emerges
3	Vocal play	4–7 months	Increasing control of the articulatory mechanisms leads to vocal play sounds (squeals, growls, yells) Onset of marginal babbling: consonant-like and vowel-like features start to occur
4	a. Reduplicated/canonical babbling	7+ months	Infant starts to produce strings of repeated (reduplicated) speech syllables (e.g. *da-da-da-da* or *goo-goo*)
	b. Variegated babbling		Infant starts to produce mixtures of syllables (variegated babbling; e.g. *ka-da-bu-ba*) N.B. Some studies suggest that canonical babbling precedes variegated babbling; Vihman argues that both begin at the same time, though variegated sequences may become more dominant with age

becoming more like each other (this is called consonant harmony; e.g. *doggy* → *goggy*). Fourth, infants often repeat syllables within words (*tummy* becomes *tum tum* and *bottle* becomes *baba*). The intriguing question is why infants make these errors, given that their ability to perceive speech sounds seems very sophisticated from a very young age (see section 2.2 above). Thus the key question we will address in this section is:

Key question: why do children make errors when they first try to produce speech?

Below we consider four possible answers. One attributes errors to problems in perception, one attributes them to problems in articulation, one proposes universal constraints on production and one proposes that the strategies that children are applying to the problem of speech production cause errors. As always, some theories are omitted, most notably the Optimality Theory. References for this theory are provided at the end of the chapter.

2.4.1 Mispronunciation due to misperception: the 'mushy mouth–mushy ear' hypothesis

The evocative subtitle for this section – 'mushy mouth–mushy ear' – has been unashamedly stolen from Lust (2006), since it captures the idea behind the theory so well. According to this view, an infant will mispronounce a word because she has mis-perceived it; thus, a mushy ear leads to a mushy mouth. For example, perhaps an infant produces *wabbit* instead of *rabbit* because she has mis-heard the word in her input and has learnt the wrong pronunciation.

On the face of it, this explanation seems to be ruled out by all the evidence presented above about how infants perceive phonemes (section 2.2). This evidence seems to indicate that infants under 12 months old are already very sensitive to differences between phonemes such as /r/ and /w/. Thus it would seem implausible to suggest that they mis-hear these phonemes when learning words. However, on a closer examination this may not be so implausible. Curtin and Werker have pointed out that simply discriminating between two sounds is a much simpler task than mapping a word to its meaning. Perhaps the difficulty of the word learning task means that children often fail to encode information about how to pronounce a word, given that they are also trying to encode information about what it means (Curtin & Werker, 2007).

There is some evidence to support this idea from research using a switch task (Stager & Werker, 1997; Werker, Fennell, Corcoran & Stager, 2002). These studies have shown that English-learning infants younger than 17 months old do, indeed, find it difficult to discriminate between minimally different pairs of words in a word learning task. In the switch task, infants have to learn which of two English-sounding nonsense words (*bih* and *dih*) is associated with which of two pictures (a crown and a molecule). To achieve this, the infants are first habituated to consistent word-object pairs: every time they hear the word *bih* they see a picture of a crown and every time they hear the word *dih* they see a picture of a molecule (of course the infants do not know what a crown and molecule actually are; the habituation phase simply teaches them to associate the picture with the word). Then the pictures are switched around so they are seen with a different word (*bih*-molecule, *dih*-crown). If the infants are sensitive to this change, they will indicate surprise by looking for longer at the pictures after the change. Thus, by measuring looking time, we can assess if the children are sensitive to the difference between /b/ and /d/ during a task where they also have to learn to associate a word (e.g. *bih*) with a particular picture (e.g. *crown*). The researchers reported that although infants registered the difference between very different sounding words at 14 months (e.g. *lif* vs. *neem*), they could not do the same for minimal pairs (*bih–dih*) until 17 months of age. This suggests that mis-perception of speech sounds in word learning contexts could be one of the reasons why infants make pronunciation errors when they produce their first words.

However, this cannot be the only explanation for errors for one simple reason. Infants make errors even with words that they do perceive correctly. Berko & Brown (1960) famously recorded the following exchange between a child and an adult, which illustrates what they called *the fis phenomenon*. In this exchange, the child could clearly perceive the difference between *fish* and *fis*, even though he could not yet pronounce *fish* accurately. This shows that infants' mispronunciations cannot all be due to mis-perception problems.

> One of us, for instance, spoke to a child who called his inflated plastic fish a fis. In imitation of the child's pronunciation, the observer said: "This is your fis?" "No," said the child, "my fis". He continued to reject the adult's pronunciation until he was told, "This is your fish." "Yes," he said, "my fis."
>
> (Berko & Brown, 1960, p. 531)

2.4.2 Articulatory constraints on production

Another possible explanation is that infants take a while to learn how to manipulate their articulatory organs to produce speech sounds correctly. For example, to produce a [s] sound, the speaker has to raise the tongue high in the mouth so that it nearly touches the roof of the mouth, thereby creating a groove in the centre of the tongue. The air stream is then forced under pressure through this groove. It seems likely that infants make errors in pronunciation until they have mastered these articulatory gestures. If we combine this with the fact that major changes occur in the anatomy of the vocal tract in the first year, we have a sensible explanation of why infants mispronounce words.

The problem with this explanation is that infants seem perfectly capable of making the relevant sounds in certain circumstances. For example, N. Smith (1973) has reported on what is now called the 'Puzzle-Puddle phenomenon'. The child he studied (Amahl) mispronounced the word *puddle* as *puggle* but mispronounced the word *puzzle* as *puddle*. Since he managed to produce the word *puddle* when the target was *puzzle*, he obviously had no problems producing the correct combination of articulatory gestures. So why, then, did he mispronounce *puddle*? The articulatory constraints theory cannot explain this puzzling phenomenon.

2.4.3 Universal constraints: Jakobson's maturational theory

A third possible explanation is that the development of speech sounds is governed by a genetically programmed universal sequence of maturation. Thus, children make errors until this programme is complete (Jakobson, 1941/68). The basis of the maturational programme is a universal inventory of *distinctive features* which is said to underlie all the possible phonemes of the world's languages (these are the same features that the motor theory proposed for speech perception; see section 2.2.1 above). These features are innately organised in what Jakobson called an *implicational hierarchy*, ranging from features that characterise every language all the way down to features that are rarely used (i.e. occur in only a few languages). Unmarked sounds – those that characterise all of the world's languages – are earliest and most easily acquired. Marked sounds – those that do not occur in many languages – will take longer to be acquired, so infants are likely to make errors with these sounds.

Importantly, the key to the theory is the idea that infants do not just acquire speech sounds, they acquire a set of contrasting sounds. This means that two contrasting sounds will be acquired at the same time. For example, the [ba]–[ma] contrast is very common across the world's languages so infants should acquire the ability to produce both [ba] and [ma] very early. Rarer contrasts will be acquired later.

Given that development is assumed to follow a genetically programmed sequence of events, this theory clearly predicts that speech sounds should be acquired in the same order across different languages. There is some evidence for this view. For example, children acquiring French, English, Japanese and Swedish all tend to use some classes of consonants (e.g. labials, stops) more frequently than others (de Boysson-Bardies & Vihman, 1991). In addition, the theory predicts that similar types of error will occur across languages and this too seems to be the case. For example, in Serbian, Swedish, German, French and English, sounds such as [k] and [g] are replaced by [t]. So in Serbian *kaka* becomes *tata*, in German, *kopf* becomes *topf*, in French *garçon* becomes *tossan* and in English *cut* becomes *tut* (all examples from Lust, 2006).

However, there are also many examples where the pattern of acquisition seems to be language-specific rather than universal, contrary to the predictions of the maturational theory (see Kiparsky & Menn, 1977). For example, labials are used significantly less frequently in Japanese and Swedish than in English and French (de Boysson-Bardies & Vihman, 1991). Similarly, Pye has demonstrated that the sounds [tz] and [l] are very frequent in the speech of young K'iche' (or Quiche) Mayan speakers in Guatemala, despite the fact that English children tend to learn these sounds very late (Pye, 1991). Finally, Bulgarian, Estonian and Swedish children seem capable of producing the sound [v] much earlier than English children (Ingram, 1992).

There are also problems with Jakobson's interpretation of babbling. Jakobson has argued that the development of speech depends on the child first recognising that sounds have meaning. As a result, babbling and speech sounds must have their origins in different production mechanisms, since babble is meaningless. However, there is plenty of evidence for continuity between babbling and the acquisition of words. Vihman and colleagues conducted an extensive analysis of the babble and speech sounds of nine English-speaking children, beginning when each child was about nine months old. They reported a "striking parallelism between babbling and words within each child, across time and within time period" (Vihman, Macken, Miller, Simmons & Miller, 1985, p. 397). For example, one child (Sean) showed an increasing use of monosyllabic babble and monosyllabic words over the same time period, showing that an increase in one was accompanied by an increase in the other. Similarly, Timmy started to use more disyllabic babble and words over the same time period. This suggests that the development of babble and words may go hand in hand. In fact, it turns out that babble can be so 'word-like' that its acoustic properties (e.g. pitch, intonation) reflect the specific language that the infant is learning. De Boysson-Bardies and colleagues, using acoustic analysis, demonstrated that the babble of French, Japanese, English and Swedish children had different characteristics which reflected the acoustic properties of the language to which the infants had been exposed (de Boysson-Bardies, Hallé, Sagart & Durand, 1989). This is contrary to the predictions of Jakobson's maturational theory, which saw no role for babbling in the development of speech sound.

2.4.4 Template theory

The final theory to be discussed, the template theory, does not explain errors in terms of universal rules but in terms of the task the child is trying to solve. The focus here is on the fact that the child is trying to learn words, so her motivation is to try to reproduce the adult target as closely as possible. Unfortunately, however, "the problem posed by the learning of a large and arbitrary set of patterned sound-meaning pairs" is a difficult one (Vihman & Velleman, 2000, p. 256). It is made even harder by the fact that the child may not have mastered the complex articulatory gestures needed to reproduce adult words accurately. The child's solution is thus to resort to *word templates* (Macken, 1995). Templates are well-practised word patterns that the child has already learnt and can produce easily and effortlessly. Errors occur when the child tries to extend these templates to words that do not fit the template. For example, children may develop a trochaic (strong–weak) stress-based template and deform words that do not fit with this template. As a result, unstressed initial syllables might be omitted (e.g. *eraser* becomes *raser* [/reɪzə/], Echols & Newport, 1992).

Analyses of children's spontaneous speech do seem to reveal evidence of templates. For example, Waterson (1971) reported that her son developed a template [vowel-ʃ] that he extended to the words *dish* [iʃ], *fetch* [iʃ], *fish* [iʃ] and *vest* [uʃ] (we pronounce the ʃ sound as *sh* as in *sheep*) Evidence for templates has, in fact, been reported for children learning a range of languages including Hebrew, Spanish, French, English, Finnish and Estonian (Berman, 1977; Macken, 1978; Menn, 1978; Vihman, 1976, 1993; Vihman & Velleman, 2000).[4] The theory also explains why mispronunciation errors sometimes occur after a period in which children have been producing the word correctly. Fikkert & Levelt (2008) found that errors in the speech of Dutch-learning children only began after a period of correct use. For example, the child Noortje pronounced the word *koek* (/kuk/ 'cookie') correctly at age 2;5,[5] but then mispronounced it as /tuk/ at age 2;8. This is something that universal theories have a particular problem with, but template theory deals with it very easily. Initially, children's words are simple and quite easy to produce. As they develop templates in an attempt to produce a wider range of more complex, difficult words, these previously correct words can get sucked into the template pattern, resulting in errors.

Finally, the theory can explain cross-linguistic differences in errors because the rhythmic patterns of each language are predicted to have a different effect on

4 Note that some of these authors do not refer to templates but the data they provide has been cited as evidence of templates.
5 This notation indicates age in years; months.

the templates that children create. For example, Vihman & Croft (2007) analysed children's speech errors across five languages, focussing on errors in which the initial consonant of words was omitted (e.g. [iʃ] for *fish*). These errors were far more frequent in Estonian, Finnish, French and Welsh than English. Vihman and Croft argued that this was because a number of factors conspire to affect the rhythm of the languages differently, so that the first consonant tends to be more salient in English than the other languages. For example, in English, the first syllable is often long and loud, with a reduced second syllable (e.g. DOCtor). In French, however, it is the final syllable that tends to be accented, not the first syllable. Welsh and Finnish both also have features that conspire to make the first consonant less salient. As a result, English children are more likely to develop word templates that preserve these initial consonants than are children in other languages.

However, children also make errors that do not seem to fit into templates, and these cannot be explained by the theory. It may be that such errors do fit a template pattern, but one that is not captured by the researchers' recordings. Alternatively it may be that some errors occur for reasons other than templates. The problem is that it is often quite difficult to isolate and identify templates given that each individual child is predicted to develop their own unique set of templates. In fact, individual differences are the norm rather than the exception. For example, Vihman reported that although consonant harmony errors were the most well-documented error that children produce, their use ranged from 1 per cent to 32 per cent across the 13 children she studied (consonant harmony errors are those where syllables within a word are assimilated to each other, becoming more like each other, e.g. *doggy* becomes *goggy*, Vihman, 1978) Within the theory, individual differences like these stem from the children developing different patterns of consonant production during the babbling stage, which are called *vocal motor schemes* (see DePaolis, Vihman & Keren-Portnoy, 2011). However, the theory at present posits no principled explanation of why a particular child will develop one set of vocal motor schemes and not another.

2.5   CHAPTER SUMMARY

We have considered the groundwork that children have to put in before they really get going on the process of language acquisition. We first focussed on speech perception, considering the key question:

How do we learn the phonemes of our language?

We discovered that infants start off with the ability to perceive many (although not all) of the sound contrasts that are important in the world's languages, but lose much of this ability as they become tuned to their native language. Researchers are still discussing the abilities children are born with and how their native language tunes these abilities. However, by the end of the first year, we do know that children are capable of distinguishing most of the sounds of their native language.

In the second section, we investigated which cues children might use to segment the speech stream, to explore the key question:

What cues might infants use to segment the speech stream?

We discussed prosodic cues, phonotactic regularities, allophonic variation, isolated words and transitional probabilities. However, although children seem to be sensitive to all these cues to word boundaries, none of the cues is likely to be sufficient on its own. An integrative approach is almost certainly required.

Whatever the solution, it is clear that children do somehow learn to segment the speech stream because they start to produce individual words at the end of the first year. However, their first attempts at words can sound very different from the words as spoken by an adult. This is the issue we turned to in the third section by exploring the key question:

Why do children make errors when they first try to produce speech?

We concluded that these mispronunciation errors could not be attributed either to perceptual problems or to problems with articulation. Jakobson's maturational theory similarly had difficulty, especially in explaining both individual differences and differences across languages. Template theory seems to deal much more effectively with individual and cross-linguistic differences but many of its predictions remain to be tested. Cross-linguistic research is likely to be the key to the next stage in our understanding. By comparing the strategies that infants apply in response to the challenges posed by different languages, we will learn more about the skills that infants bring to the language learning task.

2.6 SUGGESTED READING

Three leading researchers in the field have written very readable books:
de Boysson-Bardies, B. (1999). *How language comes to children.* Cambridge, MA: MIT Press.
Jusczyk, P. W. (2000). *The discovery of spoken language.* Cambridge, MA: MIT Press.
Vihman, M. M. (1996). *Phonological development: The origins of language in the child.* Oxford: Blackwell. A revised edition of this book should also be available from 2014.

2.7 SUGGESTED READING (ADVANCED LEVEL)

Aslin, R. N. & Pisoni, D. B. (1980). Some developmental processes in speech perception. In G. Yeni Komshian, J. F. Kavanagh & C. A. Ferguson (Eds) *Child Phonology: Perception and Production* (Vol. 2, pp. 67–96). New York: Academic Press. This is the book chapter that introduced the universal theory.

Jusczyk, P. W., Houston, D. M. & Newsome, M. (1999). The beginnings of word segmentation in English-learning infants. *Cognitive Psychology, 39*(3–4), 159–207. Jusczyk's 15-experiment paper showing infants are sensitive to English trochaic stress patterns.

Kuhl, P. K., Conboy, B. T., Coffey-Corina, S., Padden, D., Rivera-Gaxiola, M. & Nelson, T. (2008). Phonetic learning as a pathway to language: New data and native language magnet theory expanded (NLM-e). *Philosophical Transactions of the Royal Society B, 363*, 979–1000. The article in which Kuhl and colleagues introduce the NLM-e.

Saffran, J. R., Aslin, R. N. & Newport, E. L. (1996). Statistical learning by 8-month-old infants. *Science, 274*(5294), 1926–1928. Saffran's original study that showed infants are sensitive to transitional probabilities.

Vihman, M. M. & Croft, W. (2007). Phonological development: Toward a 'radical' templatic phonology. *Linguistics, 45*(4), 683–725. A very good introduction to template theory.

For reading on Optimality Theory see:

Fikkert, P. & Levelt, C. C. (2008). How does place fall into place? The lexicon and emergent constraints in the developing phonological grammar. In P. Avery, B. Elan Dresher & K. Rice (Eds), *Contrast in phonology: Perception and acquisition* (pp. 219–256). Berlin: Mouton de Gruyter.

Prince, A. & Smolensky, P. (1997). Optimality: From neural networks to universal grammar. *Science, 275*, 1604–1610.

2.8 COMPREHENSION CHECK

1. Describe the problems for the learner caused by:

   a. A lack of acoustic invariance
   b. Cross-linguistic differences in categorical perception

2. Describe the main differences between the universal theory (maintenance and loss) and attunement theories like Kuhl's NLM-e.

3. Identify which of the following segmentation cues are language universal (language general) and which differ across languages (and must be learnt by exposure to a language)

   a. Allophonic cues
   b. Stress cues
   c. Transitional probabilities
   d. Phonotactic regularities

4. What is wrong with the idea that transitional probabilities are sufficient for infants to solve the segmentation problem?

5. What are the four main types of pronunciation error (deformations) that children produce?

6. Identify one problem with each of the following theories of why children make pronunciation errors:

   a. Mis-perception: mushy mouth–mushy ear
   b. Articulatory constraints on production
   c. Jakobson's maturation theory
   d. Template theory

3

Learning the meaning of words

3.1 THE ISSUE

On the face of it, learning the meaning of words seems like a simple task. We can easily imagine what a typical word learning scene might look like. A child sits on the floor playing with her pet dog. Her (unimaginative) mother says *"That's a dog."* *"Aah"*, the child thinks, *"So this animal I'm playing with is a dog."* Put like this, the task of mapping words to their meanings seems quite simple.

Unfortunately, when we delve a little deeper we find that the task is not that simple. There are two main problems; the *reference problem* and the *extension problem*. These problems are discussed below, before we turn to some of the solutions offered by word learning theorists. The focus here is on word learning in the early years, so the reader must be aware that children continue to learn words throughout childhood, many of which they come across when they start to read books.

3.1.1 The reference problem

The reference problem was eloquently described by Quine (1960). Quine called the reference problem the *problem of radical translation* because he saw the child's task as equivalent to that of a linguist attempting to translate a previously unknown, radically different language. How might the linguist go about the task? He would probably start by listening to what words the natives used to describe observable events. For example, suppose a rabbit scurried by and the native said *gavagai*. The linguist might tentatively note down a possible translation as *rabbit*. However, the problem is that the word could equally well mean *animal* or *white* or any number of things. How is the linguist to distinguish between these possible meanings, given that he does not know enough of the language to ask the native what *gavagai* means?

The linguist's problem is the same problem that faces children in their attempt to learn words. Every time a word is spoken, there are millions of things, events or ideas that it could refer to. Xu and Tenenbaum have summed up the problem very neatly: "With each referential act, e.g., 'Look, a dog!' there are an infinite number of hypotheses for the meaning of the word '*dog*' that are consistent with the data" (Xu & Tenenbaum, 2005, p. 1). How do children learn the meaning of words, given that each word has millions, if not an infinite number, of possible meanings?

In fact, children face an even more difficult task than Quine's linguist because children have no first language (unlike the linguist) on which to base their hypotheses. Linguists can at least guess that a language is likely to have a word for rabbit and can focus on trying to figure out what that word is. Children, however, might not even know that languages usually have words to describe rabbits. For the child, the word *gavagai* might just as easily mean *we have no word for that animal in our language*. And this is just the problem inherent in learning words for observable objects. Presumably it is even harder to work out the meaning of words that do not refer to things that the child can see; words like *think* and *love*. For some words, it seems almost impossible to converge on what the word means; how on earth do you teach a two-year-old the meaning of the word *the*?

Despite this, children learn words impressively fast, so fast that Pinker famously called them "lexical vacuum cleaners" (Pinker, 1994, p. 151). By the time children reach young adulthood they will understand thousands of words and some children start this learning task very early. For example, Bergelson and Swingley tested whether six- to nine-month-old English-learning infants could understand some common words for body parts and food items using an eye tracking methodology (Bergelson & Swingley, 2012). This method takes advantage of the fact that children and adults have tendency to look at pictures of objects that they hear named. In this study, infants were shown pictures on a computer screen, then their eye movements were tracked as their parents instructed them to look at a particular object in the pictures (e.g. *look at the apple*). The researchers reported that the infants looked at the named object significantly more often than we would expect by chance, indicating that six- to nine-month-olds had already learnt the meaning of these words.

Given this finding, it is not surprising that the average American 12-month-old already understands about 50 words (Fenson et al., 1994). In fact, most children understand so many words by two years of age, and add to this list so quickly, that it soon becomes virtually impossible to keep accurate records of the number of words they understand. Children tend to produce fewer words than they can understand but even so, they can start to accumulate a production vocabulary equally quickly. Table 3.1 shows the words produced by one British English-learning child aged one year and one month old (1;1). As is usual for English children, very few of the earliest words are verbs, and the word *no* is learnt earlier than the word *yes*.

There is also evidence that children are capable of learning a word after only hearing it once or twice; an ability that is called *fast mapping*. Carey and Bartlett (1978) taught three- and four-year-old children a new colour term – chromium – simply by showing children two trays (one blue and one a sort of olive green colour) and saying *bring me the chromium tray, not the blue one, the chromium one*. The children in this study were surprisingly successful at choosing to bring the olive-green tray, despite never having heard the word chromium before. It is important to note that the children did not learn the meaning of the word very well; they retained some meaning of the word after six weeks but did not have very clear memories. Word learning is clearly much better if words are heard and practised often (Dockrell, Braisby & Best, 2007; Horst & Samuelson, 2008). But the study does show that children are capable of learning at least something about the meaning of a word very quickly.

Table 3.1
Words produced by Lara aged 1;1

Animal Noises	Nouns	People's names	Miscellaneous words
Baa baa	Bird	Daddy	Bye bye
Grrr	Teddy	Dadaw (Grandad)	Hello
Mieow	Pram	Mummy	No
Moo	Ball		Boo
Ouch	Book		Ta (thanks)
Vroom	Bath		There
Woof woof	Bottle		More
			All gone
			What's that?

3.1.2 The extension problem

Solving the reference problem is only part of the story. Even after working out what a word refers to, the child has to work out what to extend the word to. In the example given at the beginning of the chapter, we imagined a little girl playing with her pet dog, hearing her mother say *that's a dog* and, thus, learning that the word *dog* refers to her pet dog. But, of course, this is not quite enough. The word *dog* can be used to refer to all the dogs in the world, including those that look quite different from each other (e.g. Chihuahuas and Labradors). In fact, the word *dog* can even be used to refer to imaginary dogs as well (e.g. cartoon dogs in picture books). However, *dog* cannot ever be used to refer to cats, rabbits or horses. How does the child learn to extend the word *dog* correctly?

The extension problem occurs because words are not always used to denote tangible things. They are also used to denote categories (or concepts). Thus, the word *dog* is used as a word to describe all members of the dog category (we say that members of a category are *taxonomically related*). This category, by definition, includes all dogs, even those that are as different-looking as Chihuahuas and Labradors. It also excludes all other animals (cats, rabbits and horses) as well as things that are *thematically associated* with dogs (e.g. a dog basket, a lead, a bone). Thus children have to learn to extend the word *dog* to other members of the dog category but not to other animals or to things associated with dogs. To take another example, to learn the meaning of *in*, children have to learn that *in* does not just apply to one situation (e.g. *let's get you in the bath*) but extends to a whole range of sometimes very dissimilar situations (putting a ball in a box, putting the butter in the fridge) but not to others (putting the ball under the box, taking the butter out of the fridge). In other words, children have to learn the essential meaning of *in* that is common across all these situations (inclusion within a space or enclosure).

The extension problem gets even more complicated when we consider that words do not map onto categories in the same way across languages. This means that children have to learn to extend words in different ways depending on the language

Figure 3.1
Categorisation of some object placements in English and Korean. Reprinted from Bowerman and Choi (2001, p. 482, Figure 16.1).

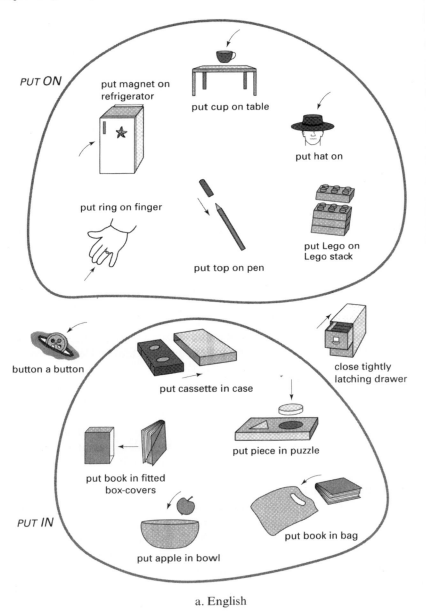

a. English

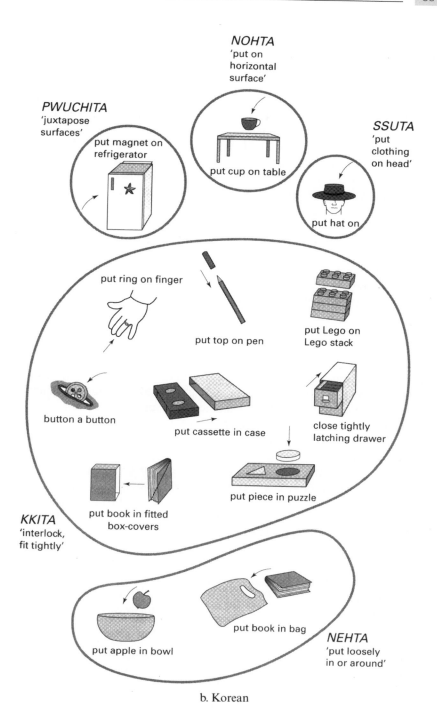

b. Korean

they are learning. For example, English and Korean differ in how they describe the location of an object in relation to other objects (spatial relations). In English, speakers have to distinguish between support relations (ON) and containment relations (IN). Objects can be *on* other things (*on the table, on the floor, on the slide*) or *in* things (*in the box, in the cup, in the drawer*). This means that English children have to learn to extend the word *on* only to objects that are on a surface (e.g. *the ring is on the box*) and to extend the word *in* only to objects that are contained inside an enclosure (e.g. *the ring is in the box*).

Korean does not have words that mean *in* and *on* because Korean does not distinguish between containment and support. Instead, Korean distinguishes between objects that are tightly fitted together and loosely fitted together. For example, the verb *kkita* is used to describe objects that are tightly fitted into another object in an interlocking manner. This verb would be used to describe putting a top on a pen or putting a ring on a finger. However, it would also be used to describe putting a jigsaw piece in a puzzle or putting a cassette in a case. A range of verbs is used to describe loose-fitting arrangements; *nehta* for 'putting loosely in or around' (e.g. putting apples in a bowl) and *nohta* for 'putting on a horizontal surface' (e.g, putting a cup on a table). Korean children thus have to learn to extend *kkita* to tightly fitting objects (whether they are on or in each other) and to use other words for loose-fitting objects (see figure 3.1).

Despite this, neither English nor Korean children have problems learning how to use spatial words appropriately for their own language. Not only do they learn the relevant words early, they extend them in language-appropriate ways from the beginning. Choi and colleagues devised an experiment to test this (Choi, McDonough, Bowerman & Mandler, 1999). They showed English and Korean 18- to 23-month-old children some videos that showed containment (*in*), support (*on*), tight- (*kkita*) and loose-fitting relations (*nehta*). For example, one video depicted Lego blocks being put on top of one another (*on/kkita*), another showed rings being put in a basket (*in/nehta*), a third showed pegs being put in a tight-fitting hole (*in/kkita*). The children saw two videos at a time and heard sentences in their own language instructing them to look at one of the videos (e.g. English: *where's she putting it in*; Korean: *Eti-ey kki-e*; "where's [she] tight-fitting it?"). From the youngest ages tested, the children showed awareness of the spatial categories of their own language. The English children looked longer at the scenes depicting containment events when they heard *in*, whether the scene depicted loose- or tight-fitting events. The Korean children looked longer at the tight-fitting events when they heard *kki-e*, whether or not the scenes showed containment (*in*) or support (*on*) events.

There is one caveat though. Children may extend words in language-appropriate ways but that does not mean that they always use them correctly right from the beginning. They make two types of error. First, they make under-extension errors, where they use words for a limited set of meanings. For example, some children initially use words like *up* and *down* only to describe events that involve motion, like walking down the hill or climbing up the tree (Smiley & Huttenlocher, 1994). Only later will they start to use them to describe static (non-moving) relations (*the man is up the ladder, the house is down the hill*). Second, children make over-extension errors where they use words too broadly and in inappropriate ways. For example, children have been known to extend *open* to the act of pulling two Frisbees apart or pulling the stem off an apple (Bowerman, 1978; Bowerman, de León & Choi, 1995; Clark, 1993). In both cases, the errors are quite sensible – pulling the stem off an apple could well be seen as an opening event – but the English language does not describe it as an opening event. In fact, over-extension errors are usually quite plausible. McDonough (2002) found that children tend to over-extend words in very sensible ways, such as to objects of the same shape or animacy. For example, children are much more likely to extend the word *bird* to other animals (e.g. a pig) than to inanimate objects (a hat).

To summarise so far, to learn the meaning of a new word, the child not only has to isolate the correct referent for a word but also has to learn how to extend it appropriately for her language (while not over-extending it incorrectly). Since languages differ in how they categorise the world, the child has to pay careful attention to how a word behaves in her language in order to learn its proper meaning. And there are thousands of words to be learnt like this. Despite this, children seem to learn words – solving both the reference and extension problems – relatively easily.

Not surprisingly, given the complexity of the task, researchers do not yet know how children learn words. However, there have been a number of influential theories over the years. Some theories argue that innate constraints help children isolate the meaning of words. Other theories argue that we do not need special constraints – they suggest children can learn words by working out the speaker's intention, or by applying powerful, but general, cognitive processing abilities to the learning task. Still others argue that some words, verbs in particular, cannot be learnt until we have mastered some aspects of grammar. A final theory – the emergent coalition model – takes all of these factors and puts them together. In the rest of this chapter we discuss these ideas in turn.

3.2 CONSTRAINTS THEORY PART I: THE ROLE OF INNATE CONSTRAINTS

Constraints theorists argue that "children's word learning is guided by a set of default assumptions or constraints on hypotheses" (Woodward & Markman, 1998, p. 379). What this means is that children have innate guidelines about how to interpret new words, and follow these guidelines when they come across a new word. Thus, our key question in this section is:

Key question: since new words can potentially refer to any aspect of an event, are we innately biased to consider some meanings before others?

For example, one proposed constraint is the *whole object assumption*, which states that, in the first instance, learners should assume that new words refer to whole objects, rather than parts of objects, actions, events or spatial relations. Thus, a child who is playing with her pet dog and hears her mother say *that's a dog* might assume that the new word applies to the whole object (the dog) rather than to a part of the object (the dog's leg).

Theorists have suggested a whole raft of such constraints to guide children's learning. As well as the whole object assumption, Markman and colleagues have proposed:

- *The mutual exclusivity assumption.* Learners should assume that objects only have one name. Thus, if you already have a name for an object (e.g. *dog*), assume that other words spoken in the presence of the dog (e.g. *leg, running*) are not alternative names for the dog but refer to something about the dog (e.g. a part of the dog, the dog's action, the dog's location).

- *The taxonomic assumption.* When learning how to extend a new word, assume that it will only extend to taxonomically related things, not thematically associated things. In other words, only extend the word *dog* to other members of the same category (dog) not things associated with dogs (e.g. bones).

Other constraints have been suggested by other authors, such as:

- *The shape bias* (Baldwin, 1992; Landau, Smith & Jones, 1988). This is said to bias children to label objects of similar shapes with the same name.

- *The function bias.* This is said to bias children to label novel objects that have the same function with the same name (e.g. objects you can use to pick up balls and deposit them in a chute; Kemler Nelson, 1999).

- *Pragmatic principles of conventionality and contrast.* 'Conventionality' refers to the idea that children assume that "there is a conventional form that should be used in the language community" (Clark, 2003, p. 142). 'Contrast' is similar to the mutual exclusivity assumption and refers to the idea that children assume that "any difference in form indicates a difference in meaning" (Clark, 2003, p. 143).

3.2.1 The evidence for and against constraints theory

Many studies support the constraints theory but the most widely cited are those by Markman and colleagues. One of Markman's first studies demonstrated that children seem to obey the mutual exclusivity assumption when learning new words (Markman & Wachtel, 1988). Markman and Wachtel showed three-year-old children pairs of pictures; one showing a familiar object (e.g. a cow) and one showing an unfamiliar object (e.g. a radish rosette maker, which is a tool for making pretty rosettes out of radishes). When asked to *show me the fendle* (where *fendle* is a made-up novel word), the three-year-old children overwhelmingly chose the novel object. The researchers argued that this supported the mutual exclusivity assumption; the children already had a name for cow, so they assumed, based on mutual exclusivity, that the new unfamiliar name must refer to the unfamiliar object. In an additional experiment in this paper, Markman and Wachtel showed children familiar objects but labelled them with unfamiliar names. For example, on one trial, they taught children the words *dorsal fin* while showing them a fish. The children were then asked *what is the dorsal fin, the whole thing* (experimenter circled the whole object with her finger) *or just this part* (experimenter pointed out the fin)? As predicted by the mutual exclusivity assumption, children tended to assume that the label *dorsal fin* referred to the part of the object not the whole thing, because they already had a familiar word (*fish*) that referred to the whole object.

In another study, Markman and colleagues reported evidence for the taxonomic assumption (Markman & Hutchinson, 1984). The taxonomic assumption states that children have a bias to assume that new words only extend to taxonomically related things (i.e. things in the same category). In this experiment, three-year-old children were shown an object that was then labelled with a novel word. For example, they were shown a cow and then told *this is a dax*. Half the children were then asked to *find another dax* from among a group of objects (the labelling condition). The other half were simply asked to *find another one* from among the group of objects (the control condition). Importantly, the group of objects included items that were taxonomically related and items that were thematically associated with the labelled object. Taxonomically related objects came from the same category as the labelled object (e.g. a pig is taxonomically related to a cow because they are both members of the animal category). Thematically associated objects did not come from the same category but associated with the labelled animal (e.g. milk and grass are associated with cows). The researchers found that the children instructed to *find another dax* were much more likely to choose objects that were taxonomically related (e.g. a pig) than the children who were instructed simply to *find another one*. This shows that the children were biased to extend the new word (*dax*) to taxonomically related objects, just as the taxonomic assumption predicts.

Constraints theories, however, also have their critics. The first criticism is about what the evidence actually shows. For example, there is a lot of debate about whether the evidence provided by Markman and Hutchinson (1984) actually provides support for a taxonomic constraint or simply for a shape bias in which the children are more likely to choose an object with a similar shape to the labelled object (Baldwin, 1992). Perhaps even more importantly, there is also a very vigorous debate about whether innate constraints work in all languages. Innate constraints, by their very nature, must be present in all children across the world, no matter what language they are learning. This means that any evidence showing that children do not use a constraint when learning a language counts against constraints theory.

For example, there is a very lively debate in the literature about whether a universal noun bias applies across all languages. Gentner (1982) first proposed this universal constraint, suggesting all children will find nouns easier to learn than other words because nouns refer to objects in the world, which are easily identifiable. Gentner called this the *natural partitions hypothesis* because it was based on the idea that all languages naturally distinguish between nouns (that refer to concrete, simple and basic objects) and other types of word (that refer to more complex things like states and events). In support of the hypothesis, Gentner (1982) reported that children's first words contain more object words (nouns) than action words (verbs) across a number of very different languages – English, German, Japanese, Kaluli, Mandarin and Turkish.

However, other research on languages such as Tzeltal, Korean and Japanese suggests that children produce more action words than Gentner predicted (Choi & Gopnik, 1995; Tardif, 1996). As a result, some researchers argue that noun bias is not universal and that children's vocabularies simply reflect the type of language that they hear. In languages like English, nouns are very salient and easy to perceive – they are always present and often occur at the end of the sentence. As a result, nouns are learnt easily and early. In languages like Japanese, however, nouns can be omitted, which means that sentences often contain only verbs. In these languages, verbs may be easier to learn than nouns. There is also some evidence that the situation in which children are tested can affect the number of nouns and verbs they appear to know. Book reading, for example, tends to encourage children to produce nouns rather than verbs (Ogura, Dale, Yamashita, Murase & Mahieu, 2006). This debate is by no means resolved (see Imai et al., 2008). The important thing to remember is that there is still an animated debate among researchers about whether there is any evidence for universal constraints that work across all languages.

A third problem is that simply relying on constraints would point children in the wrong direction for a large number of words. We do not need any studies to show that this is the case – a simple thought-experiment will do. If we consider again the little girl playing with her pet dog, this time let us imagine that she already knows that the dog's name is Fido. What will her reaction be when her mother says *that's a dog*? According to the mutual exclusivity assumption, the girl must assume that the word does not refer to the dog; she already has a word for the dog – *Fido*. So perhaps she will assume that the word refers to the dog's paws, or its fur, or its collar? But of course this would be wrong. Immediately, the mutual exclusivity assumption has led her astray because lots of objects have multiple labels: Fido, puppy, dog, mammal, animal and so on. Constraints, then, can only ever serve as initial hypotheses or what Markman and colleagues call "good first guesses as to a word's meaning" (Markman, Wasow & Hansen, 2003, p. 242). They cannot ever be the whole story.

3.3 CONSTRAINTS THEORY PART II: THE DEVELOPMENTAL LEXICAL PRINCIPLES FRAMEWORK

In response to the critics, Golinkoff and colleagues devised a version of constraints theory called the *developmental lexical principles framework* (Golinkoff, Mervis & Hirsh-Pasek, 1994). They suggested that six principles, organised into two tiers, could do the job of learning words. In the first tier are the three principles that are (probably) innately given. These three principles are essential for word learning to get off the ground and are available to the children from the beginning of the process. They are:

- *The principle of reference.* Children assume that words symbolise/stand for objects, actions and attributes.

- *The principle of extendibility.* Children assume that words do not necessarily refer to a single example but to a category of similar objects.

- *The principle of object scope.* Children tend to assume a) that words refer to objects in the first place, and only apply labels to actions and events if it is clear that the word does not refer to an object and b) that words refer to the whole object not a part of the object.

These three principles are not very powerful or constraining, so children make a lot of errors. For example, children might incorrectly over-extend words on the basis of shape similarity and use the word *ball* to refer to all round objects (including, for example, the moon). In addition, with only these constraints to help, word learning is slow and difficult. Thus, as children get older, they develop more refined, sophisticated constraints to help them learn words. This is when the second tier of principles develops. These are:

- *The principle of conventionality.* Children must learn to use the conventional meaning of words and abandon their own creations or family names.

- *The principle of categorical scope.* Perceptual similarity is no longer an adequate basis for extension. Children now know that words label taxonomic categories, first at the basic level (e.g. dog) and then at superordinate levels (e.g. mammal, animal).

- *Novel-name-nameless category principle.* Children now assume that a new word refers to an object or category that does not yet have a name. Unlike the mutual exclusivity assumption, however, the principle does not prevent children having two names for one object (e.g. *Fido* and *dog*).

Importantly, the second tier of constraints develops as a result of inborn biases combined with the child's experience of word learning. This means that the constraints are applied in a much more sophisticated way. For example, they can be overridden if they conflict with other cues, so children are far less likely to make errors in learning the meaning of words.

3.3.1 The evidence for and against developmental lexical principles

Like the original constraints theory, this account can explain why children seem to obey constraints in word learning (see the evidence discussed in the previous section). However, unlike the original constraints theory, it can also explain why children are capable of ignoring the constraints in certain circumstances. However, once again, it is not yet clear whether the cross-linguistic evidence supports the theory. In principle, the lexical principles framework is better equipped than the original constraints theory to explain cross-linguistic differences because it allows for some language-specific learning at the second tier of constraints. But the first tier of constraints is predicted to be universal, so we would expect these to apply at the start of language learning across all languages. In other words, the theory predicts that children's word extension will be based on innate (and thus universal) biases at the beginning of the word learning process, even if not later on. Unfortunately, it is still unclear whether universal initial biases exist cross-linguistically because there is both evidence for and against the idea.

Evidence for universal initial biases comes from studies that demonstrate children are sensitive to the same properties of objects and events no matter what language they are learning. For example, Pulverman and her colleagues studied whether English- and Spanish-learning children paid attention to both the path and manner of motion events (Pulverman, Golinkoff, Hirsh-Pasek & Buresh, 2008). Path refers to the direction of motion of an action in relationship to a landmark such as a house (e.g. into the house, out of the house, over the house) and is referred to frequently in both English and Spanish. Manner refers to the type of motion (e.g. running vs. walking) and occurs far less often in Spanish than English speech. This is because Spanish verbs do not encode manner, which means that Spaniards do not say *the girl ran out of the house* but must say, instead, something like *the girl exited the house, running*. Pulverman and colleagues showed cartoon videos of a star (called Starry) moving around a fixed point to English and Spanish 14- and 17-month-old children. They tested whether the children noticed when the path of Starry's motion changed (over vs. under the fixed point) and when the manner of Starry's motion changed (spinning vs. bending). Despite the differences in the way the two languages encode path and manner, English and Spanish children responded in exactly the same way and were sensitive to both changes in path and manner. The authors concluded that despite language differences, there may be universal biases (or what they called *primitives*) in how children pay attention to objects and events in the world, which could be used in the word learning task.

However, evidence against universal initial biases comes from studies that demonstrate that children are sensitive to language-specific properties of events from the beginning. An example is the study by Choi and her colleagues that we have already described above (Choi et al., 1999). They found that 18- to 23-month-old children treated events differently depending on whether they were learning English or Korean. The children in this study were shown two videos and instructed either to watch *where's she putting it in* (English children) or *Eti-ey kki-e; where's [she] tight-fitting it?* (Korean children). From the beginning, English children paid attention to the distinction between containment (IN) and support (ON) events whereas Korean children paid attention to the distinction between tight- and loose-fitting, just as their language required. Contrary to the universal constraints view and, in fact, contrary to some other studies (Hespos & Spelke, 2004), there was no evidence of an early stage of development in which the children were tempted to follow a universal bias. From the beginning, they responded to the distinctions made by their language.

The search for universal biases is likely to continue for some time. However, some researchers have moved away from this search, asking instead whether we can explain word learning simply in terms of more general cognitive processes. We consider these views below.

3.4 OTHER ROUTES TO WORD LEARNING

Key questions: do we need innate linguistic biases? What other factors might allow us to converge on the correct meaning of words?

As we have seen, a number of researchers challenge the view that universal, innate constraints underlie word learning. This is not unusual; there are usually at least two approaches in research. Perhaps more unusual here is the fact that the debate about what takes the place of innate constraints is just as rigorous as the debate about the need for innate constraints itself. Some argue that children's word learning strategies are guided by their emerging understanding of communicative intent and joint attention (the social-pragmatic account). Others argue that word learning can be explained in terms of powerful cognitive processing abilities alone (the attentional learning account). Sometimes the debate between these two is so fierce that the constraints theorists fail to get a look in at all.

3.4.1 The social-pragmatic account

Many researchers support a social-pragmatic account, including Bruner, Nelson, Ninio, Snow, Clark and Tomasello (Bruner, 1978; Clark, 1993; Nelson, 1985; Ninio & Snow, 1996; Tomasello, 2003). As is often the case, each researcher proposes a slightly different version of the theory, but all broadly share a similar view. According to this view, children do not need innate linguistic constraints. Instead, children are guided by their understanding of what speakers are trying to say. In other words, children pay attention to what Baldwin and Moses call "social clues" to learn the meaning of novel words (2001, p. 310).

In any social situation in which a speaker is talking to a listener, the speaker provides a rich and diverse set of clues that tell the listener what she is referring to. For example, speakers are likely to look at an object they are talking about or to orientate their body towards it. They may gesture towards the object or use facial expressions to indicate whether the object pleases them or not. Such cues are very useful to listeners, especially listeners who have not been giving the speaker their full attention. Social-pragmatic theorists argue that such cues can also be used to work out the meaning of new words.

Two abilities allow young children to use these cues to learn words: the ability to establish *joint attention* and the ability to understand the speaker's *communicative intent*. If we return again to the scene in which a girl is playing with her pet dog when her mother says *that's a dog*, the social-pragmatic account predicts that accurate word learning will occur for two reasons. First, both the child and mother are jointly attending to the dog; both are looking at the dog, and both know that the other person is looking at the dog. Second, the child is aware that the mother's intention (her communicative intent) is to label the dog, rather than, say, ordering the child to leave the dog alone. Knowing both of these things, the child can work out that the word *dog* is a label for the animal in front of her.

3.4.1.1 *Evidence for and against the social-pragmatic account*

How well does this theory explain word learning? There is quite a lot of evidence showing that we can use our social abilities to learn words (see Tomasello, 2003, for a review). In fact, some people have pointed out that it is no coincidence that children's word learning starts to take off at about the same time as socio-cognitive skills such as intention reading come online (between 9 and 12 months of age; see chapter 6 for more on this topic). Some of the most famous studies showing that children can use social skills to learn words are the *Toma* studies published by Baldwin (Baldwin, 1991, 1993a, 1993b). For example, in one study (Baldwin, 1993b), children were given a toy to play with while the experimenter held a different toy.[1] Half the children took part in the joint attention condition, where the experimenter waited until both she and the child were looking at the child's toys (i.e. she established joint attention with the child); only then did she label the child's toy with a novel word (e.g. *It's a toma*). The other children were tested in the discrepant labelling condition. Here, the experimenter waited until the child was looking at the child's own toy and then labelled her own (the experimenter's) toy with the novel word (i.e. she labelled the toy that the child was not looking at). All children were then shown both toys in a test phase and were asked *where's the toma?* Children aged 18 and 19 months of age (though not younger children) successfully identified the correct toy as the *toma* in both conditions. In other words, they linked the novel word with the toy that the experimenter was paying attention to, even when they themselves had been paying attention to a different toy. This is evidence that children are aware that it is the speaker's focus of attention, not their own, that matters when trying to learn the meaning of a new word.

Another advantage of the social-pragmatic theory is that it provides a good explanation of how children learn verbs. Verb learning is considered to be particularly difficult because verbs do not label objects; they label intangible events that are often very short-lived (e.g. *hitting*). In addition, most of the time when children hear verbs, the action is not even being performed. For example, Tomasello and Kruger (1992) noted that mothers very rarely use verbs to name ongoing actions (e.g. they rarely say things like *oh, you're eating*). They are far more likely to use verbs either to request that the child complete the action (*eat your dinner!*), to anticipate an impending action (*I'm going to eat my dinner*) or to comment on just completed actions (*have you eaten your dinner?*). How do children learn the meaning of verbs like *eat* when the action is not even occurring when the verb is spoken? Tomasello suggests that the solution is intention reading; children are "actively monitoring the adults' intention in the experimental situation to discover the intended referent of the new word" (Tomasello & Barton, 1994, p. 640). In other words, children make guesses about the referents of new verbs based on what they think the speaker intends to say.

Tomasello & Akhtar (1995) assessed whether children could learn the meaning of verbs in this way. They created an apparatus in which a novel toy spun round on a turntable. During the experiment, two-year-old children saw the action and heard the experimenter say a sentence that could refer either to the toy (*widget*) or to the action (*widge it!*). For example, the experimenter might say *widget, Paul, widget*. Importantly, the social cues provided by the experimenter differed in two conditions. In the *action highlighted* condition the children saw the experimenter ready the

---

1   In all studies the toys were completely novel so that the children would not already have a label for them. For example, two toys were "a green oblong extendable periscope and a disc encircled by yellow rubber suction cups" (Baldwin, 1991, pp. 878–879).

turntable for the action, place the toy on it, and then alternate her gaze between the child and the apparatus. In the *object highlighted* condition the experimenter picked up the toy and alternated her gaze between the child and the toy. As predicted, the different social cues produced different results. When later asked *can you show me widget/widge it?*, the children in the action highlighted condition were more likely to demonstrate the action than those in the object highlighted condition. The authors concluded that these children had used the socio-pragmatic cues provided by the experimenter to learn that *widget/widge it* referred to the action of spinning a toy on a turntable not to the toy being spun.

The final advantage of the social-pragmatic theory is that it can explain cross-linguistic differences in word categories, such as the fact that English distinguishes between IN and ON and Korean distinguishes between tight and loose fit (Choi et al., 1999). A child who is paying attention to speakers' intentions is presumably going to learn her own language's categories without the need for universal biases. The theory might also help explain how children learn words in cultures with very different child-rearing practices. For example, Ochs and Schieffelin (1984) report that, unlike Western European and American parents, the Kaluli of Papua New Guinea rarely engage young children in conversations because they believe that children have little or no understanding of the world around them. Akhtar and her colleagues have demonstrated that children can learn by listening to the conversations of others, which might explain how Kaluli children learn language (Akhtar, Jipson & Callanan, 2001). Children may be able to tune into the speaker's focus of attention even when they themselves are not engaged in the conversation.

The evidence that children can use social cues to learn words is, overall, quite impressive. However, as always, the theory has its critics. There are two main types of criticism. First, there are those who argue that social cues cannot be the whole story because word learning can take place in their absence. Second, there are those who argue that the evidence for social cues can be equally well or better explained simply in terms of general cognitive processes like perception, memory and attention.

The first set of criticisms centres on the idea that social cues cannot be the whole story. Particularly problematic is the fact that children seem to be capable of learning words before joint attention and intention reading skills have developed. For example, Bates and colleagues used a checklist, filled in by parents, to assess the language of thousands of American English-speaking children (the MacArthur-Bates Communicative Development Inventory; Bates et al., 1994). They reported that the average child understood over 30 words by the age of eight months and that the very fastest eight-month-olds already understood over 90 words. In fact, babies who are taught baby sign (a fun form of sign language) are able to produce signs representing food, drink and activities from about six months of age (Johnstone, Durieux-Smith & Bloom, 2005). Since these children have not yet developed joint attention and intention reading abilities (which develop between about nine and 12 months of age) they must be learning these words by other means.

Another similar problem comes from studies of children with autism, who find it difficult to interpret socio-pragmatic cues. This should cause problems in word learning according to the social-pragmatic theory and it does … in the lab. In an experiment by Parish-Morris and colleagues, the children with autism consistently chose an interesting object as the referent of a novel label, despite the fact that a different (boring) object was clearly intended as the speaker's referent (Parish-Morris, Hennon, Hirsh-Pasek, Golinkoff & Tager-Flusberg, 2007). However, in the real world, children with autism are capable of learning words, sometimes to a level indistinguishable from that of typically developing children. For example, children and adults with Asperger's syndrome can have severe difficulties in social understanding at the same time as demonstrating very few difficulties in vocabulary acquisition (Rourke & Tsantsanis, 1996). This evidence counts against the social-pragmatic theory because it shows that children with autism can learn words despite difficulties interpreting speaker eye gaze and communicative intent.

The second set of critics argues that we do not need to posit socio-pragmatic skills to explain word learning. They suggest that all the evidence for social-pragmatic theory can be explained in terms of basic cognitive mechanisms like memory and attention. For example, Samuelson and Smith (1998) suggested that the findings of an influential experiment by Akhtar and colleagues, one that is highly cited as support for the social-pragmatic theory (Akhtar, Carpenter & Tomasello, 1996), could in fact be explained in terms of a few simple cognitive biases.

In the original study, during training trials, two experimenters, the child and the child's parent played with three novel objects. Experimenter A and the parent then left the room while Experimenter B introduced a fourth object to the child. All four objects were then placed in a transparent box, after which Experimenter A and the parent returned. On returning, Experimenter A looked into the box containing all four objects and exclaimed *look, I see a gazzer. A gazzer.* During the test trials, despite all four objects being possible referents of the word *gazzer*, the children preferred to identify the fourth object as the *gazzer* when asked to *give me the gazzer.* Since none of the other objects had been given a name, the children could not be using biases like mutual exclusivity to solve the word learning task. Akhtar and her colleagues argued that the children were successful because they had correctly guessed that experimenter A's intention when she exclaimed *look, I see a gazzer* was to express surprise at seeing the new (fourth) object, the only one that had been introduced while she was out of the room. The results were interpreted as support for social-pragmatic theory.

Samuelson and Smith (1998) took issue with this interpretation. They argued that children were, in fact, grabbed by the novelty of the events surrounding the introduction of the fourth object (its *contextual novelty*). This, combined with a preference for assigning new labels to novel objects, could explain the findings. Samuelson and Smith's reasoning went like this. The first three objects were all introduced in the same context (playing with three adults on the floor). The fourth object was introduced in a completely different context (playing at a table with only one adult). So the children were not assigning the *gazzer* label to the object that was new to the experimenter, they were assigning it to the object that was introduced in a different context from the other three objects. In support of their interpretation, they re-ran Akhtar's experiment with a few changes. In the new version, Experimenter

A did not leave the room during the introduction of the fourth object, so the object was not new to her. However, the fourth object was still introduced in different surroundings from the first three objects – on a table covered with a brightly coloured cloth. As Samuelson and Smith had predicted, the children still preferred to assign the *gazzer* label to the fourth object. In other words, they argued, there is no need to attribute sophisticated intention reading skills to children to explain word learning. A few simple cognitive biases – like a preference to attend to novel or salient objects – can explain how children learn the meaning of words.

Of course, Samuelson and Smith did not have the last word. The debate about how to interpret these results continues. Social-pragmatic theorists are busy formulating and testing different interpretations of Samuelson and Smith's results (see, for example, Diesendruck, Markson, Akhtar & Reudor, 2004), and these are just as vigorously refuted by those who, like Samuelson and Smith, argue that basic cognitive learning mechanisms can explain word learning. In fact, this is the central idea behind our third theory: the attentional learning account.

3.4.2 The attentional learning account

The study by Samuelson and Smith (1998) described above neatly summarises the basic ideas behind the attentional learning account (which is sometimes called the associative learning account). The attentional learning account puts the child's cognitive abilities at the heart of language acquisition. Particularly important is the child's ability to do *associative learning*. Associative learning takes place when two cues co-occur in predictable ways. For example, if the word *fork* is always uttered in the presence of objects with a particular shape (but not when such objects are absent), the word *fork* and objects with that shape will become associated in the child's mind. Eventually, the child learns to label objects with this particular shape (forks) with the word *fork*.

This sort of learning works without any sort of special word-learning mechanism. Instead, the "general processes of perceiving, remembering, and attending ... may be sufficient *in and of themselves* to create children's smart word interpretations" (Samuelson & Smith, 1998, p. 95). As well as associative learning, three other general processes are considered to be important. First is the *attention mechanism*. Children are said to attach labels to things that catch their attention; these might be novel objects, salient objects or even objects that another person is showing an interest in. Second is the *memory system*. Memory is important because the learner has to be able to remember the different contexts in which a word has occurred in order to extend it appropriately. A third important ability is the ability to do *cross-situational learning* – to remember which situations are associated with a word and to pay attention to what object or event is common across all those situations.

For example, if we go back to our little girl playing with her pet dog when her mother exclaims *that's a dog*, the attentional learning account would predict that the girl would learn that the word *dog* refers to the animal in front of her because that is the object that is the focus of her attention. She later learns to extend the word *dog* to similar shaped animals (other dogs) because she has learnt, through her experience of the world, that similarly shaped objects often have the same name. In this way, she develops a *shape bias* (Landau et al., 1988). Importantly, though, this shape bias is not innately given, as suggested by the constraints theories we discussed above. It is learnt through experience. In fact, as children discover more about how words are associated with objects in their language, they learn more and more of these so-called *attentional biases* to help them in the word learning task.

3.4.2.1 *Evidence for and against the attentional learning account*

Evidence for the theory comes from a range of studies that show children prefer to link words to objects that are the focus of their attention or that are contextually novel. We summarised one of these in the section above by Samuelsom and Smith (1998), which, the authors argued, showed that children link novel words to objects that are salient in the environment. Another, particularly powerful study supporting the attentional learning account was that by Smith and Yu (2008). It is powerful because the researchers tested young children – children aged 12 and 14 months of age – and demonstrated that even children this young can do the type of cross-situational learning that is central to the attentional learning account.

In the experiment, the children saw lots of picture-pairs of objects accompanied by a word. For example, on the first training trial the infant might see a star-shaped object and a square object and hear the word *bosa*. On the second training trial they might see the star and hear the word *bosa* again, but this time the star would be paired with a round object. On the third training trial they might see the square and round object but hear the word *gasser*. And so on. Importantly, none of the individual training trials provided enough information for the children to associate the word with the correct object. However, there was enough information across trials for the children to do this. For example, across trials each time the word *bosa* occurred it was always accompanied by a star-shaped object. If the children could do cross-situational learning, then they would be able to associate the word with the correct object.

As predicted, the children learnt to associate the words with the correct objects. In the test trials that followed the training trials, the children looked significantly longer at the correct target object than at distracter objects each time they heard the novel word. The authors concluded that young children were capable of remembering word–object pairing across multiple different situations and using this knowledge to learn the meaning of the new words. This result is really quite striking, especially when we consider that the learning was done in the space of a four-minute experiment. The study provides strong evidence that even young children can learn the meaning of words simply by paying attention to word–object pairings across different situations.

In fact, such cross-situational learning also provides a very simple explanation of why children learn different languages so easily despite large differences in how these languages carve up the world. For example, by paying attention to how words were used across different situations, English children could learn to distinguish between containment and support (IN/ON) whereas Korean children could learn to distinguish between tight-/loose-fitting relations. Casasola, Wilbourn and Yang (2006) tested this idea by teaching Korean spatial words to English children via cross-situational learning. In a training phase, they taught English 21- and 22-month-old children some novel words paired with instances of the Korean tight-fit category (e.g. putting a top <u>on</u> a pen or putting a jigsaw piece <u>in</u> a puzzle). For example, the children would hear lots of instances of sentences with *keek* (e.g. *look, I am putting lid keek … see I put the lid keek*) but always paired with tight-fitting events (e.g. attaching a plastic lid onto a plastic cup, putting a peg in a hole in a plastic block). In the test phase, the children saw a new, different tight-fitting event, pictured side-by-side with a new loose-fitting event and were asked *where is she putting it keek?* The participants who had been trained looked significantly longer at the tight-fitting events than a control group who had not been trained with the novel word. In other words, English children had learnt a novel word for an unfamiliar Korean spatial category (tight-fitting) simply by observing how adults used the word across different situations.

When we turn to the criticisms of the attentional learning account, the arguments get a little bit more difficult to follow. This is because the criticisms are often based on re-interpreting the results of the experiments in different ways and then testing the predictions from these re-interpretations. The over-arching difficulty may stem from the fact that there is some truth in all of the theories, but this is something that we will leave to the final section of this chapter, as it is there that we will focus on attempts to integrate the different findings. In this section we will simply describe one study that has been cited as providing evidence against attentional learning theories.

This study, by Diesendruck and colleagues, criticised the attentional learning theory by re-interpreting some of its strongest findings in terms of socio-pragmatic cues (Diesendruck et al., 2004). To understand Diesendruck's criticism we need to remind ourselves of the debate between the social-pragmatic researcher Akhtar (Akhtar et al., 1996) and the attentional learning researchers Samuelson and Smith (1998) that we described in the last section. To recap, Akhtar and colleagues successfully taught preschool children to associate a novel name (*gazzer*) with the only novel object out of four that had been introduced when the speaker was out of the room. They argued that children guessed that the speaker's intention was to label the new (fourth) object rather than the three that she had already seen earlier. Samuelson and Smith (1998) re-interpreted this finding. They argued that the children assigned the *gazzer* label to the fourth object simply because it was introduced in a different context to the other three objects. Their own experiment supported this interpretation because they found that children successfully matched the word *gazzer* to the fourth object when it was simply made salient and different by being introduced in different surroundings (on a table covered with a brightly covered cloth). They argued that there is no need to attribute sophisticated intention reading skills to children to explain word learning. A few simple cognitive biases – like a preference to attend to novel or salient objects – can explain how children learn the meaning of words.

In response, the social-pragmatic researchers Diesendruck and colleagues have provided a re-interpretation of Samuelson and Smith's findings (although we should really call it a re-re-interpretation of Samuelson & Smith's re-interpretation of Akhtar's results). They argued that by introducing the fourth object in different surroundings, the experimenters were inadvertently 'telling' the child that the fourth object was special to the experimenter. As a result, when the experimenter later labelled one of the objects, they assumed that she was labelling the object that was special to her (the fourth object).

Diesendruck and colleagues tested their hypothesis by repeating Samuelson and Smith's study with two changes. First, they introduced an accidental condition in which the fourth object was introduced in a different context by accident (the experimenter accidentally let the fourth object slip out of her hands on to the table and then said *Come play with me over here. I'm already here anyway*). They argued that in this case the child should have no reason to think that the object was special to the experimenter, and should thus not associate the label *gazzer* with the new object. They were right – in this condition the children did not learn to associate the label *gazzer* with the fourth object, even though it had been introduced in different surroundings. Second, they introduced a different speaker condition where a puppet named the object (not the experimenter). Since all four objects were new to the puppet, they argued that the child should have no reason to think that the puppet was referring to the fourth object when he said *look, a gazzer*. They were right again – the children failed to associate the word *gazzer* with the fourth object. Diesendruck and colleagues concluded that, overall, the results of all of the studies (Akhtar & colleagues', Samuelson & Smith's and their own) were best explained by the social-pragmatic account not the attentional learning account after all. The children failed to associate the fourth object with the label despite its being introduced in different surroundings. They only learnt to label the fourth object as a *gazzer* if it was clear to them that the experimenter's intention was to label the object.

As always, the debate about how to interpret results like these continues. For those who enjoy the cut and thrust of theoretical debate, a very direct exchange of ideas can be found by reading the journal article by Jones, Smith and Landau (1991), the re-interpretation of the study by Booth and Waxman (2002), the reply (Smith, Jones, Yoshida & Colunga, 2003, in the unambiguously titled paper 'Whose DAM account? Attentional learning can explain Booth and Waxman') and the final response by Booth and Waxman (2003). The important thing to remember is that attentional learning theorists are still testing whether children can learn words simply by perceiving, attending to and memorising associations between words and objects in the world. Their critics are still contending, and testing, whether children need some additional knowledge or mechanisms such as innate constraints or socio-pragmatic cues. In addition, there are also those who contend that we need to take into account children's sensitivity to how the syntactic structure in which a word occurs constrains its possible meaning. This is the view proposed by syntactic bootstrapping theorists.

3.5 THE ROLE OF SYNTAX: THE SYNTACTIC BOOTSTRAPPING ACCOUNT

According to syntactic bootstrapping accounts, innate constraints, socio-pragmatic skills and general cognitive processes are (probably) all necessary to learn words.

However, none of them is sufficient (Gleitman, 1990; Landau & Gleitman, 1985). In particular, none of them explains how we learn verbs. The argument here is that verbs are too difficult to learn by these means, so children need something else as well – they need to pay attention to syntax. Thus, the key question here is:

Key question: does verb learning require knowledge of syntax?

The 'verbs are hard' argument is quite compelling. Verbs are words that refer to events rather than objects (e.g. *hitting, eating, walking*), and events are, inevitably, more ephemeral than objects – events only last for a short space of time. For example, the act of eating a cake only takes a few minutes, meaning that the child only has a few minutes in which to associate the verb *eating* with the relevant action. In addition, Tomasello and Kruger (1992) have found that adults tend to label events before the action has actually begun, which means that children rarely hear a new word at the same time as the action is taking place. For example, we are more likely to say *I am going to eat this cake* and then eat it, than we are to say *I am eating this cake* while we are eating it. Furthermore, some verbs like *think* and *know* label mental states not observable events, which makes it even more difficult to work out the verb's meaning. Finally, there are many verbs like *chase* and *flee* that differ in the perspective they take on an event, meaning that they are often used in the same situations. For example, if a child sees a dog chasing a cat and hears her mother say *look, glorping*, how does she know whether the word *glorping* refers to the action of the dog (*chasing*) or the action of the cat (*fleeing*)?

Gillette and colleagues demonstrated what a difficult task it would be if we had to learn verbs simply by trying to associate them with events or objects in the world (Gillette, Gleitman, Gleitman & Lederer, 1999). In their study, adult participants were shown videos of mothers playing with their child but, importantly, with the sound turned off. Their task was to identify mystery words spoken by the mother. The mystery word was represented by a beep, which sounded at the exact point on the video when the mother had uttered the word. Each word (beep) occurred six times, in different situations, giving the participants cross-situational evidence for the word's meaning. The participants then had to guess which nouns (e.g. *piggy, ball, mummy*) and verbs (e.g. *go, do, want*) were being spoken by the parents. The results of the study supported the researchers' claim that verbs are harder to learn than nouns. The participants were very good at identifying nouns; they correctly identified 45 per cent of the nouns simply on the basis of observing six different events (remember there was no sound so they were doing this simply by watching what was happening). However, they found it much harder to identify the verbs; they were correct only 15 per cent of the time. In fact, the verb task was so difficult that eight of the 24 verbs used in the study were never correctly identified by the participants. The researchers concluded that simply observing words paired with events, even across multiple situations, does not provide us with enough information to learn the meaning of verbs.

Since we all eventually learn verbs, the problem cannot be insurmountable. Syntactic bootstrapping theorists suggest that the solution is in the syntax. The idea is that children exploit (possibly universal) mappings between meaning (semantics) and syntax to learn verbs. They can do this because the types of sentence in which a verb can appear are, to a large degree, constrained by their meaning. For example, verbs that refer to events which involve only one participant (intransitive verbs like *fell, laugh*) tend to occur in sentences with only one noun phrase (e.g *I* in *I laughed*). Verbs that refer to causal events in which one participant causes something to happen to another (transitive verbs like *kick*) tend to occur with two noun phrases (*I* and *the ball* in *I kicked the ball*). Verbs that refer to the transfer of an object from a donor to a recipient (e.g. *give*) will tend to occur with three noun phrases (*I, Francesca* and *a cake*, in *I gave Francesca a cake*).

Using syntax–semantics correspondences like these, children can use the syntax of the sentence in which a verb occurs to narrow down the verb's meaning. If, on seeing a dog chase a cat, the child's mother had said *the dog is glorping the cat* (instead of just *look, glorping*), the child could use her knowledge of English syntax to identify that the word *glorping* refers to the action of the dog and is therefore more likely to mean *chasing* than *fleeing*. If the mother had said *look, the cat is glorping*, the child would guess that *glorping* referred to the action of the cat and therefore means something like *fleeing* or *running away*. In other words, syntactic bootstrapping theorists suggest that children can use the typical correspondences between syntax and verb meaning to narrow down the meaning of new verbs. This is called syntactic bootstrapping because the children are said to be bootstrapping from syntax to meaning.[2]

It might be tempting to interpret the theory as claiming that syntax is all that is needed to learn the meaning of verbs. If this really is the claim, then the syntactic bootstrapping theory is just plain wrong. For example, even children as old as three years of age cannot learn the meaning of verbs only from hearing them in grammatical sentences: the verb also needs to be paired with an observable scene or event (or at least some knowledge of the relevant context, see Sethuraman, Goldberg & Goodman, 1997). However, this criticism is almost certainly unfair because few proponents of syntactic bootstrapping theory claim that syntax is the only requirement. The child also has to be able to associate the word with an event and/or must be able to work out that the speaker's intention is to label the action. So all that syntactic bootstrapping theorists are really arguing is that the precise meaning of some verbs such as *chase/flee* can only be learnt if children use syntax as well as other cues.

3.5.1 Evidence for and against syntactic bootstrapping

Given the proviso above, there is plenty of evidence that supports the theory. Even very young children can use the structure of a sentence to narrow down the meaning of new words. The most famous study demonstrating this ability is one by Naigles

---

2   The word bootstrapping has been used frequently in language research for many years. It is used to describe the problem that occurs when it is difficult to see how the learning of a skill or ability could actually get started. Pinker (1994, p. 385) first used the phrase bootstrapping in this context by asking, how do children "lift themselves up by their bootstraps" in order to start the process of grammar learning?

(1990), which showed that children as young as 24 months could use syntax to help them learn the meaning of new verbs.

Naigles (1990) used a *preferential looking paradigm*, which exploited the fact that young children (and adults) have an unconscious tendency to look at things that are being spoken about. For example, if we are faced with a picture of a dog and a cat, it is very hard to suppress our tendency to look automatically at the dog on hearing *look at the dog*. Naigles showed 24-month-old children two videos, side by side, of people, dressed up as a duck and a rabbit, performing actions. On one video one character was acting on the other (the duck was pushing the rabbit into an unusual position). This causal action (one person causing another to move) would be best described using a transitive sentence such as *the duck is pushing the bunny*. On the other video, the characters were performing non-causal actions independently but in synchrony (e.g. they were making circles in the air with one arm). This action would be best described using an intransitive sentence such as *the duck and the bunny are waving*.

The actions were accompanied by an experimenter speaking a novel verb (*gorp*). Importantly, half the children heard *gorp* in a transitive sentence (*the duck is gorping the bunny*). According to syntactic bootstrapping theory, this should bias them to choose the causal action (duck pushing bunny) as the referent of *gorp*. The other half of the group heard this novel verb presented in an intransitive sentence (*the bunny and the duck are gorping*), which should bias the children to choose the non-causal (arm circling) action as the referent of *gorp*. Both groups of children were later asked to *find gorping* and behaved exactly as expected. Those who had heard the transitive sentence (*the duck is gorping the bunny*) looked for longer at the causal (duck pushing bunny) action. Those who had heard the intransitive sentence (*the bunny and the duck are gorping*) looked for longer at the non-causal (arm circling) action. This study provides good evidence that even two-year-old children can use the syntactic structure to narrow down possible meanings of new verbs, just as the syntactic bootstrapping theory predicts.

Supportive findings have even been reported for languages in which syntax is a less reliable cue to verb meaning. In Mandarin Chinese, speakers often miss out the nouns in a sentence altogether if it is obvious what is being talked about. This is perfectly legitimate in Mandarin Chinese but means that many sentences have missing nouns. For example, a Mandarin speaker is perfectly at liberty just to say *chased the cat* or even just *chased* instead of *the dog chased the cat*, as long as it is obvious from the scene or previous discourse that the sentence is referring to the dog. This means that Mandarin Chinese children have a lot less to go on when trying to do syntactic bootstrapping. Despite this, however, it seems that they are just as good at syntactic bootstrapping as English children are.

Lee and Naigles (2008) demonstrated this in an act-out experiment. They asked Mandarin Chinese children (aged 2;1 to 2;11) to act out sentences using a toy Noah's ark and associated props (e.g. toy people, toy animals). They found that the children interpreted the verb, and thus acted out the sentence, in accordance with the sentence's syntax. If the sentence contained two noun phrases (e.g. *Xiǎo zhū ná shīzi* 'little pig takes lion') they interpreted the verb as referring to a causal event and acted it out accordingly (e.g. the pig making the lion go somewhere). If the sentence contained one noun phrase (*Xiǎo gǒu lái* 'little dog comes'), they treated the verb as non-causal (e.g. the dog moving along on his own). Importantly, the children even did this when the meaning of the verb conflicted with the syntactic structure. For example, the ungrammatical sentence *Xiǎo zhū qù shīzi* ('little pig goes lion') was interpreted as meaning that the pig made the lion go (causal), not as meaning that the pig should move alone towards the lion. Lee and Naigles concluded that syntactic bootstrapping is so powerful that children are willing to bend the meaning of known verbs to be consistent with the syntax of the sentence in which they occur.

Criticisms of syntactic bootstrapping theory tend to focus on whether syntax is necessary to learn verb meanings, rather than whether it is possible to use syntax to learn verb meanings. The first set of criticisms starts from the premise that although syntax may be a useful cue, it is only available for use by older children and adults. This is the approach taken by constructivist researchers such as Tomasello who have consistently argued over the years that children learn syntax more gradually, and thus more slowly, than syntactic bootstrapping theorists assume (Tomasello, 2000). This approach will be considered in more detail in chapter 4. The important point to note here is that some argue that young children do not have the sophisticated knowledge of syntax necessary to support syntactic bootstrapping.

This claim gains support from research that shows that, in some situations, children are unable to use syntactic bootstrapping. Fisher (1996) demonstrated this in a study in which children saw videos of giving and receiving events. The children tested (aged three years and five years old) were capable of pointing correctly to the character who was *blicking the balloon to the other one* (the giver). However, they were not capable of pointing correctly to the character who was *blicking the balloon from the other one* (the receiver). This study is particularly important to critics of syntactic bootstrapping theory because this type of event – where observation of the event provides little information about whether the verb means *give* or *receive* – is often cited as a typical case in which syntactic bootstrapping is required to learn verb meanings (Gleitman, 1990). The fact that children cannot always use syntax to do the task is, thus, potentially a problem for syntactic bootstrapping theories.

The second set of criticisms focusses on the idea that syntactic bootstrapping would actually hinder verb learning in some situations. There are many situations where the number of noun phrases provides an incorrect cue to a verb's meaning. For example, short passives such as the sentence '*Pat was killed*' contains only one noun phrase (Pat) but refers to a causal event that involves two participants (Pat's killer causes Pat to become dead; see Goldberg, 2004 for this example and more). In this case, syntactic bootstrapping might bias children to make incorrect assumptions about the meaning of the verb kill.

This problem might be overcome if children were paying attention to all the sentences in which *kill* occurred. Sooner or later they would realise that kill also occurred in sentences with two participants (e.g. *John killed Pat*) and would refine their understanding of the verb's meaning accordingly. But in some languages, syntax always provides a misleading cue to verb meaning. Margetts (2008) provides an intriguing example of a language – Saliba – in which syntactic bootstrapping would cause problems for children trying to learn the verbs that mean *give*. Saliba is a language that is spoken by about a thousand people who live in Papua New Guinea, and has (at least) two verbs that refer to giving events. One verb – *mose-i* – is used if the recipient is a third person, such as in *He gave him/her one basket*. The second verb – *le* – is used if the recipient is the speaker or the listener (first or second person). In other words, this verb would be used to express *He gave me one basket* and *He gave you one basket*.

Despite the fact that both verbs express giving events, they occur in very different syntactic structures. *Mose-i* can be used with three noun phrases, like *give* in English. Saliba speakers can say the equivalent of *he gave him/her one basket* (*Bosa keesega ye mose-i-Ø*). However, *le* only occurs in simple transitive sentences: speakers can express the object (*I gave basket*) or the recipient (*I gave you*) but not both (speakers cannot say *I gave you the basket*). This is problematic for syntactic bootstrapping theorists because the required mapping between syntax and semantics simply does not exist in Saliba. Giving events are supposed to align with sentences with three noun phrases but *le* never occurs in such sentences. Thus, Saliba children should make errors when trying to learn that *le* means *give*. In addition, Saliba children should assume that *le* and *mose-i* have different meanings because they occur in different syntactic structures. However, the evidence Margetts provides (data from one Saliba-learning two-year-old) suggests that Saliba-learning children experience no difficulties learning the meaning of the two verbs. Obviously more studies are needed here because one child's data are not enough. However, if it is established that children easily learn verb meanings even when the syntax should lead them astray, we may need to downplay the importance of syntax in early verb learning, at least in some languages.

3.6 THE INTEGRATION: THE EMERGENTIST COALITION MODEL (ECM)

In what we have discussed so far, we have seen that many researchers have focussed their efforts on trying to isolate one or two mechanisms that might explain how children learn words. However, other researchers have taken a different tack. Instead of assessing evidence for one mechanism or another, they have suggested that all these mechanisms are important. These researchers propose integrated accounts, in which a number of different learning mechanisms all play a part. Thus, the key question here is:

Key question: given the weight of evidence showing a role for constraints, socio-pragmatic abilities, cognitive processing abilities and syntax, do we need an integrated account that takes some, or all, of them into account?

For example, the emergentist coalition model (ECM) proposed by Hollich and colleagues (Hollich, Hirsh-Pasek & Golinkoff, 2000) offers "a hybrid account that is sensitive to the multiple strategies children use to break the word barrier and to move from being novice to expert learners" (Hollich et al., 2000, p. 17). Three statements lie at the heart of the theory. First is the idea that children are sensitive to multiple cues in word learning – attentional cues, social cues and linguistic cues like syntax. This means that children recruit the full range of cues available to the word-learning task. For example, attentional cues might be particularly important at the start of word learning, where children's attention is captured by new and exciting objects. Children might start to use socio-pragmatic cues (eye gaze, speaker intention) a little later, as they come to realise that these cues may be more reliable guides to a word's meaning than object novelty or salience. Linguistic cues such as syntax increase in importance throughout the second year of life, as the child comes to realise that a lot of information about a word's meaning is provided by co-occurring words and by the structure of the sentence in which it occurs.

Since different cues are said to wax and wane in importance through development, the second tenet of the approach is the idea that children differentially weight certain cues over others in the course of word learning. Attentional cues are important early on but give way to socio-pragmatic and linguistic cues as children learn that these are more reliable cues to meaning. The reliability of different cues is learnt via cross-situational learning; children compute the reliability of different cues across different situations and, in this way, come to learn which cues are best. Thus, while attentional cues may win out with young infants, social cues such as eye gaze will take precedence later on.

The third and final tenet of the theory is that constraints on word learning emerge from the developmental process itself. In other words, children can move from using immature, basic constraints to more mature, sophisticated ones as they learn more about the word-learning process. This development represents a shift from domain-general attentional factors to more sophisticated language-specific constraints. As an example of how this might happen, Hollich and colleagues discuss the whole object constraint. They suggest that early in development children are biased to distinguish (or segment) whole objects from the surrounding environment. This bias is very useful for learning names for objects but it is less useful for learning other words, like names for parts of objects. As children develop, they start to use other cues in tandem with the whole object bias. For example, they may use syntactic cues to help them decide if a word refers to a whole object (*look at the fep*) or a part of the object (*look at the dog's fep*). In this way immature and often misleading domain-general constraints are gradually replaced by more complex but more accurate language-specific ones.

3.6.1   Evidence for and against the ECM

The biggest advantage that the ECM has over other theories is that the theory acknowledges that children are likely to use multiple strategies to learn words, rather than trying to explain the whole of word learning using one or two mechanisms. This intuitively seems a very plausible thing to suggest – why wouldn't a child use every strategy available to her to learn a word? It also neatly explains why different strategies may be important at different ages. For example, an apparent contradiction in the literature is the finding that 18-month-old children can correctly apply a new word to the toy that is the focus of the speaker's, but not their own, attention, but

12-month-old children cannot do this successfully (Baldwin, 1993b). This apparent contradiction is resolved by the ECM's proposal that attentional cues are used more readily by children in the early stages of word learning, but are supplanted by socio-pragmatic cues like eye gaze later on.

In addition, there are studies that specifically test and support the theory's predictions about development. For example, the idea that children move from relying on perceptual cues early on in development to paying attention to social cues later in development has been tested in experiments using an interactive form of the preferential looking paradigm (Hollich et al., 2000; Pruden, Hirsh-Pasek, Golinkoff & Hennon, 2006). In these experiments, the researchers tested whether children at different ages (from 10 to 24 months) preferred to attach a novel word to a boring toy (dull beige with no moving parts) that was the focus of the speaker's attention, or to an interesting toy (brightly coloured with moving parts) that was not. In the training phase, children saw the two toys, side by side, fixed with Velcro onto a blackboard, saw the experimenter look at one of the toys (the target) and label it with a novel name five times. In a test phase, the toys were shown again and the experimenter, now hiding behind a board, asked for the toy that was labelled (e.g. _where's the danu?_). The researchers then analysed whether the children looked longer at the labelled target toy than the distracter toy on hearing the novel word.

Importantly, there were two different conditions in the experiment. In the coincident condition, the experimenter looked at and labelled the interesting object. Not surprisingly, all the children learnt to attach the label to the interesting object in this condition. However, the critical condition was the conflict condition. Here, the experimenter looked at and labelled the boring object; meaning that the perceptual cue (brightly coloured interesting object that grabs the attention) and social cue (speaker's focus of attention) were in conflict. As predicted, the children's responses differed according to age in this condition. The 24-month-olds successfully ignored the interesting object and identified that the label applied to the boring object that was the focus of the speaker's attention. The 19-month-olds were also successful but were slightly more attracted to the perceptual cues (interesting object) than the 24-month-olds. The 12-month-old children failed to identify the boring object as the target, showing that they were not able to use the social cue to identify the labelled object. They did not mistakenly label the interesting object though, showing that they may have detected the social cues provided by the speaker, just been unsure what to do with them. The 10-month-olds were pure attentional learners. They looked for longer at the interesting object no matter which object the speaker was focussing on. This developmental sequence is precisely what is predicted by the ECM.

It is important to note here that the older children did not completely ignore the interesting object. Children at all ages did better in the coincident condition than the conflict condition, which indicates that they were influenced by the fact that the interesting object was attention-grabbing. Nor were the 12-month-olds incapable of using social cues; a series of follow-up studies showed that increasing the number of social cues available, together with labelling the object more often in the training phase, allowed even 12-month-olds to identify the target object (the researchers called this the "bludgeoning" study as they were metaphorically 'hitting the children over the head' with multiple cues; Hollich et al, 2000, p. 75). The take-home message, however, is that, as predicted by the ECM, older children were much better at ignoring the attention-grabbing interesting object and at following the speaker's focus of attention.

It is quite difficult to find criticisms of the ECM because it can explain a lot of the evidence we have discussed in previous sections simply because it incorporates multiple mechanisms of word learning. In fact, one of the dangers of integrative theories like the ECM is that they can quickly become unfalsifiable, precisely because they are potentially capable of incorporating any pattern of data from any study. However, the ECM avoids this problem because it makes quite clear developmental predictions that can be tested quite easily in the lab. For example, the model predicts that it is not until about 19 months of age that children will "use the adult's focus of attention to assign a word-to-world mapping" (Hollich et al., 2000, p. 28).

A common criticism of the ECM, however, is that it is unnecessary to propose multiple mechanisms because the same work can be done by one single mechanism, whether this is a social-pragmatic, constraint-based or attentional mechanism. For example, Akhtar and Tomasello argue that the ECM makes the task too complicated and that all the crucial work of word learning can be achieved via social-pragmatic means (Akhtar & Tomasello, 2000). Although they acknowledge that other abilities may exist (and be demonstrated in the lab), these are simply "ancillary to the fundamental social-communicative process" (Akhtar & Tomasello, 2000, p. 116). Smith (2000) takes a similar view, arguing that it is possible to build an associative learning version of the ECM, which means that all the evidence explained by the ECM could be explained in terms of associative/attentional learning.

There are also quite strong criticisms of the ECM's claim that the word learning process starts with universal biases, albeit immature ones. We discussed this issue in relation to constraints theory above, but it is worth revisiting the issue here. The point is that languages differ so dramatically in how they create categories to describe the world (and in how they use words to refer to these categories) that it is difficult to posit any universal bias that could do the job effectively across all languages. And if so many words in so many languages have to be learnt without the help of universal biases, perhaps it is simpler to assume that all words in all languages are learnt without the aid of universal biases.

This point is best explained with a hypothetical example constraint. Let us imagine that there is a constraint that naturally biases us to group together actions that perform the same function. Superficially, we could see how this might be useful; different types of eating actions, for example, would be grouped together and could then easily be labelled with *eat* in English (and *manger* in French etc.). However, this bias would be of very little use if we were learning Tzeltal, which requires us to learn three separate words for eating: one for ingesting crunchy-solid foods (e.g. carrots), one for ingesting less than crunchy-solid foods (e.g. bananas) and one that is used only for ingesting tortillas and other bread substances (all examples taken from Maratsos, 2001). As Maratsos puts it, these are not "intuitively obvious" non-linguistic categories and are unlikely to be learnt with the help of a universal bias (2001, p. 1111). But if children can learn Tzeltal categories without the aid of a universal bias, why do we need to posit a universal bias to help us learn English *eat*? Surely, English children could learn *eat* in the same way that Tzeltal-speaking children learn their words for *eat*. In fact, L. Bloom (2000) argued that the ECM has no need to posit universal innate biases at all; she stated that she was convinced, after reading Hollich and colleagues' monograph in which they describe the ECM, that all the work can be done by the children's developing knowledge of how the world works (what she calls conceptual knowledge) together with the attentional, social and linguistic cues that the ECM proposes. If Bloom is right, it might be possible to do away with universal biases in the ECM completely.

3.7 CHAPTER SUMMARY

In this chapter we have asked how children learn the meaning of words. We have seen that the word-learning task is more difficult than it might seem at first sight. Children have to work out which of potentially millions of possible referents a new word refers to (the reference problem) as well as how to extend words appropriately (the extension problem). In addition, children have to repeat the word learning process thousands of times in order to learn all the words that adults can understand. On the face of it, this seems like an impossible task, yet children not only start word learning early, they seem to learn words relatively rapidly.

A number of theories have been proposed to explain what factors help children solve this difficult task. Constraints theories argue that children are guided by innate biases (constraints) that help them home in on the possible meaning of words. Thus, work here focuses on the key question:

Since new words could potentially refer to any aspect of an event, are we innately biased to consider some meanings before others?

Social-pragmatic and attentional learning theories argue that innate constraints such as these are unnecessary. They key question in this section thus became:

Do we need innate linguistic biases? What other factors might allow us to converge on the correct meaning of words?

Social-pragmatic theories argue that children focus on trying to work out what speakers intend to say, helped by sophisticated socio-pragmatic skills such as joint attention and intention reading. Attentional learning theorists argue that both of these are unnecessary – children can learn words simply by paying attention to what objects, events or states tend to co-occur with particular words across different situations.

Syntactic bootstrapping theories argue that even together, all these skills are insufficient to learn verbs, which are particularly difficult and require knowledge of syntactic structures to help. Thus, the key question here was:

Does verb learning require knowledge of syntax?

To end the chapter, we asked one final, integrative key question:

Given the weight of evidence showing a role for constraints, socio-pragmatic abilities, cognitive processing abilities and syntax, do we need an integrated account that takes some, or all, of them into account?

We discussed the emergentist coalition model, which argues that all of these skills and abilities are co-opted into the learning process, albeit at different points in development.

Overall, none of these key questions has a definitive answer. The debates are frequent and robust. The main problem stems from the fact that the same piece of evidence can often be explained in different ways. For example, when a child shows a preference to assign a novel label to a nameless object, is she following a mutual exclusivity bias or simply making an educated guess about the speaker's intention? The most obvious answer is that both of these things can come into play at different times; the child uses each and every cue available to her in order to work out the meaning of words, as suggested by the ECM. However, even this is disputed, as we have seen above, by those who propose that one or two mechanisms are powerful enough to do the job on their own. And even if multiple cues are necessary, we do not know whether they are universally given or learnt from experience with the language. Studies with children learning two languages at once (bilingual language acquisition) may be particularly informative here. The interesting questions for the future will focus on how the child learns to distinguish which cues are important in her language, and how she then learns how to co-ordinate these cues.

3.8 SUGGESTED READING

Bloom, P. (2000). *How children learn the meanings of words*. Cambridge, MA: MIT Press.

Golinkoff, R. M., Hirsh-Pasek, K., Bloom, L., Smith, L. B., Woodward, A. L., Akhtar, N., Tomasello, M. & Hollich, G. (2000). *Becoming a word learner: A debate on lexical acquisition*. New York: Oxford University Press. Chapters and commentaries by influential proponents of constraints theory, social-pragmatic theory, attentional learning theory and the emergentist coalition model.

3.9 SUGGESTED READING (ADVANCED LEVEL)

Bowerman, M. & Choi, S. (2001). Shaping meanings for language: Universal and language specific in the acquisition of spatial semantic categories. In M. Bowerman & S. L. Levinson (Eds), *Language acquisition and conceptual development* (pp. 475–511). Cambridge: Cambridge University Press. Summarises cross-linguistic evidence on how different languages carve up the world into different types of spatial category and the implications this has for theories of word learning.

Hall, D. G. & Waxman, S. R. (Eds) (2004). *Weaving a lexicon*. Cambridge, MA: MIT Press. Articles by leading experts in the field.

Hirsh-Pasek, K. & Golinkoff, R. (Eds) (2006). *Action meets word: How children learn verbs*. New York: Oxford University Press. Chapters on verb learning by some of the most influential thinkers of the day.

3.10 COMPREHENSION CHECK

1. Summarise:

   a. The reference problem
   b. The extension problem

2. Describe a cross-linguistic study that shows that children are <u>not</u> sensitive to universal biases. How does this evidence count against the constraints approach?

3. How does the social-pragmatic theory explain how children learn verbs?

4. What four cognitive mechanisms or abilities are central to the attentional learning account?

5. Why does the study by Naigles (1990) show that 24-month-old children can do syntactic bootstrapping?

4

Acquiring syntax

4.1 THE ISSUE

Consider the following lines from Lewis Carroll's famous poem, 'Jabberwocky':

> 'Twas brillig, and the slithy toves
> Did gyre and gimble in the wabe:
> All mimsy were the borogoves,
> And the mome raths outgrabe,

As Alice herself perceptively remarks, the poem somehow "seems to fill my head with ideas – only I don't know exactly what they are" (Carroll, 1871). The reason for this – the reason Jabberwockey is not complete nonsense (although it is nearly so) – is that it follows the rules of English syntax and morphology.

We can demonstrate this by mixing up the words so that they no longer follow these rules:

> brillig the Twas slithy and toves
> gyre in and gimble the Did wabe
> mimsy the All borogroves were
> raths the mome outgrabe And

The poem no longer gives us the unnerving impression that we almost understand it. Now it really is complete gibberish.

All languages require that speakers follow syntactic rules when combining words into sentences. Despite the complexity of these rules, children seem to learn them relatively easily. Most researchers agree that children start to put words together into simple sentences when they have a vocabulary of about 50 words, although it takes a few years before they produce adult-like sentences (Nelson, 1973). For a long time, children's utterances are much shorter than adults' because children tend to omit obligatory words and word endings. For example, English children tend to omit inflections from verbs and nouns (producing, for example, *he like* instead of *he likes*). They also omit the 'little words' (so-called function words such as determiners (*a, the*), prepositions (*to, on*), auxiliaries (*can, do*) and conjunctions (*and, but*)). In fact, Brown and Fraser (1963) suggested the term *telegraphic speech* to describe children's early speech because the omission of function words makes the sentences resemble old-fashioned telegrams (like Camus's famous telegram in his novel *L'Etranger*: *Your mother passed away. Funeral tomorrow. Deep sympathy*, see Camus, 1946, p. 4).

However, it is important to note that the characteristics of children's early sentences differ from language to language. Table 4.1 illustrates the three longest sentences produced by two 2;6-year-olds,[1] one learning Italian and one learning English. The two children were the same age and had the same number of words in their vocabulary (over 500 words). Yet the Italian child used the correct verb and noun endings and function words more systematically, which makes her utterances appear more sophisticated than those of the English child.

Table 4.1

Examples of the three longest utterances produced by two-year-old English and Italian children (Caselli, Casadio & Bates, 1999)[2]

Italian two-and-a-half-year-old girl

Mamma	*non*	*voglio*	*andare*	*all'asilo,*	*ma*	*a*	*scuola*	*con*	*la*	*Costanza*
Mommy	not	want	to-go	to-the-preschool, but		to	school	with	the	Costanza

'Mommy, I don't want to go to preschool, but to school with Costanza.'

Mama	*perché*	*dondola*	*quel*	*signore*	*è*	*malato?*
Mommy	why	rocks	that	man,	is	sick?

'Mommy, why is that man rocking, is he sick?'

I	*denti*	*ci si*[2]	*lavano*	*dopo*	*mangiato,*	*vero,*	*mamma?*	*Prima*	*no.*
The	teeth	(to us)	are-wash	after	eaten,	true,	Mommy?	Before	no.

'Teeth get washed after eating, right Mommy? Not before.'

English two-and-a-half-year-old-boy

Daddy, can you help me find it please?

I wanna help wash car.

Mommy, you go to work?

As well as being shorter and simpler than adult utterances, children's speech contains some systematic errors. For example, English children take a while to

---

1 This convention indicates age in years;months.
2 *Ci* and *si* are pronouns and the use of both here is a grammatical error. The grammatical sentence would be *I denti si lavano* using the pronoun *si*. It may be that this child started to say *I denti ci laviamo*, which would mean *we brush our teeth*, and then switched to a different construction (*I denti si lavano* 'teeth get washed').

master the system of negation, producing errors such as *no go movies and I no like it* (Bellugi, 1967). Children also take a while to learn complex sentence structures such as relative clauses (e.g. *the dog that chased the cat was barking*) and passives (*the cat was chased by the dog*). However, again there are language-specific differences. For example, in English, German and Hebrew, even 11-year-olds rarely produce full passives (Berman & Sagi, 1981; Horgan, 1978; Mills, 1985). However, Sesotho-speaking children are already using passives at the age of two years (Demuth, 1990). Similarly, Italian three-year-olds use relative clauses more frequently than English children (Bates & Devescovi, 1989).

In summary, children learn the syntactic rules of their language, although they make a number of systematic errors along the way. They key question for us then is:

Key question: how do children learn the syntax of their language?

One possible answer to our key question is that children learn simply by imitating the speech they hear around them. However, this answer, which was suggested by Skinner (1957), cannot be the correct one for a very simple reason. If we learnt syntax by simply imitating what we hear around us, we would not be able to understand sentences that were completely new and unfamiliar. Yet we can both generate and understand such sentences. Chomsky demonstrated this fact with two very famous sentences (Chomsky, 1957):

> *Colourless green ideas sleep furiously*
>
> **Sleep green colourless furiously ideas*[3]

Unless you have read books on language before, you have probably never heard either of these sentences. Yet you probably know instinctively that the first sentence is grammatical and the second is not. You would not be able to do this if your knowledge of language was based on simply learning and reproducing the sentences you hear around you.

Instead, children learn a system of syntactic principles that allows them to generate (not just imitate) sentences. For example, one of the principles we learn in English is that nouns (e.g. *dog*) can combine with determiners (e.g. *a/the/this/that*) to form noun phrases (*the dog*). These can then be substituted for other noun phrases (*the dog is running* → *the cat is running*), for a pronoun (→ *he is running*) or even for a whole clause (→ *the dog that is barking is running*). These rules for using noun phrases, together with all the other syntactic rules, constitute language's "secret skeleton" of syntactic principles that govern how words are put together (Lust, 2006, p. 18).

In this chapter we will explore the theories that try to explain how we learn syntax. However, before we look at these theories, we need to consider the three challenges that complicate matters: the poverty of the stimulus problem, the bootstrapping

---

3   The star * is used to denote an ungrammatical sentence.

problem and the over-generalisation problem. In order to explain how children learn syntax, researchers have to come up with explanations of how children overcome these three challenges.

4.1.1 The three challenges

The first challenge is posed by the *poverty of the stimulus* problem (sometimes called the *learnability* problem). The poverty of the stimulus problem is captured by a logical argument that can be summarised thus:

> Language comprises a system of rules for combining words. There are only two ways to learn these rules. Either the child's environment or the child's genes (genetic inheritance) must provide the information necessary to learn the rules. Unfortunately, the child's experience does not provide her with the information necessary to learn the rules. It is not possible for the child to figure out the rules just by listening to people talking around her. As a result, since the rules of language cannot be learned from the environment, the knowledge necessary to learn the rules of language must be specified in the child's genes.

The key statement in the description above is this one: 'Unfortunately, the child's experience does not provide her with a way of learning the rules'. The basis of the poverty of the stimulus argument is the idea that the child's environment (stimulus) is impoverished in the sense that it does not provide her with the knowledge necessary to acquire syntax.

On the face of it, this argument seems a little ridiculous since children clearly learn the language they are exposed to (French children learn French, English children learn English etc.). So the stimulus clearly has an influence on language learning in this sense. However, the poverty of the stimulus argument is not about whether the stimulus has any effect at all (it clearly does) but whether it contains sufficient information to learn the underlying syntactic rules of language. Chomsky has long argued that the speech that children hear does not provide sufficient information to allow them to converge on the correct syntactic rules of their language.

In evidence, Chomsky provided an example of an apparently unlearnable rule: the English question formation rule (Chomsky, 1971). English questions, he argued, are created by moving the auxiliary (e.g. *is*) to a position in front of the sentence subject (e.g. *he*). Thus, *he is eating* becomes *is he eating?* A child trying to derive this rule on the basis of her input might be tempted to generate the rule 'move the first auxiliary to the beginning of the sentence'. However, sentences with two auxiliaries would be transformed into ungrammatical questions. For example, *the boy who is smoking is crazy* would become the error **is the boy who smoking is crazy?* So this is clearly not the right rule.

We could argue that hearing correctly formed sentences with two auxiliaries might help the child correct her error and learn to produce *is the boy who is smoking crazy?* However, although hearing these sentences would correct this particular problem, it does not solve the wider problem, which is that there are an infinite number of possible rules that the learner could hypothesise on the basis of their input. The learner might hypothesise a rule 'move the loudest auxiliary' or 'move the auxiliary that begins with the letter *i*' or anything. And unfortunately, the problem with infinity is that it is never-ending. It is physically impossible for anyone to scroll through an infinite number of possible rules in order to hit on the right one. Thus, no matter how much experience the child gets with the language, she could never amass enough experience to scroll through and dismiss an infinite number of incorrect rules. Thus, the challenge facing the child is how to acquire syntactic rules from a stimulus that does not contain all the information needed to converge on the correct rules.

One solution might be to argue that parents actively teach their children the rules of the language. For example, to help students learn to form a negative in French, a French teacher may tell them to 'sandwich the verb between the *ne* and the *pas*'. So *Je veux le chocolat* (*I want chocolate*) becomes *Je ne veux pas le chocolat* (*I don't want chocolate*). However, French mothers, unlike French teachers, do not explain the rules of negation to their children. In fact, it is not clear that parents even correct the grammatical errors their children produce (Brown & Hanlon, 1970). Instead, children learn these rules implicitly, without knowing that they are learning them. And they learn them so well that they can instinctively tell when sentences are incorrectly formed. Children will take great pleasure in correcting the grammar of non-native speakers. The challenge facing theorists is to explain how they do this.

The second challenge facing children is the *bootstrapping problem*. This problem stems from the fact that syntactic rules operate over syntactic categories such as noun and verb rather than over the words themselves. For example, the negation rule that French teachers use requires that their students know what a verb is. The rule applies to the syntactic category of verb, not to individual words. To discover the rule, students have to first figure out which words in French are verbs. In other words, before children learn the syntactic rules, they have to have some way of identifying which words are nouns and verbs in their parents' speech.

There is a problem here that the astute reader may have spotted. Knowledge of syntactic categories is required to learn syntactic rules. But in fact knowledge of syntactic rules is required to learn syntactic categories. The system is circular – you cannot learn rules unless you already know categories, but you cannot learn categories unless you already know the rules. How do children break into this system?

Let's explain this in more detail. Before children can learn to form negatives in French, they need to identify which words are verbs. But how do they identify verbs? The category of verb is not associated with a consistent meaning that they could use to identify it; many verbs refer to actions but others refer to thoughts and feelings (*love, know*) or states of being (e.g. the verb *is* in *she is a girl*). Verbs also do not occupy a fixed position in the sentence so one cannot discover verbs by, for example, identifying which words come second or third in the sentence. A word is only a verb because of the way it takes part in certain syntactic rules. A verb is a word that takes syntactic arguments (subject, object), carries tense and agreement morphology, is sandwiched between *ne* and *pas* in French negatives and so on. So to identify which words are verbs children must first identify the syntactic rules of the language and work out how words take part in these rules. But note earlier we said that children need to know which words are verbs in order to discover the syntactic rules. Now we discover that they need to know the syntactic rules in order to identify which words are verbs.

Pinker called this the 'bootstrapping problem' because it means that the child must somehow 'lift himself up by his bootstraps' to even get started on the process of learning syntax. Note that children do not have to know all the syntactic principles or categories of their language to bootstrap into syntax. But they do need to have a way of recognising at least some of them. This is the second obstacle that children have to overcome.

The third obstacle children face is learning to avoid *over-generalisation errors*. These are errors such as **don't giggle me*, **I said her no* and **I spilled the rug with juice*, which children sometimes make while learning a language (see Bowerman, 1988; Pinker, 1989). Over-generalisation errors occur because children have learnt how to generate novel sentences but have not yet learnt the limits on what kinds of verb can occur in different sentence types. Thus they are generalising too freely. Errors cease when the child has learnt the relevant restrictions. For example, English-learning children have to learn that it is possible to say *don't make me giggle* but not **don't giggle me*. The learning problem is complicated by the fact that it is not clear why these restrictions apply to some verbs and not others. For example, it is not immediately obvious why one cannot say **don't giggle me* when it is perfectly grammatical to use a whole range of other verbs in this structure (e.g. *don't tickle me*). Theories of syntax acquisition have to explain not only how children learn syntactic rules but how they learn to restrict their use appropriately.

In summary, syntax is a system of underlying principles that govern how we put words together into meaningful sentences. In order to explain how children learn syntax, we need to be able to explain how children solve the poverty of the stimulus argument, how they solve the bootstrapping problem and how they come to restrict their over-generalisations. In the next two sections of the chapter we will discuss nativist and constructivist solutions to the poverty of the stimulus and bootstrapping problems. In the final section we will discuss the over-generalisation problem.

One word of warning is required at this point. It is easy to get bogged down in the details of nativist and constructivist approaches to syntax acquisition, finding it difficult to understand what they are arguing about. It helps to bear in mind the difference between theories of syntax, which attempt to describe the rules governing syntax, and theories of syntax acquisition, which attempt to explain how syntactic rules are learnt.

There are many different theories of syntax, each of which is an attempt to describe the syntactic rules of language. Many of these theories characterise syntax as a system of rules that generates novel utterances out of individual syntactic units such as nouns and verbs. For example, underlying all Chomsky's theories is the idea that sentences are formed by a system of phrase structure rules that govern how the individual constituent parts are combined (Chomsky, 1957, 1981, 1995). Chomsky's famous sentence *Colourless green ideas sleep furiously* is thus represented by the (simplified) phrase structure tree shown in figure 4.1:

Figure 4.1

A simplified phrase structure tree for the sentence *Colourless green ideas sleep furiously.*

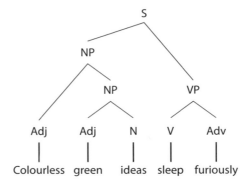

To form the sentence, the adjectives *colourless* and *green* combine with the noun *ideas* to form Noun Phrases (NPs). The verb *sleep* and adverb *furiously* combine to form a verb phrase (VPs). Both NP and VP combine to form the sentence (S).

Many nativist and generativist theories of syntax acquisition are based on such phrase structure grammars.[4] So these theories are trying to explain how children might learn phrase structure rules. Most constructivist theories of syntax acquisition, however, are far more ambivalent about phrase structure rules. Some take a strong position and deny that children are learning phrase structure rules at all. These constructivists advocate different linguistic descriptions of grammar, such as Goldberg's construction grammar (Goldberg, 1995, 2006). Other constructivist language acquisition researchers do not to commit to any particular linguistic description of syntax, following George Miller's famous admonition to "hang loose" (Miller, 1981). This means that debates between nativists and constructivists are complicated by disagreements about what is being learnt: a system of abstract rules and categories or a system of constructions, or perhaps something else entirely. Keeping this in mind will help readers interpret the material presented in the rest of this chapter.

4.2 NATIVIST THEORIES OF SYNTAX ACQUISITION

Nativist theories start from the assumption that children cannot learn syntax simply by listening to the people around them (the poverty of the stimulus

---

4   Nativist theories are those that assume that at least part of children's grammatical knowledge is innate (encoded in the genes). Generativist theories are those that assume that grammar consists of rules, like phrase structure rules, that operate over syntactic categories like nouns and verbs. All the nativist theories we discuss here are also generativist, so we simply use the term nativist. However, in principle it is possible to have a nativist theory that is not generativist and vice versa.

problem). Their solution is to build into the genetic code a basic knowledge of syntactic rules and categories. If the child's environment does not provide her with everything she needs to learn the rules, the rules must be acquired with the aid of innate knowledge pre-specified in the genes. Children's task is then not to learn syntax, but to map the language they are hearing onto their innate knowledge of syntax. On this view, the problem of the poverty of the stimulus disappears. All children need to do is identify which of their set of universal principles applies to their language. The key question, then, becomes not how children learn language, but:

Key question: what innate knowledge does the child possess?

In what follows, we will discuss some nativist approaches to language acquisition, chosen to illustrate a range of approaches to the problem. A number of influential proposals have been omitted because of lack of space, the most notable being the prosodic bootstrapping theory. Some references to this theory are provided at the end of the chapter.

4.2.1 Semantic bootstrapping theory

Pinker (1984, 1989) has suggested that children have innate knowledge of the following:

a) Syntactic categories (noun, verb), syntactic phrases (noun phrase, verb phrase) and syntactic roles (subject, object).

b) Thematic (or semantic) roles like agent, patient and recipient of the action, which specify the role that the referent plays in the action.

c) *Innate linking rules* that tell the child how to map from one to the other.

The provision of syntactic categories, thematic roles and innate linking rules solves both the poverty of the stimulus problem and also the problem of how to bootstrap into syntax. The poverty of the stimulus problem is solved because innate knowledge guides children's analysis of their input. The bootstrapping problem is solved because the innate linking rules allow children to infer syntactic categories, which are not observable from the situation, from thematic roles, which are. Once syntactic categories are identified, syntactic rules can be learnt.

How does this work? Thematic roles refer to the role that people and objects play in an action. So in the sentence *the dog bit Alec, the dog* is the agent of the action (the one who bites) and *Alec* is the patient (the person bitten). Because of this, it is relatively easy to identify the thematic roles in a sentence from observing the situation being described. With linking rules, the child can then link these thematic roles to the correct syntactic roles. For example, identifying an agent will allow the child to activate the subject role, identifying a patient triggers the activation of the object role and so on. This allows the child to identify syntactic categories and, thus, solves the bootstrapping problem.

For example, supposing a child hears the sentence *the dog bit Alec* and sees a dog biting a boy (*Alec*). The child can see that the dog is the agent of the action (the one doing the biting). She can also see that Alec is the person being bitten and is, thus, the patient of the action. So she can identify the agent and patient of the verb *bit*. Now she uses her innate linking rules to link these thematic roles to syntactic roles. Her linking rules specify that the agent of an action should be associated with the syntactic subject role. So she assigns the subject role to *the dog*. The rules also specify that the patient of an action should be assigned the syntactic object role. So she assigns the object role to *Alec*. Finally, the rule specifies that she should link the action word *bit* to the verb category. Now she has built a simple phrase structure that tells her the word order of English: SUBJECT-VERB-OBJECT. She has bootstrapped into syntax.

Not all sentences can be interpreted using linking rules. For example, more philosophical sentences such as *the situation justified the measures* have no obvious agent and patient roles so there is no canonical mapping between syntactic and thematic roles. However, this does not matter because the child can use other information to interpret the sentence (i.e. the position of words) as long as she has already learnt some of the basic syntactic rules. For example, she might use her newly acquired knowledge that English has SUBJECT-VERB-OBJECT word order to assign the first noun (*situation*) to the subject role, *justifies* to the verb category and *measures* to the object role. Further syntactic knowledge can be extracted in a similar way. For example, the child could learn to recognise that the words *a* and *the* are determiners because of the fact that they co-occur with nouns. In sum, although sentences with clearly identifiable links between syntactic and thematic roles will be acquired first, other sentences can be acquired later, by analysing the position of words in the sentence. This is called *distributional analysis* because the child is analysing the distribution of words in the sentence to determine how the syntactic rules of the language work.

4.2.1.1 *Evidence for and against semantic bootstrapping*

Evidence for the theory comes from studies showing that children's first utterances have the predicted simple, canonical, mappings between thematic and syntactic roles. For example, children's first nouns tend to refer to physical objects, their first verbs to actions and their first grammatical objects to patients (Bowerman, 1973; Brown, 1973; Macnamara, 1982; Nelson, 1973; Slobin, 1973). In addition, there is some evidence that children find it easier to learn verbs with canonical mappings between thematic and syntactic roles (e.g. agent = subject). For example, Marantz (1982) tested how easily three-, four- and five-year-old children learnt to interpret sentences with novel (made-up) verbs. Some sentences had canonical mappings in which the subject was an agent and the object was a patient (e.g. *John is mocking the table* referred to John pounding the table with his elbow). Others had non-canonical mappings in which the subject role encoded the patient and the object the agent (e.g. *the table is mocking John* used to refer to the same pounding action). The three- and four-year-olds found it much easier to learn the meaning of the verbs in the sentences with the canonical mappings, just as the theory predicted.

One problem with the theory, however is that it is difficult to see how the innate linking rules might work in other languages. The linking rules work well for English because it is a *nominative–accusative* case-marked language. Case markers indicate what grammatical role nouns and pronouns play in sentences, for example, whether a noun is a subject or an object. In nominative–accusative languages, the subjects of both transitive (e.g. *he hit the girl*) and intransitive (e.g. *he slept*) sentences are marked in the same way – with nominative case markers. Thus, the subject in a transitive sentence (called the 'A' argument) has to be marked with a nominative case pronoun (e.g. *he*). So we say *he hit the girl* not **him hit the girl*. Similarly, the subject in an intransitive sentence (called the 'S' argument) also receives nominative case (*he slept* not **him slept*). In other words, the 'A' argument of transitive sentences and the 'S' argument of intransitive sentences receive the same nominative case. However, the object being acted upon in a transitive sentence (called the 'O' role) is treated differently; it is marked by the use of an accusative case pronoun (*the boy pushed her* not **the boy pushed she*).

Figure 4.2
Representation of the difference between a nominative–accusative and an ergative–absolutive language.

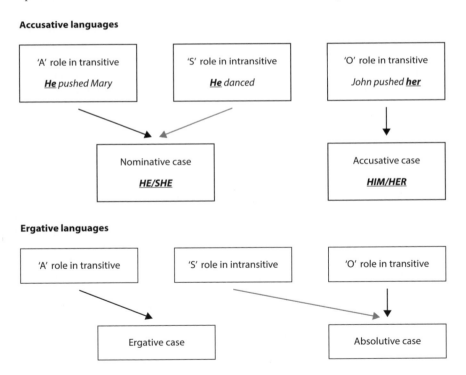

However, in *ergative–absolutive* languages, the case marking system carves up the language differently. The 'A' argument of transitive sentences and the 'S' argument of intransitive sentences are not marked in the same way. The 'A' argument of a transitive receives ergative case marking. But the 'S' argument of an intransitive sentence is marked in the same way as the objects ('O' arguments) of transitive verbs, with an absolutive case marker. So these languages group together the 'S' argument of intransitive verbs and the 'O' argument of transitive verbs, and distinguish them from the 'A' argument of transitive verbs (see figure 4.2). For example, in Hunzib, a language spoken in Russia, the 'A' argument of a transitive sentence is marked with the ergative case marker *-l* (*oždi-l kid hehe-r*, literally '*boy girl hit*'). The 'O' argument of a transitive and the 'S' argument of an intransitive both require absolutive case marking (see figure 4.2 and Comrie, 2011, for more information about case marking across languages).

How would a child with innate linking rules learn ergative languages? We might predict that the linking rules would initially mislead her. The child might link the agent ('A' argument of transitive) and the agent ('S' argument) of intransitive verbs with the syntactic subject, and then be misled into thinking they should receive the same markers. As a result, the child would mistakenly apply ergative markers to intransitive, as well as to transitive, subjects. However, this does not seem to be the case. For example, Pye analysed the speech of children learning K'iche' (or Quiche) Mayan, an ergative language spoken in Guatemala. Contrary to the prediction, Pye reported that K'iche' Mayan children do not over-generalise ergative markers to intransitive sentences (Pye, 1990).[5]

Some have suggested that this criticism is misplaced and that children could use linking rules to learn ergative languages as long as we allow them the ability to distinguish between agents in transitive and intransitive sentences from the beginning. In fact, Pinker himself suggested that linking rules could work for ergative languages in these circumstances since all the child has to do is notice whether "the case marker for the intransitive actor is identical to the marker for the transitive agent … or to the marker for the transitive patient" (1984, p. 372). However, even then, the theory would find it difficult to explain acquisition in split-ergative languages like Georgian and Hindi. These use the nominative–accusative system in some circumstances (e.g. present tense sentences) and use the ergative–absolutive system in others (e.g. past tense). Here, the theory more clearly predicts that children would find it difficult to work out how to mark grammatical roles but the data we have suggest that children do not have any such difficulty (see Siegel, 2000). Similarly, in some Mayan languages the ergative marker is extended to the 'S' argument of intransitive sentences under some circumstances. Yet, again, children learning these languages are not misled into extending the marker to all intransitives (Pye, Pfeiler & Mateo Pedro, 2013). The over-arching problem with the theory is that it predicts that children learning languages such as these should make errors, and the evidence suggests that they do not (see Bowerman & Brown, 2008, for these arguments plus

---

5   In K'iche' Mayan, the relevant ergative/absolutive markers are person markers that are added to the verb. This is different to languages like Hunzib, where the markers are case markers added to the nouns. However, the theory makes similar predictions about both types of ergative language.

more examples of languages that violate linking rules). What we need is a theory that can capture variation across languages effectively.

4.2.2 Principles and parameters theories

The principles and parameters framework was designed to explain why syntactic rules differ across languages. Within the framework, the child has two types of innate knowledge. First, she has a set of grammatical *principles* that innately specify the 'secret skeleton' that applies to languages. For example, the principles may specify that all words should be assigned to a syntactic category (e.g. noun, verb). Second, the child has a set of *parameters*, which have to be set to different values depending on the language that she is learning. For example, one possible parameter is a *null subject parameter* that affects whether a language allows sentence subjects to be omitted or not (see Hyams, 1986). English children have to set the parameter to the *obligatory subject* setting which means that the grammatical subject of a sentence cannot be omitted. Thus, English speakers have to say <u>it</u> *is raining*, not *is raining*. Spanish children have to set their parameter to the *null subject* setting, which means that subjects can be omitted (*llueve*, 'is raining'). Children set the parameters to the correct value in response to hearing trigger phrases in their input. These are certain key phrases whose grammar provides unequivocal evidence about how to set the parameter. For example hearing sentences such as *It is raining* might trigger English children to set their parameter to the obligatory subject setting.

With the aid of innate principles and parameters, the child interprets her input, slotting the words that she hears into her innate syntactic categories and then using this knowledge to set the parameters. For example, once the child has identified which words behave as nouns, she can identify which words behave as subjects. Once she has identified which words behave as subjects, she can identify, using the relevant trigger phrases, whether her language is an obligatory or null subject language. Then she simply sets the parameter to the correct setting.

Support for the theory comes from studies demonstrating that young children's knowledge is more sophisticated than we would expect if they did not have access to innate principles. For example, Valian analysed two-year-old children's speech to establish at what age they could use syntactic categories such as noun and determiner (Valian, 1986). She established objective criteria for determining knowledge of a category. For example, in order to be attributed with a determiner category, the children had to use determiners like *a* and *the* according to the following principles:

1. Determiners had to appear in the correct position, before adjectives or before nouns or before both. So children had to say *a red dog* and not *red a dog* to be attributed with knowledge of the determiner category.

2. Determiners could not stand alone as the only content of an utterance or phrase. So children should not produce *the* on its own, for example.

3. Determiners could not be sequenced incorrectly in sentences. So children should not say *there's a the dog*, for example.

Valian demonstrated that the children's use of determiners satisfied all these criteria. The children never used determiners in the wrong position, never used determiners on their own and rarely sequenced them incorrectly. The children did omit determiners, which might seem to count against the idea that they had knowledge of how to use the determiner category (e.g. saying *I want biscuit* instead of *I want a biscuit*). However, Valian argued that the fact that they used determiners correctly when they did include them made this explanation unlikely. She suggested, instead, that the children might have been unsure about which nouns require determiners (e.g. it takes a while to learn that *I want milk* is correct but *I want biscuit* is not). In sum, Valian concluded that by the age of 2;6 children already have knowledge of the syntactic rules governing a number of English syntactic categories. She interpreted this early mastery as evidence that language acquisition is guided by innate principles (though see Pine & Martindale, 1996, for criticisms of this interpretation).

However, a substantial problem for principles and parameters approaches is the fact that children make a range of frequent errors in their early sentences, particularly errors of omission. Children often omit what are called function words, such as prepositions (e.g. *to*, *in*), determiners (e.g. *a*, *the*) and auxiliaries (e.g. *can*, *do*). Why would a child with powerful innate principles and parameters omit these devices so often?

Perhaps even more puzzling is the fact that children do not just miss out words, they sometimes produce quite garbled sentences. Bellugi (1967) has documented ungrammatical use of negatives such as *I no like it* and* I not go*. Even utterances as odd as *I don't sure don't like it* are not unknown. English children also mis-order words in early questions, producing sentences such as * why the tape recorder don't lie?* (Rowland, 2007). Errors also occur in comprehension; English children misinterpret some types of passives such as *Goofy was liked by Donald*, until five, six or even seven years of age (Maratsos, Fox, Becker & Chalkley, 1985). Why would a child with powerful innate knowledge guiding language acquisition make so many errors?

4.2.2.1 *Explanations for errors within the principles and parameters framework*

Three possible explanations have been proposed within the principles and parameters framework. First, some researchers suggest that children take a while to set their parameters. For example, Hyams (1986) argues that English children start out with the null subject parameter set to the *null subject* feature, which explains why they act as if they were following Italian rules, producing sentences with missing subjects (*go park, sit chair*). A second possibility is that some aspects of innate knowledge are not present at birth but only mature later on. For example, Radford (1990) has suggested that children have access only to some grammatical categories at birth. These categories allow them to produce sentences with nouns, verbs and adjectives, but do not allow them to add the function words or to put inflectional endings on verbs. This explains why children produce sentences such as *Daddy want car* instead of *Daddy wanted a car*. A third possibility is that children do have access to the full set of universal principles, and have set the parameters early, but are unable to demonstrate their knowledge because of performance limits. Thus although their grammatical competence is adult-like, their performance is constrained by extra-syntactic factors such as a smaller working memory or a limited attention span (e.g. P. Bloom, 1990).

Each of these ideas has evidence to support it. English children do indeed omit subjects more often than English adults, as predicted by the parameter setting account (Hyams, 1986). English children also omit function words in their early speech as the maturation account predicts (Radford, 1990). And the performance limits explanation has attracted a lot of support. Crain and his colleagues, in particular, have published studies demonstrating that that children's adultlike grammatical competence has been underestimated because researchers ask them to complete experimental tasks that are too difficult for them.

For example, some studies show that even six-year-olds have difficulty understanding relative clauses, such as *the dog pushed the sheep that jumped over the fence* (e.g. Tavakolian, 1981). When asked to act out the action specified in the sentence using toy animals, children often do not act it out correctly. In the past, researchers have interpreted these errors as evidence that children have not mastered the syntactic rules governing relative clauses. However, Hamburger and Crain showed that children's errors could be attributed to difficulties with the task they were asked to perform (Hamburger & Crain, 1982). They argued that it only makes sense to say something like *the dog pushed the sheep that jumped over the fence* when there are two sheep present; one that jumped a fence and one that just stood still. This makes it sensible (i.e. pragmatically felicitous) to use the relative clause to specify which sheep the dog pushed. Otherwise, the sentence is a bit odd, which might confuse children. Hamburger and Crain modified the procedure so that the children were provided with a number of toy sheep, only one of which jumped over a fence, and then asked them to act out the sentence. Sure enough, the children's performance improved. The authors concluded that the children did understand relative clauses and could demonstrate this when given the correct type of task.

The moral of this story is that we must be careful about how we interpret children's failure to complete a task. However, acknowledging that our studies have task demands is not the same as agreeing that children have adultlike knowledge of grammar. There are still a number of problems with theories that posit late parameter setting, maturation or performance limits as an explanation of children's errors. For example, children learning languages other than English produce tensed verbs, determiners and prepositions earlier in acquisition than predicted by the maturational hypothesis (Lust lists the examples Korean, K'iche' Mayan, Hindi, Tamil, Italian, Spanish and Sesotho; Lust, 2006, p. 200). However, there is also one over-arching problem, which has proven to be the thorn in the side of most, if not all, nativist explanations of errors. This is the problem of lexical specificity in children's early utterances.

4.2.2.2 *The problem of lexical specificity in children's early utterances*

All three explanations of errors summarised above focus on broad, general restrictions on what children can produce. For example, if children are delayed at setting the null subject parameter, this should affect all subjects equally. Similarly, if function word categories mature late, as predicted by the maturational account, no words that rely on function word categories should be present in children's early speech. Equally, performance limits should affect all members of a syntactic category equally. If children omit *a* from sentences like *that's a dog* because working memory limitations stop them producing long sentences, they should be equally likely to omit *the* from the sentence *that's the dog*. None of the theories predict that some lexical items (i.e. words) within the same grammatical category should be treated differently from others. Yet this is what we see in children's speech.

Many studies have shown that children are more knowledgeable about how to use some lexical items in sentences than others, even when the lexical items come from the same grammatical category. All of these studies cause problems for theories within the principles and parameters framework because these theories posit that children are learning abstract grammatical categories and rules. For example, Pine, Lieven & Rowland (1998) analysed how 12 children used auxiliaries and verbs during the first six months after they had begun to produce sentences. The researchers recorded the children at home interacting with their caregivers and then transcribed and analysed the spontaneous speech that the children produced. They found that the children's utterances were not consistent with the idea that they were working with abstract grammatical categories and rules. Instead, it looked as if they had pockets of knowledge about how individual words behave in sentences, which we call *lexically specific knowledge*.

We use the term lexically specific to refer to the fact that the children's knowledge is restricted to how to use certain lexical items (i.e. certain words). For example, although many of the children produced a lot of different auxiliaries in total (e.g. *is, are, can, do*) there was very little overlap in the verbs that occurred with different auxiliaries in Pine's study (Pine et al., 1998). Although *can* was used with a number of verbs, these tended to be different verbs from those used with the auxiliaries *be, do* and *have*. So it looked as if the children had some restricted knowledge of which verbs could co-occur with *can* but this knowledge did not overlap with their knowledge about which verbs could co-occur with *be, do* and *have*. The authors concluded that "These data suggest that children's use of auxiliary + verb combinations can be accounted for in terms of a mixture of rote-learned and lexically specific knowledge" (Pine et al., 1998, p. 819). This means that the data were inconsistent with the predictions of principles and parameters accounts, because children with abstract knowledge of the auxiliary and verb category should be able to use all auxiliaries with all verbs.

Lexically specific effects have been found with a whole range of grammatical devices and structures including determiners, subjects, negatives, verbs, auxiliaries, questions, relative clauses and sentential complements (Cameron-Faulkner, Lieven & Theakston, 2007; Kidd, Lieven & Tomasello, 2006; Pine, Freudenthal, Krajewski & Gobet, 2013; Rowland, 2007; Theakston, Lieven, Pine & Rowland, 2001, 2005; Wilson, 2003). Some studies have even reported that most of children's early utterances can be explained in terms of lexically specific schema such as *want + X* and *me got + X* (where X stands for a category of words that can be slotted into the lexically specific frame; see e.g. Pine & Lieven, 1993). All these studies conclude that these patterns are inconsistent with principles and parameter-based accounts, which attribute children with knowledge of grammatical categories, not knowledge based around lexical items.

Still further studies demonstrate that children cannot generalise their knowledge of syntax to novel (made-up) words, as we would expect if they had adultlike knowledge of syntactic categories. Some of the most famous of these studies are so-called weird word order experiments, in which researchers produce novel verbs in wacky word orders and see if children are willing to imitate them. In the first of such studies, Akhtar hypothesised that children who have correctly set the parameters of their language, as predicted by many nativist accounts, should already know how to sequence words in sentences (Akhtar, 1999). For example, in English the basic word order is SUBJECT-VERB-OBJECT (SVO), which means we say *Elmo dacked the car* not *Elmo the car dacked* (SOV) or *dacked Elmo the car* (VSO). If young children already know this rule, as has been suggested by nativist theories (e.g. Valian, 1986), it should not be possible to prompt them to produce sentences with the wrong word order.

Akhtar (1999) tested this with two-, three- and four-year-old children. She played a game in which she and the child took it in turns to act out some novel actions (such as dropping a toy down a chute) and then described these actions with novel verbs – *dacking*, *gopping* and *tamming*. One of the novel verbs was always produced by Akhtar in the correct English SVO order (*Look! Elmo dacked the car*) and children had no problem with these. When prompted to describe the action themselves, children at all ages used the novel verb in the correct English word order, even with different actors and objects (e.g. *Tigger dacked the fork*). However, the other two verbs were produced by Akhtar in weird word orders; SOV (*Elmo the car gopped*) or VSO (*tammed Elmo the car*). Here the children's responses differed with age. The four-year-olds tended to correct the weird word orders when it was their turn to speak, producing correct English sentences like *Tigger gopped the fork*. The two- and three-year-olds, however, were significantly more likely to copy the weird word order produced by the experimenter, producing sentences like *Tigger the fork gopped* (although they did correct to English word order about half of the time). Interestingly, they did not copy the weird word order when the experiment was repeated with familiar verbs such as *push* (e.g. they did not say *Elmo the car pushed*). Akhtar concluded that "young English-speaking children do not have a general understanding of the significance of SVO order in reversible sentences; that is, they seem to rely on verb-specific formulas (e.g. NPpusher ± form of the verb PUSH ± NPpushee) to interpret such sentences" (1999, p. 339). This is inconsistent with the idea that children have knowledge of abstract categories such as subject, verb and object.

To conclude this section, the biggest problem for nativist theories is explaining why children's early utterances look like they do. Theories like the semantic bootstrapping account have difficulty explaining the cross-linguistic pattern of development. Theories within the principles and parameters framework struggle to explain why children make errors and seem so much more knowledgeable with some lexical items than others, even items within the same grammatical category. Constructivist theories find it much easier to explain lexical specificity and cross-linguistic variation. Nevertheless, they have their own problems, as we will see below.

4.3 CONSTRUCTIVIST THEORIES OF SYNTACTIC DEVELOPMENT

Many constructivists actively reject the assumption that children are learning formal rules or formal grammatical relations like subject and object. To many constructivists, labels like syntactic subject are simply quick, convenient ways to describe collections of words: in Maratsos's terms, they are "merely a device to make quick reference to a group of grammatical phenomena" (Maratsos & Chalkley, 1980, p. 152). In a constructivist view, the child's task is to learn how different words behave in sentences, categorising together words that behave in similar ways and extracting the patterns that govern this behaviour from the input they hear around them. This means that in a constructivist world, there is no need to build in innate categories or knowledge such as principles and parameters. Children build the syntax of their language from the bottom up. They exploit the fact that grammar is essentially a system of repeating patterns and build links between words that behave in the same way in sentences and between words that are used for similar functions or express similar meanings.

Adopting a constructivist view of syntax provides different solutions to the bootstrapping and poverty of the stimulus problems. In effect, the bootstrapping problem is solved because the categories and rules can be built up gradually by generalising across words that behave in similar ways. There is no poverty of the stimulus argument because the input to children does contain enough information to learn the system of repeating patterns that underlies syntax. The key question for constructivists is thus:

Key question: how do children analyse their input in order to learn the grammatical regularities of their language?

In the next sections, two constructivist theories are presented. As in the last section, some very influential theories are omitted for reasons of space, perhaps most notably Bates and MacWhinney's competition model (MacWhinney & Bates, 1989). References to work within the competition model framework are provided at the end of the chapter.

4.3.1 Semantic-distributional analysis

Semantic-distributional analysis refers to the process by which children analyse the distribution of words in the sentence, using this information to link words that behave in similar ways and have similar meanings, and extract the patterns that govern this behaviour. For example, most verbs will occur in similar positions in sentences (e.g. *I want, I like, I need*) and will occur with similar inflections (e.g. *wanted, liked, needed*). On the basis of these similarities, verbs can be linked together into a verb category.

All theories, even nativist theories, build in a role for this type of semantic-distributional analysis. Even if children start out with innately specified parameters or linking rules, at some point, they have to analyse the distribution of words in the sentence and categorise words based on the outcome of this analysis. So some researchers have suggested that semantic-distributional analysis may be all that is needed. Perhaps children build categories and rules simply by paying attention to how different words pattern with respect to other words in the input.

Braine was one of the first to suggest that children could learn syntax simply by paying attention to the distributional patterns of words in their input (Braine, 1963). He suggested that children began by building very simple two-word sentences consisting of *pivot words* (e.g. *more, no, again, it*) and *open class words*, which usually equate to adult noun, verb and adjective categories (*jump, hit, Mummy, juice*). He suggested that children construct sentences by combining pivot + open words (*more juice, no hit*) or open + open words (*Daddy car*) in the order in which they have heard them in their input. In other words, children construct fixed word order rules based on the distribution of words in their input. They then generalise across these patterns to create more flexible patterns. For example, he suggested that the children he studied developed a *more + X* pattern, which enabled them to combine the pivot word *more* with a variety of nouns, allowing them to produce a number of different, grammatically correct, but quite limited, two word combinations.

However, Braine did not make it very clear how children might then develop onwards from these pre-grammatical patterns to a full adult grammar. How does a child with a *more + X* pattern move on to learn adultlike syntactic rules? This was a problem because it very quickly became clear that children do generalise beyond these lexically specific patterns, if not from the beginning, at least from very early on. As a solution, Maratsos and Chalkley proposed a developmental semantic-distributional account (Maratsos & Chalkley, 1980). Here they suggested a way in which children may build adultlike syntax by linking together words that share similar semantic and distributional features. The idea was that children build links between words that behave in the same way in sentences and between words that are used to express similar meanings. For example, verbs in English share particular distributional properties such as appearing with a small set of inflectional endings (*-ed, -s, -ing*) and appearing directly after auxiliary verbs like *didn't* and *don't* (*didn't go, didn't see, don't know*). In addition, each verb context represents a particular meaning that remains relatively stable across different verbs. So verbs used with *-ed* are used to denote an event that happened in the past (e.g. *the dog barked*). A child who was sensitive to these patterns could learn to link together words that occurred in these contexts, forming a *de facto* verb category on the basis of semantic-distributional analysis. In this way, although children might start off with lexically specific patterns that pivot around individual verbs, these verbs would eventually be linked together via semantic-distributional analysis to form an adultlike verb category.

4.3.1.1 *Evidence for and against semantic-distributional analysis*

In support of the theory, there is quite a lot of evidence that children's utterances do look formulaic in the way Braine suggested. As we saw above, there are many analyses showing that it looks as though young children have pockets of lexically specific knowledge about how individual words behave in sentences, rather than adultlike knowledge of grammatical rules and categories (e.g. Pine et al., 1998; see section 4.2.2.2 above). There is also evidence for the idea that syntactic knowledge could emerge from distributional analysis from artificial grammar learning (AGL) experiments.

AGL experiments demonstrate that infants and adults have the ability to learn simple grammatical rules via distributional analysis, just as Maratsos and Chalkley (1980) suggested. In one of the most influential AGL studies in the literature, Gomez and Gerken tested whether 12-month-old infants could learn a simple artificial grammar in this way (Gomez & Gerken, 1999). Their study began with an acquisition phase in which infants listened to strings of one-syllable nonsense 'words' (VOT, PEL, JIC, TAM). Importantly, although the strings were of different lengths, they all conformed to an artificial (made up) grammar which meant that the 'words' always occurred in a particular 'grammatical', order (e.g. VOT PEL PEL PEL JIC was one grammatical string and PEL TAM PEL JIC was another). After the acquisition phase, the children entered a test phase. Here they heard 20 new strings of nonsense words, but only 10 of these conformed to the grammar. The other 10 were ungrammatical strings created by changing the order of some of the words in the strings. The key question was this: would the children discriminate between grammatical and ungrammatical strings by listening to them for different lengths of time? The answer was yes. The children listened significantly longer to the strings that conformed to the grammar than those that were 'ungrammatical' despite the fact that both sets of strings contained the same set of nonsense words. This study shows that infants are sensitive to the distributional patterns of words in their input and can use these to discriminate between grammatical and ungrammatical sentences. This is exactly what the semantic-distributional theory predicts that they will be able to do.

There is also evidence from computer simulations using connectionist networks that it is possible to learn syntax via distributional analysis. Connectionist networks are computer programs made up of networks of simple processing devices. They contain neuron-like units called input, output and hidden units, all connected together. Each unit receives excitatory or inhibitory input from other units, responds to that input according to a simple activation function, and then either excites or inhibits the other units to which it is connected. Importantly, networks can *learn* from their input. Learning occurs when the model outputs a signal that fails to match the correct output. In response, the model modifies the weights of the connections between its own units (i.e. how easily each unit 'communicates' with others) and then tries again. In other words, the model learns by modifying its own structure in response to the distributional characteristics of the input until it has learnt to output a new behaviour correctly.

Elman (1993) has shown that such a network can learn syntactic structures just from listening to, and responding to, the distributional information available in language-like input. Elman trained a connectionist model called a simple recurrent network to learn the grammar of a basic artificial language. The model's task was to learn to predict the next word in a sentence, which it could only do accurately if it had learnt the grammar of the language. Despite the difficulty of the task, Elman's model succeeded. Most surprisingly, it was even capable of learning long-distance dependencies between two words that were separated by a long embedded clause. For example, take the following sentence *the girls* who the teacher has picked for the play that *will be produced next month practise every afternoon.* The verb *practise* is in its plural form because it has to agree with the plural noun phrase *the girls.* In order to predict this word correctly, we must keep track of the dependency relationship between the words *girls* and *practise*, despite the fact that they are separated by no fewer than 14 other words. Elman's model learnt to keep track of long-distance dependencies of this type, albeit with shorter sentences (e.g. *boys who chase dogs see girls*).[6]

However, the most important problem that advocates of distributional analysis have to address is the problem of unconstrained generalisation. In order to learn a verb category, for example, the child has to link words together that behave in the same way in sentences. However, which features of the input should the child focus on? There are so many incorrect features she could choose. If she generalised based on rhyme, she would link *run* and *fun*, which might lead to errors such as *I am funning* or *can you fun fast?* If she generalised based on position in the sentence, she might link all words that occurred in the second position in the sentence, including verbs (*stroked* in *Alec stroked the pig*), nouns (*Alec* in *does Alec want to stroke the pig?*) and adjectives (*big* in *the big pig is happy*). In fact, even quite a conservative distributional analyser might make mistakes because there are many words that can be both nouns and verbs (Pinker, 1979). For example, it might lump together the words *climb*, *fish* and *rabbits* into one syntactic category on the basis of hearing the following four sentences:

Bears can climb

Bears can fish

Bears eat fish

Bears eat rabbits

This would cause the child to produce sentences such as *Bears can rabbits* and *Bears eat climb*, which are clearly grammatical "monstrosities" (Pinker, 1979, p. 240). In fact, Pinker (1984) has calculated that a simple seven word sentence may have

---

6   Elman's model could only learn under two conditions a) when the input it received at first was very simple, increasing in complexity over time, or b) when it was given an "incremental memory". However, subsequent models have been shown to learn without such manipulations (Rohde & Plaut, 1999).

about nine million possible grammatical properties on which a child could base her distributional analysis.

At this point, it is important to note that this problem applies to an *unconstrained* distributional analyser. The point is that the learning mechanism must be constrained to pay attention to some patterns and not others, and that these constraints must be specified within the theory. In fact, most computer models of distributional analysis are constrained in some way. Elman (1993) constrained the size of the mechanism's memory. Cartwright and Brent's (1997) model was constrained to build grammatical categories based on overlap between frequently occurring phrases (so hearing *the dog sat* and *the cat sat* frequently would enable the mechanism to put *dog* and *cat* into the same grammatical category). There are also models in which the mechanism pays particular attention to the preceding and following word in the construction of grammatical categories (Mintz, 2003; St Clair, Monaghan & Christiansen, 2010). There are also possibilities that do not seem to have been explored extensively. Slobin (1973) proposed a list of universal operating principles based on his cross-linguistic work. These include principles like *pay attention to the endings of words*, which could provide a powerful constraint (see, for example, Freudenthal, Pine, & Gobet, 2007). However, it remains to be seen if these sorts of constraint will solve the problem.

4.3.2   The usage-based model

In section 4.1 above we touched on the issue that nativist and constructivist theories often disagree fundamentally how to describe the syntactic rules of language; whether it is a system of abstract rules and categories, a system of constructions or something else entirely. Usage-based theories are often based on a description of grammar called construction grammar (Goldberg, 1995, 2006), which conceptualises the learning task in a very different way to generativist linguistic theories (see Tomasello, 2000, 2003; Lieven & Tomasello, 2008, for more detailed descriptions of usage-based theories, though also see Ninio, 2006, 2011 for a hybrid theory that combines Chomskian linguistic theory with constructivist ideas about learning).

Construction grammar characterises language as an inventory of constructions, each of which has a specific function in communication. For example, the English transitive construction takes the form *noun1 verb noun2* and is used when we want to convey that *noun1* acted upon *noun2*, causing *noun2* to be affected in some way. In order to form a sentence, speakers are said to fit appropriate items (*Biba, ball, kicks, the*) into the appropriate slots in the construction (to yield *Biba kicks the ball*). Thus, what the child has to learn is a series of constructions and which items to fit into which slots in the constructions.

According to usage-based theory, learning constructions and their meanings does not require any specialised innate knowledge of linguistic rules or principles. Instead, it can be accomplished by a mixture of general cognitive and social abilities. Four skills are of central importance. First is the ability to do *distributional analysis* (described in section 4.3.1 above). Second is the ability to do *analogical reasoning*, which allows the child to compare (analogise) across different constructions and work out what commonalities they share. Third is *competition*; the child is sensitive to differences between what she is hearing in her input and what her own knowledge of syntax predicts about upcoming sentences, so that she can correct errors in her own knowledge. Fourth is the ability to do *intention reading* – to work out what message the speaker intends to convey. For example, imagine you are a two-year-old child who sees a rabbit hopping along. You hear your mother say *glorp the gavagai*. If you believe that your mother's intention is to direct your attention to the rabbit, you will probably guess that she is saying something like *see the rabbit*. However, if you believe that your mother wants you to help catch the rabbit before it escapes, you might guess that she is saying *stop the rabbit!* In other words, the ability to guess the intention behind your mother's utterance correctly will have a strong effect on whether you interpret what she says accurately and, ultimately, on whether you learn the correct meaning of the sentence.

Intention reading is a powerful tool. Not only does it allow children to guess the meaning of words, it allows them to hazard a guess at the meaning of whole sentences. This provides an important constraint on how the distributional analyser generalises across different sentences. Effectively, the child links together sentences in which she has recognised similarities in the meaning that the speaker intends to convey, as well as similarities in the distributional properties of the sentences. This provides the constraint on generalisation needed to avoid errors like *bears can rabbits*, which were discussed in the previous section.

According to usage-based theory, language learning progresses in the following way. The child begins by learning a number of phrases directly from the input (e.g. *want biscuit, want drink, want cuddle*). Because some of these phrases have similar meanings the child links these phrases together to create what we call *a lexically specific* or *item-based schema*. She can then use this schema to convey her desire for any item (*want + desired object*). She then builds an inventory of such lexically specific schema that allows her to produce different sentence types. However, her knowledge is still restricted to these particular lexical items.

As the child learns more lexically specific schemas, the similarities between these schemas start to emerge. For example, a *want + X* and a *need + X* schema will be used with an overlapping set of nouns and may be used in similar situations. On the basis of these commonalities, the child can form analogies across similar lexically specific schemas to form a more abstract construction such as *desire verb + X*. As more and more schemas are linked together, the child's knowledge approaches the adult state. Because the child's knowledge becomes more abstract as she develops (i.e. becomes less tied to lexical items) this process is called *abstraction*.

4.3.2.1 *Evidence for and against the usage-based model*

The usage-based model of syntax development is based on the same principles as the social-pragmatic account of word learning discussed in chapter 3. In fact, most constructivist accounts assume that the same set of skills and abilities underlie syntax learning and word learning (Bruner, 1978; Clark, 1993; Nelson, 1985; Ninio & Snow, 1996; Tomasello, 2003). Thus, a lot of the evidence discussed in chapter 3 is relevant here (e.g. Baldwin's *Toma* studies, 1991, 1993a, 1993b, see section 3.3.1.1). The usage-based theory also provides a very simple explanation for why children's utterances seem to pattern lexically and why young children are unable to generalise their knowledge of syntax to novel words in weird word order tasks (Akhtar, 1999, see section 4.2.2.2 above). According to the theory, children's early knowledge is restricted to an inventory of lexically based schema, which gradually becomes more abstract. We would thus expect children's early utterances to pattern in lexically specific ways, precisely as has been identified by these studies.

Such lexically specific effects are not restricted to English. For example MacWhinney (1975) identified that over 85 per cent of the utterances of two Hungarian children could be generated by a set of lexically specific patterns. Even in free word order languages like Turkish, where it is possible to combine words in a number of ways and still maintain the same meaning, children's early patterns seem to fit the most frequent word order of their language (Küntay & Slobin, 1996). In addition, Matthews and colleagues have replicated the findings of Akhtar's weird word order study with French children (Matthews, Lieven, Theakston & Tomasello, 2007). Interestingly these researchers also compared high and low frequency real verbs and found that children were significantly more likely to reproduce the weird word order of the experimenter's sentence with low frequency verbs than with high frequency verbs. This, they concluded, supported the usage-based theory because "children showed more robust preferences for the canonical orders of their language when using lexical items they knew well" (Matthews et al., 2007, p. 401).

There is also evidence that children are faster to interpret words if they are presented as part of a lexically specific frame. Fernald and Hurtado (2006) ran a looking-while-listening experiment using some of the lexically specific frames identified as highly frequent in children's input frames. Eighteen-month-old infants were shown two objects on a screen and heard sentences directing them to look at one of the objects. For example, the child might see a dog and a baby and be instructed to *look at the doggie*. The researchers found that the children were much quicker and more accurate at identifying the correct object when the word was presented in a frequent frame. For example, they looked at the dog much more quickly if they heard *look at the doggie* than if they just heard *Look! Doggie!* Bannard and Matthews (2008) similarly found that three-year-old children were quicker and more accurate at repeating words that occurred in highly frequent four-word strings such as *sit in your chair* than lower frequency strings such as *sit in your truck*. This evidence all suggests that young children are learning, and using, lexically specific schemas.

However, one problem is that most of the evidence we have cited in support of the theory focusses on what children can say (production). When we look at what children understand (comprehension) a different pattern emerges. In fact, many comprehension studies seem to show that children's knowledge of syntax is much more abstract, and perhaps more adultlike, than the usage-based model predicts.

For example, Gertner and colleagues tested the claim that young children have only lexically specific knowledge (Gertner, Fisher & Eisengart, 2006) In particular, they tested the prediction that two-year-old children will know how to interpret sentences with familiar verbs, but will not be able to generalise this knowledge to novel verbs (Tomasello, 1992). According to the usage-based model, two-year-olds will be able to interpret sentences such as *the rabbit kicked the duck* because they have a lexically specific *kick* schema that tells them how to use *kick* (e.g. a kicker-kick-kickee schema). However, they will not yet have build up the abstract SUBJECT-VERB-OBJECT schema required to interpret sentences with completely novel verbs, such as *the rabbit glorped the duck*.

Gertner and colleagues tested this prediction in a preferential looking experiment (Gertner et al., 2006). Twenty-five-month-old children watch two synchronised videos of a duck and a bunny performing novel actions (n.b. the videos showed people dressed up as a duck and a bunny, not a real duck and bunny). In one video, the bunny wheeled the duck back and forth in a wagon. In the other video the duck rocked the bunny, who was sitting in a rocking chair. As they watched the videos, the children heard transitive sentences with a novel verb that directed them either to look at *the bunny is gorping the duck* or to look at *the duck is gorping the bunny*. Crucially, because the verb was novel, the children could only interpret the sentence correctly, and look at the target action, if they understood the significance of the sentence's word order. Yet, despite the difficulty of the task, these very young children succeeded. They looked significantly longer to the screen matching the directed audio than we would expect by chance. In a follow-up experiment, the effects were replicated with children as young as 21 months. The researchers concluded that "Even before children reach their second birthday, their representations of sentence meaning and form are not strictly tied to particular words" (Gertner et al., 2006, p. 689). Similar evidence for more abstract knowledge in comprehension tasks has been found in other laboratories (see Dittmar, Abbot-Smith, Lieven & Tomasello, 2008; Kidd, Bavin & Rhodes, 2001; Naigles, 1990; Noble, Rowland & Pine, 2011). These results are difficult to explain within the usage-based model. In fact, it is now quite widely accepted that children are capable of showing more abstract knowledge in comprehension than in production, although the reasons for this and the implications for the usage-based account are still hotly debated (see Tomasello & Abbot-Smith, 2002).

There is also evidence that children are capable of going beyond lexically specific patterns even in production under certain circumstances. For example, Bencini and Valian conducted a syntactic priming task, which showed that three-year-old children generalise their knowledge beyond lexically specific patterns (Bencini & Valian, 2008). Syntactic priming tasks exploit the fact that children and adults are likely to re-use sentence structures that they have just heard. This happens even when the sentence they produce shares no lexical items with the sentence they have just heard. For example, when faced with the task of describing a picture showing a boy eating a cake, we are more likely to describe this picture with a passive sentence (*the cake was eaten by the boy*) if we have just previously heard someone use a passive sentence to describe a different picture (e.g. *Biba is being kissed by Cecily*). The consensus is that children can only show these priming effects if they have abstract knowledge of syntactic structure, since the prime and target sentences share no lexical items except for the word *by*. Thus evidence of sensitivity to priming is considered to be evidence of abstract syntactic knowledge.

Bencini and Valian (2008) showed that three-year-old children can be primed to produce passive sentences. In their task, the child and the experimenter took it in turns to describe pictures in a picture book. First the experimenter described a picture (which the child had to repeat). Then the child had to describe a different picture. Half of the children heard the experimenter use an active transitive sentence (*the spoon stirred the milk*) and the other half heard the experimenter use a passive sentence (*the milk was stirred by the spoon*). Sure enough, the children primed with the passive produced significantly more passive sentences when it came to their turn to speak than the children primed by the active. Bencini and Valian concluded that under the right circumstances young children could demonstrate abstract knowledge of quite complex syntax even in production tasks (though there were large individual differences across children; see Kidd, 2012). In summary, although the usage-based account explains lexically specific effects in children's utterances very well, it has difficulty explaining why young children show evidence of more abstract knowledge in other tasks, especially when such knowledge can be ascribed to very young children. This discrepancy remains to be explained.

4.4 HOW DO CHILDREN LEARN TO CONSTRAIN THEIR PRODUCTIVITY?

Above we considered different theories of how children learn syntactic rules and categories, each of which provides a solution to the poverty of the stimulus and bootstrapping problems. However, we have not addressed the third challenge; how to avoid over-generalisation errors. This is the topic of this final section.

Once the child has mastered the syntactic rules of her language, she only has to hear a word a few times in order to know how to use it appropriately. Sometimes, just once is enough. If I tell you that *yesterday Samuel glorped his sister Orla*, you can then produce any number of novel sentences yourself: *really? Why did he glorp her? Doesn't he know that glorping your sister is wrong?* This productivity is at the heart of language.

However, a child who has learnt the syntactic rules of her language still has one final challenge to face: how to constrain her productivity so that she avoids making over-generalisation errors. Over-generalisation errors are errors such as *don't giggle me*, *I said her no* and *I spilled the rug with juice*, which children make while learning a language (Bowerman, 1988; Pinker, 1989). They occur when children have learnt how to generate new sentences of their own, but have not yet learnt the limits on what kinds of verb can occur in different sentence types. Thus, they are generalising too freely.

This problem is sometimes called *Baker's paradox* after one of the first researchers to outline the problem (Baker, 1979). The paradox is this. Children have to generalise across utterances in order to formulate novel utterances. Thus, their language learning mechanism must allow them to hear a novel verb in a sentence like *Orla glorped* and extrapolate from this the hypothesis that it is also possible to say *Samuel glorped Orla*. However, children must also learn that this generalisation is not possible under certain circumstances. It is not appropriate to make this generalisation with the verb *giggled*, for example (**Samuel giggled Orla*). Thus, the key question is this:

Key question: how do children learn to constrain their generalisations so that they converge on only grammatical utterances?

The three solutions that have been proposed are discussed below.

4.4.1   Solution I: negative evidence

When we answer incorrectly in school our teachers correct us. They tell us that we are wrong and then (hopefully) provide the correct answer. When they do this they are providing *negative evidence*. Negative evidence is very important because without it we might never correct false beliefs. We might go through life thinking that two plus two equals five, or that a tomato is a vegetable (if you thought it was a vegetable let me provide the relevant negative evidence – it is a fruit).

Because negative evidence is crucial for correcting false beliefs in many areas of learning, it seems plausible to suggest that it might apply to language learning. Perhaps parents respond· to syntactically ill-formed utterances with explicit corrections. Children might learn to avoid over-generalisation errors by having their errors corrected. Brown and Hanlon investigated this possibility by analysing what parents said immediately after their children had produced errors (Brown & Hanlon, 1970). Contrary to the prediction, there was no evidence that parents corrected their children's syntax errors. Instead, parents tended to comment on the truth value of their children's utterances not the syntax. Eve's claim *Mamma isn't a boy, <u>he</u> a girl* was met with the approving *that's right*, not a correction of her misuse of *he*. Sarah's syntactically well-formed *There's the animal farmhouse* was followed by her mother's *No, that's a lighthouse*. In fact, since many of children's errors are very amusing, some mischievous parents are more likely to repeat errors than correct them, as in the following conversation between a two-year-old girl and her mother (Stefanowitsch, 2011):

Anne: I don't sure don't like it.

Mother: You don't sure you don't like it?

However, it is possible that parents provide negative evidence indirectly, by responding to children's errors in a certain way. One influential idea is that parents reformulate (*recast*) their children's utterances, repeating the sentence back in correct form (see Saxton, 1997, 2000), as in the following example:

Child: He wiped <u>him</u>.

Adult: He wiped <u>himself</u>.

Child: Yes, he wiped <u>himself</u>.

(Saxton, 2000)

Here the adult has recast the child's sentence, thus modelling the correct sentence. The child then picks up on this and repeats the correct sentence. Saxton suggested that the same process might apply to all types of error, including over-generalisation errors. For example, what if Bowerman had responded to her daughter Chrissie's *I said her no* with a recast such as *You said no to her?* (Bowerman, 1988). We can imagine that this might provide Chrissie with negative evidence, albeit indirect evidence, that her own sentence was not well formed.

There is good evidence that parents do provide this type of negative evidence. For example, Chouinard and Clark analysed how three English-speaking and two French-speaking parents responded to their young children's errors in natural conversation (Chouinard & Clark, 2003). They found that parents recast their children's errors significantly more frequently than they repeated their correct utterances, especially when the children were young. Importantly, the parents responded in this way to all types of error: phonological errors, lexical errors, morphological errors and syntax errors. There was also some evidence that the children were sensitive to these recasts. In other words, although parents may not explicitly correct their children's errors they do provide the information necessary for children to correct themselves.

However, recasts cannot be the full explanation for how children learn that over-generalisation errors are ungrammatical for one very important reason. In grammaticality judgement studies, adults and children reject ungrammatical utterances with verbs that are so infrequent in the language that they have almost certainly never produced them, let alone had them corrected (e.g. **the joke chortled me*). In fact, they even reject ungrammatical uses of novel verbs that we know they have never produced, because the experimenters just made them up. Ambridge and colleagues showed this quite clearly by demonstrating that five- and nine-year-old children and adults identified transitive sentences like *the joke tammed Lisa* as ungrammatical if they had previously been taught that *tam* meant 'to laugh in a particular way' (Ambridge, Pine, Rowland & Young, 2008). The participants in this study based their responses on the sentence's similarity in meaning to other laughing verbs, which would also be ungrammatical in this sentence (**the joke giggled/laughed Lisa*). In other words, although children do respond to indirect negative evidence, it cannot explain results like those of Ambridge and colleagues so it is unlikely to be the full explanation of how children learn to restrict their generalisations.

4.4.2   Solution II: the semantic verb class hypothesis (Pinker, 1989)

Pinker's solution to the over-generalisation problem was to take another look at the apparently arbitrary restrictions on which verbs can and cannot occur in certain syntactic structures. At first sight, there seems neither rhyme nor reason to these restrictions. For example, there are restrictions on the verbs that can occur in the double object dative (a structure used to express the transfer of an object or information). We can say *I told Mo something* but not **I said Mo something*. *Told* and *said* seem to mean very similar things so why is *told* allowed but not *said*? Pinker's answer was to argue that the restrictions on use are not actually arbitrary but are based on subtle differences in meaning. One difference, for example is that *told* implies that the information is successfully transferred to a listener whereas *said* carries no such implication. One can *say* a sentence out loud even when no one else is in the room.

Pinker (1989) suggested that the key to restricting over-generalisation errors was learning these subtle semantic differences. This learning process occurs in three stages. The child first learns a set of *broad range rules* that work on the basis of the meaning associated with each sentence structure. For example, the meaning associated with the double object dative sentence structure is *cause to have*. Thus, the sentence *I gave Mo a book* implies that I caused Mo to have the book. However, the meaning associated with the prepositional dative (an alternative way to express transfer) is *cause to go*. Thus *I gave the parcel to Mo* is grammatical because it implies that I caused the parcel to go to Mo. Verbs like *give* incorporate both *cause to go* and *cause to have* meanings so they can occur in both datives. These rules are innately specified in the child's Universal Grammar, which means that children can learn very quickly how to apply them in their language.

There are also, however, *narrow range rules* that further subdivide verbs into more fine-grained verb classes, some of which contain verbs that can alternate between the two structures and some of which do not. For example, 'verbs of giving' (*send, give*) can occur in both prepositional and double object datives (e.g. *I gave Morton a book/I gave a book to Morton*). Verbs of 'accompanied motion' however, can only occur in the prepositional dative (which means that **I pulled Morton the box* is ungrammatical but *I pulled the box to Morton* is fine). Importantly, children learn these narrow range classes in the second stage of acquisition, by paying attention to the input. Once they have gathered evidence that verbs in a particular narrow range class can occur in both structures, they label that verb class as an alternating class. Other verb classes will never be labelled as alternating verb classes, because their verbs are never heard in both structures.

At some point "presumably around puberty" the third stage occurs, in which the child abandons broad range rules in favour of narrow range classes (Pinker, 1989, p. 349). Now the verbs in verb classes that have been labelled as 'alternating' are free to alternate (e.g. *give*). Verbs in other classes are not free to alternate and will only be used in one structure (e.g. *I pulled the box to Morton*). Until they reach this point, however, children will make over-generalisation errors, either because they have not yet learnt the narrow range classes and are over-applying the broad range rule or because they have not yet learnt how to fit the verb into a verb class. For example, on this account, a child might say **I pulled Morton the box* because she has mis-categorised *pulled* into an alternating verb class. As she slowly learns the correct meaning of *pull*, she will correct her error.

Pinker's theory provides a very neat explanation of how children can learn the correct use of verbs that they have never heard before. As long as a new verb is incorporated into an existing non-alternating verb class, adults and older children will assume that it cannot alternate. For example, we learnt in the previous section that the participants tested by Ambridge and colleagues had no problems rejecting sentences like **the joke tammed Lisa* if they had previously been taught that *tammed* meant 'to laugh in a particular way' (Ambridge et al., 2008). Pinker's theory predicts this very result. By teaching the participants that *tamming* meant 'to laugh in a particular way', the researchers had taught the participant that *tamming* was a member of the 'verbs of laughing' semantic class, which is not permitted in transitive causative constructions (c.f. *the joke laughed Lisa). Other studies report similar findings with novel verbs (Brooks & Tomasello, 1999).

There is also some tentative evidence to support the idea that children make over-generalisation errors when they have not yet learnt the correct meaning of a verb. Gropen and colleagues found that children who made errors with the verbs *fill* and *empty* were also likely to misinterpret the verbs' meaning (Gropen, Pinker, Hollander & Goldberg, 1991). To assess this, they first elicited sentences from different groups of children aged two to five years in order to see if they would make over-generalisation errors. Many did (e.g. *the man filled water into the sink). Then, in order to test whether children understood the meaning of the verbs, they showed them pictures of actions that either focussed on the manner of motion of an action (e.g. a woman <u>dripping</u> or <u>pouring</u> water into a glass) or the end state (a <u>full</u> glass but no woman). The design was quite complicated but the bottom line was that some children seemed to think that the manner of motion was important to the meaning of the verb *fill*. The children had a tendency to answer as if the word *fill* was only appropriate if the water was <u>poured</u>, not <u>dripped</u>, into the glass. They did not, however, misinterpret the meaning of *pour*. Importantly, the children also tended to make many more syntactic over-generalisation errors with *fill* than with *pour*. The authors concluded that the children made over-generalisation errors with precisely those verbs whose meaning they have misinterpreted, just as the theory predicted.

There is, however, one very robust effect in the literature that the semantic verb class theory cannot explain. This is the effect of frequency on over-generalisation errors. A number of studies have shown that children and adults are much more likely to reject an over-generalisation error if the verb is one they have heard often; a high frequency verb. For example, Ambridge and colleagues (2008) found that older children and adults rated * The clown laughed Lisa as much less acceptable than *The clown giggled Lisa. Similarly, they rated *The magician disappeared Bart as much less acceptable than *The magician vanished Bart. The authors explained this effect in terms of frequency. *Laugh* is a much higher frequency verb than *giggle* in the speech that children hear. *Disappear* is, similarly, a higher frequency verb than *vanish*. In essence, over-generalisation errors are more acceptable with low frequency verbs than high frequency verbs, even when these verbs come from the same semantic class. This is an effect that cannot be explained in terms of the semantic verb class theory, which states that verb class, not frequency, should determine how a verb can be used. Thus, like the negative evidence hypothesis, the semantic verb class hypothesis provides a partial, but not a full explanation of how children learn to restrict their generalisations.

4.4.3 Solution III: the role of frequency (entrenchment and pre-emption)

Above we discovered that high frequency verbs are more resistant to over-generalisation errors than low frequency verbs. In other words, the more often you hear a verb used, the more likely you are to consider it ungrammatical in unattested constructions. This is the basic tenet of the entrenchment hypothesis, which was proposed by Braine and Brooks (1995). On this view, hearing a verb frequently in one structure and never in another will lead the child to assume (unconsciously) that the verb is ungrammatical in the second structure. For example, since *laugh* will have been heard frequently in intransitive structures such as *Bart laughed*, and never in transitive structures like *The clown laughed Bart*, children assume that it is ungrammatical in transitive structures. However, *giggle* is less frequent in children's input, so children's knowledge about its status is less clear-cut. As a result, it sounds 'less bad' in the transitive than *laugh* and is more likely to attract over-generalisation errors. In essence, over-generalisation errors occur with verbs whose correct usage has not yet been firmly *entrenched*.

A related proposal, also based on frequency, is the pre-emption hypothesis (Braine & Brooks, 1995; Clark & Clark, 1979; Goldberg, 1995; MacWhinney, 2004). In one way, this hypothesis is similar to the entrenchment hypothesis because it is based on the idea that hearing a verb frequently in one structure and never in another will lead the child to assume that the verb is ungrammatical in the second structure. However, the pre-emption hypothesis ascribes a special role to the similarity in meaning between two structures. For example, let us say that a parent wants to tell her child that a magician made a ball disappear when doing magic tricks. Her child might note that the parent uses the periphrastic causative structure (*the magician made the ball disappear*) not the transitive (*the magician disappeared the ball*) to describe this event. According to the pre-emption hypothesis, the more often the child hears the periphrastic causative, when she might well expect to hear a transitive, the more likely she is to infer that the transitive cannot be used with the verb *disappear*. Note that it is the fact that the periphrastic causative expresses a similar meaning to the causative transitive that leads the child to make this inference. In other words, the use of the periphrastic causative pre-empts the use of the transitive.

Children seem to show both entrenchment and pre-emption effects. In terms of entrenchment, many studies have found that both adults and children rate low frequency verbs as more acceptable than high frequency verbs when asked to judge if they are grammatical in the 'wrong' structures (Theakston, 2004; Wonnacott, Newport & Tanenhaus, 2008). We reported on one of these in the previous section (Ambridge et al., 2008). Similarly, Brooks and colleagues reported that three-, five- and eight-year-olds were three times more likely to make over-generalisation errors with low frequency verbs (e.g. *vanish*) than high frequency ones (e.g. *disappear*; Brooks, Tomasello, Dodson & Lewis, 1999). This is precisely what we would expect if hearing a verb frequently in one structure and never in another leads the child to assume that the verb is ungrammatical in the second structure.

There is also evidence that hearing a verb in a pre-empting structure reduces the number of over-generalisation errors that children make with that verb. Brooks and Tomasello (1999) taught children novel verbs to describe novel actions and then encouraged the children to use the verbs themselves to describe what was going on. Importantly, in the training session, half of the children heard the novel verbs in pre-empting constructions as well as other constructions. For example, all of the children learnt that the verb *meek* was an intransitive-only verb that described how a car moved up a ramp when a puppy pulled on a string (*look, the car meeked up the ramp*). However, half of the children also heard it used in the pre-empting periphrastic causative as well (*look, the puppy made the car meek*). As predicted, the six- to-seven-year-olds who had heard the pre-empting structure (though not the two- and four-year-olds) produced significantly fewer over-generalisation errors than the control group when they later came to describe the action themselves. For example, they used far fewer transitives (**the puppy meeked the car*). Hearing the pre-empting construction seemed to have allowed the children to infer that the over-generalised use of the novel verb was ungrammatical.

Ambridge and Lieven have identified a possible problem in these results because it turns out that hearing pre-empting structures blocked transitive uses of all the novel verbs, even those that should have been allowed in the transitive. "Pre-emption served not to selectively reduce the number of overgeneralizations, but simply to reduce the number of generalizations across the board" (Ambridge & Lieven, 2011, p. 255). In other words, in this study, pre-emption was so powerful it took out children's ability to form novel utterances even when they were grammatical. This is not what happens in natural language learning since we know children are capable of forming novel, grammatical utterances. However, Ambridge himself has since provided independent evidence that pre-emption does block over-generalisation errors (Ambridge, Pine, Rowland, Freudenthal & Chang, 2012). In a large scale study testing 301 dative verbs, these authors reported that the frequency with which a particular verb occurs in a pre-empting structure predicts the extent to which children and adults consider over-generalisation errors with that verb to be ungrammatical.

However, one problem with both the entrenchment and the pre-emption hypotheses is that they cannot explain the semantic class effects that we discussed in the previous section, especially those that occur with novel verbs. Children and adults reject ungrammatical uses of novel verbs as well as real verbs, and they do this on the basis of the verb's meaning (**The clown laughed/giggled/tammed Lisa*; e.g. Ambridge et al., 2008). According to the entrenchment hypothesis, only hearing a verb frequently in one (or more) construction can lead to its being treated as ungrammatical in unattested structures. According to the pre-emption hypothesis, only hearing a novel verb in a pre-empting construction can lead to its being treated as ungrammatical in unattested structures. Novel verbs like *tamming* have never been heard before. The implication, yet again, is that the hypotheses provide only a partial explanation of how children learn to restrict their over-generalisations.

To conclude, the clear, but prosaic, conclusion to this section has to be that children probably use many factors to help them retreat from over-generalisation: recasts, semantics, entrenchment and pre-emption. However, this statement is not a theory per se, it is merely a summary of the evidence. The key to a successful theory in future will be in explaining how these factors interact.

4.5 CHAPTER SUMMARY

In this chapter, we discovered that there is more to the process of learning syntax than just copying the sentences of others. Syntax comprises a hidden skeleton of rules and categories that are not immediately observable from the language that we hear every day. In order to learn syntax, the child has to overcome three obstacles: the poverty of the stimulus, the bootstrapping problem and the problem of how to avoid over-generalisation. The first key question to be answered, then, is this:

How do children learn the syntax of their language?

Nativist theories answer our key question by positing powerful innate principles that guide the child through the learning process. As a result, the follow-up key question for nativists becomes:

What innate knowledge does the child possess?

We discussed the semantic bootstrapping hypothesis and theories within the principles and parameters framework. All have difficulties that stem from the fact that the innate knowledge ascribed to children predicts different patterns from those we see in children's early language. The semantic bootstrapping theory has difficulty explaining cross-linguistic patterns of development. Theories within the principles and parameters framework find it difficult to explain why children make errors and why they seem so much more knowledgeable with some lexical items than others, even items within the same grammatical category.

Constructivist theories propose that children build the syntax of their language from the bottom up. They exploit the fact that grammar is essentially a system of repeating patterns and build links between words that behave in the same way in sentences and between words that express similar meanings. The key question for them is:

How do children analyse their input in order to learn the grammatical regularities of their language?

They too have their problems. Theories that focus solely on distributional analysis need to have some built-in constraints in order to explain why children do not make inaccurate generalisations. Yet no one has successfully pinned down what these constraints may be. Usage-based theories propose constraints on generalisations but have difficulty explaining why children show evidence of abstract knowledge in comprehension and priming tasks.

Where do we go from here? Although it is too early to evaluate their success, there are some new theories emerging within the constructivist tradition that posit a larger role for abstract knowledge earlier in development (Abbot-Smith, Lieven & Tomasello, 2008; Chang, Dell & Bock, 2006). There are also some new ideas emerging in the nativist tradition. For example, Fisher (2001) has proposed a one-to-one mapping bias, which leads children to assume a different semantic role for each noun that occurs in a sentence. Thus, children are biased to assume that sentences such as *the bunny glorped the frog* refer to actions in which one character acts upon another. It is interesting that this type of innate knowledge is far closer in principle to the type of cognitive primitives now being proposed by constructivists. Readers must bear in mind that the two theories disagree about whether such biases stem from innate language-specific knowledge or general cognitive principles (see Goldberg, 2004, for a more detailed discussion). However, an optimist might conclude that the theories may be moving closer to a consensus.

In the final section, we discussed the retreat from over-generalisation error, asking the key question:

How do children learn to constrain their generalisations so that they converge on only grammatical utterances?

The clear conclusion to this section was that children probably use all four factors to help them retreat from over-generalisation: recasts, semantics, entrenchment and pre-emption. The key to a successful theory in future will be in explaining how these factors interact.

4.6 SUGGESTED READING

Ambridge, B. & Lieven, E. V. M. (2011). *Child language acquisition: Contrasting theoretical approaches.* Cambridge: Cambridge University Press. This very readable book has three detailed chapters on simple and complex syntax (chapters 6, 7 and 9) as well as a chapter on theoretical approaches to grammar acquisition (chapter 4).

Clark, E. (2009). *First language acquisition.* 2nd edition. Cambridge: Cambridge University Press. Chapters 7 and 9 give readers a detailed picture of exactly what types of utterance children produce at different ages. Clark is a constructivist, and her book reflects this.

Lust, B. (2006). *Child language: Acquisition and growth.* Cambridge: Cambridge University Press. An interesting introduction to language acquisition from a nativist perspective.

4.7 SUGGESTED READING (ADVANCED LEVEL)

Some papers that provide details of the two major theories omitted in this chapter are as follows. For information about the competition model:

Bates, E. & MacWhinney, B. (1987). Competition, variation, and language learning. In B. MacWhinney (Ed.), *Mechanisms of language acquisition* (pp. 157–194). Hillsdale, NJ: Lawrence Erlbaum Associates.

Bates, E., MacWhinney, B., Caselli, C., Devescovi, A., Natale, F. & Venza, V. (1984). A crosslinguistic study of the development of sentence interpretation strategies. *Child Development, 55*(2), 341–354.

For information about prosodic bootstrapping:
Christophe, A., Millotte, S., Bernal, S. & Lidz, J. (2008). Bootstrapping lexical and syntactic acquisition. *Language & Speech, 51*, 61–75.
Christophe, A., Guasti, M. T., Nespor, M., Dupoux, E. & van Ooyen, B. (1997). Reflections on prosodic bootstrapping: Its role for lexical and syntactic acquisition. *Language and Cognitive Processes, 12*(5–6), 585–612.

The following exchanges illustrate the cut and thrust of the nativist-constructivist debate:
Debate about constructivism:
Tomasello, M. (2000). Do young children have adult syntactic competence? *Cognition, 74*(3), 209–253. The seminal article that outlines Tomasello's usage-based theory.
Fisher, C. (2002). The role of abstract syntactic knowledge in language acquisition: A reply to Tomasello (2000). *Cognition, 82*(3), 259–278. A reply from the nativist camp.
Tomasello, M. & Abbot-Smith, K. (2002). A tale of two theories: Response to Fisher. *Cognition, 83*(2), 207–214. The response to the reply.
Debate about nativism:
Valian, V. (1986). Syntactic categories in the speech of young children. *Developmental Psychology, 22*(4), 562–579. Valian's original paper attributing knowledge of syntactic categories to children.
Pine, J. M. & Martindale, H. (1996). Syntactic categories in the speech of young children: The case of the determiner. *Journal of Child Language, 23*(2), 369–395. Pine and Martindale suggest that Valian's (1986) criteria could be satisfied by children who know only lexically specific schema. They suggest a different measure of syntactic knowledge: the overlap measure, which demonstrates that children do not have adultlike knowledge.
Valian, V., Solt, S. & Stewart, J. (2009). Abstract categories or limited-scope formulae: The case of children's determiners. *Journal of Child Language, 36*(4), 749–778. Valian and colleagues accept Pine and Martindale's criticism but apply a critique of their own and demonstrate that children do seem to have adultlike knowledge.
Pine, J. M., Freudenthal, D. & Krajewski, G. (2013). Do young children have adult-like syntactic categories? Zipf's law and the case of the determiner. *Cognition, 127*(3), 345–360. Pine and colleagues identify some problems with Valian's analysis and re-analyse the data, concluding that children do not have adultlike knowledge of the determiner category.

4.8 COMPREHENSION CHECK

1. In your own words, explain what is meant by:

   a. The poverty of the stimulus problem
   b. The bootstrapping problem
   c. The problem of over-generalisation

2. Give an example of:

   a. A transitive sentence
   b. An intransitive sentence
   c. A passive sentence
   d. A relative clause
   e. A syntactic subject
   f. A syntactic object
   g. A thematic role

3. Describe in your own words <u>one</u> problem with each of the following theories:

   a. Semantic bootstrapping theory
   b. A principles and parameters theory that explains errors in terms of performance limitations
   c. A semantic-distributional account
   d. The usage-based theory

4. Describe briefly how the following explain how children retreat from over-generalisation error:

   a. Negative evidence
   b. The semantic verb class hypothesis
   c. The entrenchment hypothesis
   d. The pre-emption hypothesis

5

Acquiring morphology

5.1 THE ISSUE

In the last chapter we looked at how children learn syntax – the process of putting words together into sentences. We learnt that in languages like English we change the meaning of a sentence by changing the order of words. For example, if you heard someone say *man bites dog* you would probably be more surprised than if you had heard them say *dog bites man*. However, in languages like Turkish or Russian we can change the order of words without changing the meaning as long as we use the right word endings. For example, *man bites dog* in Russian is:

Человек	кусаем	собаку
Man (biter)	bites	dog (bitten)

However, the order of words does not matter, so speakers can swap the words round without changing the meaning:

Собаку	кусаем	человек
Dog (bitten)	bites	man (biter)

This sentence also means *man bites dog* because it is the endings on the nouns, not the word order, that tell us who did what to whom. We call these endings inflectional endings, or simply inflections.

Inflections like these are examples of morphemes, which are "the smallest meaningful constituent of words that can be identified" (Haspelmath & Sims, 2010, p. 3). For example, the word *nuts* is made up of a stem word (*nut*) and an inflectional marker (*s*), both of which are morphemes. The *-s* inflectional marker makes the word plural, making it refer to more than one nut (the official terminology is that the *-s* inflectional ending adds the grammatical feature of number: see below for an explanation).

Research on morphemes (morphology) focusses on how we use two different types of morpheme: inflectional morphemes and derivational morphemes. In this chapter, we look at inflectional morphemes, because these have attracted most attention from child language researchers (see Saxton, 2010, for a brief review of work on derivational morphology). The reason for the spotlight on inflection is the puzzling errors that children make, which theories of morphological development have to be able to explain.

In this chapter we will outline what inflectional morphology is, before describing some of the errors that children make and how different theories attempt to explain them. We will first cover the debate on why children sometimes omit inflection or use the wrong inflection. We will then discuss the separate, but related, debate about why children sometimes over-generalise inflectional endings incorrectly.

5.2   WHAT IS INFLECTIONAL MORPHOLOGY?

Inflectional morphology is used to express the different *grammatical features* of a language, such as tense, number and person. An example is the English past tense marker *-ed*, which is applied to verbs (e.g. to turn *walk* into *walked*). Using this, we can indicate to the listener that the event being described took place in the past. For example, we can turn *Look out, you are going to <u>walk</u> into that lamp post*, which refers to an event that is just about to occur, into *never mind, you <u>walked</u> into the lamp post anyway*, which refers to an event that occurred in the recent past. Children need to learn how to use inflection in their own sentences and how to interpret them in the speech of others.

The child's task of learning inflection is complicated by two factors. First, across the world's languages, inflections can encode a range of possible grammatical features. So children have to be prepared to learn a large number of markers to mark a large number of possible features. The most common features marked in inflection across languages are as follows:

- *Tense and aspect.* Tense markers encode the location of an event in time (i.e. when an event took place) and are usually added to the verb. For example, in English, we can add *-ed* to indicate past tense (*kick* becomes *kicked*). To indicate that an event is occurring in the present we use either a null marker that does not visibly change the form of the verb (e.g. *to kick* becomes *I kick*) or we add an *-s* (*to kick* becomes *Cecily kick<u>s</u>*), depending on the person marking of the sentence subject. Aspect markers are used to encode how the event is to be viewed with respect to time, such as whether it is completed (*Cecily has kicked the ball*) or ongoing (*Cecily is kicking the ball*). In English tense and aspect are usually marked using inflections on the verb (e.g. *kicks*) or by adding an auxiliary such as *is* or *has* (*has kicked, is kicking*).

- *Person.* Person marking allows us to add a marker, usually to the verb, to distinguish between the person speaking (first person; *I kick, we kick*), the listener (second person; *you kick*) and other people not involved in the conversation (third person; *he kicks, she kicks*). Person marking is impoverished in English because we do not have many different inflectional verb forms (*I, you, we* and *they* usually take the same verb form, for example, *I kick, you kick, we kick, they kick*). It is richer in a language like Spanish, where each person has a different marker. Thus, *jugar* ('to play') becomes *juego, juegas, juega, jugamos, jugáis, juegan* ('I play', 'you play', 'he/she/it plays', 'we play', 'you (plural) play', 'they play').

- *Number.* Number marking indicates the number of people or objects under discussion; distinguishing whether an event involves one person (singular: *I, it, dog, cat*) or many (plural: *we, they, dogs, cats*). Some languages also have a third form to indicate that there are two people or objects only (duality: e.g. Classical Greek's *adelphō* 'two brothers'; see Haspelmath & Sims, 2010). Many languages make use of person and number marking together, so that the marker used depends both on the person and on the number of the grammatical subject. In English, for example we use *am* with first person singular subjects (*I am*), *is* with third person singular subjects (*he is*) and *are* with third person plural subjects (*they are*). This is called subject-verb agreement. It is particularly useful in languages like Spanish where omitting the grammatical subject from a sentence is allowed. Here, subject-verb agreement allows the listener to reconstruct which subject was omitted. So, a Spanish speaker hearing the verb *juego* can infer that the speaker means *I play* because *juego* is the first person singular form of the verb. Similarly, if the speaker said *juegan*, the listener could infer that the speaker meant *they play*, because *juegan* is the third person plural form.

- *Case.* Case marking indicates what grammatical role nouns and pronouns play in the sentence. For example, in German, if we want to say that *the dog bit the man*, we use different case marked determiners in front of each noun to indicate that the dog is the biter and the man is the person bitten (e.g. *der, den*). We use a nominative case marked determiner for the doer of the action (*der Hund* 'the dog') and an accusative case marked determiner for the person acted upon (*den Mann* 'the man'). Thus we say *der Hund biss den Mann*. Conversely, if we want to say *the man bit the dog*, we must use nominative case for the man and accusative case for the dog (*der Mann biss den Hund*). In Finnish, the case marking occurs on the noun. So, for example, *the man shot the dog* becomes *mies ampui koiran*; *mies* is the nominative form of the word for 'man' and *koiran* is the accusative form of the word for 'dog'. In fact, Finnish is generally considered to have about fourteen cases (see http://www.cs.tut.fi/~jkorpela/finnish-cases.html). Other languages like Modern Greek have very few.

- *Gender.* In many languages, nouns are classified into different categories such as masculine, feminine and neuter. These are known as gender-based classification systems. In these languages, the gender of a noun usually has an effect on the form of words related to the noun (e.g. determiners, pronouns, adjectives). For example, the French word for 'bread' (*pain*) has masculine gender, which means we use the masculine article *le* rather than the feminine *la* (so *the bread* is *le pain* not *la pain*). In many languages, the gender of the noun is not determined by the meaning of the word but by the word's morphology or phonology. For example, in Spanish, words that end in *-a* are usually assigned feminine gender even when the word refers to a man (e.g. the word *persona* 'person' is feminine, even when the person referred to is a man).

These features – tense, aspect, person, number, case and gender – are quite common across the world's languages. However, there are many other features that can be encoded by the inflection system. In different parts of the world, there are languages that use inflections to indicate humanness (whether the object under discussion is human or not), distance (how far away the object under discussion is from the speaker) and the source of the evidence (whether the speaker witnessed the event under discussion or heard about it from a third party). Children, thus, have to learn to mark whichever features their language requires.

The second complication for children learning inflection comes from the fact that there are different methods of marking these features across languages. Here are a few:

- In most languages, we can add markers to the end of words (*kick* becomes *kicked*, *dog* becomes *dogs*). These markers are called suffixes.

- In many languages we can add markers to the start of words (prefixes). For example, in Sesotho, a language spoken in Lesotho and parts of South Africa, prefixes are added to nouns to mark number and nouns class (e.g. *mo-sali* 'woman' becomes *bo-sali* 'women').

- In some languages we can change the vowel in the middle of the word (English: *sing* becomes *sang*).

- In some languages, we can add a marker in the middle of the word (infix). For example, in Nuuchahnulth, a native American language: *t'an'a* 'child' becomes *t'a-t-n'a* 'children'. In Lepcha, a Himalayan language, *mák* 'die' becomes *m-y-ák* 'kill'.

- In languages like German, we can combine prefixes and suffixes to create a circumfix; a marker that wraps around the word (e.g. in German, *fahr* 'drive' becomes *ge-fahr-en* 'driven').

- Sometimes the form of a word changes completely. For example, in English, the past tense of *go* is *went* (not **goed*)[1] and in French, the first person form of the verb *être* 'to be' is *suis* (*je suis* 'I am').

- Sometimes, grammatical features are marked by adding an additional, separate, word to the sentence. For example, in English, we commonly add an auxiliary such as *is*, *are* or *were* to mark tense, aspect, person and number (*he is going, we are going, they were going*).

Many languages use a single marker to mark multiple features all at once. For example, the English suffix *-s* marks person, number and tense in verbs. For example, in the sentence *Cecily wants a cake,* the *-s* ending on the verb indicates to the listener that the subject *Cecily* is referred to in the third person, is singular not plural and

---

1   A star * indicates an ungrammatical utterance.

that the event is taking place in the present (Cecily wants a cake at the moment). Languages like English are called fusional or synthetic languages. However, other languages use a different marker to mark each feature (agglutinative languages). This can give us long complex words made up of many morphemes. For example, in K'iche' Mayan the phrase *you are hitting me* is expressed by a single word (*kinach'ayo*) made up of five morphemes:

k-	*in-*	*a-*	*ch'ay-*	*o*
present tense	first person singular object (me)	second person singular subject (you)	hit	present tense

To summarise, in order to devise a successful theory of how children learn inflection, we must specify how children learn how to encode any one of a large number of features (e.g. tense, case) using any one of a large number of different methods (e.g. suffixes, prefixes). Strangely enough, children seem to learn inflection relatively easily, despite the complexity of the system. However, devising a theory to explain how they do this has proved challenging, as we shall see below.

One final question is worth addressing. How do we know that people are adding inflectional markers to words when they speak? Perhaps they simply retrieve the inflected form from memory. For example, perhaps speakers do not add an -*ed* when they want to create a past tense form of the verb *love*. Perhaps they simply store the past tense form *loved* separately from the present tense form *love* in memory, and retrieve *loved* when they want to talk about a lost love.

It is quite easy to show that this is not the case using a simple thought experiment. Read and complete the following sentence:

Last week I said that I wanted to pilk and you know what ... yesterday I did it! Yesterday I ...

Most native English speakers have no difficulty finishing the sentence off with the correctly inflected verb *pilked*. However, we know that they cannot do this by retrieving *pilked* from memory because people can only store words that they have heard before, and most people have never previously heard the work *pilked* (unless they have read a lot of studies on language; *pilk* is a nonsense word that was invented some years ago for language experiments). So they must have constructed the word *pilked* by adding the correct past tense inflectional ending to the verb stem *pilk*.

One of the first researchers to demonstrate that we add inflectional endings to words in this way was Jean Berko, who created the famous *wug test* (Berko, 1958). She used nonsense words like *pilk* and *wug* to demonstrate that adults and children do not simply store inflected forms in memory but are capable of adding them to any new word productively. So, given that we know adults use inflections productively, how do children learn them?

5.3 HOW DO CHILDREN LEARN THEIR LANGUAGE'S INFLECTIONAL SYSTEM?

Young children, to varying degrees, make errors when they first start to learn to use their inflectional system. This is not unexpected. As we have seen, inflectional systems are complex. However, children often produce correctly inflected utterances at the same time as they make errors. Thus, the focus of many theories of inflection acquisition has been on explaining why children make errors and why these errors co-occur with correct utterances. So the key question for this section is:

Key question: why do children make errors at the same time as they produce correctly inflected utterances?

A common error among two-year-olds learning languages like English is to use what we call a bare stem (or bare root) form, which has no inflectional ending at all. So an English child may say *Rover lick my face* instead of *Rover is licking my face*. To illustrate, table 5.1 lists some of the sentences produced by Lara at age two years five months (2;5). As the table shows, Lara sometimes omitted the inflectional ending used to mark tense (e.g. *finish* instead of *finished*). She also omitted the auxiliaries that are often used in English to mark tense and agreement features. For example, she said *what you doing* instead of *what are you doing*. In fact, it is very common for young English-speaking children to omit auxiliaries in their speech.

Table 5.1
Errors and correct sentences produced by Lara aged 2;5

Errors	Correct sentences
I finish now	I've finished, Mummy
Mummy coming, Amy	I'm playing
what you doing	what's that in there
I just eat little bit	I don't want a bib on
dolly lie down here	I'm stuck now

In some languages, such as Dutch and German, it is relatively common for two-year-old children to use the uninflected (or infinitival) form of the verb instead of an inflected form. For example, in German, a child may say of his pet, *Rover mich lieben*, using the infinitival form of the verb love (*lieben*). The literal translation of this sentence in English is *Rover me to love* which is not grammatical in German. The correct way of saying this would be to use the inflected form *liebt* to produce *Rover liebt mich* 'Rover loves me'. We should also point out, because it will be important later, that the word order of the two sentences differs. When German and Dutch children use a infinitival form, they tend to put it at the end of the sentence, which is the correct place for an infinitive verb in these languages (*Rover mich lieben*) but not for an inflected form. When they use an inflected verb form, children tend to put the verb in its correct position; here the correct position would be after the word *Rover* (*Rover liebt mich*).

In many languages, children also make errors where they use the wrong inflectional ending on a verb given the person and number marking of the sentence's subject. These are called subject-verb agreement errors, because the verb form does not agree with the subject. For example, instead of using *do* for plural subjects (*do cats scratch?*), English children sometimes use *does*, the form that should be used with singular subjects (e.g. *does cats scratch?*). In fact, children learning a whole range of different languages make these types of error, but not very often. For example, Hoekstra and Hyams provide a summary table of the results from four studies across four languages: Spanish, Catalan, Italian and German (Hoekstra & Hyams, 1998, p. 84). Rates of agreement errors were never higher than 4 per cent overall, which means that the children produced the correctly agreeing verb form at least 96 per cent of the time.

Children also sometimes use the wrong case on nouns and pronouns, producing case errors. In English, for example, some children go through a stage in which they use accusative pronouns like *me* and *her* instead of nominative pronouns like *I* and *she* (Rispoli, 1998). For example, children might say *me do it* instead of *I do it*, or *her love you* instead of *she loves you*. Children learning Polish also make case errors in which they use the genitive case ending on nouns where the dative case ending is required (Dąbrowska & Szczerbiński, 2006). There are also reports in some languages of errors in gender marking, in which children over-use one gender marker. For example, both German and French children may over-generalise the masculine articles (*der, le*), using them incorrectly with feminine nouns (and neuter nouns, in the case of German; Boloh & Ibernon, 2010; Szagun, Stumper, Sondag & Franik, 2007).

Importantly, the rate at which children make errors differs widely across languages. English-learning children make a lot of errors in which they use the bare root form instead of an inflected form for an extended period of time (e.g. *Rover lick face*). Sesotho-learning children also produce bare stem noun forms without the prefixes that Sesotho requires to mark noun class and number, though these errors have largely disappeared by the time the children are two-and-a-half years of age (Demuth, 1988). However, bare stem errors are much rarer in other languages. For example, Aksu-Koç and Slobin (1985) have suggested that Turkish children never produce bare stem forms and only rarely make other types of error. Similarly, Smoczyńska (1986) has argued that Polish children make errors with gender and agreement marking for a much shorter period of time than Russian children. Rates of infinitive errors like *Rover mich lieben* also differ across languages. Freudenthal and colleagues compared infinitive errors in different languages and found that they were quite common in German, Dutch and French but were infrequent in Spanish, accounting for fewer than 21 per cent of the verbs that the children used (Freudenthal, Pine & Gobet, 2010).

Finally, it is important to note that all of the errors discussed above co-occur with correctly inflected forms, sometimes for quite a long period of time. If we look again at table 5.1, we can see that Lara does not always omit inflectional endings and auxiliaries; she produces grammatical sentences too. Thus, the difficulty is this. On the one hand, children make errors that suggest that they have not learnt how to use their language's inflectional system. On the other hand, the same children are clearly capable of producing correctly inflected utterances. This pattern of co-occurring correct use and error has proven particularly difficult for theorists to explain.

Theories on this topic can be grouped into those that explain errors in terms of maturation, parameter setting and learning. We will focus on three theories that illustrate the strengths and weaknesses of each approach. As always, there are many more theories that we have left out, simply because it would take too long to discuss them all (e.g. Hoekstra & Hyams, 1998; Hyams, 1986; Pinker, 1984; Radford, 1990; Rizzi, 1993; Slobin, 1973).

5.4 NATIVIST ACCOUNTS I: MATURATIONAL THEORIES

Nativist (or generativist) accounts of inflection propose that children get a helping hand from innate knowledge, which is what Chomsky called Universal Grammar (or UG; Chomsky, 1981).[2] Within UG are the rules that help children construct the inflection system of any language. Since children have access to this innate knowledge, the task of learning inflection becomes much simpler. For example, UG could contain the knowledge that languages can use inflections to mark tense (whether the event occurred in the past, present or future). On this model, children learn inflectional systems by first figuring out whether their language marks tense (like English) or not (like Mandarin Chinese) and, if so, then learning how their language marks tense. Importantly, once the child has learnt how her language marks tense, she should be able to apply this knowledge across the board. For example, once a child has learnt that tense can be marked in English by adding a past tense marker (e.g. *-ed*) she can immediately generalise this knowledge across many verbs, even novel ones (*kick* becomes *kicked*, *love* becomes *loved* and *pilk* becomes *pilked*).

The problem is that children make errors for quite a long time, which does not fit with the idea that children can immediately generalise their knowledge of inflection across verbs. So some nativist theorists have proposed that *maturation* plays a role. They suggest that only some of the all-important innate knowledge is available to children at the start of the language learning process. Other knowledge, in particular, the knowledge needed to build the inflection system, matures at a later date.

There are a number of maturational accounts but we will focus on Wexler's *Agreement/Tense Omission Model* (ATOM; Schütze & Wexler, 1996; Wexler, 1998). Within the account, errors occur because there·is competition between two constraints in the child's grammar. One constraint specifies that tense and agreement inflections must be applied (e.g. to produce *he kicks*). This constraint tells the child

---

2   Nativist theories assume that at least part of children's grammatical knowledge is innate (encoded in the genes, see chapter 4). Generativist theories assume that grammar consists of rules that operate over linguistic categories like nouns and verbs. All the nativist theories we discuss are also generativist, so we simply use the term nativist.

that she must produce sentences <u>with</u> inflections. However, there is an additional constraint in young children's grammar called the *Unique Checking Constraint* (the UCC). This constraint prohibits the child from applying both tense and agreement at the same time (the official terminology is that the constraint prevents the child checking items against more than one functional category). As a result, the child is prohibited from using a verb that is correctly inflected for tense and agreement (e.g. *kicks*) so uses an infinitive form instead (*kick*). Children, thus, swing from obeying the UCC one moment to obeying the 'apply tense and agreement' constraint the next.

What does this mean in practice? Well, when the child obeys the UCC, she produces utterances without inflection. In other words, she produces uninflected forms such as *John like Mary*. When she obeys the 'apply tense and agreement' constraint, she produces correctly inflected utterances such as *John likes Mary* or *John liked Mary*. Because children treat uninflected forms as a grammatical option, this stage of development is known as the *optional infinitive* stage. This stage does not last forever, however, because the UCC withers away in time due to "UG-constrained maturation" (Wexler, 1998, p. 63). After this point, children can use tense and agreement inflections correctly.

5.4.1   Evidence for and against the ATOM

The ATOM'S strength is that it provides one explanation for a whole range of findings. In particular, it explains both why children produce bare stem forms in English (*Rover love me*) and why children produce infinitive errors in German (e.g. **Rover mich <u>lieben</u>*, see section 5.3 above). Both types of error are produced because the child is simply obeying the UCC and omitting tense and agreement marking. This results in a bare root form in English (*Rover <u>love</u> me*) and an infinitive form in German (*Rover mich <u>lieben</u>*). The ATOM also explains why errors co-occur with correctly inflected verbs. Correctly inflected verbs are produced when the child is obeying the 'apply tense and agreement' constraint and errors occur when she is obeying the UCC. Finally, the ATOM explains why children sometimes make case-marking errors such as **me do it*. This explanation is a bit complicated but, put crudely, case is assigned by subject-verb agreement and when agreement is missing, the child cannot apply case marking properly. Thus, she resorts to the default form (which, in this example, is *me*).

In fact, the ATOM is quite successful at explaining the pattern of errors across a wide range of different languages. For example, according to the ATOM, children learning languages that require the grammatical subject to be present in the sentence are predicted to go through a stage in which they sometimes produce bare stem or infinitive errors (an optional infinitive stage).[3] These are languages like Danish, Dutch, English, Faroese, Icelandic, Norwegian, Swedish, French, Irish and Russian. Null subject languages, which allow the speaker to omit the grammatical subject, do not go through an optional infinitive stage (see chapter 4 for more on null subject

---

3   There is a quite complex reason for this, to do with the grammatical subject being taken on by the agreement category in null subject languages but not in obligatory subject languages. Interested readers should read Wexler (1998) for a fuller explanation.

languages). These are languages such as Italian, Spanish, Catalan, Tamil and Polish. Sure enough, cross-linguistically, the data support this prediction. Children learning languages such as Danish, Dutch and English seem to go through an optional infinitive stage. Children learning languages like Italian and Spanish do not (Wexler, 1998).

However, the ATOM is not wholeheartedly supported by the evidence. There are three main problems. First, children make errors that the theory cannot explain. In particular, children make subject-verb agreement errors in which they use the wrong verb inflection given the subject. For example, they may say *the dogs is barking* instead of *the dogs are barking*. According to the ATOM, these errors should not occur because, when tense and agreement are applied, they should be applied correctly, according to the principles laid down in UG. However, we know that such errors do occur: Hoekstra and Hyams (1998) cite studies in four different languages that report agreement errors in the speech of young children.

In fact, Wexler acknowledges that agreement errors occur but he argues that they are "vanishingly rare" and only occur if the child does not yet know which morpheme to use (Wexler, 1998, p. 42). For example, a child who has not yet learnt the word *are* might produce *the dogs is barking* for a while. However, Rubino and Pine have shown that such errors can be quite frequent even after the child has learnt the necessary markers (Rubino & Pine, 1998). They tape-recorded, transcribed and then analysed the speech of one three-year-old child learning Brazilian Portuguese. Although overall rates of agreement error were very low (3 per cent), error rates with plural verb inflections were very high; over 28 per cent of plural verbs had the wrong inflection on them. In other words, when the child tried to use verbs with plural grammatical subjects (e.g. *they*, *we*), he put the wrong inflection on the verb nearly one-third of the time. Importantly, the child still made errors after he had started to use the plural verb inflection correctly so we cannot say that these errors occurred simply because he did not know the correct inflection to use. It is difficult for the ATOM to account for these results.

Second, infinitive errors pattern in a way not predicted by the theory. According to the ATOM, whether a verb is produced correctly (*he likes*) or as an error (*he like*) should not differ according to the identity of the verb. However, there is quite a lot of evidence that certain verbs are much more likely to occur as errors than others. For example, in Russian, Dutch and French, researchers have pointed out that errors are much more likely to occur with eventive verbs than stative verbs (Ferdinand, 1996; Gvozdev, 1949; Hoekstra & Hyams, 1998; van Gelderen & Van der Meulen, 1998; Wijnen, 1996). Eventive verbs are verbs like *hit*, *kiss*, *eat* that refer to particular events that have a clear start and end point. These are frequently produced as infinitive errors by Russian, Dutch and French children. Stative verbs refer to situations or states of affairs without clear start and end points; verbs like *know* and *love*. Russian, Dutch and French children rarely produce these as infinitive errors. This distinction is not predicted by the ATOM, which predicts that children should simply oscillate between correctly inflected forms and infinitive errors randomly.

Similarly, Wilson and Pine have reported that English children are much more likely to produce a correctly inflected verb when the sentence subject is a pronoun than when it is a noun (Pine, Conti-Ramsden, Joseph, Lieven & Serratrice, 2008; Wilson, 2003). For example, in Pine's study, the children were more likely to produce *he eats* correctly than they were to produce *the dog eats* correctly. There is also evidence that children are more likely to produce a correctly inflected verb when the subject is *it* than when it is *I* (Pine et al., 2008; Theakston, Lieven, Pine & Rowland, 2005). These findings are difficult for the ATOM to explain.

Third, there are differences across languages that the ATOM struggles to explain. The ATOM very simply predicts a clear categorical dividing line between languages in which children make optional infinitive errors and those in which children do not. However, there is, in fact, a gradient of error rates across languages. English and Swedish attract a lot of errors, Dutch, French and German attract a moderate amount, and Spanish and Italian attract very few (Phillips, 1995). There is even a gradient of errors among languages in which errors should occur. English, Dutch and French children are predicted to produce errors at approximately equal rates during the optional infinitive stage but, in fact, English children make a lot more errors than Dutch and French children (Phillips, 1995). It is difficult for the ATOM to explain why this should be the case.

5.5 NATIVIST ACCOUNTS II: PROBABILISTIC PARAMETER SETTING

As we saw in the last chapter, the *principles and parameters framework* provides the basis of many nativist theories of grammar acquisition. To recap, the idea is that the child's innate knowledge of grammar (Universal Grammar) consists of both principles and parameters. The *principles* are a set of universal principles that are said to apply across all languages. The *parameters* are a set of parameters that the child sets to a certain value after gaining experience with her own language. Parameters explain how children can learn the grammar of any language despite the fact that these grammars can differ dramatically.

Since languages differ in how they use inflection, it seems plausible to propose some *inflection parameters* that children set after experience with their language. For example, since Mandarin Chinese does not use inflection to mark tense but English does, we could posit a tense parameter that English children set to ON and Chinese children set to OFF after they have gathered enough experience of their language. It is possible then, that we can explain why English children make errors with inflection in this way; they start with the parameter set to OFF and make errors until they have learnt enough about their language to set it to ON. Unfortunately, this simple explanation does not work because inflection errors co-occur with correctly inflected forms. These correct forms should not occur if the English children's tense parameter is set to OFF.

As a solution to this problem, Yang has proposed a parameter-setting theory that can explain why correct forms and errors co-occur. This is the *variational learning model* (VLM; Legate & Yang, 2007; Yang, 2002). According to this theory, children start out with the principles specified in UG and with parameters that have to be set to ON or OFF depending on the characteristics of the language. So far, the theory is similar to other parameter setting theories (e.g. Hyams, 1986). However, Yang also suggests that each parameter is associated with a probability, which "changes adaptively in response to the linguistic data in the environment" (Legate & Yang, 2007, p. 319). When the child hears a sentence, she selects a particular grammar (e.g. tense parameter = ON) and tries to analyse the sentence with this grammar. If the analysis is successful, the grammar will be rewarded. This means that this grammar is more likely to be selected to analyse sentences next time. If the grammar fails to analyse the sentence, the grammar will be "punished" (Yang, 2002, p. 27). This means it is less likely to be selected next time.

Because the right grammar will almost always result in a successful analysis, it will rarely be punished. All the other grammars will be punished quite often though, which means that they will increasingly become less likely to be selected. Thus, with time, the child selects the right grammar more and more often. Eventually, all the incorrect grammars will be "driven to extinction by the target grammar" (Legate & Yang, 2007, p. 319). In this way, the child eventually ends up with the correct grammar for her language.

5.5.1   Evidence for and against the VLM

The variational learning model can explain why correctly inflected forms and errors co-occur in children's speech. They co-occur because children are yo-yoing between a grammar that requires tense marking (a +*Tense* grammar) and one that does not (a -*Tense* grammar). The rate of errors decreases over time, because each time the child hears an utterance with a Tense marker (e.g. *he kicked*), the +*Tense* grammar is rewarded and the -*Tense* grammar is punished. Eventually, the -*Tense* grammar will be driven to extinction. However, while it is still a possibility, children will make errors.

The variational learning model also explains why the period of error can last for such a long time. Sometimes, adults speaking a language with a +*Tense* grammar will produce ambiguous sentences which seem to have no tense markings and which are thus mis-analysed by the child. For example, when we produce a sentence such as *I like broccoli*, the use of *like* is correctly tensed. However, it actually sounds identical to the untensed *like* in the sentence *I want to like broccoli but I can't*. Because of this, the sentence *I like broccoli* is not unambiguously tensed and does not reward the child's +*Tense* grammar. Sentences like this delay the process of choosing the +*Tense* grammar and thus delay the acquisition process.

This account can also explain why children who are learning different languages make errors at different rates. This occurs because the amount of evidence for the +*Tense* grammar differs across languages. English children make a lot of errors for a long period of time because English contains lots of ambiguous sentences like *I like broccoli*. This delays the setting of the +*Tense* grammar. Spanish children, however, converge on the +*Tense* grammar early and make very few errors because most Spanish utterances are unambiguously marked for tense and agreement (e.g. *juego* 'I play', *juegas* 'you play', *jugamos* 'we play' all sound different to the infinitival form *jugar*). French children make a moderate number of errors for a moderately long period of time because French has an intermediate number of ambiguous sentences.

Thus French children converge on the *+Tense* grammar more quickly than English children but less quickly than Spanish children.

In fact, the variational learning model might even be able to explain individual differences between children learning the same language. Hadley and colleagues have reported that it is possible to predict the rate at which different English-learning children produce bare stem errors by the input informativeness of their own mother's speech (Hadley, Rispoli, Fitzgerald & Bahnsen, 2011). In other words, if a particular child's mother produced a lot of ambiguous utterances like *I like broccoli*, that child tended to produce a lot of errors.

In sum, the strengths of the variational learning model are that it can explain why errors occur, why errors co-occur with correctly inflected verbs, and why error rates differ across languages and across children. However, once again, everything is not plain sailing. A major problem with the model comes from the fact that it cannot explain why different verbs attract different rates of error. For example, above we discovered that Russian, Dutch and French eventive verbs like *hit* and *kiss* attract more errors than stative verbs like *know* and *love*. Like the ATOM, the variational learning model cannot explain why this might be, because, like the ATOM, the model predicts that children should simply oscillate between correct forms and errors randomly.

A similar problem was identified by Freudenthal and colleagues (Freudenthal et al., 2010). These researchers directly compared the variational learning model with a constructivist theory, which they implemented in a computer model called MOSAIC (see section 5.6.1 below). MOSAIC had no built-in knowledge of syntax or morphology. Instead, it rote-learnt strings of words from its input and generalised across these memorised strings of words on the basis of what we call distributional commonalities. For example, the model might link the word *like* with the word *love* because the two words tend to occur in the same position in sentences (*I like cake, I love cake, we like biscuits, we love biscuits*). MOSAIC made errors because it started to learn from the beginning and end of a sentence. So, on hearing *Cecily wants to eat cake*, MOSAIC might just learn *Cecily* and *eat cake*, which it then reproduced as *Cecily eat cake* (a bare stem error). As learning progressed, the errors slowly ceased as MOSAIC learnt to produce longer and longer sentences.

Freudenthal and colleagues directly compared how well the variational learning model and MOSAIC explained the rate of error across five different languages: English, Dutch, German, French and Spanish. They analysed the spontaneous speech produced by 14 mothers and their children across the five languages. They first calculated whether the variational model accurately predicted the children's error rates based on the mothers' input informativeness. They then ran the mother's speech through MOSAIC and analysed the errors that MOSAIC produced, comparing them to the errors produced by the children. They reported that the VLM and MOSAIC predicted the children's error rates equally well for all analyses except one; MOSAIC managed to predict which verbs would attract error whereas the VLM did not. For example, children were more likely to produce errors with *eat* than with *know*. The variational learning model could not explain this finding because the *+Tense* and *-Tense* grammars are supposed to apply equally across all verbs. Thus, a child learning in the way suggested by the variational model would not be expected to produce more errors with some verbs than others. The authors concluded that the variational learning model could not explain the pattern of errors that children make when learning to use inflections (the reason why MOSAIC explains this pattern of results is discussed below).

5.6 CONSTRUCTIVIST THEORIES

In chapter 4, we introduced constructivist theories of syntax acquisition. Constructivist ideas about inflection learning are based on similar processes (Clark, 2003; Freudenthal, Pine, Aguado-Orea, & Gobet, 2007; Pine et al., 2008; Theakston et al., 2005). Constructivists claim that children do not come equipped with innate knowledge of grammar – neither principles nor parameters. The learning mechanism, instead, rote-learns strings of words from the input (in the same way that it rote-learns words) and generalises across these memorised strings of words on the basis of commonalities in both form and meaning. Thus, children's early knowledge of grammar, both syntax and morphology, is based around strings of lexical items, and gradually develops into more abstract (adultlike) knowledge via a process of abstraction.

In terms of inflection learning, constructivist theories propose that children will begin with unanalysed forms. At the beginning of the process of acquisition, children are unaware that inflected words (e.g. *wanted*) should be analysed as a stem word (*want*) plus an inflectional ending (*-ed*). However, because most inflected words tend to occur over and over again in the same sentence position and in the same contexts (e.g. when the speaker is talking about a past event), children can generalise across these words to extract the common factor: the inflectional ending (*-ed*). For example, let us assume that a child has learnt *he wanted*, *he walked* and *he liked*. By generalising across these three forms, the child's learning mechanism can extract a *he VERB-ed* pattern, which the child can then apply with new verbs, even novel ones (*he pilked*). We call these *slot and frame patterns*, because they contain slots in which the word can vary (*walk, pilk*) and static frames that cannot (*he* and *-ed*). The child then generalises across slot and frame patterns (e.g. *he VERB-ed, she VERB-ed, Mummy VERB-ed*) to form new patterns, eventually discovering that the inflectional ending can be applied productively to a whole number of verbs (see figure 5.1).

Figure 5.1
Schematic representation of constructivist-style learning.

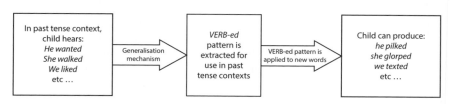

5.6.1 Evidence for and against constructivism

The main advantage of this theory is that it predicts that children will be better at applying inflection to some verbs than to others. Thus, the theory not only explains, but explicitly predicts, the patterning of errors that proves so problematic for the VLM (see the previous section). Within the theory, bare stem errors such as *Cecily eat cake* are explained in terms of children learning, piecemeal, parts of so-called compound finite sentences. These are sentences with two verbs, one of which occurs in inflected form and one of which occurs in uninflected form (e.g. *Cecily wants to eat cake*; see Ingram & Thompson, 1996; Theakston, Lieven & Tomasello, 2003). Verbs that occur frequently in uninflected form in compound finite sentences in the children's input are predicted to occur as bare stem errors (e.g. *eat* in *Cecily wants to eat cake*). However, verbs that children hear more often in their finite form (e.g. the verb *wants* in *Cecily wants to eat cake*) are predicted to be produced in inflected form.

This idea was tested in the study by Freudenthal and colleagues that we discussed above (Freudenthal et al., 2010). They analysed the spontaneous speech produced by 14 young children and their mothers across five languages: English, Dutch, German, French and Spanish. They analysed which verbs the children produced in uninflected form and how often their mothers produced these verbs in compound finite sentences. They reported that there was a significant correlation between the children's and mothers' uses. What this means is that the verbs that occurred frequently in compound finite sentences in the children's input (e.g. *he will eat it*) were much more likely to occur as infinitives (e.g. **he eat them up hisself*; an error produced by Lara, 2;8) in the children's own speech. The verbs that the children heard more often in their finite form (e.g. *he wants some cake*) were more likely to be produced correctly by the child (e.g. *she wants to hold my hand*; Lara, 2;11). They concluded that the results "provide strong support for the idea that OI [optional infinitive] errors are learned from compound finite constructions in the input" (Freudenthal et al., 2010, p. 663). What is particularly convincing about this study is that the results explain acquisition across five different languages. The different rate of compound finites in the five languages predicted the different rates of error across the languages. Thus, the theory also explains why we find optional infinitive errors occurring at different rates across many different languages.

A second point in favour of constructivist theory is that it can explain why children make subject-verb agreement errors such as *does cats scratch?* and why these errors are more common with some auxiliaries and with some inflectional endings than others. According to constructivist theory, auxiliaries and inflections that occur frequently will be learnt much earlier than those that have occurred rarely. As a result, high frequency auxiliaries and inflectional endings will attract fewer errors than low frequency ones. This seems to be the case. For example, Rubino and Pine reported that the Brazilian child they studied was very good at applying inflectional endings that occurred frequently (e.g. the third person singular ending that is required when the verb occurs with *he, she* or *it*; see Rubino & Pine, 1998). However, he made errors with less frequent inflectional endings (e.g. the third person plural ending required for verbs that occur with *they*). In fact, he would often use his well-learnt third person singular ending in place of the correct plural form, producing a subject-verb agreement error. This supports both the prediction that error rates are low with inflections that occur frequently and the prediction that error rates are high with low frequency endings because the child takes longer to amass evidence about how to use them.

Finally, the theory predicts that the acquisition of the inflectional system will be gradual, with the earliest uses restricted to rote-learnt high frequency forms. This prediction is also supported by some studies. Gathercole and colleagues studied the inflections used by one Spanish child and reported that initially the child produced only one inflectional form per verb (Gathercole, Sebastián & Soto, 1999). For example, some verbs were produced only in the imperative tense, which is used for commands (e.g. *mira* 'look'), while other verbs were produced only in the preterite, used to denote past completed events (e.g. *acabó* 'finished'). There was no evidence that the child could use other inflections with these verbs. The child then gradually extended the use of inflections across different verbs as she accumulated more knowledge. In fact, a number of researchers have reported a similar pattern of gradual development in a number of languages (e.g. for Hebrew, see Berman, 1985, and for Italian, see Pizzuto & Caselli, 1992).

In sum, the constructivist theory is good at explaining why some verbs occur with inflections more often than others, which is precisely the pattern of errors that cause such problems for nativist theories. It is also good at explaining why some inflections attract more errors than others and why children make errors for such a long time in some languages. However, the constructivist theory has its own problems.

First, English children seem to make a lot more bare stem errors than we might expect, given their input. This was demonstrated in the study by Freudenthal and colleagues that was described above (Freudenthal et al., 2010). To recap, these researchers built a constructivist computer model called MOSAIC that rote-learnt strings of words from its input and generalised across these memorised strings of words on the basis of distributional commonalities. Like children, MOSAIC made bare stem or infinitive errors when given Dutch, German and English input but not when given Spanish input. Thus, it was good at modelling the pattern of errors across languages. However, when it learnt Dutch it made more errors than when it learnt English. This is different from the pattern we find in children; Dutch children make fewer errors than English children. So MOSAIC, and the constructivist theory as a whole, cannot explain why English children make so many more errors than Dutch children (though see Räsänen, Ambridge & Pine, in press, for a possible explanation).

A second problem comes when we take another look at some of the evidence for constructivism. For example, constructivists have reported that sentences with pronouns (e.g. *he's going*) are protected from error because the child produces them using high frequency slot and frame patterns learnt from the input (e.g. *he's VERB-ing*, which is a very frequent pattern in children's input; Pine et al., 2008; Theakston et al., 2005). Sentences with lexical subjects (e.g. *the dog is going*) attract higher rates of error because the child has not yet learnt a pattern on which to base his sentence. At least three studies support this prediction (Pine et al., 2008; Theakston et al., 2005;

Wilson, 2003). However, Guo and colleagues have provided conflicting evidence (Guo, Owen & Tomblin, 2010). They developed a design in which they studied children in a narrow age range (2;8 to 3;4) using an elicitation task, using targeted questions to encourage children to produce auxiliary *is* with different types of subject. They then analysed how often the children produced *is* correctly in their responses. Although some of the less advanced children produced auxiliary *is* less accurately with noun subjects (e.g. *the dog is going*) than pronominal subjects (*he is going*), across most of the children, there was no difference between pronoun subjects, high frequency lexical subjects and low frequency lexical subjects. In other words, overall, the children produced auxiliary *is* correctly equally often with all three different types of subject. The authors concluded that "Counter to some assertions in the literature (e.g., Tomasello, 2000), average 3-year-olds in the study seem to have acquired quite abstract grammatical representation" (Guo et al., 2010, p. 1733). In summary, although constructivist models explain lexical variation and some of the cross-linguistic data very well, they do not explain why English children make so many bare stem errors or why some of the lexical effects disappear so quickly once the children reach three years of age.

5.7 HOW DO WE STORE AND PRODUCE INFLECTIONS?

So far we have discussed how children learn inflection, focussing on why children make errors. However, there is one very important error that we have ignored – the over-regularisation error. We have ignored it because the issues it raises are different from those discussed above. In particular, the literature here concentrates not on how children learn inflections, but on explaining how children and adults store inflections in memory and how they then produce them. Below we describe the error that started off the whole debate. We then move on to two accounts of why children make this error and some of the studies that provide evidence for and against these accounts.

5.7.1 The over-regularisation error

The *over-regularisation* (or over-generalisation) error is probably the most intensively studied error in the literature. It has stimulated hundreds, if not thousands, of articles and books. It occurs when children apply a *regular inflection* to a verb or noun that should actually occur in an *irregular form*.

What do we mean by this? Many inflectional paradigms have exceptions; verbs or nouns that do not take the usual, regular inflectional ending. The English plural is a classic example. The regular rule here is *add -s*; so *rat* becomes *rats* and *cat* becomes *cats*. However, this regular rule does not apply to all nouns. Thus, *mouse* becomes *mice*, not **mouses*, and *woman* becomes *women*, not **womans*. We find the same thing with the English past tense. The regular rule is *add -ed,* so *jump* becomes *jumped* and *skip* becomes *skipped*. However, again there are some irregular endings. *Run* becomes *ran*, not **runned*, and *fly* becomes *flew*, not **flied*.

The verbs in a language that do not take regular ending are called irregular verbs. When learning inflections, children make errors in which they seem to over-use the regular form inflection instead of producing the correct irregular verb. For example, at the age of 22 months Lara came out with *Lara <u>doed</u> it instead of Lara did it. When she was nearly three years old, instead of saying I don't like men she said *I don't like mans. In other words, she produced over-regularisation errors.

These errors do not appear right at the start of the learning process but follow a stage at which children seem to use inflections correctly. Then they finally disappear. This developmental pattern was neatly described by Cazden, who analysed the speech of the most famous children in the child language literature: Adam, Eve and Sarah (Cazden, 1968). Adam, Eve and Sarah were recorded in conversation with their caregivers every week or so, then their speech was transcribed and analysed (see Brown, 1973, for a full description of the corpus of data from these children). Cazden analysed the words and sentences the children produced and noted four stages in the development of the plural inflection. In stage A the inflection was absent. For example, in response to *what are those?*, the children might say *shoe* instead of *shoes*. The next stage – stage B – was "defined by occasional production with no errors or overgeneralisations" (Cazden, 1968, p. 436). In other words, the children started to produce both regular and irregular plurals correctly although they did not produce very many of either. Then, in stage C, the children started to produce a lot more plurals, but also made over-regularisation errors where they applied the plural *add -s* rule incorrectly. Cazden gives examples such as *two <u>mans</u>* and – my favourite – *you pull my <u>pantses</u> down* (Cazden, 1968, p. 445). Finally, in stage D, children started to use the plural ending correctly nearly all the time. This type of developmental pattern – correct use (stage B) followed by errors (stage C) followed by correct use again (stage D) – is called *U-shaped learning* because if you plotted it on a graph with time on the X axis and proportion of correctly inflected words on the Y axis, the resulting curve would be U-shaped (see figure 5.2).

Figure 5.2
A hypothetical U-shaped learning curve. The stages A to D correspond to the stages of plural inflection development described by Cazden (1968).

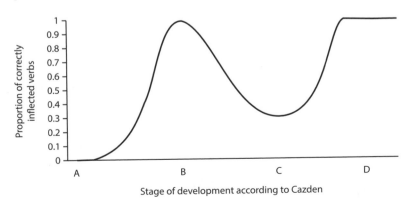

There are two final things we need to know about these errors. First, they do not always occur at the same age in different children. In Cazden's study, Eve was only 27 months old when she reached stage D, during which she produced correct plurals 98 per cent of the time. At the same age, Adam and Sarah were still at an earlier stage of development, producing correct plurals only 36 per cent and 13 per cent of the time respectively. Second, different verbs tend to have their own individual patterns of development, with some verbs attracting over-generalisation errors early on in development, others attracting such errors later in development and some never attracting any at all (Maratsos, 2000). However, importantly, all English children seem to produce some over-regularisation errors. They produce words like *mans instead of *men* and *waked up* instead of *woke up*. It looks as if they have learnt the regular rules *add -s* and *add -ed* but are over-using them.

Given that children seem to over-use rules like *add -s* and *add -ed*, many researchers have concluded that this is how we form all regular plurals and past tense forms. In other words, the brain stores these rules and then applies them as needed to nouns and verbs. For example, if I wanted to tell my friend that my legs were hurting because I jogged five miles yesterday, I would retrieve the verb *jog* from memory and apply the *add -ed* rule to produce the past tense verb *jogged* (*Suzanne, yesterday I jogged five miles and now my legs are killing me*). This seems, on the surface, like a plausible explanation of how we form the plural and the past tense. However, there are other researchers who disagree. These researchers argue that we do not use rules like *add -ed* but form past tenses by analogy to stored examples. As a result, the question that exercises the field is the following:

Key question: are regular inflectional forms produced using a rule or by analogy to stored examples?

5.7.2 The dual route model

According to the *dual route model*, there are two ways to produce the plural and past tense in English (Marcus et al., 1992). The first route involves simply retrieving a word from memory. The second route involves generating and applying a grammatical rule. Because both words and rules are used, the theory is sometimes called the *words and rules theory*.

Route one is for the production of irregular forms like *men* and *ran*. Irregular verb forms are learnt one by one and are stored in the memory as *lexical entries*. Each lexical entry stores essential facts about the word, including meaning, pronunciation and usage. When the speaker wants to produce a past tense form, she simply retrieves the correct past tense verb from memory. For example, if I wanted to tell my friend that I ran five miles yesterday, I would simply retrieve the lexical entry for the irregular verb *ran* from memory. Alternatively, if I did not have the correct past tense stored, I might be able to generate it by analogy to other similar-sounding past tense forms (these were christened phonological 'friends' by Marchman, 1997). However, I could only do this if these 'friends' were stored in my memory. So for example, the past tense of *throw* (*threw*) could either be retrieved directly from memory or produced by analogy to similar-sounding phonological 'friends' (*blow/blew* and *know/knew*), as long as these 'friends' had already been learnt.

Route two is for the production of regular past tense forms like *jogged*. Regular past tense forms are not stored in memory. Instead they are constructed, as needed, by applying a morphological rule. So, when a speaker wants to produce a past tense form, she retrieves the verb stem from memory and applies the rule *add -ed*. For example, if I wanted to tell my friend that I jogged five miles yesterday, I would retrieve the verb stem *jog* from memory, apply the rule *add -ed* and concatenate the stem and *-ed* marker to produce a single word *jogged*. Saxton characterises this process very well. He writes that the process is "a mental production line that puts words together at the time of speaking" (Saxton, 2010, p. 166).

Figure 5.3
Schematic representation of the dual route model.

a. Process of retrieval when the correct irregular form is stored in memory

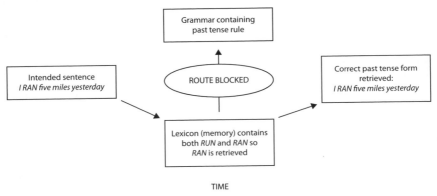

b. Process of retrieval when the correct irregular form has not yet been learnt

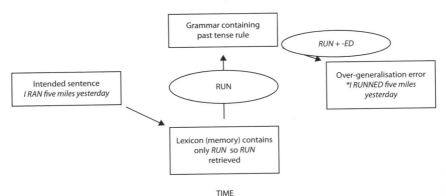

Why, then, do children make over-regularisation errors? According to the dual route model, errors occur for two reasons (see figure 5.3). First, although the rules are learnt quickly, the irregular verbs have to be learnt one by one, which takes time. So, until children have learnt the correct irregular form (e.g. *ran*) or similar sounding 'friends', they will default to the grammatical rule, producing over-regularisation errors (e.g. **runned*). Errors will gradually cease as children learn the correct irregular forms, which block the production of the over-regularisation error. Second, errors can occur if the child has already learnt the correct irregular but fails to retrieve it from memory. This will especially affect low frequency verbs that have not been heard often, because these will not have laid down strong memory traces. Because the irregular verb form is not retrieved, the rule mechanism is not blocked and the child will produce an over-regularisation error.

5.7.2.1 *Evidence for and against the dual route model*

A study by Marcus and colleagues provided supporting evidence for the dual route model (Marcus et al., 1992). They analysed the past tense verbs produced by 88 children, though they focussed most of their analyses on the speech of a smaller number of children. The data were gathered from transcripts of the children recorded in conversation with their caregivers. The children's age range was very wide; the youngest was 1;3 at the start of testing and the oldest was 6;6 at the end. The data showed that children started to produce over-regularisation errors at about the same time as they consistently started to apply the regular past tense ending. The fact that both appear in children's speech at the same time supports the dual route prediction that both correct regulars and over-regularisation errors are produced as soon as the child has learnt the regular past tense rule.

Marcus and colleagues also noted that over-regularisation errors occurred most often with low frequency irregular verbs – verbs for which the correct form is learnt late or is harder to retrieve from memory. This is also just as predicted (Bybee & Slobin, 1982, reported a similar effect). They also noted that over-regularisation errors occurred less often with verbs that had a lot of similar-sounding 'friends', which supported their prediction that the correct irregular past tense form could be produced by analogy if it had not been rote-learnt. Finally they reported that the median rate of over-regularisation error was very low; just 2.5 per cent across 25 children. This is in accordance with the dual route account, which suggests that error rates should be low because the blocking mechanism should be successful most of the time.

The evidence supporting the dual route account does not just come from studies of English. Marcus, Clahsen and colleagues have reported that German speakers also use two routes when producing plural nouns (Clahsen, Rothweiler, Woest & Marcus, 1992; Marcus et al., 1995). There are a number of ways to produce a plural in German; one can add *-en*, *-er*, *-s*, *-e* or add no ending at all. One might assume that this would make it more difficult for children to identify a regular ending, and thus harder to learn a plural rule. However, this seems not to be the case. Clahsen and colleagues (1992) analysed the errors produced by 19 dysphasic children and one clinically normal child learning German (dysphasic children have a disorder affecting their speech and language). They reported that the children made an unexpectedly large number of over-regularisation errors that used the plural ending *-s,* just as we would predict if they had learnt an *add -s* rule. Interestingly, *-s* is not the most frequent ending in the language (*-n* is just as frequent, if not more frequent) Clahsen and colleagues called this a *minority default* behaviour because the children seemed to be defaulting to the *-s* ending, despite the fact that it was not the most frequent (majority) ending.

The first problem for the dual route account comes when we start to look more closely at the development of inflection in other languages. The dual route model proposes that children learning all languages should be programmed to look for one default inflection. Thus, the account predicts that when over-regularisation errors occur, children should consistently use only one of the inflectional endings they hear. However, children often use more than one ending in their over-regularisation errors. In fact, even the German children studied by Clahsen and colleagues, and cited as evidence for the dual route model above, made errors in which they over-generalised the ending *-en* as often as they over-generalised the default ending *-s.* Similar findings have been found for other languages. For example, Dąbrowska tested the dual route explanation against the speech of young Polish children learning the inflections for the genitive singular case (Dąbrowska, 2001, 2004). Genitive case markers are added to the end of nouns in Polish to mark a possessor (e.g. in the sentence *John's cake, John* would take the genitive ending). Dąbrowska reported that the children in her study produced over-regularisation errors using all three genitive singular inflections (*-a, -u* and *-y*), although none was over-regularised frequently. She concluded that there was no evidence that children had identified one single inflection as the default regular ending. Keuleers and colleagues have made a similar argument with respect to the Dutch plural, showing that the problem is not restricted to Polish (Keuleers et al., 2007).

A second problem comes when we re-evaluate the claim that over-regularisation errors are very rare. Marcus and colleagues initially reported that error rates were low in children's speech (3 per cent) but this figure was derived by averaging across a number of different verbs. When we look at individual verbs, error rates can be much higher. For example, Maratsos reported that some of the verbs produced by the children he studied attracted very high rates of error; over 50 per cent (Maratsos, 2000). This means that the children actually produced an error more often than the correct form with some verbs. Now, this is not a devastating problem for the dual route model, which concedes that some past tense verb forms may be difficult to retrieve from memory, and may attract high rates of error. However, it is difficult to understand why the memory retrieval mechanism fails so often. For example Maratsos estimated that some verbs would have been produced and heard correctly hundreds of times by the children, yet they still attracted high rates of error. Maratsos argued that we would expect this number of instances to be large enough for the child to learn and retrieve the past tense form successfully.

The final problem comes when we turn to the issue of phonological 'friends'. The dual route model predicts that a child can sometimes generate irregular past tense verb forms by analogy to similar-sounding past tense forms stored in memory (phonologically similar 'friends'). So *threw* might be produced by analogy to *blew* and *knew*. However, similarity should not affect the production of regular past tense verbs, which are always generated by the application of the past tense rule. Albright and Hayes, however, have shown that, contrary to this prediction, phonological similarity does affect the production of regular past tense verbs (Albright & Hayes, 2003).

To test this, Albright and Hayes made up four sets of novel verbs, based on what they called *islands of reliability*: groups of novel (made up) verbs whose past tense forms can be reliably predicted by the sound of the verb itself. The first set of novel verbs were created to sound similar to existing *irregular islands of reliability*. For example, they created *gleed* because it sounds similar to the group of verbs *feed*, *speed* and *bleed* which all undergo the same vowel change in the past tense (*fed/sped/bled*). Another set of novel verbs was created to sound similar to existing *regular islands of reliability*. For example, they created *bredge* because it sounds similar to the group of regular verbs that includes *pledge*, *wedge*, *allege* and *dredge* (*pledged/wedged/alleged/dredged*). The third set of verbs was similar to both regular and irregular islands, and the fourth was similar to neither regular nor irregular islands.

The researchers then asked adult English speakers to produce past tense forms for each novel verb and to rate how well formed both irregular and regular past tense forms were. They found that the islands of reliability influenced which past tense forms the participants produced themselves and how they rated different past tense forms of the verbs provided by the researchers. Importantly, these findings applied to both irregular and regular past tense endings. The participants were more likely to produce regular endings for verbs that fitted into a regular island of reliability and were more likely to produce irregular endings for verbs that fitted into an irregular island of reliability. The dual route model can explain why this effect occurred for irregulars. However, it cannot explain why it occurred for regulars because the past tense rule should not be sensitive to phonological similarity. In other words, contrary to the prediction, phonological similarity to existing real regular verbs affected whether participants were willing to produce and accept a regular past tense form for a novel verb.

It is important to note that dual route theorists have made modifications to incorporate these problems. For example, some theorists have suggested that high frequency regular verbs may be stored in memory (see for example, Alegre & Gordon, 1999; Hartshorne & Ullman, 2006). However, the question then arises: if all the hard work is being done by the memory-based route, what is the role of the rule-based route? Ramscar (2002) suggests that we should apply Occam's razor here, which is the scientific principle that the simplest explanation that fits the data should be preferred. In other words, if all the data can be explained by a single route, why do we need to posit a second route? Ambridge and Lieven make a similar point: "on the grounds of parsimony, it would seem wise to avoid positing an additional default rule, unless there is compelling evidence that it is required" (Ambridge & Lieven, 2011, p. 187). They conclude that the challenge for dual route theorists in future is to provide this compelling evidence.

5.7.3 Single route accounts: analogy not rules

Single route accounts created a bit of a stir when they first appeared. For the first time in decades, the dominant view of language as a rule-based system had a challenger. In fact, MacWhinney and Leinbach describe the accounts as "Streaming forth from their banishment in the Skinnerian dungeon … a major challenge to the *ancien régime* – a definitive revolution in the way in which we understand the human mind" (MacWhinney & Leinbach, 1991, p. 122).[4]

Many different single route theories have streamed forth but all share the basic assumption that we use only one route to produce inflections (no surprises there, given that they are called single route accounts; see Bybee, 1995; Rumelhart & McClelland, 1996). This route is identical to route one in the dual route model; it stores past tense forms as *lexical entries* in memory. The correct past tense form is retrieved directly from memory if possible. If not, the correct form can be created by analogy to other stored verbs that sound similar (i.e. phonological 'friends'). So for example, the past tense of *throw* (*threw*) can either be retrieved directly from memory or can be produced by analogy with other verbs that sound the same (*blow/blew* and *know/knew*). However, the important difference between the single route and the dual route account is that the single route account suggests that <u>all</u> past tense verbs are formed in this way – regular verbs like *kicked* as well as irregular verbs like *threw*. There is no need for a second, rule-based, route.

Figure 5.4
The basic structure of the single route model. Reprinted from Rumelhart and McClelland (1986, p. 222, Figure 1).

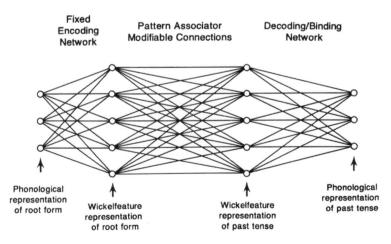

4   Skinner was a behaviourist psychologist whose non-rule-based views about how language was acquired were heavily criticised by Chomksy (1959). MacWhinney and Leinbach (1991) were referring to the fact that Chomskian-type rule-based theories dominated research in language acquisition for decades after the publication of Chomsky's critique, meaning that any accounts that, like Skinner's, were not based on rules were banished to a metaphorical dungeon.

The first demonstration of a single route model came not from the speech of children, but from a computer program, a connectionist network built by Rumelhart and McClelland (1986). Connectionist networks are computer simulations that learn to produce certain behaviours. They consist of networks of neuron-like units called input, output and (in more recent networks) hidden units, all connected together. They learn by adjusting the connections between these units if the answer provided by the model (the output) is different from the correct answer (input). In other words, the connections between the units in the model (crudely, how it is wired up) change in response to the input until the model has learnt to output a new behaviour (see figure 5.4).

Rumelhart and McClelland's connectionist network learnt to produce past tense forms in this way, without access to grammatical rules. It had 406 input and 406 output units, each associated with a particular sound (these units were coded as *wickelfeatures*). Verb stems were fed into the model, which switched on the input units associated with the sounds in that verb stem (e.g. *run*). Activation then travelled through the network, activating output units, which outputted a response. If the model outputted the correct form it was given a 'correct' signal by a 'teacher' signal, which reinforced the strength of the connections that led to this correct output. This made those connections more likely to be activated next time the model heard the same verb. If the model was given an 'incorrect' signal, it reduced the strength of the relevant connections, making subsequent activation less likely. The model continued to change the strengths of all the connections in response to the input, until it always received a correct signal. At this point we say that the model had learnt to produce the past tense.

It is important to remember that the model was simply learning to associate the sounds of the verb stem with the sounds of its past tense form. So the model was generating phonologically based links (sound-based links) between words. There was no second, rule-based route. Even so, the model learnt to produce regular, as well as irregular, past tense forms. It could even generate correct past tenses of verbs that it had never seen before. Perhaps more importantly, it went through a period of producing over-regularisation errors, demonstrating U-shaped learning, just like children. These errors occurred because, as the model learnt more and more regular verbs, it learnt to associate more and more verb stem sounds with the past tense sound -*ed*. These new links sometimes overwhelmed existing links to the verb's correct irregular past tense form, resulting in an over-regularisation error. The errors then gradually ceased as the model received more incorrect signals from the teacher signal in response to the error and adapted accordingly. What this means is that the very errors that seemed to provide evidence for a rule could, in fact, be generated simply by analogies based on sound patterns. This seemed to be strong support for the single route account. In fact, the excitement generated by the success of the model was perhaps a little over the top. One reviewer apparently described the implications of the model as "awesome" (see Sampson, 1987).

5.7.3.1 *Evidence for and against single route accounts*

In effect, single route accounts can explain how children learn to produce regulars and irregulars and why they produce over-regularisation errors. They also have a ready explanation for data that the dual route account cannot explain, especially data showing that the same factors influence irregular and regular inflections. For example, we discovered above that the similarity of a verb to phonological 'friends' influences how people inflect it for tense. This applies to both regular and irregular verbs (Albright & Hayes, 2003). This is contrary to the prediction of the dual route account, but is directly predicted by the single route model, which assumes regular and irregular past tense forms are produced in the same way.

Single route accounts are also compatible with studies that show a close relationship between a child's verb vocabulary and her success at applying both regular and irregular inflections. For example, Marchman and Bates (1994) have suggested that children start to produce over-regularisation errors soon after the number of verbs that they have learnt reaches a *critical mass*. This is compatible with the idea that as the child learns more and more regular verbs, she associates more and more verb stem sounds with the past tense sound *-ed* (see Marchman & Bates, 1994 for evidence from English and Kidd & Kirjavainen, 2011, for evidence from Finnish).

However, a whole raft of criticisms has been levelled at single route accounts, especially Rumelhart and McClelland's model. In fact, Pinker and Prince find enough criticisms of the model to fill 120 pages (Pinker & Prince, 1988). We focus here on three that have attracted a lot of attention. The first of Pinker and Prince's criticisms was that the modellers 'cheated'. Pinker and Prince argued that the model only produced over-regularisation errors because the modellers gave it different input at different stages of development. During the first phase of learning the model heard mostly irregular verbs. Then, during the second phase of learning, it was swamped by regulars (80 per cent of the verbs it was given were regulars). It was at this point that the model started to produce over-regularisation errors. So the U-shaped learning – correct use followed by errors followed by correct use again – was actually a direct consequence of the modellers changing the input to the model. Rumelhart and McClelland argued that this training regime was designed to reflect the fact that irregulars are highly frequent in the input and, thus, will be learnt first. However, Pinker and Prince suggested that the model would not have produced over-regularisation errors if it had actually heard regular and irregular verbs in the proportions that children hear them.

A second criticism of single route accounts is that they cannot deal with minority default behaviour. We came across this type of behaviour before. Clahsen, Marcus and colleagues demonstrated that the regular ending for German plurals, and the one that German children used in their errors, was not the most frequent ending in the language (Clahsen et al., 1992; Marcus, Brinkmann, Clahsen, Wiese & Pinker, 1995). Single route accounts cannot account for this finding because models like that of Rumelhart and McClelland will learn the most frequent ending as the default (regular) ending. So these models cannot learn to produce minority default behaviour (though see Hahn & Nakisa, 2000, for a rebuttal).

A third criticism is that single route accounts cannot deal with homophones. Homophones are words that sound the same but have different meanings. For example, the words *break* and *brake* sound identical when spoken but they mean very different things; having a *brake* in the car is far less worrying than having a *break* in the car. Importantly, they also take different past tense endings. *Brake* is a regular verb so the past tense is *braked* (*I braked suddenly when the dog ran into the road*). Break is *irregular* so the past tense is *broke* (*I broke the car by running it into a tree*). A single route model that created past tense forms by linking words based on sound patterns would find it difficult to learn to produce both past tense forms. In fact, Rumelhart and McClelland's model could not deal with homophones at all (Pinker & Prince, 1988).

It is important to note that subsequent models have been built to deal with these issues. Newer models add a layer of *hidden units* between the input and output units that optimise the model's performance, use more powerful learning algorithms, or make other modifications that allow them to deal with many of the problems raised (see for example, Plunkett & Marchman, 1991). In fact, there have been many more models since, as well as many more arguments made for and against the dual and single route accounts. This is a debate in the true sense of the word, the issues swing back and forth in a battle of evidence and counter-evidence, argument and counter-argument.

Long-standing debates like this can sometimes be characterised as stale and unproductive, with each side unwilling to give ground. However, this would be an inaccurate characterisation. Each new round of evidence and arguments tells us something new about how children and adults learn and store inflections. The discovery that regular verbs have phonological 'friends', in particular, has inspired some new and exciting ideas. For example, Albright & Hayes (2003) suggest that the data cannot be accounted for by either single or dual route approaches, and propose a new multiple rules account. We have not discussed this view here as there is not yet enough evidence to evaluate it effectively, but this evidence will build up over the next few years. Discussions are likely to continue for some time.

5.8 CHAPTER SUMMARY

In this chapter we have asked how children learn and store inflectional morphology. We have learnt that most, if not all, languages use inflectional morphology to mark grammatical functions. The child's task is to learn what functions are marked with inflection in her language (tense, gender, case, etc.) and how inflection is used to mark this function (adding a suffix, adding a prefix, etc.). We discovered that children make quite a lot of errors while learning inflectional morphology, so the key question that many theorists have asked is:

Why do children make errors at the same time as they produce correctly inflected utterances?

Answering this question is tricky. Errors co-occur with correctly inflected forms, sometimes for quite long periods of time. Some errors are quite frequent and others are rare overall, though they may be common in certain parts of the inflection paradigm. Error rates differ across languages and, sometimes, across different lexical items.

We evaluated three answers to this question: the ATOM, the variational learning model and the constructivist account. None of these theories can, as yet, explain all the findings. The ATOM does not explain why there is a gradient of error rates across languages, from English and Swedish, to Dutch, French and German, to Spanish and Italian. Nor does it explain why errors are more frequent with some verbs than others. The variational learning model provides a better explanation of the pattern across languages but not the pattern across different verbs within a language. Constructivist models explain lexical variation and some of the cross-linguistic data but do not explain why English attracts such high rates of bare stem errors.

We then turned to the lively and long-standing debate about how children (and adults) store and produce inflections; addressing the key question:

Are regular inflectional forms produced using a rule or by analogy to stored examples?

We discussed dual route and single route models, evaluating their strengths and weaknesses.

Overall, the difficulty for theories of inflectional morphology is trying to capture the vast array of different patterns that we see across languages. No two languages are alike either in the grammatical features they mark with inflections or in the inflections they use to do so. English is considered to have a very impoverished inflectional system, but even this very simple system has been difficult to capture in any one theory. That said, we have learnt a lot simply by testing these theories against the pattern of errors we see in children's speech. Across languages there are differences in how often errors occur, so there are clues to be found by looking at why different languages attract different rates of error. Within languages, there are systematic patterns to be explored: some errors seem widespread, others are more common on low frequency words and in low frequency parts of the inflectional system. Computational models have also featured widely in this field. They have also told us a lot about what kind of learning mechanism might be able to explain acquisition.

5.9   SUGGESTED READING

Ambridge, B. & Lieven, E. V. M (2011). *Child language acquisition*. Cambridge: Cambridge University Press. A very readable more in-depth discussion of the theories and issues raised here.

Saxton, M. (2010) *Child language: Acquisition and development*. London: Sage. A very enjoyable textbook that covers a broad range of material.

5.10 SUGGESTED READING (ADVANCED LEVEL)

Pinker, S. (1999) *Words and rules: The ingredients of language*. New York: HarperCollins. Pinker always writes well-explained, enjoyable books and this is no exception.

Seidenberg, M. S. (1992). Connectionism without tears. In S. Davis. (Ed.), *Connectionism: Theory and practice* (pp. 84–122). New York: Oxford University Press. A great introduction to connectionist networks.

Here are three classic articles describing the three different theories of how children learn inflection:

Freudenthal D., Pine, J. M. and Gobet, F. (2010) Explaining quantitative variation in the rate of optional infinite errors across languages: A comparison of MOSAIC and the Variational Learning Model. *Journal of Child Language, 36*(3), 643–669.

Legate, J. & Yang, C. (2007) Morphosyntactic learning and the development of tense. *Language Acquisition, 14*(3), 315–344.

Wexler, K. (1998). Very early parameter setting and the unique checking constraint: A new explanation of the optional infinitive stage. *Lingua, 106*(1–4), 23–79.

The journal *Trends in Cognitive Science* published a very frank exchange of views on the over-regularisation error in 2002. There is an opinion article, a reply and a reply to the reply:

Pinker, S. & Ullman, M. (2002a) The past and future of the past tense. *Trends in Cognitive Science, 6*(11), 456–463.

McClelland, J. L. & Patterson, K. (2002) Rules or connections in past-tense inflections: What does the evidence rule out? *Trends in Cognitive Science, 6*(11), 465–472.

Pinker, S. & Ullman, M. (2002b) Structure and combination, not gradedness, is the issue (Reply to McClelland and Patterson). *Trends in Cognitive Science, 6*(11), 472–474.

For advanced readers who want to know more about how gender, agreement and number manifest in different languages across the world, the following are recommended:

Corvette, G. (1991). *Gender*. Cambridge: Cambridge University Press.

Corvette, G. (2000). *Number*. Cambridge: Cambridge University Press.

Corvette, G. (2006). *Agreement*. Cambridge: Cambridge University Press.

5.11 COMPREHENSION CHECK

1. Give a brief explanation of the function of:

   a. Tense markers
   b. Person markers
   c. Number markers
   d. Case markers
   e. Gender markers

2. Summarise how the following theories explain why children make errors:

   a. The ATOM
   b. The variational learning model
   c. Constructivist theory

3. Which theory (ATOM, VLM, constructivist) can explain why children make more errors with eventive verbs than stative verbs, and why?

4. Describe the methods by which English speakers produce past tense forms, according to the dual route model.

5. Which of the methods you gave in answer to question four above are also proposed by the single route accounts?

6

Learning to communicate

6.1 THE ISSUE

By the time they start school, children will have learnt most of their language's sounds, words and grammatical rules. However, this is still not enough for successful communication. Imagine a student, Lauren, offering a coffee to her friend quite late on in the evening (example adapted from Stephens & Matthews, 2013). She receives the reply *coffee keeps me awake*. Whether Lauren makes a coffee for her friend depends on her knowledge of her friend's situation and state of mind. If her friend has a difficult, exhausting day planned for tomorrow and needs to sleep well, *coffee keeps me awake* is probably a rejection of the offer. If her friend plans to work on an essay into the small hours of the morning, however, the response should be interpreted as an implicit *yes*. Similarly, imagine if Lauren's teacher hands back an essay with a muttered *good work*. If she received a high grade, it is likely that the teacher's intended meaning was praise. However, if she received a very low grade, it is far more likely that the teacher was being sarcastic.

These examples illustrate that successful communication relies on more than just an understanding of speech sounds, words and grammar. In order to communicate effectively we have to a) interpret the sentence's literal meaning by drawing on our knowledge of phonology, vocabulary and grammar and b) infer the speaker's intended meaning, by drawing on our knowledge of the situation, the real world and the mental state of the speaker. Thus, in order to communicate successfully, children must learn both to interpret the sentence's literal meaning and the speaker's intended meaning.

In fact, we require even more than this. According to Grice, the ability to converse also requires that both communicative partners follow certain rules (maxims) governing how conversations should be conducted (Grice, 1989). They are as follows:

1. Maxims of Quantity

   - Make your contribution to the conversation as informative as necessary.

   - Do not make your contribution to the conversation more informative than necessary.

2. Maxims of Quality

- Do not say what you believe to be false.
- Do not say that for which you lack adequate evidence.

3. Maxims of Relation

- Be relevant.

4. Maxims of Manner

- Avoid obscurity of expression.
- Avoid ambiguity.
- Be brief.
- Be orderly.

By following these rules, a speaker can ensure that a conversation progresses successfully. By violating these rules, the speaker can induce a range of different effects such as deceit (telling lies), humour (saying something unexpected) and sarcasm or irony (saying the opposite of what is meant). Thus, to become successful communicators, children must learn to follow the rules governing conversation, and to identify when they have been violated.[1]

The study of the development of communicative competence is called developmental pragmatics and it is the focus of this chapter. We begin by discussing the abilities of pre-verbal infants, assessing whether they can already infer the intended meaning behind the speech and actions of others. We then move to the development of children's own conversational skills, focussing on children's ability to interpret scalar implicature and reference words, and their ability to take turns in conversations. Finally, we look at what happens when the ability to communicate breaks down, as happens in autistic disorders and pragmatic language impairment.

6.2 COMMUNICATION WITHOUT WORDS

An infant's communicative life does not begin when she starts to talk. Adults and infants have been engaging in successful communication for quite a few months before the infant utters her first word. In fact, Stephens and Matthews have argued that "first words are in reality an end point for infants, which emerges only after they have reached several fundamental milestones" (Stephens & Matthews, 2013, p. 1).

For example, imagine a scenario in which 12-month-old baby Amy is happily making music, banging on a drum with a drumstick. Suddenly, the drumstick flies out of her hand. She looks up at her father, who points to the location of the missing drumstick. Amy looks in the direction of the pointing finger and retrieves the

---

1   The accuracy of some of Grice's maxims has been debated in the literature (Moore, 2013). However, even if some of the details are wrong, it is undeniable that they capture the flavour of successful conversations.

drumstick. No speech has taken place but Amy and her father have undoubtedly been engaged in communication.

How much does Amy understand about the communicative intention behind her father's pointing gesture? One possibility is that she follows the pointing finger because she recognises that her father is trying to help her retrieve the drumstick. She makes an inference that his intention is to help her find the drumstick, and thus interprets his point as an attempt to help. This is known as the *rich interpretation* view of infant communicative behaviour (e.g. Tomasello, Carpenter & Liszkowski, 2007). However, another possibility is that she simply recognises that the pointing finger signals the location of an interesting object. On this *lean interpretation* view, Amy is not interpreting the intentions behind her father's pointing behaviour, but is simply responding to the action itself (e.g. Moore & Corkum, 1994). It is often difficult to distinguish between these two interpretations of early infant behaviour. Thus, the key question in this area of research is:

Key question: are infants and young children capable of interpreting the communicative intentions of others?

The extent to which infants can interpret the communicative intentions of the people around them is important because it has implications for the development of language itself. If infants can already communicate with gestures before they can talk, the task of learning words becomes much easier. It may be a relatively simple step to replace the gestures with words. Similarly, if infants can interpret the intentions behind their caregivers' gestures, it may be a relatively short leap to interpreting their words. Thus, a second key question is:

Key question: what role do infants' early communicative abilities play in word learning?

6.2.1 Infants, communicative intent and joint attention

Infants seem to recognise that people are somehow special from very early on in life. Newborns prefer human speech sounds over artificially produced sounds and prefer infant-directed speech to adult-directed speech (Cooper & Aslin, 1990; DeCasper & Fifer, 1980). Two-month-old infants respond differently to people and dolls, producing more positive vocalisations such as cooing and gurgling when interacting with people (Legerstee, Pomerleau, Malcuit & Feider, 1987). At this age, infants also prefer their mothers to respond naturally to them in interactions, showing distress when the mothers behave in an odd or unexpected manner (Markova & Legerstee, 2006).

However, according to rich interpretation theorists, communication between infants and other people takes a huge leap forward at what is called the *nine-month revolution* (Stephens & Matthews, 2013). According to this theory, infants between nine and 12 months of age are said to reach crucial milestones in the development of communication (Tomasello, 2003, 2008). As evidence for the nine-month revolution, Carpenter and colleagues videotaped and then analysed the interactions of parents and their infants at different ages, and reported that many types of communicative behaviour emerge very soon after the infant reaches nine months of age (Carpenter, Nagell & Tomasello, 1998).

For example, Carpenter and colleagues reported that between nine and 11 months of age, the infants started to engage in *joint engagement* in which the infant showed evidence of shifting attention from a toy to the face of the adult she was playing with, and then back again to the toy. Carpenter and colleagues interpreted this as the infant becoming aware that she is engaged in a joint activity with someone else and noting that person's focus of attention. Second to emerge was the ability to follow the attentional focus of another person. Thus, between 11 and 12 months the infants started·to follow reliably the trajectory of adult points and eye gazes, accurately locating the adult's focus of attention. Infants at this age also demonstrated the ability to imitate adult actions, such as touching a button to make a light flash. Finally, at 12 to 13 months of age, the infants learnt to direct the attention of adults themselves, by pointing to objects or locations and then monitoring the adult's face to check that the adult had responded.

On the basis of these results, the rich interpretation theorists have concluded that the period between nine and 12 months represents a sea-change in infants' understanding of the attention and intentions of others. It marks the start of the infant's ability to attend jointly to, and thus communicate about, objects and events in the world. It allows infants to learn, via communication, all about their environment, their culture, their society and their language. It is "the cross-roads where human infants meet the world of collective cognition in which they will reside for the rest of their lives" (Carpenter, et al., 1998, p. 2).

However, lean interpretation theorists explain these results differently. They suggest that, in all of these seemingly communicative behaviours, the infant is not interpreting the adult's intentions, but is simply responding to the action itself. For example, lean interpretation theorists have argued that infants turn to look in the direction in which adults are looking (i.e. follow eye gazes) because the looking behaviour attracts their attention to the location of an interesting object (Butterworth & Jarrett, 1991; Corkum & Moore, 1995). On this view, the infants are not inferring the communicative intention behind the adult's eye gaze but are simply responding to the behaviour in the expectation of discovering something exciting.

As evidence for this view, Corkum and Moore (1995) tested how six- to 19-month-old infants reacted to an experimenter's eye gaze shifts and head turns. They argued that if the infants' motivation was to look where the adult was looking, in an attempt to infer the experimenter's communicative intent, the infants should follow the experimenter's eye gaze whether or not it was accompanied by a turn of the head in the appropriate direction. However, they found that infants did not reliably follow eye gaze in the absence of a head turn until 18 months of age. They concluded that before 18 months, infants are simply responding to a head turn cue, which they interpret simply as a signal to the location of an interesting object or event.

The literature on infants' own pointing behaviour has also attracted different interpretations. Two different types of infant pointing behaviour emerge between nine and 12 months of age (Bates, Camaioni & Volterra, 1975, were the first to suggest this distinction). First are proto-imperative points, which are used by infants to request or demand objects or actions. These are relatively uncontroversial because most researchers agree that proto-imperatives are simply used by the infant to achieve a desired outcome. Second are proto-declarative points, which infants use to point out objects or activities of interest to others. There are many disagreements about the interpretation of these. Rich interpretation theorists argue that proto-declarative points are purely communicative from the beginning. Thus, infants point in order to attract someone's attention to an object or activity of interest, with the goal of communicating about it. However, the lean interpretation view is that infants use proto-declaratives, like proto-imperatives, simply to "elicit an adult response towards him- or herself rather than seeking to direct the adults' attention to the object" (Moore & D'Entremont, 2001, p. 110). In other words, they are not interested in whether or not the adult attends to the object, they simply want to get a reaction.

To illustrate, let's imagine a little boy (referred to as A), who pointed through the window to the sky when he heard an aeroplane noise (Tomasello, 2008, p. 114). On the rich interpretation view, A's pointing gesture was motivated by a desire to communicate the existence of the aeroplane to others. On the lean interpretation view, it was simply an attempt to elicit a response from others, without any understanding of why the pointing action might achieve the desired result.

As evidence for the lean interpretation view, researchers call attention to the fact that infants often point at objects that adults have already seen. This suggests that they cannot be pointing in order to direct their parent's attention to an interesting object, because the parent is already attending to it. For example, Moore and D'Entremont tested one- and two-year-old infants by showing them an interesting object and observing whether they pointed to attract their parent's attention to the sight (Moore & D'Entremont, 2001). They reported that the one-year-old infants pointed at the object whether or not their parent had already seen and registered it previously. Two-year-olds, however, pointed more when the parent had not already seen it. They concluded that the one-year-olds were only pointing to "enhance the interaction", not to direct their parent's attention (Moore & D'Entremont, 2001, p. 123). Thus, pointing was not truly communicative until about two years of age.

However, subsequent studies by rich interpretation theorists have challenged these conclusions. For example, Liszkowsi and colleagues assessed the lean interpretation hypothesis that 12-month-old infants point only to attract attention (Liszkowski, Carpenter, Henning, Striano & Tomasello, 2004). They did this by assessing how infants reacted when their pointing gestures elicited different types of adult response. In their study, each infant sat on the floor with their mothers and were shown hand puppets, who popped out of a door for ten seconds and then disappeared. This action, not surprisingly, elicited frequent pointing gestures from the infants. Immediately after the infant pointed to the puppet, an experimenter produced one of four types of reaction. In the *Joint Attention* condition, the experimenter alternated looking at the puppet and the child's face, talking excitedly about the puppet (*Oh, wow! Are you showing Grover to me?*). In the *Face* condition, the experimenter still talked excitedly, but not about the puppet and only looked at the child's face not at the puppet (*Oh I see you are in a good mood!*). In the *Event* condition, the experimenter looked only at the puppet and did not speak or show any emotions. In the *Ignore* condition the experimenter ignored both the child and the puppet.

Understandably, infants did not react well to the *Event* and *Ignore* conditions. However, the crucial comparison was in their reaction to the *Joint Attention* and *Face* conditions. On the lean interpretation view, the children should have been equally happy with the responses they received in these conditions since they received equal amounts of attention from the experimenter. However, this was not the case. The infants only seemed satisfied with the experimenter's response in the *Joint Attention* condition. In the *Face* condition, the infants kept repeating their points to the puppet, which implied they were dissatisfied with the experimenter's lack of attention to the puppet. As the experiment went on, the infants also became less likely to point at the puppet when it first popped up, as they became more and more discouraged by the lack of the appropriate response. The authors concluded that the only plausible interpretation of these results was that infants pointed in order to direct the experimenter's attention and interest to the interesting object, not simply to gain the experimenter's attention. This is consistent with the rich interpretation view of early communicative behaviour.

6.2.2   Understanding intentions and imitating actions

Following eye gaze and using and understanding pointing gestures are not the only ways that infants can demonstrate their understanding of communicative intent. There is also a large body of research on how infants interpret other types of action. Particularly relevant are studies that find that infants tend to imitate the intended outcome of an action, rather than the actual movement itself. These studies suggest that infants can discern the purpose behind people's actions from a very early age, consistent with the rich interpretation view.

For example, Meltzoff has tested whether infants would successfully complete an action that an experimenter had tried, but failed, to perform (Meltzoff, 1995). In this study, 18-month-old infants viewed videos of an experimenter either completing an action successfully or trying and failing to complete it. For example, in the target condition the experimenter picked up a stick tool and used it to press a button, which made a buzzer sound. In the intention condition, the experimenter tried to press the button with the stick but he always missed. Surprisingly, despite never having seen the completed action in the intention condition, the infants imitated the target action in both conditions equally often. In other words, even though they had never seen the experimenter successfully push the button in the intention condition, the infants would themselves use the stick to press the button successfully. Interestingly, they did not behave the same way when a mechanical toy demonstrated the actions. Meltzoff concluded that the infants were interpreting the movements of the experimenter, but not the mechanical toy, in terms of their intention; they inferred what action the adult intended to complete and imitated the target action, even when they had never seen it completed.

Gergely and colleagues demonstrated a similar ability in children as young as 14 months (Gergely, Bekkering & Király 2002). Infants viewed a video of an experimenter carrying out a goal in an unusual way: using her head to turn on a light-box that was placed on a table. Importantly, in one condition there was no discernible reason why the experimenter had used her head, not her hands, to press the light. Sixty-nine per cent of infants who were shown this video copied the experimenter's unusual movements when their turn came to carry out the action. They, too, turned the light on with their heads. However, in another condition, the experimenter pretended to be cold and held a blanket around her body, thus demonstrating a valid reason why she could not use her hands to turn on the light. Only 21 per cent of the infants who viewed these videos copied the unusual head action, preferring to turn the light on with their hands. These results seem to indicate that the infants had understood why the experimenter had used her head not her hands. They had reasoned that it was not necessary to emulate the experimenter's actions, just as long as they achieved the same goal (turning the light on). In other words, they were capable of judging the motivations behind the experimenter's actions and responding accordingly, just as rich interpretation theory predicts.

One word of warning is necessary here, though. It is tempting to conclude that if 14-month-olds can interpret the intentions behind actions like turning on a light, they must be able to interpret communicative actions like pointing and gestures in the same way. However, it is important to note that the children in Meltzoff's and Gergely's studies were not interpreting adults' attempts at communication. Thus, we cannot rule out the possibility that it may take infants longer to learn to infer the intentions behind adults' communicative gestures, just as lean interpretation theorists suggest.

6.2.3 The role of early communicative abilities in language learning

Above we discussed whether infants and young children can interpret the intentions behind the communicative acts of others. In this section, we discuss the role these early abilities may play in the development of language itself.

An influential constructivist theory of language development, the *social-pragmatic theory*, suggests that skills like understanding communicative intent are fundamental to language learning (see chapter 3 and Bruner, 1978; Clark, 1993; Nelson, 1985; Ninio & Snow, 1996; Tomasello, 2003). The idea here is that adults provide a lot of information about word and sentence meanings in the context of interacting with their children. Children can use this information to make inferences about word meaning. To do this, children use the context of the conversation, their ability to infer what message the speaker intends to convey and two important principles of communication – conventionality and contrast (Clark, 1987, 1990). The principle of *conventionality* refers to the idea that children's aim in learning language is to match the language of the adults around them (i.e. to learn the conventions of language). The child understands that words have conventional meanings, so her goal is to learn these meanings. The principle of *contrast* refers to the idea that children understand that different words tend to have different meanings. Thus children are aware that when a speaker uses two different words she is likely to be expressing slightly different meanings, even if the words appear to refer to the same object. For example, if the speaker refers to an animal both as a *dog* and a *puppy*, this indicates that the two words must have slightly different meanings.

According to the social-pragmatic theory, then, language acquisition is built on "specific social-cognitive skills on part of the child" (e.g. joint attention, intention reading) and "specific types of social interaction in which the child is exposed to social conventions that constitute her native language" (Carpenter, et al., 1998, p. 130). On this view, it is not a coincidence that the nine-month revolution, in which a whole range of communicative abilities emerges, is swiftly followed by the emergence of a child's first words. It is the emergence of these communicative abilities that allows language to develop.

Social-pragmatic theorists suggest that parents provide children with a huge amount of information about word meanings simply by interacting with them. For example, when adults introduce new words into conversations, they often offer additional information about the word's referent, as exemplified in the exchange below between a child and mother looking at a book together:

Mother: Do you know what that one is?

Child: Ummm.

Mother: I don't know if you know what that one is.

Child: That's a snake.

Mother: It looks like a snake, doesn't it? It's called an eel. It's like a snake only it
            lives in the water. And there's another one.

> (reported in Clark & Wong, 2002, p. 201;
> example originally from Gelman et al., 1998).

This type of interaction provides children not only with the relevant label (*eel*) but with additional information about the properties of the eel (that it lives in water; see Clark & Wong, 2002). Adults also accompany new words with informative gestures. For example, Clark and Estigarribia (2011) have reported that adults often use *demonstrating gestures* while discussing how a new object works (e.g. picking up a spoon and making a stirring gesture) but *indicating gestures* when discussing an object's parts or properties (e.g. pointing at or tapping the bowl of the spoon). This provides the child with exactly the information she needs to learn the meaning of new words.

Further evidence for the theory comes from the finding that infants' early communicative ability predicts how quickly they later learn language. For example, Carpenter and colleagues studied how often children aged nine, 10 and 11 months engaged in joint engagement with their mothers, and then assessed how many words infants understood and could produce at different ages (Carpenter et al., 1998). Joint engagement was measured in terms of the time that the infant and mother spent jointly attending to an object, activity or event during a ten minute videoed play session. For example, "an infant might push a car towards her mother, look up to her mother's face, and then look back to the car while the mother watches and comments 'You're pushing it'" (Carpenter et al., 1998, p. 48). The researchers reported that the amount of time the infants spent in joint engagement had a significant effect on later language development. The infants who began to participate in joint engagement by 12 months of age understood more words than those who did not start joint engagement until after 12 months of age. This is an important finding because it is precisely these types of social interaction that are predicted to promote language according to the social-pragmatic theory.

There is also evidence that children's proficiency with pointing predicts how early and how quickly they learn language. Colonnesi and colleagues conducted a meta-analysis of 25 studies conducted between 1978 and 2009 on the role of pointing behaviour in language development in 734 children (Colonnesi, Stams, Koster & Noomb, 2010). A meta-analysis is a particularly robust methodology because it takes the findings of a number of studies and analyses them together, providing a comprehensive view of whether, on balance, a hypothesis is supported by the literature. On the basis of this meta-analysis, Colonnesi and colleagues reported that there was a strong relationship between proto-declarative pointing and language development. Most importantly, there was a *predictive* relationship between the two, which means that infants' ability to use and understanding pointing gestures early in development predicted their language development later on. They concluded that "the pointing gesture is a key joint attention behaviour involved in the acquisition of language" (Colonnesi et al., 2010, p. 352).

There is, thus, a substantial body of evidence supporting the social-pragmatic theory of language learning. However, there is one problem with this picture, which results from the fact that all of the studies referenced above were conducted with Western, mainly American and German, parents and children. This is an important omission because social-pragmatic theory relies on the assumption that abilities like pointing and joint attention are crucial for language development. Thus, an important prediction of this theory is that these behaviours should occur universally, across all cultures, if children are to learn language. In other words, if the social-pragmatic theory is correct, we should see similar patterns of development across different cultures.

At first sight, the literature suggests that at least some features are indeed universal. In particular, there is now good evidence that communicative behaviours might emerge at about the same age across cultures. For example, Liszkowski and colleagues assessed the onset of pointing behaviours across seven cultures and reported that there was very little difference in the age of onset; all infants started pointing at about nine months of age, regardless of the culture in which they were raised (they tested children in Papua New Guinea, Indonesia, Japan, Peru, Canada, and in Tzeltal and Yucatek Mayan societies in Mexico; Liszkowski, Brown, Callaghan, Takada & De Vos, 2012). Similarly, Callaghan and colleagues studied a range of communicative behaviours across three cultures (Western middle-class Canada and two traditional rural villages, one in Peru and one in India, Callaghan et al., 2011). They measured gaze following, pointing, imitation, helping, collaboration and joint attention and reported that all these communicative behaviours emerged at approximately the same time across the three cultures. Thus, we are now beginning to amass some good evidence that infants start to produce communicative behaviours at about the same age across different cultures.

Nevertheless, we still need to discover whether the emergence of these behaviours is universally followed swiftly by the onset of language. This is more problematic. Only a few studies have looked at the role of early communicative behaviours in later language development across different cultures and these have produced conflicting results. For example, Childers and colleagues (2007) found that joint engagement episodes were predictive of the language development of children in a rural Nigerian community, which mirrors the results from Western children. However, Mastin and Vogt (2011) reported that there was no such relationship in their study with infants and mothers in rural Mozambique.

On balance, the evidence we have supports a role for early communicative behaviours in language development, although we cannot be certain of our conclusions until we have more evidence from children in non-Western cultures. However, why this should be the case remains an important unresolved question. One possibility is that there is a direct relationship between the two. Thus, children with good non-verbal communication transition smoothly into language learning later on (for proponents of this view, see Bates et al., 1975; Brooks & Meltzoff, 2005; Camaioni, 1993). However, an equally plausible alternative is that adults find it easier to talk to children who are capable of more sophisticated communicative behaviours. As a result, these children hear more language more often, which then helps them to learn language more quickly (for proponents of this view, see Dobrich & Scarborough, 1984; Kishimoto, Shizawa, Yasuda, Hinobayashi & Minami, 2007; Petitto, 1988). As a third alternative, it may be that both of these factors play a part in language development; children with more sophisticated communicative abilities both find it easier to learn language and encourage adults to interact with them more often, thus benefiting from a richer linguistic environment.

6.3 COMMUNICATING WITH LANGUAGE

Above we discussed the evidence that infants can interpret and convey messages before they start to talk. These skills should stand them in good stead as they begin to communicate in speech. Successful conversations require that speakers adjust what they are saying in accordance to listener characteristics (e.g. listener's prior knowledge) and that the listener interprets the message behind the speaker's words. Given children's early competence in these areas, we might expect them to be very good at this.

However, work with both preschool and school-aged children suggests that they have difficulties interpreting many types of message. For example, five- and six-year-olds find it difficult to interpret ironic comments, which superficially express the opposite meaning to that intended. (e.g. *You only got 9 out of 10? What went wrong?*; Hancock, Dunham & Purdy, 2000). This seems puzzling given the weight of evidence suggesting that even very young children are sensitive to the meaning behind adults' gestures and actions. Thus, our key question here is:

Key question: why is successful conversation so difficult for children?

Below we address this question by discussing three areas in which children's abilities to communicate seem to lag behind their growing ability to produce and understand words and sentences: computing scalar implicature, using referring expressions and taking turns in conversations.

6.3.1   Choosing what to say I: scalar implicature

By choosing to use a particular word in a sentence, we implicitly exclude many alternative interpretations of that sentence. For example, adults often use the word *some* when they want to imply that they do not mean *all*. Imagine our student, Lauren, looking for cheese in the fridge, and asking her flatmate *Did you eat the cheese?* If the flatmate replies *I ate some of the cheese* she is likely to infer that her flatmate did not eat all of the cheese, unless her flatmate then qualified his statement (e.g. *I ate some of the cheese, in fact I ate it all*). In other words, when a speaker uses the word *some*, he or she is implicitly asking the listener to exclude the meaning *all*.

This is a little strange, since logically use of the word *some* does not exclude the possibility of *all*. If the instructions on a mathematics exam stated that *some of the answers are above 20*, we would be foolish to assume that some of the answers must also be below 20. In fact, all of the answers might be above 20. However, in conversation we regularly interpret *some* as meaning *not all*, presumably because we assume that the speaker would have said *all* if they meant *all*. This type of reasoning is called an inference (inferring something not explicitly stated) and is explained by one of Grice's Maxims of Quantity, which state that *speakers should be as informative as necessary, no more and no less* (see section 6.1. above, Grice, 1989). If we assume that the speaker is striving to be as informative as necessary, we can assume that he would have said *all* if he meant *all*. Thus, it is legitimate for the student to assume that her flatmate's response *I ate some of the cheese* meant that he ate some, not all, of the cheese.

The inference we make when we assume that *some* means *not all* is an example of a scalar implicature. It is called an *implicature* because it concerns what the use of a term implies, and *scalar* because the words lie on a scale of informativeness from informationally strong terms (*all*) to informationally weak terms (*some*). In conversation, listeners assume that speakers who use an informationally weak term like *some* are implying that the informationally stronger term (*all*) is not true. Some other examples of scalar implicatures are *or*, *and* and *possible*, *certain* and the same inference rules apply to these terms as to *some*, *all*.

Unlike adults, children do not routinely compute scalar implicatures. The first systematic study on this topic was that of Noveck (2001), who simply asked English and French adults and children to judge the truthfulness of under-informative statements such as *some giraffes have long necks*. The adults in the study rejected sentences like this 59 per cent of the time, explaining that they were false because, for example, all giraffes, not just some giraffes, have long necks. In other words, they assumed that the use of *some* implied *not all*. However, eight- to ten-year-olds accepted the statements as true 85 per cent of the time (i.e. only rejected them 15 per cent of the time), responding as if the word *some* was compatible with the meaning *all*. In other words, unlike adults, most of the children did not compute scalar implicatures. Subsequent studies across a range of languages including Greek, Italian, English and French, and with children aged between five and nine years, have confirmed that children are much less likely to reject under-informative sentences than adults, with performance improving gradually as the children age (Guasti, Chierchia, Crain, Gualmini & Meroni, 2005; Katsos & Bishop, 2011; Papafragou & Musolino, 2003; Pouscoulous, Noveck, Politzer & Bastide, 2007).

Why do children find scalar implicatures difficult for such a long time? The most obvious answer is that they lack the ability to reason about the speaker's intent. This is known as the *pragmatic delay hypothesis*. However, most researchers reject this hypothesis for two very good reasons. First, children are capable of similar types of reasoning from a very young age in different contexts. For example, two-year-olds who know the word *one* will assume that an unfamiliar number word (e.g. *five*) must refer to a group of objects, rather than to a single object on its own. They do this, presumably, by reasoning that if the speaker had meant to refer to the single object, she would have used the word *one* (Condry & Spelke, 2008). This inference "requires all of the processing resources that an ordinary implicature would require, as well as several of the same steps" (Barner, Brooks & Bale, 2011, p. 87).

Second, children are capable of computing scalar implicatures if given the right type of support. For example, Papafragou and Musolino tested various ways to help Greek children compute scalar implicatures (2003). In this study, children took part in a training session in which they were shown pictures of objects and were then encouraged to help Minnie Mouse choose the best description of the picture.[2] For example, the children might be shown a picture of a dog and asked whether the sentence *This is a little animal with four legs* was a good description of the picture or not. If the child failed to identify that this was not a good description, the experimenter would do so for them (e.g. *Minnie didn't say that very well. This is a DOG*). As well as training, a background storyline was given, which highlighted to the participants the importance of judging the sentences precisely. For example, in one story, it was very important for the outcome that Mickey Mouse got all (not just some) of the hoops around the peg. The researchers argued that these modifications would highlight to the children that it was important to judge the sentences based on whether they were completely accurate or not. This should help them to compute scalar implicature. They were right. As predicted, five-year-olds went from computing scalar implicature 20 per cent of the time in the standard task, to 45 per cent of the time when training and a storyline were added. In other words, the children started to judge sentences with *some* as if they excluded the meaning *not all*, just like adults.

2 Note that the examples are translated into English but the participants were actually tested in Greek. The scales used in testing were *oli*, *meriki* ('all, some'), *tris*, *dio* ('three, two') and *teliono*, *arxizo* ('finish, start').

The authors concluded that the training and storyline had provided a context which helped the children more readily compute the implicature.

These results do not support the pragmatic delay hypothesis but are compatible with an alternative hypothesis, the *pragmatic limitations hypothesis*. On this view, computing scalar implicature requires cognitive effort, which make it difficult for children whose language skills are less efficient and less well practised than those of adults. Making the experimental task easier, by adding practice sessions or providing a context that highlights the goal of the experiment, helps children overcome these difficulties.

Further evidence for the pragmatic limitations hypothesis comes from studies investigating the role of the questions that children are asked. In most studies, children are asked to judge the truthfulness of under-informative sentences such as *some giraffes have long necks*. Katsos and Bishop have argued that children may be aware that the sentence is not quite right but tend to accept it because it is not clearly and obviously wrong (Katsos & Bishop, 2011). After all, it is not an obviously false statement like *giraffes have short necks*. In other words, it may be that children do compute scalar implicatures, but are more tolerant of subtle pragmatic violations than adults, reserving their 'reject' judgements for statements that are clearly inaccurate.

To test this, Katsos and Bishop devised a method in which the child had to reward the speaker of the sentence, Mr Caveman, with different sized strawberries, depending on the truthfulness of the sentence (Katsos & Bishop, 2011). They reasoned that this method would allow children to differentiate between sentences without requiring them to reject the under-informative sentences outright. If children are sensitive to scalar implicature we would expect them to reward the speaker with smaller strawberries when the sentences are under-informative than when they are completely accurate (optimal). For example, if Mr Caveman said *the turtle played with some of the balls* when, in fact, the turtle played with all of the balls, we would expect the child to reward him with smaller strawberries. This is exactly what they found. Five- to six-year-old English children tended to reward Mr Caveman with big strawberries when his sentences were under-informative, but with huge strawberries when his sentences were optimal. The children were also, however, more tolerant of under-informative utterances than false utterances, since they tended to give Mr Caveman even smaller strawberries in response to sentences that were simply untrue. Thus, the children demonstrated both an ability to detect scalar implicature violations and a tolerance towards them, just as Katsos and Bishop suggested.

In sum, the evidence that children can compute scalar implicature when task and processing demands are reduced is very strong. However, it must be borne in mind that children do not reach adult levels of performance even in the most supportive experimental environments. This means that the pragmatic limitations hypothesis may not explain all the differences between adults and children.

6.3.2 Choosing what to say II: using reference words

Work with infants tells us that they are very good at taking the perspective of the listener into account. For example, Moll and Tomasello (2007) reported that

14-month-old German children responded differently to questions such as *where is the other toy… can you give it to me?* depending on which toys the speaker had previously played with. If the speaker had not previously played with one of the toys, the children would give her that toy, presumably by reasoning that this must be the desired toy since it was the toy she had not previously seen. Thus, by 14 months of age, children seem sensitive to other people's current state of knowledge. Given this, we might expect children to learn quickly how to take account of their listener's knowledge once they learn to talk.

Taking note of a listener's prior knowledge is particularly important when choosing which word to use to identify an object, person or event (reference words). For example, when English speakers first introduce an object into a conversation, they will tend to use an indefinite article (*a*) rather than the definite one (*the*). So they might say *look there's a cat*. However, when they refer back to the cat subsequently in the conversation they are likely to use an definite article (*the*) in order to indicate that they are still referring to the same cat (*the cat's drinking some milk, isn't he?*). Alternatively, they might subsequently use a pronoun, as long as the intended referent remains unambiguous (*he's drinking some milk, isn't he?*).

Reference terms such as these lie on a scale of *accessibility*, determined by "the degree to which the referent is active in the hearer's consciousness" (Graf & Davies, 2013). If the referent has recently been introduced into the conversation, the speaker may assume that it is highly accessible in the hearer's mind, and that a pronoun is appropriate. If the referent is completely new, or if the use of a pronoun would not sufficiently discriminate between a number of possible referents, then the speaker will use a more specific, clearly identifiable word or phrase (e.g. *the cat*). Choosing the correct referring word requires the child to take the listener's perspective and knowledge state into account. Given the sophisticated abilities of pre-verbal infants discussed in section 6.2 above, we might expect them to learn quickly how to choose the correct referring expression once they have learnt to talk.

Most of the work on this topic suggests that children are, indeed, sensitive to the factors governing the use of reference words from an early age. However, they take a while to use them in an adultlike way in their own speech. For example, Allen (2007) has summarised research from three studies on Korean, Inuktitut and Italian all of which analysed the spontaneous speech of children aged between about one-and-a-half and three years of age (e.g. Allen, 2000; Clancy, 2003; Serratrice, 2002). In all three of these languages it is possible to omit referent words from a sentence if the referent is very accessible (e.g. it is grammatical to say simply *drinking some milk*). Allen reports that across all three languages, the children tested seemed sensitive to this constraint. Like adults, the children tended to omit reference words when the referent was easily identifiable from the previous discourse or from the situation. However, if the referent was not easily accessible, the children tended to produce a word to identify it, often a full noun phrase (e.g. *the cat*).

However, the children in these studies were not performing as well as they could. They were under-informative over 50 per cent of the time, omitting words for new referents that had not yet been mentioned in the conversation. The equivalent in English would be a child saying *drinking some milk* when it is not possible to identify who or what is drinking the milk. To illustrate, in the example below, an Inuit child has introduced a new topic of conversation without identifying who she is referring to. This, not surprisingly, leads to a request for clarification from the child's mother (from Allen, 2007, p. 201):

Child: Uvattinunngi

           uvatti-nut-uq-nngit

           our.place-ALLATIVE[3]-go-NEGATIVE

           '(He/she/it) isn't coming to our house.'

Mother: Suna?

           'What?'

Allen has also reported that the children tended to be over-, as well as under-informative, using words to identify referents unnecessarily (Allen, 2007). The equivalent in English would be a child saying *look at the cat. The cat's having some milk*, even though the second use of *the cat* is unnecessary. In a similar vein, Hickman and Hendricks (1999) have reported that children use less than optimal strategies when using newness markers. Newness markers differ across languages but all share the function of the English indefinite article, *a* (e.g. *a cat*), which is used to introduce new referents. Hickman and Hendricks reported that children do not systematically use newness markers to introduce new referents until seven years of age, a trend which held across four different languages (English, French, German and Mandarin Chinese; Hickman & Hendriks, 1999). For example, they found that the English children tended to introduce new references into the conversation with definite articles (*there's the cat*) rather than indefinite ones (*there's a cat*).

Why might children be sensitive to the conditions governing the choice of referring expressions but not consistent in applying this knowledge? One possibility is that children are more accurate than we give them credit for, but that our analyses have missed some of the features they pay attention to. In particular, Clancy has suggested that children may use less informative terms in situations in which the referents can be identified by a gesture or eye gaze (Clancy, 2003). For example, if one simultaneously gestures towards the cat to indicate that the cat is the object referred to, it may be perfectly appropriate to introduce the cat with *he's drinking some milk* (or *drinking some milk* in a null subject language like Inuktitut).

Allen investigated how Inuktitut children used gestures but found no evidence to support the idea that children used gestures to replace missing words (Allen, 2007). However, she suggested that children may instead use gestures to accompany pronouns, like *it, he, she, this* and *that* (e.g. *this one/he is drinking some milk*). This might explain why children tend to overuse pronouns when introducing new referents; the

---

3   Allative case marker.

gesture makes it clear what the referent is. She also reported some evidence for the role of joint attention, in that children were more likely to omit referent words if they and their caregiver were jointly attending to the referent object. Skarabela reported a similar finding: Inuktitut children omitted more referent words and produced more pronouns like *this* and *that* in joint attentional contexts (Skarabela, 2007). Thus, it may be that children use less informative terms when they know that the referent will be easily identified by the listener by other means.

There is also another possible explanation of over- and under-informative referencing. Matthews and colleagues have suggested that substantial experience is required to learn all the factors that contribute to reference word choice, which means that children may learn some of these factors before others (Matthews, Lieven, Theakston & Tomasello, 2006). They tested at what age English children became sensitive to two of these factors: *perceptual availability* (whether the listener could perceive the referent, study 1) and *prior mention* in discourse (whether the referent had already been named, study 2). To test perceptual availability, they manipulated whether the listener could see the video that the child was describing. This was achieved simply by having the experimenter sit either next to the child (*addressee can see* condition) or opposite the child behind the television (*addressee can't see* condition). The results showed that three- and four-year-olds, but not two-year-olds, were significantly more likely to name the referent with a full noun in the *addressee can't see* condition (e.g. to say *the clown is jumping*). They were more likely to give pronoun or verb-only responses in the *addressee can see* condition (e.g. *he's jumping* or just *jumping*). In other words, by three, but not by two, years of age, the children were capable of taking account of what the listener could see and adapting their use of referring expressions appropriately.

In study 2 the researchers tested the effect of prior mention in discourse, by having a second experimenter ask the child to comment on what happened in the video. Importantly, in one condition (*noun given* condition), the second experimenter first introduced the referent before asking the question, thus establishing prior mention (e.g. *Was that the clown? Oh! What happened?*). In the other condition (*no noun* condition), the experimenter did not introduce the referent (*That sounds like fun! What happened?*). This time, even the two-year-olds showed evidence of adapting their use of referring expressions appropriately. They were significantly more likely to use full nouns (e.g. responding with *the clown's jumping*) in the *no-noun* condition than the *noun given* condition.

These two studies suggest that children become sensitive to different cues at different ages; sensitivity to prior mention occurs at a younger age than sensitivity to perceptual availability. However, the results of a later study by Salomo and colleagues suggest that even this picture may be over-simplified (Salomo, Graf, Lieven & Tomasello, 2011). In this study, the researchers manipulated whether the experimenter, rather than the child, heard the referents in prior discourse. The child was always present when the referent was mentioned but, in some conditions, the experimenter was not. In these circumstances, even the three-year-olds did not take account of prior mention, in the sense that they did not alter their answers to take account of whether the experimenter had heard the referents named in prior discourse. Taken together with the studies of Matthews and colleagues (2006), these findings suggest that children apply their knowledge of reference inconsistently because they are in the process of learning all the factors that they have to take into account.

In summary, it seems to take time for children to learn all the factors that influence referential choice. This is not surprising since there are many factors to pay attention to. It is likely that the child learns these constraints through increasing experience with conversations, especially situations in which their utterances are misunderstood by the listener. For example, Matthews, Butcher, Lieven & Tomasello (2012) reported that providing English two- and four-year-old children with specific feedback in the form of clarification questions increased the appropriateness of their use of referring expressions. The feedback helped children learn to adapt their expressions to the demands of the situation, providing more identifying information as and when needed.

6.3.3 Learning how to take turns

Holding a conversation requires two people to take turns at speaking. This requires the child to master a number of skills. First, the child has to pay attention to the topic of the conversation in order to decide what contribution she wants to make. Second, she has to plan her utterance carefully to ensure that it does not lead to communicative breakdown (i.e. to ensure that the listener will understand her). Third, she has to ensure that her utterance is both relevant and informative; it must build on what the previous speaker has said and add something new. Fourth, it has to be timed correctly; too quickly and she will interrupt the previous speaker, too slowly and there will be an embarrassing pause.

Research with infants suggests that the pattern of conversational turn-taking begins almost from birth. However, for the first few months, this interaction is governed exclusively by adults not infants. For example, in one of the first published studies on turn-taking, Snow (1977) analysed videos of two mothers interacting with their infants from three months of age. The following type of exchange was typical with three-month-old infants (Snow & Ferguson, 1977, p. 12):

Mother	Ann
	(smiles)
Oh what a nice little smile!	
Yes isn't that nice.	
There.	
There's a nice little smile.	(burps)
What a nice wind as well!	
Yes that's better isn't it?	
Yes.	

Yes.   (vocalises)

Yes!

There's a nice noise.

In fact, all of the children's burps, sneezes, coughs, yawns, smiles, laughs and vocalisations were commented upon and responded to by their mothers, as if they were playing a part in a conversation. Even when the mothers sang songs or nursery rhymes they did so as part of an interactive game in which the infant took turns providing actions, gestures or vocalisations.

Parents establish this pattern of turn-taking from very early on but the interactions become more sophisticated throughout the first three months of life. This probably occurs because infants become more responsive to their caregivers as they develop, starting to attend to and smile at others and to produce positive vocalisations such as cooing. Henning and colleagues analysed the interactions of German infants and mothers and reported significant changes in how the mothers interacted with their infants between one and three months of age (Henning, Strianoa & Lieven, 2005). At one month, the mothers tended to talk in simple sentences, but these became longer as their infants aged, incorporating a greater diversity of words. This progression seemed to reflect a change in the mothers' goals from simply establishing contact with, and preventing fussiness in, their one-month-olds to a focus on real communication with their three-month-olds. By three months of age, it seems that parents are already engaging in a simple form of turn-taking behaviour, in which they treat the infants as communicative partners in a conversation.

Given that infants have been engaging in turn-taking behaviour from three months of age, we might expect them to be very good at it when they later learn to talk. In support, there is evidence that children are good at turn-taking in certain situations, in the sense that they are able to engage in a fluent conversation with a caregiver. For example, an important part of turn-taking is that the child makes his contribution relevant and appropriate given the previous speaker's turn. Children as young as two years of age seem to be capable of this. Dunn and Shatz analysed the conversations between 24-month-old English children and their mothers and reported that 89 per cent of the infants' responses to the speech addressed to them was appropriate to the topic of conversation (Dunn & Shatz, 1989). By two years of age, then, children seem capable of taking turns successfully to maintain conversations.

However, these findings are based on conversations between the child and a highly cooperative conversational partner who is likely to be tolerant of children's mistakes. Thus, it may be that the conversation continues successfully simply because of adult willingness to adapt to the child rather than because of the child's turn-taking skills. In support of this view, research looking at how children engage in turn-taking in multi-party conversations shows that young children's turns are often irrelevant, off-topic and are frequently ignored. For example, Dunn and Shatz (1989), in the study reported above, also analysed the infant attempts to join in with conversations between their mother and an older sibling. They found that two-year-olds were far less successful at this aspect of turn-taking. Approximately 51 per cent of their intrusions were irrelevant to the ongoing conversation, as in the example below:

Child to mother:	I want a drink. [Mother ignores request.]
[2 min later]:	
Mother to sibling:	Daddy brought the box home for you.
Sibling to mother:	Has it got a lock?
Child to mother:	I want a drink.

(Dunn & Shatz, 1989, p. 403)

Even when they were relevant, the infants' intrusions often failed to add new information to the conversation, an important part of maintaining the flow of a conversation:

Sibling to mother:	I got my shopping list in.
Child to mother:	I got my shopping list!

(Dunn & Shatz, 1989, p. 403)

Timing is another aspect of turn-taking that children find difficult. It has been estimated that in adult conversations, the gaps between speaker turns are only about 250 milliseconds long (Stivers et al., 2009). The gaps between turns in conversations between three-year-olds are much longer: about 1.5 seconds (Lieberman & Garvey, 1977). This is a factor that affects infants' contributions to multi-party conversation in particular; they often miss their turn in the conversation because they find it difficult to anticipate the end of the previous speaker's utterance and to plan their own contribution accordingly. Children's difficulties with timing are probably made more severe by the fact that they may not have mastered the use of 'floor holders' such as *um* and *ah*, which adults use to indicate to listeners that they are planning a contribution to the conversation (Clark & Fox Tree, 2002; Hudson Kam & Edwards, 2008). In conversation with one adult, especially if that adult is a familiar caregiver, these delays matter less.

Thus, even though infants are exposed to turn-taking behaviour from a very young age, it takes them many years to master it, especially in multi-party conversations. Paradoxically, it may be the most challenging conversational situations that are the most useful for the child's learning. Conversational breakdowns, in which the listener fails to understand the child's utterance, are more frequent in conversations with unfamiliar adults, who are consequently more likely to request that the child repeat or clarify her utterance (Mannle & Tomasello, 1987). Berko Gleason (1975) has suggested that these types of challenging interaction can serve as learning experiences, helping children identify what aspects of their conversations are problematic and helping them learn how to address these difficulties.

6.4 COMMUNICATIVE IMPAIRMENTS

Many children have impairments that affect successful communication. Children with autism famously have communication difficulties, even though other aspects of language such as syntax are often unproblematic. Children with specific language impairment can also have difficulty communicating, although in this case the problems are usually caused by language impairments, particularly in phonology and syntax. Children with pragmatic language impairment have similar difficulties to children with autism, but without some of the impairments in social interaction that come with autism.

However it has proven difficult to identify what causes these difficulties and to establish how they link with other language and socio-cognitive difficulties. For example, many autistic children seem to develop good competence in phonology, syntax and vocabulary, despite sometimes severe communicative impairments. What, then, causes their communication difficulties? Also at issue is the question of how to distinguish between different categories of impairment, and to what extent these impairments overlap. In this section we will discuss both these issues by addressing the key question:

Key question: why do some children have communication impairments?

6.4.1 Children with autism

Children who have been diagnosed with one of the autistic spectrum disorders such as autism or Asperger's syndrome often find it difficult to communicate their own thoughts effectively and to infer the communicative intentions behind the utterances of others. In fact, impairments in communication are one of the three diagnostic features of autistic disorder (see figure 6.1 for the diagnostic criteria).[4] These difficulties are apparent in a number of areas.

Unlike typically developing children, children with autism often fail to produce and comprehend gestures such as proto-declarative pointing (Baron-Cohen, 1989). Children with autism are also reported to use language for a restricted range of functions. In particular, they tend not to use language to call for attention or to talk about their own beliefs, ideas and understanding (Tager-Flusberg, 1992). Pronoun reversal errors are also more common in the speech of children with autism; for example, using *you* instead of *I* and vice versa (e.g. *pick you up* instead of *pick me up*, Lee, Hobson & Chiat, 1994). Both children and adults with autism often find it difficult to take turns appropriately in a conversation, either introducing irrelevant information or failing to add new information (Tager-Flusberg & Anderson, 1991). Finally, perhaps the most famous characteristic of autistic communication is a

---

4   The criteria in figure 6.1 are taken from the DSM IV, as described in the APA Manual (2000). This was replaced in 2013 by the DSM V. However, some researchers and clinicians have expressed concerns about the classification of autism and other developmental disorders in the DSM V, so the DSM IV diagnostic criteria are referenced here (see Norbury, 2013, for a discussion).

Figure 6.1

Diagnostic criteria for autistic disorder. Reprinted from American Psychiatric Association (2000).

A. A total of six (or more) items from (1), (2), and (3), with at least two from (1), and one each from (2) and (3):

(1) qualitative impairment in social interaction, as manifested by at least two of the following:

    (a) marked impairment in the use of multiple nonverbal behaviours such as eye-to-eye gaze, facial expression, body postures, and gestures to regulate social interaction

    (b) failure to develop peer relationships appropriate to developmental level

    (c) a lack of spontaneous seeking to share enjoyment, interests, or achievements with other people (e.g. by a lack of showing, bringing, or pointing out objects of interest)

    (d) lack of social or emotional reciprocity

(2) qualitative impairments in communication as manifested by at least one of the following:

    (a) delay in, or total lack of, the development of spoken language (not accompanied by an attempt to compensate through alternative modes of communication such as gesture or mime)

    (b) in individuals with adequate speech, marked impairments in the ability to initiate or sustain a conversation with others

    (c) stereotyped and repetitive use of language or idiosyncratic language

    (d) lack of varied, spontaneous make-believe play or social imitative play appropriate to developmental level

(3) restricted repetitive and stereotyped patterns of behaviour, interests, and activities, as manifested by at least:

    (a) encompassing preoccupation with one or more stereotyped and restricted patterns of interest that is abnormal either in intensity or focus

    (b) apparently inflexible adherence to specific, non-functional routines or rituals

    (c) stereotyped and repetitive motor mannerisms (e.g. hand or finger flapping or twisting, or complex whole body movements)

    (d) persistent preoccupation with parts of objects

B. Delays or abnormal functioning in at least one of the following areas, with onset prior to age 3 years: (1) social interaction, (2) language as used in social communication, or (3) symbolic or imaginative play.

C. The disturbance is not better accounted for by Rett's Disorder or Childhood Disintegrative Disorder difficulty interpreting non-literal and figurative language, including the use of irony and metaphor (see Happé, 1993). Irony and metaphor can only be understood if the listener can distinguish between an utterance's literal and intended meaning. This is because the utterance itself, taken literally, either expresses the opposite meaning to that intended in the case of irony (e.g. *You only got 9 out of 10? What went wrong?*) or is nonsensical in the case of metaphor (e.g. *it's raining men*). A difficulty understanding the speaker's intended meaning is characteristic of autism and is apparent both in children and adults. In fact, many of the communicative difficulties that are characteristics of autism are just as prevalent in adults as in children (see Tager-Flusberg, 2000, for a review).

The cause of these problems in autism is unknown. One possibility is a deficit in understanding *theory of mind*. Theory of mind refers to our ability to guess what may be going through the minds of others. In other words, theory of mind allows us to infer "the full range of mental states (beliefs, desires, intentions, imagination, emotions etc.) that cause action" (Baron-Cohen, 2000, p. 3). For example, if you heard that a friend had passed an important exam you would probably infer that she would be feeling happy and excited. You might also assume that she was likely to go out to celebrate. You can only do this because you have theory of mind, which allows you to guess your friend's likely state of mind. A deficit in theory of mind understanding is a classic symptom of autism, and may have an important role in the communicative impairments of children, given that successful communication relies on being able to infer what message the speaker intends to convey.

There is some evidence for this view in the fact that performance on theory of mind tasks correlates with the communicative abilities of children and adults with autism. For example, Happé (1993) compared the performance of three groups of adults with autism on a metaphor task.[5] The first group had previously failed to pass even the simplest theory of mind tasks (*no-ToM* group), the second group had passed simple but not complex theory of mind tasks (*1st order-ToM* group) and the third had passed both simple and complex tasks (*2nd order-ToM* group). For the metaphor task, the children simply had to complete metaphorical sentences by choosing an appropriate word from a list (e.g. on hearing *The dancer was so graceful. She really was a …*, the appropriate word to choose would be *swan*). The *no-ToM* group chose the wrong word significantly more often than either of the other groups, despite the fact that the groups were of roughly the same age and cognitive ability level. In other words, the ability of children with autism to comprehend metaphor was predicted by their theory of mind ability.

However, other aspects of communicative difficulty are not so easily explained by a theory of mind deficit. Norbury (2013) gave inference as an example of an ability that is impaired in children with autism but is difficult to explain in terms of theory of mind. Inference is important for inferring missing elements in a sequence of sentences. For example, on hearing *John walked into the room and reached into the bag for his torch*, most listeners would normally make the inference that the room

---

5   Happé also examined simile and irony understanding but we have not reported these results here.

was dark. This inference does not rely on the listener interpreting John's state of mind but on integrating the information given in the sentence with prior knowledge of the world (that one needs a torch in the dark). It is, thus, difficult to see how the inferencing problems of children with autism might be caused by a theory of mind deficit.

As a result, others have suggested that the communication difficulties of children with autism can be attributed to *weak central coherence* (Frith, 1989). This is the idea that people with autism find it difficult to integrate different sources of information into a coherent whole. On this view, inference is difficult because it requires integrating knowledge of the world (e.g. that one needs a torch in the dark) with the information given in the sentence (e.g. that John reached for his torch). In support, there is evidence that individuals with autism do not integrate different pieces of information in a sentence when interpreting homograph pairs. Homographs are words that are spelt the same but have different sounds and meanings (e.g. *tear in the eye* vs. *tear in a dress*). This means that reading homographs requires the reader to pay attention to the information given in the rest of the sentence in order to extract the correct meaning and pronunciation.

Happé (1997) asked teenagers with autism (mean age 17 years) and younger typically developing children (mean age seven years) to read aloud sentences containing homographs. Half of the homographs were preceded by a context that gave clues to the correct pronunciation (e.g. *Molly was very happy, but in Lilian's eye there was a big **tear***). In these sentences, by the time the children came to read the homograph, they had already received relevant information that should help them decide which pronunciation to use. The teenagers with autism were significantly less likely than the typically developing children to use the clues to help them pronounce the homographs correctly. Interestingly, this was the case even for the children with autism who passed advanced theory of mind tests. This suggests that their problems using context cannot be attributed to deficits in theory of mind understanding. Happé concluded that individuals with autism have problems integrating information in context, supporting the weak central coherence theory of communicative impairment.

However, there is also evidence that the severity of communicative impairments in autism might stem from delayed language acquisition. Although many children with high functioning autism often develop language to the same levels as typically developing children, some children with autism have a range of language difficulties. For example, Kjelgaard and Tager-Flusberg (2001) administered a battery of language tests to 89 children with autism aged four to 14 years and reported that about three-quarters of the children scored significantly below age expectations in the tests of phonology, vocabulary and syntax. Thus, it may be that the communicative impairments we see in autism can be attributed to difficulties understanding words and sentences.

However, just showing that some children with autism have language difficulties does not tell us whether these cause the communicative impairments. For this, we need to compare the performance of children with and without language impairments on communication tasks. These comparative studies do indeed suggest that language difficulties play a part in communication difficulties. For example, Norbury (2005) assessed the performance of children with autism with and without language impairment on a lexical ambiguity test. This test assessed the children's ability to integrate different bits of information within a sentence to determine the meaning of an ambiguous word. For example, on hearing the sentence *the man fished from the bank*, it is possible to use the meaning of the word *fished* to infer that the most likely referent for the word *bank* is a river bank (not a building in which we deposit money).

The children were instructed to listen to a sentence containing an ambiguous word (e.g. *bank*) and then decide whether a picture would 'fit' the meaning of the sentence (e.g. a picture of a river bank). Some of the sentences contained cues to the meaning of the ambiguous word that could facilitate the children's response to the picture (e.g. *the man fished from the bank*). Other, control, sentences contained no facilitating information (e.g. *he ran from the bank*). The researchers reported that the performance of children with autism who had no diagnosed language impairment was similar to that of a control group of typically developing children. Both groups were more accurate at responding to the pictures after hearing a sentence with facilitating information. This information, however, had little effect on the performance of the children with autism who had associated language impairment. In fact, their performance was similar to that of a group of children diagnosed with specific language impairment who did not have autism. In other words, both groups of children with language impairment, those with and without autism, found it difficult to use contextual information to determine the fit between a sentence and a picture. Norbury concluded that the data did not support the central coherence theory, because that theory predicts difficulties with facilitation across all children with autism, not just those with language impairment. Instead, difficulties with facilitation seemed to be related to language ability, regardless of autistic status.

However, language difficulties cannot be the sole cause of communication difficulties in autism for one simple reason. Many children with the communicative difficulties so characteristic of autism, perhaps a quarter, have language skills within the normal range (see Kjelgaard & Tager-Flusberg, 2001). In addition, children's problems with vocabulary and syntax are often much less severe than their problems with communication and are less likely to continue into adulthood (Lord & Paul, 1997; Rapin & Dunn, 2003). These findings mean that it is unlikely that the communication difficulties of children with autism can be attributed solely to problems learning language.

In summary, children with autism are universally impaired in their ability to communicate with others. However, it is not clear why this is the case. There is evidence for a role for theory of mind deficits, for weak central coherence and for poor structural language skills, but none provides a complete explanation. The conclusion of most researchers is thus summed up by Tager-Flusberg: autism is "clearly understood to be a complex and heterogeneous set of related developmental disorders in which no single cognitive mechanism or cause can account for the variety of symptoms and range in their expression" (Tager-Flusberg, 2007, p. 311).

6.4.2 Pragmatic language impairment

Since the mid twentieth century researchers and clinicians have been discussing how to classify language impairments effectively. There are children with autism who clearly have difficulties with the pragmatic aspects of language. There are children with specific language impairment (SLI) who have difficulties with the structural aspects of language, especially phonology and syntax. There may even be children with autism who have an associated diagnosis of SLI. However, some researchers have proposed a third distinct group of children whose profile seems to fit neither that of autism nor that of SLI (Bishop & Rosenbloom, 1987; Rapin & Allen, 1983, 1987). These children were originally identified as having a 'semantic-pragmatic disorder'. However, the word 'semantic' was later dropped when researchers reported that tests of semantic ability did not distinguish these children from those with specific language impairment (Bishop, 1998). The term *pragmatic language impairment* (PLI) was proposed as an alternative by Bishop and is now more widely used (see Bishop, 2000).

Children with PLI have problems using language in social situations, despite sometimes good structural language skills (phonology, vocabulary and syntax). They may be able to produce fluent, complex, expressive speech but they tend to use this language in an atypical way (see Bishop & Rosenbloom, 1987; Rapin & Allen, 1983, 1987 for fuller descriptions). For example, children with PLI may have difficulty maintaining the topic of a conversation, with a tendency to interject information that is off-topic or to provide too much or too little background information. Like children with autism, they may misunderstand jokes, metaphors and irony and have problems making inferences (e.g. to infer that the room is dark from hearing *John walked into the room and reached into the bag for his torch*). A characteristic problem is difficulty retrieving words to describe pictures in word finding tasks, producing some very unusual errors. For example, Botting and Conti-Ramsden (1999) noted that, faced with a picture they could not name, children with PLI tended to join words together in unusual ways, producing *stickfire* (for matches), *bedtime uniform* (for pyjamas) and *bumblenest* (for beehive). In contrast, children with SLI, faced with the same problem, tended to rely on a more typical strategy of substituting alternative words with similar meanings such as *bottle* (for jar) or *weigher* (for scales).

The communication problems experienced by children with PLI are very similar to those experienced by children with autism. This has prompted a challenge from researchers who argue that PLI is simply a form of high-functioning autism (see Gagnon, Mottron & Joanette, 1997). On this view, children with PLI have communication difficulties simply because they have an autistic disorder. Evidence for this view comes from studies demonstrating that children with PLI and autism show very similar profiles of impairment. For example, Shields and colleagues assessed children with PLI (though they called it semantic-pragmatic disorder) on tests of socio-cognition, which measure how well we process information in social situations (e.g. theory of mind abilities, detecting the direction of someone's eye gaze; Shields, Varley, Broks & Simpson, 1996). A range of difficulties in these abilities is characteristic of autism, so similar problems in children with PLI might indicate that these children should be diagnosed with an autistic spectrum disorder.

Shields and colleagues administered four socio-cognitive tests to children with PLI and children with autism, and compared their performance with that of groups of typically developing children and children with specific language impairment (SLI). All children were English and were aged between seven and 11 years. Across all four measures, the children with PLI and those with autism had significantly lower scores than the typically developing and SLI groups. However, there were no significant differences in performance between the children with PLI and those with autism. In other words, the children with PLI showed the same characteristic problems in socio-cognition as children with autism. The authors concluded that the results "support the opinion that 'semantic-pragmatic disorder' is a disorder of the autistic spectrum" which, like autism, "may result from, or be associated with, an underlying cognitive deficit which is not primarily linguistic in nature" (Shields et al., 1996, p. 492).

In response, however, a number of authors have noted that some children with pragmatic language impairments do not have other autistic features. To be diagnosed with an autistic disorder according to the DSM-IV (see figure 6.1), children must have impairments in social interaction and show evidence of restricted or stereotyped patterns of behaviour, as well as having impairments in communication. Studies suggest that many children with communication impairments do not meet these criteria (Bishop, 1998, 2000; Bishop & Norbury, 2002; Botting & Conti-Ramsden, 1999).

For example, Bishop and Norbury (2002) identified children with PLI (aged seven to nine years) and assessed their abilities in language, communication and social interaction. To assess communication and language skills, teachers were asked to rate the children's abilities on a rating scale called the Children's Communication Checklist (CCC; Bishop, 1998). Data were also obtained from three 'gold standard' autism scales; the Autism Diagnostic Observation Schedule, the Autism Diagnostic Interview and the Social Communication Questionnaire (Berument, Rutter, Lord, Pickles & Bailey, 1999; Lord, Rutter & Le Couteur, 1994; Lord et al., 2000). These are designed to assess whether children can be diagnosed with disorders like autism by assessing their abilities in social interaction, communication, play/imagination and repetitive behaviours. The study found that a substantial number of children who met the criteria for PLI did not meet the criteria for autism. Using conventional diagnostic criteria for autism, they showed that only 21 per cent of the children identified with PLI also met the criteria for autism. The other 79 per cent of children had good social interaction skills and showed no evidence of the repetitive non-verbal behaviour that is characteristic of autism (e.g. hand or finger flapping).

Bishop and Norbury were, however, very keen to emphasise that they do not consider PLI and autism to be completely separable categories. They wrote "the findings of these studies have reinforced our view that there are no sharp dividing lines between SLI and PLI on the one hand, and PLI and autistic disorder on the other" (Bishop & Norbury, 2002, p. 927). As we find in autism, there seems to be a range of structural language difficulties among children with PLI, some of which are similar to those seen in typical SLI (Norbury, Nash, Baird & Bishop, 2004).

Furthermore, some of the children with PLI studied by Norbury and Bishop met the criteria for autistic disorder, and others would have met less stringent criteria (e.g. meeting the criteria on one of the autism measures but not on the others). In fact, even some of the children with a diagnosis of typical specific language impairment were reported by their parents to have some autistic symptoms.

As a result, many researchers advocate a dimensional, rather than a categorical, view of language impairments. For example, Bishop proposed a continuum model with two dimensions on which children can vary; one dimension for communication and another for social relationships and interests (Bishop, 2003). Children with impairments on both the communication and the social dimension would be diagnosed with autism. Children with impairments in social interaction but not communication would be diagnosed with Asperger's syndrome. Children with communication difficulties but unimpaired social interactions would be diagnosed with PLI.

The dimensional model provides a neat way to capture the differences between social and communicative impairments but one cautionary note must be sounded. Many studies have demonstrated that the pattern of impairments can change substantially with age, which means that young children who meet the criteria for autism may no longer do so if assessed in adolescence or adulthood. Mawhood and Howlin demonstrated this quite conclusively in a study in which they contacted adults (aged on average 24 years) who had originally been studied by Bartak and colleagues at seven or eight years of age (Bartak, Rutter & Cox, 1975; Mawhood & Howlin, 2000). In the original study, it had been relatively simple to distinguish children with structural language impairment from those with the communication difficulties typical of autism. However, these differences were far less pronounced in adulthood. In fact, the adults who were originally diagnosed with language impairment experienced a much wider range of communication difficulties than the researchers expected, so much so that it was often difficult to distinguish them from adults who were originally diagnosed with autism. Typical difficulties included problems sustaining conversations and reporting on events, as well as immature syntax and what the researchers called "prosodic oddities" (odd speech rhythm, speech stress or intonation; Mawhood & Howlin, 2000, p. 555). It is not clear why this is the case. It may be that sophisticated language abilities become far more important for communication in adulthood, so that those with language impairments find it hard to communicate successfully. However, it is clear that the age of the child at test must be taken into account when identifying similarities and differences between children with language impairment and autism.

6.5 CHAPTER SUMMARY

In this chapter, we discovered that successful communication requires that the child learns both to interpret a sentence's literal meaning and to interpret a speaker's intended meaning by drawing on her knowledge of the situation, the real world and the mental state of the speaker.

Successful communication between children and adults begins before children learn their first word, through the use of communicative actions such as pointing gestures. However, the extent to which infants are interpreting the communicative intention behind the gestures of others is disputed. Thus, the first key question was:

Are infants and young children capable of interpreting the communicative intentions of others?

We discussed research showing that from about nine months of age, infants behave as if they understand what others are trying to communicate. They also seem capable of interpreting intended and accidental actions differently soon after their first birthday. However, there are two possible interpretations of these behaviours; the rich and the lean interpretation views, with disagreements centring on the age at which knowledge of communicative intent can be attributed to infants.

We also debated whether the early communicative abilities of infants provide them with a crucial first step in the language learning process, as suggested by social-pragmatic theorists. Here we addressed the key question:

What role do infants' early communicative abilities play in word learning?

There is some evidence to support social-pragmatic theory, but nearly all of it comes from Western cultures. More evidence from different cultures is required to determine whether the link between early abilities and later language learning is universal.

Given the early sophisticated communicative abilities of infants, we might expect them to be very good at holding conversations once they learn to talk. However, research suggests that children find it difficult to adjust what they are saying in response to their listener and to interpret the message behind a speaker's words. Thus, we asked the key question:

Why is successful conversation so difficult for children?

We addressed this question by exploring three areas: the development of scalar implicature, the use of referring expressions and learning how to take turns. In some cases, it turned out that children were more proficient than we originally thought. The apparent problems stemmed from the fact that our experimental designs were not sensitive enough to reveal children's knowledge. In other cases, the children's lack of ability could be explained by the fact that holding a conversation requires children to master a range of different skills, some of which require extensive experience with the language. In fact, in some cases, children may learn most from their unsuccessful attempts at conversation, as these can help them identify what aspects of their conversations are problematic.

Finally, we looked at communicative impairments, focussing on autism and pragmatic language impairments. We addressed the key question:

Why do some children have communication impairments?

We first looked at autism. Communicative impairments are central to a diagnosis of autism, yet the reasons why are unclear. Three explanations were discussed – theory of mind theory, central coherence theory and language deficit theory – but none fully explains the pattern of impairments. We then discussed pragmatic language impairment, which, like autism, is characterised by difficulties in communication. We debated whether pragmatic language impairment should be seen as separate from autism. However, one factor that makes the accurate diagnosis of communication impairment difficult is the fact that children change so substantially through development. This means that children who meet the criteria for one diagnosis when young may no longer do so in adolescence or adulthood. It is crucial that researchers and clinicians take account of both the age of the child and how the child's profile of impairment changes with development.

6.6 SUGGESTED READING

Matthews, D. E (2013). *Pragmatic development in first language acquisition.* Amsterdam: John Benjamins. A comprehensive overview of the latest research in pragmatic development.

6.7 SUGGESTED READING (ADVANCED LEVEL)

Clark, E. V. M. & Amaral, P. M. (2010). Children build on pragmatic information in language. *Language and Linguistic Compass, 4*(7), 445–457. A concise summary of the literature.

Kita, S. (Ed.). (2003*). Pointing. Where language, culture, and cognition meet.* Hillsdale, NJ: Erlbaum. An in-depth summary of pointing research across ages, cultures and species.

Ninio, A. & Snow, C. (1996). *Pragmatic development.* Boulder, CO: Westview Press. A thorough, readable summary written by two influential social-pragmatic theorists.

Two readable, comprehensive overviews of the literature on communicative impairments:

Bishop, D. V. M. (2000). Pragmatic language impairment: A correlate of SLI, a distinct subgroup, or part of the autistic continuum? In D. V. M. Bishop & L. B. Leonard (Eds), *Speech and language impairments in children: Causes, characteristics, intervention and outcome* (pp. 99–113). Hove, UK: Psychology Press.

Tager-Flusberg, H. (2007). Language and understanding minds: Connections in autism. In S. Baron-Cohen, H. Tager-Flusberg and D. J. Cohen (Eds), *Understanding other minds: Perspectives from developmental cognitive neuroscience* (2nd ed.; pp. 1–45). Oxford: Oxford University Press.

6.8 COMPREHENSION CHECK

1. What is the key difference between the rich interpretation and lean interpretation views of infant communicative behaviours?

2. According to the social-pragmatic theory of language development, what is required for children to learn language?

3. Explain what is meant by the term scalar implicature.

4. Explain what is meant when we say that reference words lie on a scale of accessibility.

5. What does the study by Dunn and Shatz (1989) tell us about children's ability to take turns in a) a conversation with familiar caregivers and b) a multi-party conversation?

6. Briefly describe the a) theory of mind theory, b) weak central cohesion theory and c) language deficit theory of communicative impairment in autism.

7. What are the key differences between specific language impairment, pragmatic language impairment and autism?

Multilingual language acquisition

7.1 THE ISSUE

Many of us who live in Western Europe or in the USA tend to assume that learning one language in childhood is the norm. However, this is not the case. In 1982, Grosjean estimated that half of the world's children grow up in multilingual environments (Grosjean, 1982). For many of these children, multilingualism is necessary if they are to communicate effectively. For example, Ethnologue lists 69 languages spoken in Kenya, including the two official languages Kiswahil and English (see www. ethnologue.com). In the Philippines, children learn one of up to 70 languages at home, before being introduced to English and Tagalog at school (Galang, 1988). Even in predominantly monolingual speaking countries like Britain and the USA, there are large bilingual and even trilingual communities.

This means that if we want to learn how all children acquire language we need to study multilingual children. However, this is not simple. The basic problem is one of definition – what do we mean by a multilingual child? On one level the answer is simple – a multilingual child is a child who speaks and understands more than one language. However, it is not really possible to lump all multilinguals together in the same category. In fact, multilinguals differ quite substantially from one another when it comes to their language acquisition.

One factor that has a major effect on multilingual language development is the age at which the child starts to learn each language (*age of acquisition*). Some children learn two languages in the home from birth (*simultaneous multilingualism*). Other children start to learn one language first and then learn another later in life (*sequential multilingualism*). Many of these children are from migrant families who have settled in a country where most people speak a different language. Still other children live in bilingual communities, where two languages are used freely (e.g. parts of Quebec in Canada) or where the language used in school and at work is different from the home language (this is often the situation in countries like Kenya and Nigeria, which were formerly part of the British Empire).

A second issue to consider is the type and amount of input that the children are receiving. Sometimes, both languages are provided by the parents, so the child will be exposed to both languages in the home in roughly equal proportions. Alternatively, the second language may be provided by a grandparent or a nanny, which means that the amount of exposure to the second language will depend on how much time the grandparent or nanny spends with the child. In other families, the parents only speak one language, so the child only hears the second language outside the home. This is the case for many immigrant families.

A third factor to consider is the situation. Children who are equally competent in two languages (*balanced bilinguals*) are relatively rare. For most, one language is dominant, and this is often the community language rather than the home language. However, even for balanced bilinguals, competence may differ according to the situation. Children who have learnt Hindi at home and English at school may be better at talking about home-related topics in Hindi (cooking a meal, doing household chores, talking about family members) and better at academic topics in English (maths, history, literature). Or they may be better at holding a conversation in Hindi, but be better at reading and writing in English.

These factors, as well as others, make it difficult to study multilingualism. In designing our studies we have to be careful to ensure the results can be attributed to multilingualism and not to a different aspect of the children's situation. For example, what might we conclude from a study that shows that bilingual children develop language more slowly than monolingual children? We might want to conclude that bilingualism slows down development. But this would be premature. Many bilingual children are from immigrant families whose social and economic circumstances are difficult. Since children in difficult circumstances tend to develop language more slowly, the delay in language development may be caused by the difficult circumstances, not bilingualism per se. The only way to be certain is to include family circumstances in our analyses. We might record details of family background and control for this statistically. Alternatively, we could restrict our participant groups to children from one socio-economic group, and compare their development with monolingual children from a similar background. Because of these problems, evaluating research on multilingual children is always tricky. The reader should always ask him- or herself this question: what other factors could have contributed to these results and have the researchers controlled for these?

Despite the difficulties, we now know quite a lot about how bilingual children – children exposed to two languages – learn language. Unfortunately we know far less about children learning three or more languages, because nearly all of the studies that have been published refer to bilingual acquisition. It may be, for example, that the trilingual and bilingual children learn language in very similar ways but we cannot make this assumption until we know more about trilingualism. As a result, the focus here will be on bilingualism. Research on bilingual language falls into three broad camps: research investigating how children represent their two languages, research investigating what predicts a successful outcome for bilingual acquisition and research investigating the effect that bilingualism itself has on cognitive development in general.

7.2 ONE SYSTEM OR TWO?

Key question: are the bilingual child's two languages learnt via two distinct and separate systems or is there a single representation incorporating both languages?

How quickly and easily do children learn to distinguish between the languages that they hear? A very influential view for a number of years was the idea that children are unable to distinguish between their two languages, at least in the early stages. The most famous paper advocating this *unitary language hypothesis* was that of Volterra and Taeschner (1978). These authors proposed a three-stage model of bilingual development, based on their observations of three children who were growing up bilingual; one English–German speaking child and two Italian–German speaking children.

At *stage one* of development, Volterra and Taeschner suggested that the children had only one language system, which included words from both languages. At this stage, the children had very few *translation equivalent words*; which means that if they had a word in one language they tended not to have a word with a similar meaning in their other language. When they did have similar words, they tended to use them for different meanings. For example, Lisa (aged 1;10)[1] used the Italian word for *there* (*là*) for things that she could not see and the German word (*da*) for things that were clearly present and visible. In other words, the children behaved as if they did not know that they were learning two languages.

It was not until *stage two* that the children became capable of distinguishing between the words of the two languages (i.e. they had two *lexical systems*). However, even at stage two, they still seemed to apply the same syntactic rules to both languages (one *syntax system*). For example, to speak Italian and German correctly, the speaker must use different rules to indicate possession; Italians use one word order (*di*; e.g. *I capelli di Maria*, lit., 'the hair of Maria') but Germans use another (*s*; e.g. *Marias Haare* 'Maria's hair'). German–Italian learning Lisa used the same word order in both languages for a time, producing both *Giulia Buch* ('Giulia's book') in German and *Giulia giamma* ('Giulia's pyjamas') in Italian. It was not until *stage three* that the children started to use two separate lexicons and two separate systems of grammar.

7.2.1 Language-mixing: evidence for the unitary language hypothesis?

The problem with Volterra and Taeschner's (1978) study was that they did not provide solid evidence for their hypothesis. They gave examples of the types of utterance that the children produced, but there was no evidence that these were commonplace or typical of the children's speech. Better evidence for the unitary language hypothesis came from numerous reports of language mixing in bilingual children's utterances. Mixed language utterances are those which contain elements from both languages mixed together; for example, Giulia's *Mama ich will prendere ja?* ('Mummy, I want to take, yes?') is a mixture of German and Italian (see Volterra & Taeschner, 1978). Mixed utterances have been reported in most studies of bilingual development and are considered to be typical of bilingual development (see McLaughlin, 1978, for a summary). Most common seems to be lexical mixing, where one or two words from one language are inserted into a sentence made up of words from the other language.

---

1   1;10 indicates that Lisa was aged one year and 10 months.

However, we also find *phonological mixing, morphological mixing, syntactic mixing* and *pragmatic mixing*. Table 7.1 illustrates some examples of language mixing taken from Genesee (1989).

The prevalence of mixed utterances in bilingual children's speech gave the unitary language hypothesis more weight. It seemed logical to assume that children switch between the two languages because they think they are learning one language (Deuchar & Quay, 1998; Redlinger & Park, 1980; Swain, 1972, 1977). Further support was provided by studies indicating that the amount of language mixing reduced as the children aged, which is consistent with a developmental progression from an initial unitary system to two separate systems. Language mixing seemed to provide good evidence for the unitary language hypothesis.

Table 7.1
Types of language mixing described in Genesee (1989)

Type of language mixing	Example	Explanation of mixing
Lexical/phrasal mixing	*Putzen Zähne con jabón* 'Brushing teeth with soap'	The first two words are German and last two are Spanish.
Phonological mixing	*Kats* 'cat'	A mixture of Swedish *katt* (cat) mixed with Estonian *kass* (cat)
Morphological mixing	*pfeifting* 'whistling'	German word combined with the English progressive ending (-*ing*)
Syntactic mixing	*A house pink*	English phrase with French word order
Pragmatic mixing	*Laisse les barrettes, touche pas les barrettes, Papa. Me's gonna put it back in the bag so no one's gonna took it.* translation of French: 'Leave the hair slides alone, don't touch the hair slides, Daddy'	Child switches from French to English to elicit parental attention and emphasise that her father must not take away the hair slides.

This evidence also led some to conclude that bilingualism is disadvantageous; that children who hear two languages from birth will be confused by their input and will be delayed. Unfortunately, this view meant that some educators and paediatricians advised parents not to bring their children up as bilingual speakers. I say unfortunately, because it turns out that language mixing does not mean that children are confused about their two languages. Bialystok makes the relevant point very neatly: "It is one thing to notice that children appear to use languages interchangeably in the early stages, but it is another to argue that this behavior indicates a lack of differentiation in children's minds" (Bialystok, 2001, p. 108). In other words, just because children mix up their languages in their speech does not necessarily mean that they mix up their languages in their mind.

The evidence against the idea that language mixing results from a unitary language system can be broadly divided into two categories: studies demonstrating flaws in the methodology of the original studies, and studies supporting alternative explanations of why language mixing occurs. The most influential methodological critique of the unitary language hypothesis of mixing was provided by Genesee (1989). He pointed out that most of the evidence for the hypothesis consists of simple descriptions or illustrative examples of mixed utterances produced by bilingual children, rather than systematic investigations of why language mixing might occur in particular contexts. The evidence, Genesee claimed, was "simply not sufficient to support" the theory (Genesee, 1989, p. 165). For example, Redlinger and Park (1980) reported that the rate of mixing in four bilingual children's speech reduced with development. They concluded that this occurred as the children started to develop two different language systems. However, as Genesee (1989) points out, the researchers failed to rule out a plausible alternative explanation: that the children mixed because they had a limited vocabulary in both languages and thus borrowed words from the other language to make themselves understood. Redlinger and Park should have included vocabulary size as a predictor in their analysis. This would have allowed them to test whether children used language mixing as a strategy to make themselves understood when their vocabulary let them down.

The second type of evidence against the hypothesis shows that when we test alternative explanations of language mixing against the unitary language hypothesis, the alternative explanations fare better. For example, as we saw above, one alternative explanation is that bilingual children use language mixing to fill in gaps in their vocabulary knowledge (the gap-filling hypothesis; see Deuchar & Quay, 2000). Genesee and Nicoladis (2006) described an unpublished study (Genesee, Paradis & Wolf, 1995) in which the researchers tested this explanation using diary data from two bilingual children. They asked the parents of the children to keep diary records of everything their children said between 1;8 and 2;0 years of age. They then investigated the situations in which the children mixed their languages. They were particularly keen to know whether children mixed in order to fill gaps in vocabulary knowledge. For example, when a child used the English word *dog* instead of the French word for dog (*chien*) during a conversation in French, was this because he did not know the word *chien* (the *translation equivalent*)? The results showed that this was, indeed, the case. The children were much more likely to slot words from the 'wrong' language into their speech when they did not know the appropriate word in the 'right' language. In fact, one of the children, Wayne, only mixed those words for which he had no appropriate translation equivalent. The researchers concluded that the data support the idea that language mixing is used by children as a sensible strategy to fill in gaps in their vocabulary.

Another alternative explanation is that language mixing actually reflects a sophisticated understanding of when it is appropriate to use each language. What the unitary language theorists had failed to recognise was that language mixing also occurs in adult bilinguals (where it is called code switching; Sridhar & Sridhar, 1980). Studies of adult code switching have demonstrated that bilinguals often switch between languages in the course of a conversation for a variety of reasons; for emphasis, to quote what a third person said, to narrate a story or to acknowledge the identity of a new listener. When researchers started to study child language mixing in the light of these studies on adults, it emerged that children used it for similar communicative purposes.

For example, Genesee and colleagues have provided evidence that bilingual children switch between languages in response to the language proficiency of their listener. In one study, they reported that two-year-old English–French bilingual children used more of their mother's language while interacting with their mother but more of their father's language while interacting with their father (Genesee, Nicoladis & Paradis, 1995). Two-year-old bilingual children are even capable of this type of subtle adjustment when interacting with strangers. Genesee and colleagues (1996) studied four two-year-old bilingual children interacting with monolingual strangers who spoke only French or English but not both. In each case the children adjusted their speech to the stranger's level of understanding, using more of the stranger's language when speaking with the stranger than when speaking with a parent who understood both languages. In other words, they took account of the fact that the stranger could not understand one of the languages and used less of this language in their speech. Genesee and colleagues pointed out that this shows that children are not just using learnt associations between parents and languages (i.e. they are not just learning that mum speaks English and dad speaks German). In order to adjust to a stranger's language in this way, these two-year-olds must be making sophisticated adjustments about which language is appropriate, given the listener.

A final alternative explanation for language mixing is simply that children mix languages because they hear adults mix languages. Once again, there is more evidence for this explanation than the unitary language hypothesis. Particularly noteworthy are studies showing that the number of mixed utterances that children hear predicts the number of mixed utterances that they produce. For example, Goodz (1989) analysed the speech of 17 English–French bilingual children and their caregivers and reported that the frequency with which the children produced mixed utterances correlated with the frequency with which their mothers produced mixed utterances. It turns out that it is very difficult for bilingual parents to avoid producing mixed utterances. Even parents who adopt the "one person one language" rule (where one parent consistently speaks to the child in one language and the other parent in the other language) occasionally use utterances from the other language (Nicoladis & Genesee, 1996). In fact, parents who strongly insist that they only ever speak one language to their children have been shown to produce mixed utterances when the tapes of their conversations with their children are transcribed (Goodz, 1989).

In summary, the evidence that language mixing occurs because bilingual children are working with one unitary language system is far from conclusive. As a result, many, if not most, researchers now agree that language mixing does not result from a unitary language system.

7.2.2 Two language systems: implications for bilingual development

If we accept that bilingual children are capable of discriminating between their two languages from relatively early on, we then face a new question: how much do the two language systems interact with each other? There are two possible answers to this question. One explanation is given by the *autonomous systems theory* (also called the *differentiation hypothesis* by Meisel, 2001, or the *separate development hypothesis* by De Houwer, 1990). On this view, the two languages develop in near-complete isolation, with one having very little influence on the other, so the children learn the phonology, lexicon and grammar of each language independently.

The other explanation is the *interdependent systems theory*. On this view, the child's two language systems interact, so that developments in one affect subsequent developments in the other (i.e. there is *cross-linguistic influence* or *transfer*). For example, we might find a type of *bilingual bootstrapping* where the acquisition of a syntactic rule in language A makes it easier for the child to acquire that rule in language B (i.e. boosts the child's ability; Gawlitzek-Maiwald & Tracy, 1996). Alternatively, if the two languages require that the child learn very different syntactic rules, the acquisition of the syntax of language A might delay the acquisition of the syntax of language B. Other possibilities are that the rules from the dominant language will be used instead of those from the weaker language for a time (Yip & Matthews, 2000).

Much of the literature on bilingual acquisition over the last few years has focussed on this issue of cross-linguistic influence, assessing evidence for and against the autonomous and interdependent systems theories. Many of the relevant studies focus on the acquisition of grammar, so we shall begin with this research. However, there is increasingly more work on phonological acquisition, as we shall see below, and very recently some work on lexical acquisition, which is addressed in one of the online activities associated with this book.

7.2.2.1 *Learning the grammar of two languages: separate or interdependent?*

Many studies have looked for evidence of cross-linguistic influence in how bilinguals develop the grammar (i.e. syntax and morphology) of their two languages. As usual, there is evidence for both sides of the debate.

In favour of the autonomous development view are studies showing that bilingual children develop syntax and morphology early, easily and in accordance with the target grammar of each language. These studies seem to show there is no cross-linguistic influence between languages. For example, Paradis and Genesee (1996) studied English and French bilingual children aged between two and three years of age. They tested whether French–English bilinguals develop the correct use of inflection in English earlier than monolinguals as a result of cross-linguistic influence of their knowledge of the French inflectional system (the inflectional system is used to mark words and phrases for grammatical features such as tense, person and number).

They assessed acquisition in three areas of inflection. First, they looked at inflected verb forms. French monolingual two-year-olds already produce quite a lot of correctly inflected verb forms (e.g. *Elle tombe*; Philippe, 2;2) whereas English two-year-olds tend to use uninflected forms much more frequently (e.g. they say *He bite my fingers* instead of *He bit my fingers*; Nina; 2;0; all examples from Paradis &

Genesee, 1996). If there was influence across languages, we might expect bilinguals to learn correctly inflected forms in English more quickly as a result of their superior knowledge of how to use French inflections. The second area investigated was negation. According to Paradis and Genesee, young French children sometimes produce sentences with the negator *pas* before the verb and at other times produce sentences with the negator after the verb (*pas* is a word that makes a sentence negative in French). For example, Phillipe (aged 2;1) said both **pas chercher les voitures* 'not look for the cars' and **Ça tourne pas* 'that turns not'.[2] However, English monolingual children only place negators like *no* and *not* before the verb (they may say **me no go home* but never **me go no home*). If the children's French influenced their English, we might expect bilingual children to place negators both before and after the verb in both languages (e.g. to say **me go no home* as well as **Ça tourne pas*). Third, the researchers investigated the use of pronouns. English monolingual children go through a stage in which they make errors in how they use verbs with nominative pronouns like *he* and *she*. So English children make errors in which they say *he eat* as well as producing correct sentences like *he eats* or *he is eating*. French monolingual children, on the other hand, rarely use the wrong form of the verb with similar pronouns in French (so-called "weak" pronouns, Paradis & Genesee, 1996, p. 7). For example, a French child will produce the correct *il mange* (*he eats*) and is unlikely to produce errors like **il manger* (*he eat*). However, they theorised, bilingual French–English children might do this, if English influences French. In other words, if cross-linguistic influence occurs, bilingual children might be expected to use these pronouns with both inflected and non-inflected verbs in French as well as English.

Paradis and Genesee (1996) tested their predictions by analysing the speech of three French–English bilingual children growing up in Quebec with an English-speaking mother and a French-speaking father. They videoed the children playing with their parents at ages 2;0, 2;6 and 3;0, transcribed the conversations and analysed the children's speech. They reported three main findings, all of which support the autonomous systems view. First, at each of the three stages of development, the children used more inflected verbs in French than in English. In other words, the children's ability to produce inflected verbs in French did not help them learn inflected verbs in English any earlier. Second, the children used negatives differently in their two languages; there was no evidence that they placed negators after the verb in English as well as in French. In fact, all English negative sentences had pre-verbal negators (*me no go home*). Third, there was no evidence of transfer in the children's use of pronouns. Pronouns like *il* and *elle* occurred only with inflected verbs in the children's French utterances but the English equivalent (*he/she*) occurred with both inflected and non-inflected verbs in their English utterances. The authors concluded that there was no evidence for cross-linguistic influence. Instead, "the acquisition of finiteness, negation and pronominal subjects in these bilingual children follows the same patterns as those of monolinguals" (Paradis & Genesee, 1996, p. 19).

However, as is often the case, there is also contradictory evidence. Contrary to the autonomous view, other studies demonstrate that in certain situations, cross-

---

2   A star * indicates an ungrammatical utterance,

linguistic influence does seem to occur. An extremely influential theory proposing cross-linguistic evidence is that of Müller and Hulk (Hulk & Müller, 2000; Müller & Hulk, 2001). These authors suggested that cross-linguistic influence is most likely to occur under two conditions. First, cross-linguistic influence will occur in the parts of language which are also difficult for monolingual children (so-called *vulnerable areas* of grammar). In particular, cross-linguistic influence is most likely to occur at the interface between the syntax system and the discourse-pragmatic system. Here we mean the aspects of grammar that are influenced by prior discourse and other pragmatic constraints. For example, let us assume that I wanted to tell you what my cousin Alec did yesterday. I might first refer to Alec by name (e.g. *Alec went swimming yesterday*) but I would probably then refer to him with a pronoun (e.g. *and then he went to work*). It would be odd (infelicitous) to use his name again (*Alec went swimming yesterday and then Alec went to work*). My choice of a pronoun here is thus motivated by (or constrained by) the prior discourse. It is these aspects of grammar that Müller and Hulk suggested are vulnerable to cross-linguistic influence.

The other constraint is partial overlap; cross-linguistic influence is most likely to occur in parts of the grammar where the structures of the two languages partially overlap. This idea of partial overlap is a tricky concept to grasp so let us turn to a bilingualism expert to explain it for us. Serratrice (2013, p. 7) writes:

> The other condition that would make cross-linguistic influence "probable" (Hulk & Müller, 2000, p. 2) … *would be partial structural overlap between the two languages with respect to the structure of interest*. If the child's grammatical analysis of a structure X in language A is potentially ambiguous and lends itself to analysis 1 and analysis 2, and the same structure X can only match analysis 1 in language B, then the prediction is that there will be unidirectional influence from language B to language A. The overlapping analysis 1 will be selected by bilingual children more often than by monolinguals.

In other words, the child attempts to figure out which analysis best explains the languages she is learning and will, perhaps erroneously, favour the analysis that seems compatible with both languages. She will then base her own speech in both languages on this analysis "to a high degree and for a long period" (Müller & Hulk, 2001, p. 2).

To make this clearer, let us take an example from Müller and Hulk (2001). They identified object drop as an area that satisfies both their criteria for cross-linguistic influence. In the Germanic languages German and Dutch, in certain conditions, it is appropriate to omit the syntactic objects in sentences (e.g. to say *I like* instead of *I like the dog*).[3] Romance languages like French and Italian do not allow object drop in the adult language. However, monolingual children learning all of these languages routinely go through a stage in which they drop objects frequently and freely in their speech, as if they think it is grammatical. German and Dutch children omit objects

---

3 In these languages, object drop is allowed when the object is in topicalised (sentence initial) position and has been previously introduced in the discourse.

under the wrong circumstances, as well as the right ones (e.g. in German **Joost heft getrokken*, literally translated as 'Joose has pulled' instead of *Joose has pulled it*, Jakubowicz, Muèller, Riemer & Rigaut, 1997). French and Italian children also omit objects despite the fact that object drop is ungrammatical. Importantly, however, children learning Romance languages like Italian and French drop objects far less often than those learning Dutch and German, probably because they do not hear object drop sentences in their input.

According to Müller and Hulk's analysis, object drop will be susceptible to cross-linguistic influence between Germanic and Romance languages, because it satisfies both criteria for an area of vulnerability. First, it lies on the interface of syntax and discourse-pragmatics as its use is governed by knowledge of syntax and by knowledge of the appropriate discourse conditions. Second, there is partial structural overlap, in the sense that a bilingual child learning a Germanic and Romance language may at first, erroneously, favour the analysis that seems compatible with both languages (that object drop is allowed). In other words, bilingual children will apply analysis 1 (that object drop is allowed under some conditions) to both their Germanic language (correctly) and to their Romance language (incorrectly). This will result in bilingual children omitting objects in their Romance language substantially more often than monolingual children.

This is, in fact, what they found. They analysed the speech of three bilingual children video- or audio-recorded in conversation with their parents. All three children spoke one Romance language (French or Italian) and one Germanic language (German or Dutch). In their Germanic language productions (German/Dutch) the children performed at a similar level to monolingual German and Dutch children; they left objects out of their speech relatively frequently. However, they also left out objects in their Romance languages (French/Italian) much more often than monolingual French and Italian children. They said things like **Ivar répare* (*Ivar repair* instead of *Ivar repair it*; Ivar aged 2;4) and **J'ai déjà raconté* (*I have already told* instead of *I have already told it*; Anouk, aged 3;1). The authors argued that the increased incidence of object drop in Romance languages provides evidence for cross-linguistic influence. The children adopted one strategy for both languages, making object drop errors more often than expected in their French and Italian speech.

Other work also seems to support Müller & Hulk's interdependent systems theory. For example, Serratrice, Sorace & Paoli (2004) found evidence for cross-linguistic influence in an English–Italian bilingual child's use of subject drop. In English subjects are almost always obligatory. In Italian, the subject of the sentence (e.g. *he* in *he likes cake*) must be dropped in certain contexts. In particular, subjects must be omitted if the referent has already been established as the topic of the discourse. This means that the phenomenon occurs at the interface of syntax and discourse, fitting the criteria of an area of vulnerability. Serratrice reported that the bilingual child they studied over-used overt subject pronouns in inappropriate contexts in his Italian utterances more often than monolingual Italian children. This suggests that his Italian was influenced by his knowledge of English, which does not allow subject drop in these contexts. This work seems to demonstrate that cross-linguistic influence does occur in bilingual acquisition.

However, others have failed to replicate these results in other languages, suggesting that cross-linguistic influence may not occur each and every time we expect it. For example, Zwanziger, Allen & Genesee (2005) studied subject drop in bilingual children learning English and Inuktitut (a language from the Eskimo-Aleut family). Unlike English, subject drop is allowed in Inuktitut, which means that speakers can omit the sentence subject (e.g. *wants cake* instead of *he wants cake*). Thus, if there is transfer, we might expect the different rules governing subject drop in the two languages to interact. However, there was no evidence of this. The researchers reported that the bilingual English–Inuktitut children omitted sentence subjects at the same rate as monolingual children in each language: frequently in Inuktitut and infrequently in English, just as we would predict if they were learning the two languages independently.

A second problem with the evidence for cross-linguistic influence is that differences between monolingual and bilingual children may be due to differences in the input, not cross-linguistic influence. Bilingual children often hear speech from non-native speakers, who may speak the language differently from native speakers. Thus, apparent cross-linguistic influence effects may simply result from children copying their input. Paradis and Navarro (2003) studied subject drop in the speech of two monolingual Spanish children and one bilingual Spanish–English child and reported this very finding. The monolingual Spanish children omitted subjects often, as we would expect since Spanish allows subject drop. The bilingual child (M) omitted subjects in her Spanish far less often, which is consistent with the idea that her Spanish was influenced by her knowledge of English (English does not allow subject drop). However, the researchers also reported that M's mother was a native English speaker who spoke Spanish to M and, importantly, used more overt subjects in her Spanish than a native Spanish speaker would. In other words, M might have used overt subjects more often than monolingual children simply because she heard her mother use them more often. Paradis and Navarro's results illustrate a wider problem, which is that there are such large differences between the language environments of monolingual and bilingual children that it is difficult to assess how often we would expect them to omit subjects and objects, given what they are hearing.

An alternative way to study cross-linguistic influence is to study very different languages that have very different grammatical rules. In many studies, the bilingual children studied are learning two typologically similar languages: English and French, or German and Italian for example. When looking for evidence of cross-linguistic influence, however, choosing two languages that are similar could be seen as equivalent to weighting the dice against yourself – the fewer differences there are in the grammar of the two languages, the less likely we are to see evidence of cross-linguistic influence in children's speech. By studying children learning two very different languages, we give ourselves more opportunity to find language transfer, if it exists. This is particularly the case if the two languages require the child to learn two diametrically opposing ways of forming sentences.

For example, Cantonese and English are very different languages and thus enable us to study forms of cross-linguistic influence that could not occur if we were studying pairs of European languages. Yip and Matthews (2000, 2007) studied the speech produced by bilingual Cantonese–English children and reported that there was "strong evidence for interaction between the two developing grammatical systems" (Yip & Matthews, 2007, p. 257). In particular, the children frequently produced English wh-questions with Cantonese word order. For example, at two years of age, Timmy, whose mother was a Cantonese speaker and whose father was English, produced English wh-questions in which the wh-word was at the end of the sentence, as is required in Cantonese questions (e.g. *This on the what? You go to the what?*). The rate at which Timmy produced these errors was much higher than the rate at which monolingual children produce them (67 per cent vs. 1.6 per cent; Yip & Matthews, 2000). There was also evidence for cross-linguistic influence in the children's use of object drop and relative clauses (a clause headed by a pronoun such as *that* or *who*, which qualifies or modifies the noun e.g. *the boy <u>that Alec saw</u> is happy*). The researchers concluded that there was a high degree of interaction between the two languages, resulting in distinctly different profiles from those that we see for monolingual English and Cantonese children. This supports the interdependent systems view of bilingual language acquisition.

7.2.2.2 *Learning the sounds of two languages: separate or interdependent?*

There is also some evidence about cross-linguistic influence in phonological (sound system) development. Research on this topic was sparse up until a few years ago. The first study is usually considered to be that of Bosch and Sebastián-Gallés, which was only published in 1997. However, since then, some exciting findings are emerging, partly because we have more sophisticated ways to study very young infants nowadays. Below we focus on a small number of studies to illustrate what they are starting to reveal.

We have already seen in a previous chapter that different languages have different phonological (or sound) systems. First, there are differences in phoneme boundaries. For example, English distinguishes between the phonemes /r/ and /l/ (so *rake* and *lake* are perceived as different words) but Japanese has only one intermediate /r/ sound.[4] Second, there are differences in the cues used to identify different words. For example, in Mandarin changing the tone of a word also changes its meaning. This can result in much hilarity when non-native speakers use the wrong tone; for example, *mā* (high level tone) means 'mother' but *mǎ* (falling then rising tone) means 'horse'. Third, there are differences in rhythm; some languages are stress-timed (e.g. English) and some are syllable-timed (French).

Do bilingual children learn the sound systems of two languages separately and independently? Mehler and colleagues argued that this must be the case because otherwise it is difficult to see how children could even start learning a language (Mehler, Dubpoux, Nazzi & Dehaene-Lamertz, 1996). They wrote "because multilingual environments are the norm rather than the exception, infants must have the capacity

---

4   Phonemes are the speech sounds that we combine into syllables and ultimately words. We use the symbol / to identify a phoneme. So /r/ refers to the phoneme *r* as in *rat*.

very early in life to distinguish one language from another. Without such a capacity, infants might acquire linguistic systems that amalgamate properties of different languages. The ensuing confusion would be overpowering" (Mehler et al., 1996, p. 101).

However, learning to distinguish between the sounds of two languages might be easier said than done. The parents of bilingual children are likely to be bilingual themselves and will address the child in both languages, at least some of the time. Non-native speakers of a language are unlikely to reproduce the sounds of a language perfectly, which means that bilingual children are likely to hear a much wider range of pronunciations. For example, a native Japanese parent talking to a child in English may not pronounce /r/ and /l/ in exactly the same way as a native English speaker, since these phonemes are very difficult for Japanese speakers to reproduce. Thus, as well as being exposed to two sound systems, bilingual children are probably exposed to a greater range of different pronunciations within each language. A final problem is that the two languages will overlap in some respects but differ in others. For example, the child may have to learn the phonemes /b/ and /t/ in both languages, but also learn that the phoneme /v/ is only present in one language. As a result, the child has to work out which aspects of the sound system are shared between the two languages, and which differ.

Some studies find little evidence of cross-linguistic transfer. In particular, learning to identify the rhythmic pattern of a language does not seem susceptible to cross-linguistic transfer. Research on monolingual infants has shown that two-day-old infants can recognise the rhythmic properties of their own language and actually prefer to listen to languages with these rhythmic properties (Mehler et al., 1988; Moon, Cooper & Fifer, 1993). This is almost certainly something the infants picked up in the womb, from hearing their mother's voice. Bilingual children, however, will often hear two languages in the womb. Do they recognise both languages and, perhaps more importantly, can they distinguish between these two languages?

Byers-Heinlein, Burns & Werker (2010) tested this with the newborn infants of bilingual English–Tagalog mothers. Tagalog is a language spoken in the Philippines and comes from a different rhythmic class to English. English is a stress-timed language, which means that stressed syllables occur at regular intervals and unstressed syllables are shortened to fit this rhythm (a sort of dee-DA-dee-DA-dee-DA pattern; e.g. *i WANT to GO to SCHOOL*). Tagalog is a syllable-timed language, which means that each syllable takes up approximately the same amount of time and is given approximately the same amount of stress (a Da-Da-Da-Da rhythm). The mothers of the infants tested reported that they had spoken each language between 30 and 70 per cent of the time during pregnancy, so we know that the infants had been exposed to both languages while in the womb.

When the infants were between 0 and 5 days old, a high-amplitude sucking procedure was used to test whether they could discriminate between the two languages. In this method, sentences are played to infants whenever they suck harder on a pacifier (dummy) than normal. The researchers found (study 1) that monolingual English children much preferred to listen to English language; they sucked harder on the pacifier when this produced a string of English speech than when it resulted in a string of Tagalog speech. However, the bilingual English–

Tagalog children showed no preference; they sucked equally hard in response to both stimuli, which indicated that both languages were equally familiar to them. Perhaps more importantly, however, the researchers also demonstrated that the newborns could discriminate between their two languages (study 2). They played one language continuously to the bilingual infants until the rate of sucking declined (*habituation*). Then they played the other language to the infants. In response, the infants' rate of sucking increased, indicating that they had perceived the change in the language. In other words, despite being familiar with both languages (study 1), the infants were still able to discriminate between them (study 2).

This finding illustrates that, like monolingual infants, bilingual infants are capable of discriminating the rhythmic patterns of their two languages from birth. There is no evidence for interdependence or for a delay in acquisition compared to monolinguals. However, in other areas of phonological acquisition, there is some evidence of interference between the two languages. One of these areas is learning to distinguish the sounds that differentiate words.

For example, to learn the difference between *bat* and *pat*, we have to pay attention to the difference between the sounds /b/ and /p/. These sounds – /b/ and /p/ – differ only in Voice Onset Time (VOT), which refers to the amount of time that occurs between releasing the consonant from the mouth and vibrating the vocal cords in the throat. In both English and French, changing VOT causes a change from a /b/ to a /p/ and thus changes the word spoken (*bat* to *pat* in English, *bain* 'bath' to *pain* 'bread' in French). Therefore, it is important to pay attention to the VOT boundary in order to learn words in both English and French. However, in Canadian English and French, the VOT boundaries that distinguish /p/ and /b/ are different. In fact, a 28ms VOT is heard as /p/ in Canadian French but /b/ in Canadian English. This means that in order to be able to distinguish *pat* and *bat* in English and to distinguish *bain* and *pain* in French, Canadian French–English bilinguals have to treat the VOT boundary of 28ms differently, depending on whether they are listening to French or English input.

Fennell, Byers-Heinlein & Werker (2007) tested whether bilingualism had a knock-on effect on children's ability to use VOT boundaries to distinguish between words. They tested groups of 14-, 17- and 20-month-old bilingual infants, all of whom were exposed to English and one other language. The infants were given a switch task, which required them to learn which of two English-sounding nonsense words (*bih* and *dih*) was associated with which of two objects (a crown and a molecule). The infants were first habituated to consistent word–object pairs (e.g. *bih*-crown; *dih*-molecule). For example, every time they heard the word *bih* they saw a crown and every time they heard the word *dih* they saw a molecule. Then the objects were switched around so they were seen with a different word (*bih*-molecule, *dih*-crown). Please note that these infants do not know what a crown and molecule actually are. The aim of the habituation phase is simply teach the infants to associate a word with a particular object so that we can test whether they detect the 'switch' between *bih* and *dih*. We know that infants who detect the 'switch' will indicate surprise by looking for longer at the objects after the change. So by measuring looking time, we can assess if bilingual children are sensitive to the contrast between /b/ and /d/

and whether they can use this to learn to associate a particular word (*bih*) with a particular object (*crown*).

As we saw in chapter 2, monolingual children succeed in this task at 17 months of age (Stager & Werker, 1997; Werker et al., 2002). However, Fennell's study showed that bilingual children could not succeed until three months later, at 20 months of age. The researchers concluded that "bilinguals ... use relevant language sounds (e.g. consonants) to direct word learning developmentally later than monolinguals, possibly due to the increased cognitive load of learning two languages" (Fennell et al., 2007, p. 1510). This study thus provides good evidence that learning the sounds of two languages simultaneously has a knock-on effect on infants' ability to use sounds to learn words.

To conclude this section on cross-linguistic influence, the research does not yet allow us to come to a clear conclusion about the extent to which the two languages influence each other throughout development. On the one hand, there is evidence that children develop the grammar and phonological systems of their two languages in parallel and to the same developmental timetable as monolingual children, as predicted by the autonomous systems view. On the other hand, there is some evidence for interdependence in syntax learning and in parts of the phonological system, as predicted by the interdependent systems view. Overall, it seems to be the case that some aspects of the language system are more affected by bilingualism than others. However, it may also be that the degree of language transfer is determined by differences in the amount of exposure the child has to each language and/or the typological similarity between the languages being learnt. We are still discovering how these factors affect cross-linguistic influence, which means there is a lot of scope for future work on these issues.

7.3 PREDICTORS OF SUCCESSFUL BILINGUALISM

There is no doubt that some children learn two languages more successfully than others. Although balanced bilinguals – children who can speak two languages with equal proficiency – are relatively rare, many bilinguals are able to converse fluently in both languages. However, there are also bilingual children who have problems in one, or even both, of their languages. For example, Oller and Eilers (2002) have reported that children who are educated in English but who speak another language at home tend to enter school with English skills well below those of monolingual children. This has a knock-on effect on their achievement in the school years (Garcia, McCardle & Nixon, 2007). In fact, bilingualism is considered a risk factor for poor academic achievement in the US, although this is largely due to the fact that many bilingual children in the US come from disadvantaged backgrounds (Office of National Statistics, 2002). This leads us to pose our key question:

Key question: why are there individual differences in how well bilingual learners acquire language?

In one sense the answers to this question are the same as in those provided in the next chapter (chapter 8) on individual variation – bilingual children are different from each other for all the same reasons that monolingual children are different from each other. However, there are particular issues that bilingual children have to face that monolinguals do not. It is also possible that the factors that influence monolinguals affect bilinguals in different ways. Below we investigate three important influences on bilingual acquisition: a) age of acquisition, b) amount and type of input, and c) attitudes to bilingualism.

7.3.1 The effect of age of acquisition

The first question to consider is whether age of acquisition has an influence on how successfully bilinguals learn language. Up until now we have focussed on studies of children who are exposed to two languages from birth. However, a lot of children learn one language from birth and only start to learn the second language later in childhood. These children may be exposed to their second language in the course of everyday interactions (for example, children who move to another country in childhood) or they may learn the second language through formal education at school. Learning a second language in later life is often much more effortful than learning two languages from birth and there is a very healthy debate concerning the effect of *age of acquisition* – the age at which someone first starts to learn his or her second language – on language learning.

Much of this debate focuses on the question of whether it is possible to achieve native-like competence in a language if the learning process starts in adolescence or adulthood. This is not the focus of the present chapter because Ortega's book in this series, *Understanding Second Language Acquisition* (Ortega, 2009), provides a thorough evaluation of this issue. What we focus on here is the effect of age of acquisition on children who start to learn their second language early on in life, albeit not from birth.

A very popular view is that children who are exposed to two languages in childhood can achieve native-like competence in both languages, even if they have not been exposed to both from birth. This is a very influential view and stems from a number of studies that compare early learners, who started learning their second language in childhood, with late learners, who started learning their second language in their teenage years or in adulthood.

For example, some brain imaging studies seem to demonstrate that the brains of early learners and learners who are bilingual from birth show similar patterns of activation in syntactic tasks, but that the brains of late learners demonstrate different patterns of activation (Dehaene et al., 1997; Pallier et al., 2003). These seem to suggest that early learners and those who are bilingual from birth process language in the same way. We have to bear in mind that these results are still controversial; for example, Osterhout suggests that the differences are due simply to practice effects, with early learners being more practised at the language than late learners (see e.g. Osterhout et al., 2008). However, the important point for our discussion is that it is generally assumed that there are few, or even no, differences between children who are exposed to two languages from birth and those who start learning their second language slightly later, but still in childhood. In fact, Ortega concludes from the literature that "by and large, learners who begin acquiring the L2 [second language] before a certain age, which these studies locate to be around puberty, will tend to exhibit intuitions that are very close to those of native speakers of that language" (Ortega, 2009, p. 19).

Recently, however, this conclusion has been challenged. Some work is starting to show that age of acquisition might be important much earlier than previously thought. This is particularly the case when it comes to phonological development. We have already seen in previous chapters that newborns are sensitive to many speech sound patterns, but lose the ability to distinguish sound patterns that do not occur in their native language very early in life (Werker & Tees, 1984, see chapter 2). Therefore, it seems plausible that children who start learning a second language later in childhood may find it difficult to acquire the sound patterns of their new language. Research is starting to support this conclusion. Sebastián-Gallés and colleagues tested whether Spanish–Catalan bilingual adults could distinguish real Catalan words from non-words based on the difference between /e/ and /ɛ/, two phonemes that sound different to Catalan speakers (Sebastián-Gallés, Echeverría & Bosch, 2005). For example, the Catalan word *galleda* 'bucket' is pronounced with one vowel sound (written as /e/ in the International Phonetic Alphabet) which means that when we pronounce it with a different, though similar, vowel sound (/ɛ/), it becomes a different, non-existent, nonsense word. Importantly, the contrast between these two vowel sounds is not found in Spanish, so monolingual Spanish-speakers cannot distinguish between the word for bucket (*galleda*) and the nonsense word *gallɛda*. The researchers found that the Spanish–Catalan bilingual speakers who had learnt Catalan before the age of four years were significantly better at distinguishing between the two sounds than those who had learnt Catalan after age four, despite the fact that all were fluent Catalan speakers. This study shows that age of acquisition can have an effect on bilingual speakers' knowledge of the sound patterns of their languages even if the second language is learnt early in childhood.

In fact, there may be subtle age of acquisition effects across a range of different language tasks. Abrahamsson and Hyltenstam (2009) tested second language learners of Swedish on 10 tasks designed to measure a number of language abilities in detail, from the perception of phonemes to familiarity with idioms. As expected, none of those who started to learn Swedish after the age of 12 years performed like native speakers. More surprisingly, however, only three of those who started to learn Swedish early – between one and 11 years of age – performed like natives across the 10 tasks. The authors argued that, although superficially the two groups looked the same when assessed with simple tests, detailed tests of the more complex aspects of language reveal there are a number of subtle differences. These tests indicate that age of acquisition has an important role to play even early in childhood.

7.3.1.1 *The case of international adoptees*

An informative line of research on age of acquisition concerns the language development of international adoptees. International adoptees are children who are adopted by a family who live in a different country and speak a different language. For example, in recent years, a number of Chinese and Eastern European orphans have been adopted by American or Canadian families. From the moment of adoption, the children rarely hear their birth language but are exposed to a completely new language. Thus, these children constitute a special case of language learning. De Geer (1992) suggests that they are learning a second first language.

These children will be exposed to their new language in much the same way as monolingual children who have learnt the language from birth. They will hear only one language typically, and they will hear it at home, at nursery and in the wider environment every day. However, age of adoption varies substantially within this group of children, with some children adopted soon after birth and others only adopted years later. This means that by studying international adoptees, we can study the effect of age of acquisition on language learning.

It is important to bear in mind that there are socio-environmental factors to consider as well as age when studying these children. Often the children who have been adopted later in childhood have had a very difficult life up to the point of adoption. This means that we have to be cautious about our conclusions – their rate of language learning is bound to be affected by their early experiences as well as their age of adoption. We also have to be careful who we compare these children with. Parents who adopt children tend to be of higher socio-economic status (SES) than the general population, and we know that SES has an effect on language development (Hart & Risley, 1995).

Nevertheless, some interesting findings are emerging about the role of age of acquisition in these populations. For example, Glennen and Masters (2002) reported that Chinese children who are adopted into English families before the age of 12 months develop English in the same way as monolingual English children exposed to English from birth. In their study, there were no substantial differences in the age at which these international adoptees reach the important language milestones when they were compared with monolingual children. The language development of children who had been adopted between 12 and 24 months was slightly delayed compared to those who had heard the language from birth (one to three months difference) but only children who were adopted after 24 months were substantially delayed in their language development (eight to ten month delay). Interestingly, even these early delays may disappear after sufficient exposure. Roberts and colleagues found no delays in the language of Chinese children adopted into American English speaking families two years after adoption (Roberts, Krakow & Pollock, 2003). What is important about their study is that they studied children between the ages of three and six years, some of whom were quite old when they were adopted (e.g. 25 months). Despite this, 85 per cent of them scored within or above the normal range on tests of vocabulary and articulation, as well as on tests of general language ability. The researchers concluded that early delays may disappear after sufficient exposure, especially if the children are exposed to language-rich environments.

However, we must bear in mind that these studies tend to rely on a small number of standardised tests to assess the children's language. They do not provide the detailed assessment of a range of language abilities that Abrahamsson and Hyltenstam (2009) claimed is necessary to distinguish native speakers from second language learners. It may be that studies that focus on more complex aspects of language will reveal pockets of long-lasting difficulty. Gauthier, Genesee & Kasparian (2012), for example, have provided some preliminary evidence that Chinese children adopted into French families may have more problems producing object clitics than native French children, despite being of a similar standard in standardised language tasks. Object clitics like *me* and *les* in French are similar to object pronouns like *me* and *them* in English. They are used when it is not necessary to identify the referent by name because it is clearly identifiable from the discourse or situation (e.g. *les* in *Julie les nouritt* 'Julie is feeding them'). In sum, although age of acquisition may not have a substantial effect on bilingual language development in childhood, we cannot conclude yet that these children are no different from those exposed to both languages from birth.

7.3.2 The effect of the input

A second possible influence on the success of bilingual language acquisition is the amount and type of input that children hear. At first sight, the amount of language that bilingual children hear does not seem to matter. Bilingual children must hear much less of each language than monolingual children, because the speech that they hear is distributed across two languages, yet they seem to reach the major language milestones at about the same age as monolingual children. For example, bilingual children produce their first word, their first two-word combination and achieve a 50-word vocabulary at about the same age as monolingual children, even when one of their languages is a sign language (Petitto et al., 2001; Petitto & Kovelman, 2003).

However, it turns out that, just like monolingual children, bilingual children are affected by the amount of language that they hear. The more language a child hears, the quicker she will develop language. In fact, we have known for a while that the rate at which bilingual children learn vocabulary in each of their languages is influenced by the language that they hear, particularly the language that they hear in the home (see, for example, De Houwer, 2007; Hoff et al., 2011; Oller & Eilers, 2002; Pearson, Fernández, Lewedeg & Oller, 1997). A much cited study is that of Pearson and colleagues (Pearson et al., 1997). Here, the researchers used the MacArthur-Bates Communicative Development Inventory (CDI) to collect information on the vocabulary development of 25 bilingual English–Spanish children aged between eight and 30 months of age. MacArthur-Bates CDIs are very useful checklists that researchers can give to parents to report on their children's language development. Since the MacArthur-Bates CDIs are available in both English and Spanish versions, the researchers in this study were able to collect data for both languages in the same way. They also asked parents to estimate how much Spanish and English the children heard (they acknowledge that this is a relatively crude measure of exposure but the results seem to indicate that it is an effective one).

They reported that the proportion of time spent in a Spanish-speaking environment (as opposed to an English one) was positively correlated with the proportion of the children's vocabulary that was Spanish (as opposed to English). In other words, the children who heard more Spanish than English produced more Spanish words, and the children who heard more English than Spanish produced more English words. Interestingly, there was no threshold effect. Some have speculated that there is an exposure threshold below which a child cannot learn a language; for example, that a child who hears Spanish only 20 per cent of the time may not learn any Spanish at all. Pearson and colleagues did not find any evidence for such a threshold. The nine children who were exposed to Spanish less than 25 per cent of the time learnt Spanish words at a rate commensurate with the amount of exposure they received. The authors concluded that "the number of words learnt in each language is, to a large extent, proportional to the amount of time spent with speakers of the language" (Pearson et al., 1997, p. 51).

Finally, there is evidence that bilingual acquisition is affected by the type of input children hear, as well as the amount of input. Hoff and Place (2012) found that the rate of vocabulary development (though not grammar development) was predicted by the number of different speakers the child heard and the percentage of the input that was provided by native speakers. The influence of native speakers is particularly interesting here, especially since other research has also found that children learn a language more successfully when they hear that language spoken by native speakers (De Houwer, 2007). We do not currently know why this is. It may be that the language is spoken more often in the home if a native speaker lives there (see Alba, Logan, Lutz & Stults, 2002). It may be that native speakers have more articulatory clarity than non-native speakers (i.e. they speak more clearly) and are thus easier to understand. It may be that native speakers tend to use a wider vocabulary and a greater range of grammatical structures, providing the children with "rich and supportive" input (Hoff & Place, 2012, p. 20). More work is needed on this issue.

In summary, bilingual children will often hear less input in each of their languages than monolinguals, which has a direct effect on the speed with which they learn each language. However, it is very important to remember that this is not the same as saying that bringing children up bilingual will harm their language development. A substantial amount of research indicates that bilingual children are progressing at the same rate overall as monolingual children, it is just that their learning is distributed across two different languages.

For example, Hoff et al. (2011) found that bilingual children were slower at developing English than monolingual children. However, they also found that the bilingual children were identical to the monolingual children when they considered both languages together. Figure 7.1 shows the pattern of vocabulary development for monolingual and bilingual children in this study. Figure 7.1a shows their scores when only vocabulary from one language is taken into account. This clearly shows that the bilinguals lag behind monolinguals in both English and Spanish; they know far fewer words at each age in English and even fewer in Spanish. Figure 7.1b shows vocabulary scores when both languages are combined (i.e. when we add together the words they know in Spanish and the words they know in English). Here it is clear that the bilinguals are virtually identical to the monolinguals in the number of words they know at each age. What these graphs together show is that the bilingual children are learning words at the same rate as monolingual children, but that their words are divided between the two languages.

Figure 7.1

English vocabulary scores for monolingually developing children together with (a) English and Spanish vocabulary scores for bilingually developing children and (b) total vocabulary scores (English+Spanish) for bilingually developing children at 1;10, 2;1 and 2;6. Reproduced from Hoff et al. (2011, pp. 7–8, Figures 1, 2).

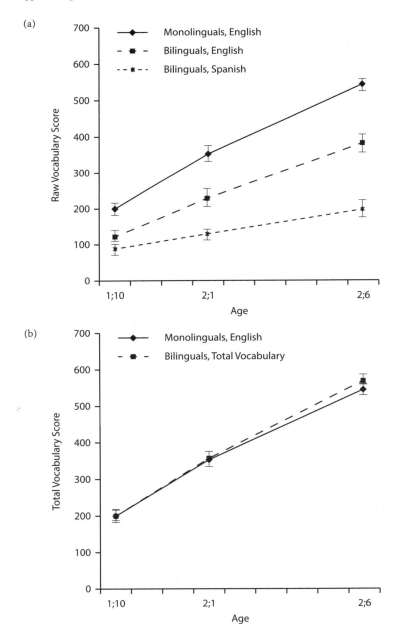

7.3.3   The effect of attitude, beliefs and behaviour

The third and final influence on the success of bilingualism concerns the attitude, beliefs and behaviour of the people around the child, as well as the attitude and beliefs of the child herself. Many parents make the decision to bring up their children as bilingual language learners. However, just making the decision does not guarantee success.

For example, De Houwer (2007) collected questionnaire data from 1899 bilingual families who lived in a Dutch-speaking area of Belgium (Flanders) and who spoke at least one other language in the home as well as, or instead of, Dutch (the other language was termed language X since the group of families as a whole spoke 73 different languages). From the questionnaire, it was clear that, although both languages were spoken in the family home, only one quarter of the children managed to learn language X as well as Dutch. To explore why this was, De Houwer collected information about the children's home life. She found that two strategies were particularly effective at helping children become bilingual. One was a strategy in which both parents spoke the other (non-Dutch) language at home (language X). The other was a strategy where one parent just spoke language X and the other spoke both language X and Dutch. The other strategies (e.g. both parents speaking both languages) were less successful.

In other words, although all the children who took part in the study heard both languages, their success at learning the minority language depended on the languages their parents chose to use while in the home. De Houwer suggested that the decisions that bilingual parents make are critical in their children's language development and that these decisions relied on the parents' *impact belief*, the belief that they as a parent can have an impact on their children's language development. Those parents who realised the impact of their own language behaviour on their children's language learning were most likely to have children who learnt both languages. However, those who did not understand the importance of their own behaviour were less successful. De Houwer (2009) describes some very sad case studies of common misunderstandings among parents about their own role in language learning. For example, she cites the case of Henry, an English-speaking American living in the Netherlands, who saw his daughter's lack of English learning as a form of rejection. In fact, it reflected the fact that she heard very little English because he was the only English speaker she heard and he was not at home very often. This father failed to recognise the impact of his own behaviour on his daughter's language learning.

In fact, it is not just the attitude of parents that is important. The wider society in which a child is raised will have a large effect. The experiences of a bilingual child growing up a bilingual society (e.g. a bilingual English–French child in Montreal, Canada) are very different to those of a bilingual child growing up in a largely monolingual country (e.g. a Gujurati–English bilingual child in Britain). Research has identified a number of influential factors including language status (Tuominen, 1999), the provision of national policies to support bilingualism (Spolsky, 2004), the availability of bilingual education (Zentella, 1997) and the role of the wider social circle (e.g. friends and family; see Shin, 2002).

For example, Gathercole and Thomas (2009) reported that English–Welsh bilingual speakers seem to acquire English to the same level of proficiency whether they come from English- or Welsh-speaking homes. In these cases, they argued, the influence of the home language was over-ridden by three other factors, all of which influenced the learner to learn English to a higher standard than we might expect. The first was the fact that English was dominant in the wider society; both in Welsh-speaking communities (all speakers in Wales know English whereas only some know Welsh) and in the larger society (Wales is part of the United Kingdom, where English is the dominant language). Second, English is seen as the language of power, because Welsh was suppressed and in decline until the 1970s. Third, English is perceived as the language of opportunity because nearly all higher education and employment opportunities require good knowledge of English. All these factors conspired to make English the dominant language even when Welsh was spoken in the home.

To conclude this section, age of acquisition, amount and type of input and the attitudes, behaviour and beliefs of the child, family and wider community affect the success of bilingual acquisition. However, it is important to note that, all else being equal, bilingual children learn language just as successfully as monolingual children. In fact, there are some who argue that bilingualism has a positive effect on a number of different cognitive developments, as we shall see in the next section.

7.4 EFFECT OF BILINGUALISM ON COGNITIVE DEVELOPMENT

In the early days of bilingual research, some suggested that bilingual children were likely to be delayed in cognitive development as a whole (see, for example, Saer, 1923). An opposing, equally influential, view was that bilingual children are more intelligent than monolingual children. Neither of these views is correct. It is now generally accepted that many of the early studies were flawed because they failed to control for factors such as socio-economic status in bilingual children's development (Grosjean, 1982). However, there may be some cognitive tasks in which bilinguals excel and others in which they tend to lag behind. In other words, bilingual and monolingual speakers may develop different patterns of cognitive skills due to the different language environments they experience. Below we look at three areas of cognition: one in which bilingualism confers a clear advantage, one in which 'the jury is still out' and one in which the evidence suggests that bilingualism may be a disadvantage. While discussing these areas we focus on the key question:

Key question: do bilingual children have different cognitive skills and abilities from monolingual children?

7.4.1 Control of attention

Quite a lot of work shows that bilingual speakers activate both language systems even when they are only conversing in one language (Brysbaert, 1998; Francis, 1999;

Gollan & Kroll, 2001; Smith, 1997). This requires a good deal of *attentional control*. The speaker must select the correct word to express the message she wants to convey and must make sure that this word is from the target language, not the competing language. In other words, during linguistic tasks, bilinguals must constantly inhibit one language and activate the other but must be capable of switching quickly from one language to another if required. These sorts of attention switching skills are considered to be under the control of the *central executive* mechanism in the brain, which is said to control and regulate a large number of cognitive processes such as planning, memory and attention. Since the central executive is involved in a large number of different tasks as well as language switching, the intriguing question is this – are bilinguals better at other cognitive tasks because of their experience of switching between two languages?

The answer seems to be yes, especially for so-called conflict tasks which require us to pay attention to particular cues and ignore other, conflicting, cues. These tasks require good attentional control, exactly the type of skill that bilingual speakers use in everyday conversations. There is now robust evidence that bilinguals outperform monolinguals on these tasks, much of it provided by Bialystok and her colleagues. For example, Martin-Rhee and Bialystok (2008) tested bilingual and monolingual four- and five-year-old children on the Simon task (Simon, 1969). In this task, a red square and a blue square are presented on a computer screen and the participants have to press a red button in response to the red square and a blue button in response to the blue square. Sneakily, for half of the trials, the squares occur on the opposite side of the screen to the corresponding keys. So for example, the red square might appear on the *left* side of the screen, requiring the child to press the red button on the *right* side of the computer keyboard. People's instinctive reaction in this task is to press the key on the same side as the stimulus, so inhibiting this reaction requires a good level of cognitive control and slows down their reaction times. Martin-Rhee and Bialystok found that bilinguals responded faster than monolinguals because they were quicker at resolving the conflict between the two possible responses. They concluded that bilinguals are better at selectively attending to conflicting cues because "they must constantly control attention between two active and competing language systems" (Martin-Rhee & Bialystok, 2008, p. 91). Other studies with young adults, middle-aged adults and older adults show similar results, demonstrating that this bilingual advantage is sustained into adulthood (see Bialystok, 2006; Bialystok, Craik, Klein & Viswanathan, 2004).

Why might cognitive flexibility be an advantage? The ability to switch attention quickly and easily is bound to be useful in a variety of everyday activities. In driving, for example, the ability to switch attention quickly from an irrelevant detail (a tree at the side of the road) to an important one (a pedestrian waiting to cross) could be critical. But there are also signs that this aspect of bilingualism might provide a level of resistance against the cognitive decline that often accompanies old age. Bialystock and her colleagues found that a group of older bilinguals, who ranged in age from a sprightly 60-year-old to a distinguished 88-year-old, were faster in the Simon task than monolinguals, as well as making fewer errors (Bialystok et al., 2004). The authors concluded that bilinguals who have used both languages regularly throughout their lifespan are protected from the decline in attentional control that usually accompanies old age. Bilingualism confers a clear advantage here.

7.4.2 Metalinguistic awareness

In other areas of cognitive development the results are less clear-cut. One of these areas is the development of metalinguistic awareness. Metalinguistic awareness refers to the ability to reflect on and think about the nature of language and its functions. It seems plausible to suggest that bilingual children, who have experience of swapping between two languages, may have enhanced metalinguistic awareness.

However, the evidence for enhanced metalinguistic awareness in bilingual children is mixed because most studies report advanced capacities in some tasks but not others (Ben-Zeev, 1977; Bialystok, 1986a, 1986b; Galambos & Goldin-Meadow, 1990). For example, work on phonological awareness (awareness of the sound system of a language) has produced contradictory results. Bruck and Genesee (1995) reported that bilingual children showed better performance on an onset-rime segmentation task at age five years (separating words into the onset and rime; *swift* into *sw* and *ift*) although the advantage disappeared a year later. However, monolingual five-year-olds were better than bilinguals on a phoneme-counting task (e.g. identifying that the word *run* has three phonemes). Similarly, Bialystok, Majumder & Martin (2003) found that Spanish–English, but not Chinese–English bilinguals, were better at a phoneme segmentation task (e.g. segmenting *run* into /r/, /ʌ/ and /n/).[5] However, they also reported no difference between groups on a phoneme substitution task (e.g. substitute /s/ for /k/ to make *sat* out of *cat*). These mixed results suggest that the pattern of performance may not be straightforward. It is probably the case that other factors are equally influential in these tasks; factors such as the child's age, her ability in her two languages, the task she is performing and even perhaps the nature of the two languages she is learning (see Galambos & Hakuta, 1988, for more on this suggestion). More research is needed here before we can draw strong conclusions.

7.4.3 Language proficiency and fluency

Finally, there seems to be evidence that bilinguals are disadvantaged compared to monolinguals in some tasks. In particular, studies have shown that bilinguals may have more difficulty accessing words from memory. For example, bilinguals tend to be slower at rapid picture naming tasks and tend to experience more 'tip of the tongue' phenomena, which happen when a speaker just cannot bring the right word to mind (Gollan & Kroll, 2001; Gollan & Silverberg, 2001). They also score more poorly on tasks in which they have to produce as many words as possible within a given category. For example, Gollan and colleagues gave different language tasks to Spanish–English bilingual adults (Gollan, Montoya & Werner, 2002). These were

---

5 We use the International Phonetic Alphabet (IPA) to represent these phonemes. This alphabet allows us to represent the sounds of language more accurately than standard letters. For example, the symbol /ʌ/ is used to represent the *u* sound of *run*, and /k/ is used to represent a hard *c* sound of *cat*. See http://www.langsci.ucl.ac.uk/ipa/ipachart.html for details.

semantic tasks, where the goal was to produce as many members of a given category as possible in 60 seconds (e.g. animals or fruits), *lexical tasks* where the goal was to produce as many words beginning with a certain letter as possible, and *proper name tasks* where the goal was to produce proper names beginning with a certain letter (e.g. *Mandy, Melissa, Morton*). The bilingual speakers scored more poorly than the monolinguals in all tasks, especially the semantic tasks, where the competition from the non-target language could be expected to be most problematic. Many have suggested that these problems stem from the fact that in order to retrieve words in one language, bilinguals have to resist competition from the equivalent word in the other language (Green, 1998), although there are also alternative possible explanations (see Gollan et al., 2002). What is important to note for our purposes is that bilinguals seem to find word retrieval harder and more effortful than monolingual speakers.

7.5 CHAPTER SUMMARY

This chapter has provided an overview of the most influential debates in multilingual acquisition, focussing on bilingual acquisition, where most of the work has been done. Research in bilingual acquisition is difficult. There are a number of factors that researchers in monolingual acquisition do not have to contend with: the influence of age of acquisition, type and amount of input in the two languages, the situation in which each language is heard. Despite these problems, a huge amount has been achieved over the last few decades. The first and largest section in this chapter focussed on the following key question:

Are the bilingual child's two languages learnt via two distinct and separate systems or is there a single representation incorporating both languages?

Although very few researchers propose a unitary language hypothesis nowadays, there is still a lively debate about the extent to which a child's two languages influence each other in development. On the one hand, there is evidence that children develop the syntactic and phonological systems of their two languages separately, and to the same developmental timetable as monolingual children. On the other hand, there is some evidence for interdependence in both systems.

The second section looked at the predictors of successful bilingual acquisition and focussed on the key question:

Why are there individual differences in how well bilingual learners acquire language?

The conclusions here seem a little more straightforward. Age of acquisition, the amount and type of input, and the attitudes, behaviour and beliefs of the family and wider community all play a role. However, the details of exactly how these factors affect bilingual children and, in particular, how they interact, are still to be fleshed out.

Finally, we looked at some of the new, emerging work on the effect of multilingualism on cognitive development to address the key question:

Do bilingual children have different cognitive skills and abilities from monolingual children?

There is not as much work on this question as for the other areas we investigated but to date, the answer here seems to be a yes for control of attention, a no for language proficiency and awareness but a resounding '*we don't know*' for metalinguistic awareness. Once again, this is an area where more work is needed to resolve the issue.

7.6 SUGGESTED READING

De Houwer, A. (2009). *Bilingual first language acquisition.* Clevedon, UK: Multilingual Matters. An engaging textbook, with useful appendices that summarise the relevant studies on a number of issues.

McCardle, P. D. & Hoff, E. (2006). *Childhood bilingualism: Research on infancy through school age.* Clevedon, UK: Multilingual Matters. Contains a range of chapters written by some of the leading researchers on monolingual and bilingual acquisition.

Serratrice, L. (2012). The bilingual child. In T. K. Bhatia & W. C. Ritchie (Eds), *Handbook of bilingualism* (pp. 87–108). Oxford: Blackwell Publishing. A summary of the most influential recent research.

Sorace, A. (2006). The more, the merrier: Facts and beliefs about the bilingual mind. In S. Della Sala (Ed.), *Tall tales about the mind and brain: Separating fact from fiction* (pp. 193–203). Oxford: Oxford University Press. A summary of some common misconceptions with explanations of why they are false.

7.7 SUGGESTED READING (ADVANCED LEVEL)

Bialystok, E. (2009). Bilingualism: The good, the bad and the indifferent. *Bilingualism: Language and Cognition, 12*(1), 3–11. A summary of current perspectives on how bilingualism might influence cognitive development.

Döpke, S. (2000). *Cross linguistic structures in simultaneous bilingualism.* Amsterdam: John Benjamins. A detailed investigation of the issues of language mixing and cross-linguistic influence from a number of influential researchers.

Genesee, F. (1989). Early bilingual development: One language or two? *Journal of Child Language, 16*(1), 161–179. Perhaps the most influential critique of the unitary language hypothesis and very readable.

Hoff, E., Core, C., Place, S., Rumiche, R., Señor, M. & Parra, M. (2011). Dual language exposure and early bilingual development. *Journal of Child Language, 39*(1), 1–27.

Meisel, J. (2001). The simultaneous acquisition of two first languages: Early differentiations and subsequent development of grammars. In J. Cenoz & F. Genesee (Eds), *Trends in bilingual acquisition* (pp. 11–41). Amsterdam: John Benjamins. Meisel supports the autonomous development view, so this chapter provides an in-depth critique of the evidence that supports the interdependence view.

7.8 COMPREHENSION CHECK

1. Define:

    a. Lexical mixing
    b. Phonological mixing
    c. Morphological mixing
    d. Syntactic mixing
    e. Pragmatic mixing

2. Language mixing probably does not indicate that children are confusing their two languages. What alternative explanations are there?

3. Explain:

    a. The autonomous systems view of bilingual development
    b. The interdependent systems view of bilingual development

4. What did Abrahamsson and Hyltenstam (2009) conclude about age of acquisition effects?

5. List five factors that are important in a bilingual child's success at learning both languages.

6. Explain which group is best at the following tasks – bilinguals or monolinguals:

    a. Conflict tasks
    b. Phonological awareness tasks
    c. Verbal fluency tasks (e.g. semantic and lexical tasks)

Explaining individual variation

8.1 THE ISSUE

Language is an extremely tenacious skill. It does not need careful tending or special treatment but develops without much effort on the part of either the parent or the child. In fact, it takes some pretty exceptional circumstance, either of deprivation or cognitive impairment, to prevent language developing.

However, that is not the same as claiming that everyone learns language in exactly the same way; there is substantial individual variation. Some children learn language extremely fast, producing their first words before one year of age. In fact, some children speak before they can crawl. Others are much slower to develop: for these, walking comes first. Some children are adventurous at combining words, producing strings peppered with grammatical errors. Others seem more cautious, only combining words when they are absolutely sure they have the grammar right. And still others struggle to produce even single word utterances, often because of some underlying cognitive impairment such as autism or specific language impairment.

Individual differences in language development fall into three distinct types. First, there are individual differences within the typically developing normal population. These are children who follow a typical timetable of development and are never diagnosed with any sort of impairment. All these children will reach adultlike competence in the normal way, but some of these children will be much slower than others (differences in *rate*) or will follow a different developmental pathway (differences in *style*). Second, there are children who find it difficult to develop language because of what we will call *physical barriers*. These could be caused by a problem in the environment (e.g. the severe social deprivation suffered by neglected and feral children) or a physical impairment such as deafness. Third, there are those whose difficulties are caused by *cognitive impairments* such as specific language impairment.

We consider these three groups separately because their difficulties may have different origins. For example, the difficulties experienced by slow learners who eventually develop good language may have a different source from the difficulties of those who are slow because they have a clinical disorder. It is important never to assume that two seemingly identical problems must have the same origin.

8.2 INDIVIDUAL VARIATION

Key question: what factors influence how quickly and easily children learn their language under normal circumstances?

Why do two children who have no cognitive or physical impairment nevertheless learn language at different rates and perhaps in different ways? The first possible answer is that we can explain it by genetics. Perhaps some children are innately more skilled at learning language. The second possible answer is that the two children have different environments. Perhaps some children just hear less language and thus learn more slowly. The third possible answer is that some children develop the cognitive skills that help language learning more quickly than others. Some children may process information faster, for example. Here we address all these possibilities. However, first, we look at what individual differences need to be explained.

8.2.1 Differences in the rate of acquisition

There is no doubt that some children learn language faster than others. Many studies document individual differences in the rate of acquisition. We will focus here on just one study in order to illustrate how very different children can be. This is the norming study for the MacArthur-Bates Communicative Development Inventories (the CDIs; Fenson et al., 2007).

CDIs are very famous, very useful checklists that we give to parents to report on their children's language development. In the first studies using CDIs, over 1000 American parents were given checklists containing questions about their children's language development. The results revealed huge differences in the rate at which American children develop language (Fenson et al., 2007). For example, at 10 months of age, the fastest 10 per cent of children understood over 100 words whereas the slowest children understood fewer than seven. At 16 months the very fastest children understood over 300 words but the slowest children understood fewer than 80 (see Fenson et al., 2007, p. 117). This means that the fastest children not only started learning words earlier, they also learnt more words per day than the slowest children.

We see similar results for the word production measure, which tested how many words the children could produce, and for the grammatical complexity measure, which tested how many inflectional markers and function words the children were using (for example, whether they said *Daddy's car* (with the possessive *s*) rather than *Daddy car*). The children did not start so early at these tasks. Half the children did not produce a single word until 10 months, and inflections and function words did not appear even in the fastest children until 16 months (Fenson et al., 2007, pp. 119, 131). However, once the children got going, similar profiles were seen as for vocabulary comprehension. There were large individual differences in the number of words produced and in the complexity of utterances, differences that increased with development. What is particularly striking about the grammatical complexity measure is the difference in the age of onset between the fastest children, who started to use inflections and function words at about 16 months, and the slowest children, who were still not using them a whole year later.

The MacArthur-Bates CDI has been translated into over 40 dialects and languages and similar individual differences are reported in these other languages (Bleses et al., 2008; Dale & Goodman, 2005; Maital, Dromi, Sagi & Bornstein, 2000). A precise comparison of five languages can be found on the CLEX database website (http://www.cdi-clex.org/), which gives CDI scores in five different languages (Danish, Croatian, Swedish, Mexican Spanish, American English). Importantly, the data here are only from studies where the sample was representative of the population of the country (i.e. not drawn from a specific group such as only middle-class families) and where the language-specific adaptations to the CDI were similar, making cross-linguistic comparisons valid.

These cross-linguistic comparisons showed large individual variation across all languages. For example, the number of words that children understood at 10 months ranged from 0 to 279 in American English, 0 to 168 in Danish and 0 to 348 in Mexican Spanish. Also, across all languages, we find that girls tend to be slightly faster than boys, at least at the early stages, and that children from high socio-economic status (SES) groups (e.g. whose parents have more money or are more highly educated) are faster than those from low SES groups (see Bleses et al., 2008 for Danish gender differences; Hart & Risley, 1995 for English SES differences; Maital et al., 2000 for Hebrew gender differences; Ninio, 1979, 1980 for Hebrew SES differences).

Finally, individual differences can persist into later childhood and even adulthood. School-age children differ in the extent that they use and understand more complex sentence structures (C. Chomsky, 1969; Goodluck, 1981; Loban, 1976; Scott, 1984). There are even differences among adults in their ability to interpret complex sentences such as reversible passives (e.g. *the soldier was hit by the sailor*) and quantifiers (e.g. *every basket has a dog in it*; Street & Dabrowska, 2010). Individual differences are, therefore, large, universal and long-lasting.

8.2.2 Do individual differences have a genetic basis?

It is sometimes assumed that theories which emphasise the innate aspects of language (nativist theories) cannot explain individual differences because they posit a universal process of acquisition. As a result, some nativists dismiss individual differences as unimportant; for example, Chomsky wrote "it is plausible to suppose that apart from pathology ... such variation as there may be is marginal and can safely be ignored across a broad range of linguistic investigations" (Chomsky, 1986, p. 18). But of course it is not true that variation can tell us nothing about the genetic basis of language. In fact, the methodology used to study the influence of genes on behaviour (*behavioural genetics*) relies on the presence of individual differences, particularly those that can be attributed to the fact that different individuals inherit different combinations of genes from their parents.

The most common method used in behavioural genetics is the twin study. Here researchers compare the behaviour of monozygotic twins (those that share 100 per cent of their genes because they developed from the same zygote) and dizygotic twins (those that share 50 per cent of their genes on average because they developed from two different zygotes). Researchers measure how similar one child is to his/her co-twin in how he/she develops language. Differences between the children in a twin pair are attributed to non-shared environment – the experiences that one twin has that are not shared by the other (e.g. different illnesses, different friends). Similarities between the children in a twin pair are attributed to shared environment (similar conditions in the womb before birth, same family, same school). However, crucially, if monozygotic twins are more similar to each other than dizygotic twins are to each other, this difference (called *the heritability estimate*) is attributed to genetic variations, because monozygotic twins share 100 per cent of their genes, whereas dizygotic twins share only 50 per cent of their genes on average. In this way, researchers can estimate the effect of a) shared environment, b) non-shared environment and c) genetic inheritance, on language development.

Unfortunately, most twin studies only look to see if there is a genetic component to language disorders rather than studying individual differences within typically developing children. This is problematic for our purposes because the origin of language disorder and of individual differences within the normal population may be very different (in fact some behavioural genetic studies suggest that they are). However, a few studies have looked at language variation in typically developing twins and these mostly report a moderate correlation between the twins' performance on language tasks (see Stromswold, 2001, for a review of all the studies published to that date). In other words, our genes have a moderate effect on individual variation in language acquisition.

For example, Kovas and colleagues (2005) studied 787 twin pairs (either monozygotic, same gender dizygotic or different gender dizygotic twins), all of whom were taking part in the famous TEDS study based at King's College in London (TEDS stands for Twins Early Development Study; see http://www.teds.ac.uk/). The children were tested on a battery of verbal and non-verbal tests at the age of four-and-a-half years (4;6). The researchers reported an average heritability estimate of 0.40.[1] This means that about 40 per cent of the variation in the language ability of the twins could be attributed to genetic variation. Fifteen per cent was attributable to shared environment and 45 per cent to non-shared environment and measurement error.

These results are backed up by other twin studies in the literature (see Stromswold, 2001, for a review). Overall, then, the literature suggests a 'moderate' effect of genetic variation on the rate at which children develop language. It is, perhaps, more interesting, though, to look at whether different language components, such as vocabulary and syntax, yield different heritability estimates. If so, this would suggest that different components of language might arise from different gene combinations. Stromswold (2001) certainly concludes that the evidence supports this idea, based on the studies that she reviewed. However, we must be cautious here because the

---

1   To learn more about the twin method and how to calculate heritability estimates see Plomin, DeFries, McClearn & McGuffin (2001).

studies reviewed by Stromswold all used different tests. For example, if test A requires the children to have a good memory as well as good language skills, but test B only measures language ability, the two tests can yield different heritability estimates simply because test A is measuring the heritability of memory as well as language. This might also be why the heritability estimates for grammar produced by some studies are so much higher than those produced by others. For example, Ganger, Pinker, Chawla & Baker (1999) reported an 81 per cent heritability estimate for grammar, while Dale, Dionne, Eley & Plomin's (2000) was only 40 per cent. We also need to bear in mind that heritability estimates measure the relative contribution of genes and the environment, which means that any changes in the environment will affect them. For example, if the environment starts to contribute more variation (e.g. two twins start to attend different schools) the heritability estimate will decrease. This makes it very difficult to extrapolate from a particular study to the whole population.

Thus, it is incredibly difficult to assess whether different genes really do influence different components of language. The study by Kovas and colleagues (2005) that we described above is probably quite reliable because the researchers controlled for as many confounds as possible. With these robust controls in place, they reported very similar results across nine different language tasks that measured a range of language components from expressive syntax (whether the child can construct grammatical sentences) to receptive phonology (judging whether phonemes presented in different words are the same or different). The authors conclude that the results suggest that the same genetic and environmental factors underlie different language components.

8.2.3   The role of the environment in explaining individual variation

Even with a moderate amount of individual variation attributable to genetics, that still leaves a big component that has to be explained by the child's language learning environment. What in the environment might cause one child to develop more quickly than another? The most obvious answer – and the one most often researched – is the amount and type of speech that children hear.

There is no doubt that speech addressed to children sounds very different from speech spoken among adults (Garnica, 1977; Phillips, 1973; Snow, 1972, 1977; Snow & Ferguson, 1977). *Child Directed Speech* (CDS, also known as *motherese*) is characterised by some very distinctive features including:

a) *phonological features* such as higher pitch, exaggerated intonation, slower rate of speech and clearer enunciation of individual words

b) *lexical features* including the use of diminutives (e.g. *doggie* instead of *dog*) and a high degree of repetition of words (e.g. *there's a doggie, can you see the doggie?*)

c) *syntactic features* including the use of nouns instead of pronouns (*give it to Mummy* instead of *give it to me*), use of simpler and shorter phrases and the use of simpler grammatical structures

d) *communicative features* including a more restricted range of topics tied to the immediate context, more questions and fewer declaratives. In CDS, speakers are also more likely to repeat back the child's own utterance, either *expanding* it or *recasting* it into a more sophisticated grammatical form (so for example the child's *Daddy car* might be repeated as *yes, that's Daddy's car, isn't it?*).

The characteristic CDS style of speech is almost certainly an adaptation that speakers make when conversing with someone with limited language. Speakers tend to use the same type of speech when talking to foreigners and animals. It is also common across languages; Ferguson (1964) and Fernald et al. (1989) both document characteristic CDS patterns across six languages as well as citing a number of other studies that report similar findings in languages as diverse as Spanish and Sinhala. Thus, the use of CDS is certainly widespread. However, it is not universal. Four case studies have famously reported little evidence of a characteristic child directed speech style: Schieffelin's study of the Kaluli people of New Guinea, Ochs's study in American Samoa, Smith-Hefner's study of the Javanese and Heath's study of a black community in the Piedmont Carolinas (Heath, 1982, 1983; Ochs & Schieffelin, 1984; Smith-Hefner, 1988).

This poses the question – does CDS actually help children learn language? In the 1970s and 1980s, a large number of studies attempted to answer this question by looking for correlations between how often parents used characteristic features of CDS and the rate at which their children learnt language. For example, Furrow, Nelson & Benedict (1979) studied the speech addressed to children by seven mothers, who were recorded when the children were aged between 1;6 and 2;3. The results showed that mothers who used simpler sentences and who asked a lot of yes–no questions tended to have children with faster language growth. Mothers who used more words, verbs and pronouns per utterance were less likely to have children with fast language growth.

These results, if replicated, would provide strong support for the idea that CDS helps language growth. Unfortunately, the results of other studies are contradictory. For example, Newport, Gleitman & Gleitman (1977) found no relationship between the simplicity of the input and language growth in the child. Their conclusions need to be considered carefully because they tested children at different ages, not taking account of the fact that CDS might have different effects at different ages. However, others also have failed to replicate Furrow's results (Hoff-Ginsberg, 1985; Scarborough & Wyckoff, 1986).

Similar problems arise when we look at other aspects of CDS. Some studies have reported that mothers who use a lot of recasts and expansions have children with faster language growth but others report no relationship at all (Hoff-Ginsberg, 1985; Newport et al., 1977; Scarborough & Wyckoff, 1986). Similarly, some studies have reported that mothers who use a lot of yes–no questions (e.g. *can you do it?, do you want some dinner?*) have children who produce more auxiliaries (e.g. *can, do*) or learn them more quickly. However, once again, other studies have found no relationship (for the debate, see Barnes, Gutfreund, Satterly & Wells, 1983; Furrow et al., 1979; Hoff-Ginsberg, 1985; Scarborough & Wyckoff, 1986).

The lack of agreement across different studies probably stems from three sources. First, each study codes the data in different ways, which will have contributed to the discrepancies (e.g. different definitions of what to include as a yes–no question). For example, when Richards (1990) reanalysed the data from Barnes et al. (1983) using a slightly different coding procedure, he reported results that went in the opposite direction. Unlike Barnes, he found a correlation between the number of yes–no questions in the input and the development of auxiliaries in the children's speech. Second, different studies analyse children at different ages, and the age of the child at the time of testing is likely to be important. Simple input might be really useful when the child is very young and trying to get a foothold into language but might be less helpful when the child is older and trying to learn how to produce more complex utterances. Third, and perhaps most worryingly, since many of the studies correlated a large number of input measures with a large number of child language measures, there is always the possibility that the significant correlations arose by chance, which would certainly explain why they are not replicable.

More recently, there has been a second wave of research that takes advantage of more sophisticated statistical techniques to pinpoint the role of the child's input more precisely. For example, *principal component analysis* allows us to create composite scores incorporating a number of the characteristics of CDS. This reduces the number of analyses we have to perform, limiting the possibility of finding spurious significant relationships by chance. Similarly, using regression models or structural equation modelling rather than correlations allows us to estimate whether the input has a big, moderate or small influence on the child's language. It also allows us to test whether the mother's speech has an effect over and above other influences such as the child's own cognitive ability.

Two clear findings emerge from these studies. First, children who hear more speech develop language more quickly. Many studies have shown that parents who speak more and who use a greater variety of different words tend to have children whose vocabulary develops more quickly (Hart & Risley, 1995; Hoff, 2003; Hoff-Ginsberg, 1998; Huttenlocher et al., 1991). Similarly, many studies have shown that parents who frequently use a syntactic structure have children who learn that structure more quickly. For example, Hoff-Ginsberg (1998) showed that the average number of noun phrases that parents use predicts the number of noun phrases in children's speech, and Naigles and Hoff-Ginsberg (1998) found a similar relationship for verb use. Even the findings that first-born children tend to develop language more quickly than second borns may have its origins in the amount of language addressed to these children. Hoff-Ginsberg (1998) has shown that this difference can be partly explained by the fact that parents use longer utterances to first borns than to later borns.

In fact, the amount of speech addressed to children may be predictive of language development even in cultures where adults direct very little speech to children. For example, Shneidman and Goldin-Meadow reported that Yucatec Mayan parents rarely engage children in conversation so children hear little CDS (Shneidman & Goldin-Meadow, 2012). Despite this, however, it was the number of different words directed to Mayan two-year-olds by adults (and not the number of word types overheard by children or directed at them by other children) that predicted the children's vocabulary size a year later (at 35 months). The researchers concluded that "adult talk directed to children is important for early word learning, even in communities where much of children's early language input comes from overheard speech" (Shneidman & Goldin-Meadow, 2012, p. 659).

Second, children who hear more diverse language and more complex language develop language more quickly. For example, Huttenlocher and colleagues (Huttenlocher, Vasilyeva, Cymerman & Levine, 2002) showed that four-year-old children whose parents produced a lot of complex utterances containing more than one clause tended to be good at producing and understanding complex sentences. Interestingly, the researchers performed the same analysis on the children's teachers and found a similar effect. Since there is no biological relationship between a teacher and the children in her/his class, the results cannot be due to the adult and child sharing genes. The effect must be attributed to the input the teacher is providing. The researchers reported that there was no relationship between the children's language and the teacher's input at the start of the school year (i.e. before the teacher and children had much interaction). However, the speed at which the children developed grammar (measured by the rate of syntactic growth) was strongly predicted by the proportion of complex sentences their teacher produced in her/his speech. In other words, children developed syntax more quickly when their teachers used a lot of complex, multi-clausal sentences. This shows quite conclusively that exposing four- and five-year-old children to more diverse, complex speech speeds up the rate at which they develop language.

It is important to note, however, that this relationship might hold only for older children, not younger children. Studies on young children (e.g. Furrow et al., 1979) have shown that mothers who used simpler sentences at the early stages of language development may have children with faster language growth. In addition, other factors may be more important at younger ages. Carpenter and colleagues have found that the type of interaction that parents engage in with their children has an effect at the younger ages (Carpenter et al., 1998). More specifically, they found greater language gains for young children whose parents engaged in a lot of joint engagement activities with their children (see chapter 6). Thus, it is highly likely that different factors might be important at different ages.

There is one final finding that deserves a mention. Many studies report that children of high socio-economic status (SES) tend to learn language earlier and faster than those of low socio-economic status (see Hart & Risley, 1995). SES is usually defined in terms of the amount of education that parents have had, but sometimes in terms of occupational prestige or income. The most likely explanation is that more educated and advantaged parents talk more to their children and use more complex, varied language (Huttenlocher, Waterfall, Vasilyeva, Vevea & Hedges, 2010; Rowe, 2008). In fact, Hart and Risley (1995) estimate that children from high SES families might hear as many as 1100 utterances per day whereas children from low SES families might only hear only about 700 utterances per day. In other words, children of high SES parents are more likely to experience a language-rich environment than children of low SES parents, which then affects their language development.

At the time of writing, we do not know why this is the case. There are two possibilities. First, it may result from the different language abilities of the parents. Street and Dąbrowska (2010) have shown a very strong relationship between adults' level of education and their ability to process complex sentences, so parents with more education may simply provide richer language input. A second possibility is that parents from different SES groups have different beliefs and ideas about child development, which affects how they speak to their children. Rowe (2008) provides some support for this idea. She found that high SES parents were more likely to answer questions about child development correctly (e.g. to answer *I disagree* to statements like *infants understand only words they can say*; *the way a child is brought up has little effect on how smart he is*). This subsequently affected how they communicated with their children; these parents tended to use more diverse vocabulary and longer utterances, for example.

Rowe's view seems to gain support from the fact that cultural beliefs affect how parents talk to their children across the world. For example, Ochs and Schieffelin (1984) have reported that the Kaluli of Papua New Guinea believe that children are helpless and have little or no understanding of the world around them. As a result, they rarely engage young children in conversations. Pye (1992) reports that the K'iche' Mayan people of Guatemala have similar beliefs, and thus, "vocal interaction between infants and parents is minimal, although there is some variation between parents in this regard, particularly among different economic classes" (Pye, 1992, pp. 242–243). So, we know that cultural beliefs affect child rearing practices. However, we do not know whether this then affects the speed of language development. Some preliminary evidence comes from Callaghan and colleagues, who compared acquisition in Canada, Peru and India (Callaghan et al., 2011). They reported that vocabulary comprehension was largely unaffected by cultural background, but language production was faster in the Canadian children. However, much more work is necessary to establish the effect of the child's environment on language development.

8.2.4 Characteristics of the child and their role in individual variation

The final part in the jigsaw concerns individual differences within the child herself. Are there differences in how different brains receive the language input and what they do with that input?

One robust finding is the effect of gender. On average, in Western industrial cultures, boys tend to acquire language more slowly than girls in the early years (Fenson et al., 1994). This may be the result of the fact that girls tend to mature earlier than boys, which would give them a slight advantage in language learning. However, there is also evidence that girls and boys experience different socialisation processes. Parents might talk more to girls than to boys or talk to boys and girls about different things. For example, Bouchard reported that boys tended to learn transportation-related words like *bateau* (boat) and *camion* (truck) before girls (Bouchard, Trudeau, Sutton, Boudreault & Deneault, 2009).

Another question is whether there are inherent individual differences in the speed at which a child is able to process information. Adults process between 10 and 15 speech sounds (phonemes) per second, a feat which requires extremely fast, efficient information processing (Cole & Jakimik, 1980). Given this, it seems likely that children who are quicker at processing information are more likely to learn language faster.

We have known for decades that infants understand more words as they age. However, we only discovered recently that infants respond with increasing efficiency and speed to individual words as they age. Fernald and colleagues have been using what they call a looking-while-listening procedure to track where infants look when listening to sentences. Using this, they measure how quickly infants shift their eye gaze to look at a target picture on hearing a word (e.g. how quickly infants shift their eyes to look at an apple on hearing *where's the apple?*). In one study, they found that 15-month-old children responded only after the end of the target word had been presented. However, 24-month-old children shifted their eyes much more quickly, after hearing only the first half of the target word. They concluded that infants become much more efficient at processing and thus recognising familiar words in speech over the course of the second year of life (Fernald et al., 1998).

Importantly, individual differences in how quickly children process words might be related to later language development. Marchman and Fernald (2008) reported that children with a faster processing speed at 25 months of age also performed better on language production tests at eight years of age. Fernald and colleagues suggest that the richness of the input might be behind this all; initiating a "positive feedback loop" (Fernald, Perfors & Marchman, 2006, p. 114). Children with rich language input begin to talk sooner, so they have more experience of both hearing and producing language than those with less rich input. These children could develop faster processing speeds as a result of their increased experience with the language – they get more practice at monitoring clues to a word's meaning.

A third factor concerns stylistic differences in the way in which children learn language. In the 1970s and 1980s, researchers reported recording two different speech styles in young children's early multi-word speech (Peters, 1977; Peters, 1983). First, there was what is called 'analytic' speech, which was the favoured model of communication of *referential* children (Nelson, 1973). Children who favoured a referential style tended to focus on naming things in their speech. They started off by producing clear simple single word utterances (e.g. *doggie, daddy*), progressing in an orderly manner to two-word utterances and then to increasingly long and complex multi-word sentences.

Second was the 'Gestalt' or 'holistic' style of speech. This speech style was favoured by *expressive* children, who used language more to express their emotions and desires and to engage in social routines. Gestalt or holistic learners attempt from the start to produce whole sentences, reproducing the characteristic melodic features of the utterance and certain key sounds (e.g. reproducing the number of syllables, the rhythm of speech and reproducing the first phoneme of the utterance correctly). However, since the children were often unable to articulate the individual words in the sentence clearly, many of their utterances were difficult for adults to interpret (Peters called it the "mush mouth" style, 1977).

Out of these observations came the idea that there might be two fundamentally different styles of language development. Children who favour the analytic style of learning begin to talk by naming things (referential style). There is then a clear transition between one-word utterances (e.g. *Mummy, doggie*) and the beginning of the two-word stage (*Mummy car, doggie go*), which may accompany a sudden and rapid increase in vocabulary. These children go on to display a *telegraphic style* in their first word combinations – linking together content words only, avoiding function words and pronouns (e.g. *want biscuit, open door*).

Children who favour the holistic style of learning start out with a more varied vocabulary. They have fewer names for things and a greater number of verbs, adjectives and function words, often combined in "frozen [unanalysed] phrases" (Peters, 1977). For example, Peters (1977) reports that one child produced *silli-in-it* (*silly, isn't it?*) at age 1;2, despite the fact that none of the separate words ever appeared in other utterances. The transition to multi-word speech is far less obvious and tends not to be marked by a rapid increase in vocabulary. When these children start to combine words together, they use more function words and pronouns from the beginning (e.g. *I want biscuit, you open door*).

Bates has argued that these two speech styles represent two different routes into language; a segmenting 'parts before the whole' mechanism (which learns parts of speech first and only later puts them together), and a suprasegmental 'whole before the parts' mechanism, which learns whole strings and later separates them out into distinguishable parts (Bates, Bretherton & Snyder, 1988). Both of these mechanisms are available for all children to use but for some reason, some children rely more on one than the other in the early stages of language learning. For example, some children may be more willing to take risks with their language development whereas others are more shy or cautious in what they are willing to say (Horgan, 1981). Alternatively, Nelson (1973) suggested that children differ in what they think language is for; with some focussing on objects and others focussing on people. Similarly, Peters (1994) suggests that the holistic approach might be used more often by blind children who are more dependent on speech as a means of social interaction.

However, although we have categorised stylistic differences as 'characteristics of the child' (by placing them in this subsection), some have argued that these differences can be attributed to the child's input. For example, there is some evidence that analytic children have mothers who use more nouns and who focus more on describing objects, whereas holistic children have mothers who focus more on social routines and spend more time directing the child's behaviour (see Pine, 1994, for a review). Similarly, Landau and Gleitman (1985) suggest that mothers of blind children may use more directives and fewer yes–no questions, thus explaining why blind children are more likely to adopt a holistic style. There is also evidence that these input style differences might contribute to cross-linguistic differences. Fernald and Morikawa (1993) report that American mothers label objects more consistently and frequently than Japanese mothers and, as a result, their infants have larger noun vocabularies. Similarly, Lieven (1994) argues that in cultures in which speech to pre-linguistic infants is discouraged (e.g. Kaluli and K'iche' Mayan) children rely on other aspects of the social interaction, such as overheard speech, for language and thus are more likely to take the holistic route. The children learn language by rote-learning chunks of language that they have overheard in conversation, only later analysing these chunks into their component words. In other words, different types of input may lead to different styles of language development.

To conclude this section, it is clear that children differ both in how they learn language and in how quickly they learn language. Research has focussed on three explanations: genetic variation, environmental differences and characteristics of the child herself. However, despite individual differences, all these children end up developing language normally. In the next section we discuss what happens when language outcomes are less successful because children hear very little or even no language in the early years.

8.3 EXTRAORDINARY LANGUAGE ACQUISITION

The key question to be addressed in this section is:

Key question: how robust is language learning under extraordinary circumstances?

There are two important issues here. First, we want to know what happens when children do not hear very much language at all in the early years. But equally importantly, we want to know whether the age at which children are exposed to language matters. Can we learn language if we are only exposed to it later in life or do we have to learn it early on? In other words:

Subsidiary question: is there a critical/sensitive period in language development?

The *critical period* hypothesis has been attributed to Lenneberg (1967) but it has been championed by many other famous researchers (e.g. Pinker, 1994). Lenneberg studied children and adults with brain injury and argued that while adults invariably found it difficult to re-learn their language after brain injury, children almost always fared substantially better (although it is a myth that their language is completely unaffected, see Avila et al., 2010). After studying patients of various ages, Lenneberg concluded that language cannot develop later in life because "after puberty, the ability for self-organisation and adjustment to the physiological demands of verbal behaviour quickly declines" (Lenneberg, 1967, p. 158). The idea is that after puberty the brain is no longer capable of learning language, either for maturational reasons or because of reduced plasticity with development (i.e. the more we know, the harder it is for our brain to adapt to new information). Nowadays, researchers refer to a *sensitive period* more than a critical period. This is because the word *critical* implies that it is impossible to learn language after the period has ended and we know this to be untrue. The term sensitive period more accurately captures the essential characteristic of the hypothesis that language learning should be easier and more effortless in the preschool years.

Clearly, in order to test the critical period hypothesis, we need to study children who have no exposure to language early in life. Do they learn language as easily later in life? Evidence comes from feral and neglected children and from children who are deaf.

8.3.1 Feral and neglected children

Figure 8.1
Victor's portrait from the front cover of Itard (1802).

Throughout history there have been cases of children raised alone in the wild, who were brought into human society only later in life. Many cases of these *Homo ferus* (a classification coined by Linneaus in 1758) are almost certainly apocryphal. However, the case of Victor, the wild boy of Averyon, is well documented by the doctor who studied him, Jean Marc Gaspard Itard (see Lane, 1976). Victor was discovered in 1797, after having spent the first 10 or so years of his life living wild and alone in the forests of southern France. Of course, he had no language at all when he was discovered so Itard set about trying to civilise him and to teach him to speak.

Victor initially showed quite good progress at understanding language and at reading some simple words. He eventually learnt to understand the meaning of action words, for example. However, he never learnt to speak. Famously he had only two words, *Oh, Dieu* 'Oh God' and *lait* 'milk', and his progress soon halted at what Itard called a rudimentary level. Itard eventually concluded that as a result of his early deprivation, Victor was effectively an unteachable deaf-mute: "the ear of our savage … was not … an organ which discriminates the various articulate modifications of the human voice; it was there simply as an instrument of self preservation, which informed him of the approach of a dangerous animal or of the fall of some wild fruit" (Itard, 1802, pp. 78–79). In other words, because Victor had no exposure to language in the early years of his life he had lost the ability to learn language.

A similar case is that of Genie, who was discovered at the age of 13 in Los Angeles and studied by Susan Curtiss and the Genie Team (Curtiss, 1977). From about 20 months to 13 years of age Genie was maltreated by her father; by day she was strapped to a potty, unable to move anything but her hands and feet and at night she was transferred into a restrictive sleeping bag. She was kept in a bare room with very little to stimulate her senses and raised in virtual silence. Her father would beat her if she attempted to produce sounds.

When discovered, Genie did have some language. Rymer (1993) reported that she understood a few words (*mother, walk, go, red, blue, green*) and could produce two expressions, which were, sadly, *stop it* and *no more*. However, the results of the intensive training she was given in language after she was discovered were mixed. On the one hand, she did learn to speak and understand several hundred words and was capable of putting words together in the correct order for English sentences (e.g. she said *bus have big mirror* not *bus big mirror have*). However, her language learning was much slower and more effortful than that of younger children and she never developed full competence in some aspects of grammar. In particular, Genie took a very long time to learn morphology and never really mastered the use of function words like pronouns and auxiliaries or complex syntax. Typically, Genie was much more likely to produce *Dentist say drink water* than *The dentist said I must drink water* (omitting the determiner (*the*), past tense marking (*-ed*), pronoun (*I*) and auxiliary (*must*)). Genie's pronunciation was also odd and she never developed a native accent. As with Victor, then, Genie's case has been taken as support for the critical/sensitive period hypothesis.

However, the final child we will discuss, Isabelle, had a much happier outcome (Davis, 1947). Isabelle was discovered in Ohio at the age of six-and-a-half years. Isabelle had spent these years isolated in a darkened room with her mother, with no language input because her mother was deaf and mute. When discovered, Isabelle could only make croaking noises, but she made such rapid improvement that she had caught up with other children of the same age by the time she was eight years old. However, although Isabelle's case had a much better outcome than Genie's or Victor's, even Isabelle required explicit intensive training to learn language.

These distressing case studies tell us two things, as well as the extent of man's inhumanity to man. First, in the face of severe social, emotional and communicative deprivation, language acquisition is not robust at all. Second, it is difficult to compensate for severe deprivation in early childhood, and perhaps impossible to do so after the end of childhood. The difference between Genie and Isabelle has been cited as evidence that the age at which language acquisition starts is crucial. Isabelle was first exposed to language at the age of six years, with an excellent outcome. Genie, who was not exposed to language until 13 years of age, was never able to reach adultlike competence.

However, the problem with all of these studies is that the children were not just deprived of language. They were deprived of all normal day-to-day human interaction: social contact, informal education, emotional bonds and so on. As a result, even the children who may not have begun with cognitive, social and emotional disabilities ended up with them. This means that it is not clear whether the children developed language problems because they had passed a critical period or because all the other cognitive, social and emotional problems caused by their deprivation got in the way of effective learning. For example, there is speculation that Victor might have originally been abandoned because he had learning disabilities. Similarly, it turns out that Genie processed language using the right hemisphere of her brain as the left hemisphere was atrophied, perhaps as a result of lack of use (Curtiss, Fromkin, Krashen, Rigler & Rigler, 1974). And it is likely that Isabelle had a better childhood than Genie, albeit without verbal communication, which means she may have had fewer severe cognitive, social and emotional problems than Genie. Her mother cared for her, displayed love and affection and, very importantly, communicated with her in rudimentary ways using gestures. So although these studies tell us that exposure to language is essential to learn language, they do not definitively tell us that this exposure must take place in the early years.

In order to investigate critical periods in a more robust way, we have to look at what happens when only language is missing from a child's experience. We need to turn to children who enjoy all the privileges of a normal upbringing, who are loved, cared for and educated, but are not exposed to language.

8.3.2 How do deaf children learn language?

Research on deaf children's language tells us the importance of early exposure. Deaf children learn sign language just as easily as hearing children learn spoken language as long as they are exposed to it in the same way. Sign languages are the equivalent of spoken languages in nearly all fundamental ways, differing only in modality; in spoken languages, we use the voice, in sign language we use the hands, arms and face. Like spoken languages, sign languages develop naturally in deaf communities, then change and evolve. Like spoken languages, we can categorise sign languages into language families (e.g. English, New Zealand and Australian sign languages are closely related enough to be mutually intelligible and could be considered dialects of the same language; Johnston, 2002). Like spoken languages, sign languages have different dialects (signers from Devon in the UK sometimes have problems understanding those from Scotland). At the time of writing, the Ethnologue website lists 130 sign languages, all of which share the same richness and complexity as spoken languages (http://www.ethnologue.com).

Sign and spoken languages also contain equivalent components (words, grammatical structure) and are processed in similar ways (MacSweeney, Capek, Campbell & Woll, 2008). For example, verbs in American Sign Language (ASL) are polycomponential just like verbs in some spoken languages. This means that the sign (word) is made up of a number of meaningful markers. For example, the sign for *walking forward/walk to* in ASL is "hand … placed palm down with an inverted V pointing downwards; the hand moves forward while wiggling the fingers" (Slobin, 2006, p. 31). Slobin suggests this sign is made up of four components, equivalent to morphemes in spoken language:

a)   a property marker [two legs]

b)   a posture marker [erect]

c)   a path marker [forward]

d)   a movement marker [wiggle]

Importantly, the lexicon and grammar of a sign language are often completely different from that of the surrounding spoken language. For example, to ask a question in English we can use a different word order from declaratives (we can say *was she there?* as well as, or instead of, *she was there?*). In ASL, questions and declaratives have the same word order (*she was there*). The questioning element is simply added by the speaker raising the eyebrows. Similarly, ASL uses space rather than word order to indicate who did what to whom. To sign *I see Mary*, the sign for *see* [a horizontal V-handshape] moves from the face of the signer to the location associated with Mary. To sign *Mary sees me* the sign moves from the location associated with Mary to the signer.

Whatever specialisation humans have for language, it seems to work just as well in the signing domain as in the verbal domain. Across many of the different sign languages, the process of acquisition is very similar (see evidence from American, Australian, Brazilian, Danish, French, Japanese, Dutch and Quebec sign language; Mayberry & Squires, 2006). Deaf babies start off with manual babbling (e.g. making a fist or an index finger point). This is followed by the one-word (or semantic one-sign) stage, then the production of simple multi-sign utterances, finishing with the acquisition of morphology and complex syntax. Sign language learners even make grammatical errors, just like spoken language learners. For example, to sign *Abi goes* in American Sign Language, the signer first sets up a location that represents Abi (e.g. a location slightly to the left of the signer) and then performs the sign in that location. Loew (1984) discovered that young children often failed to sign in the correct location, instead using the 'citation' location (in front of the signer's body). Consistent use of these location markers did not occur until age four.

There are even similar individual differences in development across signed and spoken languages. Woolfe and colleagues assessed 29 deaf native British Sign Language users aged eight to 36 months. The researchers used a special

Communicative Development Inventory designed expressly to test British Sign Language (Woolfe, Herman, Roy & Woll, 2010). Because this inventory was based on the MacArthur-Bates Communicative Development Inventory described at the beginning of this chapter and used extensively for spoken language assessment, we may feel fairly secure in making comparisons between sign and spoken language development. Also, although Woolfe's study tested a much smaller number of children, their sample still represents half the deaf signers at this age in the UK at the time, which is a substantial proportion of the population.

The deaf children assessed showed similar individual differences to those reported for spoken languages (Woolfe et al., 2010). Between eight and 11 months of age, the average child understood about 10 signs but there was a huge range of individual differences – the slowest child did not know any signs at 11 months but the fastest child knew 84. The authors also reported that receptive vocabulary (i.e. the number of signs the children understood) exceeded their expressive vocabulary (i.e. the number of signs they produced), as is the case in spoken language. They also found that the amount of BSL training that parents had experienced was related to the children's development. This suggests that in sign languages, as in spoken languages, the amount of language children experience and the complexity of that language has an effect on how quickly children learn language.

However, although the modality of the language (sign vs. spoken) does not seem to affect the course of language development, the timing of exposure to the language does seem to be important, as predicted by the critical/sensitive period hypothesis. Only about 10 per cent of deaf children grow up with fluent signing parents so 90 per cent of children have to learn either sign language or spoken language by other means, usually at a later stage in development. And the result, in these cases, is often far less successful.

Attempts to teach spoken language to deaf children have had very mixed results. There are reports that deaf children have problems acquiring complex syntax and function words like pronouns and auxiliaries, and may even have problems acquiring a large vocabulary (LaSasso & Davey, 1987). Phonology is particularly affected so that the speech of many deaf children is extremely hard to interpret. For example, many deaf learners omit sounds at the ends of words and sounds embedded in consonant clusters, which makes speech difficult to understand (Wolk & Schildroth, 1986). In fact, the results of attempts to teach deaf children spoken language are so inconclusive and variable that teachers cannot even agree on how best to teach language; different methods wax and wane in popularity every year (Schirmer, 2001). For children with some residual hearing, hearing aids are useful but in most cases they do not restore enough hearing to allow the successful development of language. Cochlear implants, which can be implanted in the first few months of life, have resulted in many more successes, but the results vary widely from child to child (see Schauwers, Govaerts & Gillis, 2002).

Attempts to teach sign language to older deaf children and to adults are perhaps more successful but still not perfect. There can be substantial differences between the language ability of children exposed to sign language in early life and those taught it later. Newport (1988, 1990) studied three groups of deaf ASL learners:

1) native learners, who were exposed to ASL from birth by deaf parents, 2) early learners, who started learning it between 4 and 6 years of age, and 3) late learners, who started learning ASL after the age of 12 years. Importantly, Newport controlled for the amount of exposure; all participants had been learning and using ASL for 30 years at the time of testing. She reported that late learners did significantly worse than native learners on a number of tests, but particularly tests of morphology. Even early learners did not always reach native-like competence. Other studies have demonstrated that language processing is distributed across different brain regions in early and late learners, suggesting that they may achieve language competence by different routes (Newman, Bavelier, Corina, Jezzard & Neville, 2002; Wuillemin, Richardson & Lynch, 1994).

Overall, then, the literature on language acquisition in deaf children demonstrates the importance of early exposure. The evidence, thus, seems to provide important support for the critical/sensitive period hypothesis. Before we draw this conclusion, however, we must consider one important fact. When we talk about a critical or sensitive period, we tend think in terms of maturational changes; the older our brains get the less they are able to learn. However, we have to bear in mind that the learning situation is very different in early and late childhood. Children brought up with signing parents are exposed to very similar conditions as children learning spoken language (total immersion in the language during the waking hours, continual interaction in sign language, focus of conversations on the here and now). Older children learning sign language are exposed to a very different environment. They are explicitly taught in a classroom or learn by interacting with a hearing parent, who is usually also a 'novice' sign language learner. Such children have also often already developed a rudimentary gesture-based communication system, which they then have to unlearn. Thus, learning sign language in later childhood is more similar to learning a second language than learning a first.

Even when deaf children are provided with some language input (e.g. provided with a hearing aid or a cochlear implant), their learning situation might still be very different from that of hearing children. In particular, parents may speak differently to deaf children. For example, Kyle and colleagues studied 11 deaf families with both deaf and hearing children and a control group of hearing families with hearing children (Kyle, Ackerman & Woll, 1987; see also Woll & Kyle, 1989). These researchers reported that deaf mothers produced less language overall (speaking or signing) with their pre-linguistic infants and asked fewer questions. It is not yet clear what effect this may have on their language development. In sum, it is difficult to draw strong conclusions about why there is a critical/sensitive period in language acquisition.

8.4 THE RELATIONSHIP BETWEEN LANGUAGE AND COGNITIVE IMPAIRMENT

So far, we have only looked at children who are perfectly capable of learning a language as long as they get the right environment. In this final section we turn our attention to children who have cognitive or language impairments. The study of such children is interesting, partly because the more we know about their disability the better we are able to help them learn a language. However, these studies can also tell us a great deal about development itself. The most hotly contested issue, and the one we will focus on here, is whether there is evidence for a dissociation between language and cognition.

Key question: is there a dissociation between language and cognition?

In the adult brain, particular areas are specialised to perform particular functions. If the visual cortex is lesioned, a person's ability to see is destroyed but not his language. If Broca's area is lesioned, vision is unaffected but language is severely compromised. These facts are undisputable. However, it is not clear whether this is the case with young children. Are we born with a brain centre specialised for language, or even for different subsystems within language, or does the brain become specialised as we grow? This question cuts to the heart of the nature–nurture debate. If we can find children whose problems can only be explained by language-specific mechanisms that operate independently of general learning mechanisms, we can conclude that our brains are specialised for language from the very beginning. However, if we can trace these problems back to more general cognitive processes such as a memory deficit, we can conclude that language learning utilises more general cognitive mechanisms, just as any other cognitive developmental task. Here we debate this issue by focussing on one disorder that has been extensively studied in the literature: children with specific language impairment (research on Williams syndrome, which has also been central in this debate, is omitted for lack of space but is considered in chapter 9 and the online resources accompanying this book).

8.4.1 Who are children with specific language impairment (SLI)?

At first sight, children with SLI are perfect candidates for the dissociation theory. The diagnostic criteria of SLI are that the children show a significant impairment in language learning in the absence of any other impairment. Children with SLI have no hearing impairment, non-verbal intelligence test scores in the normal range and no neurological damage. The fact that we can find children with a language disorder and no other problems seems to support the view that we are born with special mechanisms dedicated to language acquisition alone.

However, we need to be careful about drawing this conclusion. It may be that language relies on certain cognitive mechanisms more than other learning tasks, meaning that a problem with these mechanisms affects language more than other tasks. For example, the ability to remember words and to process stimuli quickly are both critical to language learning so impairment to the mechanisms that govern these abilities may affect language more than other cognitive functions. However, these mechanisms are not language-specific mechanisms. In order to look at whether SLI provides evidence for specialised language acquisition mechanisms, we need to look carefully at what problems the children have. Below we outline some of the main findings about SLI and then consider three theories that try to explain why it occurs:

one that suggests a language-specific impairment and two that suggest that more general cognitive deficits underlie the disorder.

SLI is a heterogeneous disorder, meaning that different children can present very different profiles. However, all children will tend to have some delay across the board in language learning. The traditional method of testing the extent of these delays is to compare children with SLI with two groups of typically developing children: a) age-matched controls, who are children of the same age who are developing language normally, and b) language-matched controls, who are younger typically developing children who have the same level of language ability (usually measured by mean length of utterance or MLU, which measures the average number of words per sentence).

Most studies show that children with SLI are delayed in many aspects of language. They produce their first word later than other children and they learn words, especially verbs, at a slower rate (Trauner, Wulfeck, Tallal & Hesselink, 1995). They also need to hear words more times in order to learn them. In one study, researchers found that children with SLI needed to hear a word 10 times before they remembered it (Rice, Oetting, Marquis, Bode & Pae, 1994). However, the pattern of deficits can vary substantially across children. In fact, Conti-Ramsden and Botting have identified six different clusters of deficits in children with SLI (1999). For example, children in Cluster 5 had problems with all aspects of languages, children in Cluster 1 had poor understanding of grammar though adequate expressive vocabulary, and children in Cluster 6 had good vocabulary and adequate grammar but had problems retelling a story.

In many children, however, one area of language seems to be particularly affected – inflectional morphology. Here we are referring to the inflectional markers that mark tense and agreement (*he plays, he played*) and function words (auxiliary verbs like *is/are/do*, see also chapter 5). Children with SLI tend to leave these out very frequently, so that their language often seems very babyish for their age. For example, instead of saying *Abi wants a ball* a child with SLI may say *Abi want ball*, omitting the inflectional marker on the verb (*wants*) and the indefinite article (*a*). Children with SLI seem delayed even compared with younger children who have the same overall language ability (language-matched controls). In other words, learning morphology seems particularly difficult, even when we take into account the fact that children with SLI learn language at a slower rate than other children (see Bishop, 1997; Leonard, 1998). This problem is so characteristic of SLI that it is considered to be a *diagnostic clinical marker*, used by clinicians and researchers to identify children who have SLI.

This weakness with morphology is not restricted to English children. Leonard and his colleagues have reported that morphology is an area of weakness across many languages, including German, English, Italian, Spanish, Hebrew and Swedish (see Leonard, 2000, for a review). In particular, tense and agreement markers are very frequently omitted in children's speech across languages. However, the specific pattern of impairment varies according to the language. For example, in English, children with SLI frequently omit the third person singular present tense agreement marker '-*s*' (e.g. they say *he play* instead of *he plays*). However, Italian and Hebrew speaking children do not omit the corresponding marker more than language-matched control children. In Italian and Hebrew, a more frequent error is to use the wrong inflectional marker given the context. So in Italian, *dormono* ('they sleep') becomes *dorme* ('he sleeps') and in Hebrew, *hitgalsha* ('she slid') becomes *hitgalesh* ('he slid'). Similarly, English children produce pronouns at the same rate as language-matched control children (e.g. *Jill saw him*) yet Spanish and Italian children frequently omit similar object clitics (e.g. Italian: *Paula vede* 'Paula sees' instead of *Paula lo vede* 'Paula sees him'). In other words, the impairment produces slightly different patterns of results across different languages.

At the same time, children with SLI produce over-generalisation errors, using morphology in novel and productive ways. For example, English children with SLI may produce past tense over-regularisation errors such as **runned* and **goed*, just like younger, typically developing children (see Leonard, Eyer, Bedore & Grela, 1997). The fact that children over-use the past tense marker tells us that the problem does not stem from ignorance of what the marker is and what it does. The children clearly know that you can add *-ed* to verbs to talk about the past. It is just that they do not use it appropriately.

In summary, children with SLI are slower at developing language overall than typically developing children, and seem to have a particular problem with tense and agreement markers. This problem exists across all the languages studied so far, although it presents itself in slightly different ways across languages. This suggests that the deficits interact with the structure of the language in some way, so that some markers are more problematic in some languages than others.

8.4.2 Theories of SLI: evidence for a dissociation between language and cognition?

Now we know what facts we need to explain, we turn to the possible explanations. There are too many theories of SLI to cover them all, so we will focus on the three that have been most well studied. There are, however, many other accounts (e.g. Gopnik, 1990; van der Lely, 1994; Gathercole & Badderley 1990). Leonard (1998) covers all of these, and more, in detail.

8.4.2.1 *A language-specific deficit? The extended optional infinitive stage*

Rice and colleagues have proposed that SLI is caused by a problem in a dedicated language-specific mechanism (Rice, Wexler & Cleave, 1995). At the heart of this theory is the fact that, across languages, children with SLI omit tense and agreement markers and auxiliaries (e.g. they say *he play* or *he playing* instead of *he played* or *he is playing*). Rice argues this is the core underlying deficit in children with SLI.

The starting point for the *extended optional infinitive theory* is Wexler's theory of typical development (Wexler, 1998, see chapter 5). The underlying idea is that children learning certain languages go through a stage of acquisition in which they think that tense and agreement marking is optional in main clauses (example of these languages are Danish, Dutch, English, Faroese, Icelandic, Norwegian, Swedish, French, Irish and Russian). According to the theory, typically developing children go through a stage in which they sometimes omit tense and agreement marking because the mechanism responsible for obligatory tense marking has not yet fully matured. As a result, instead of using the inflected verb form (*yesterday I walked*), preschoolers use an uninflected form (*yesterday I walk*). In English, these errors surface as bare stem forms (**he play* instead of *he plays*). However, in other languages the children clearly use infinitival forms. For example, in French, a child might say *la poupée dormir* (literally, 'the doll to sleep') instead of *la poupée dort* 'the doll sleeps'. As children develop, their mechanism matures and they come to realise that tense and agreement markers are obligatory.

Rice's explanation of SLI is simply that children with SLI spend longer in this stage and, sometimes, never learn that all sentences need tense and agreement marking (i.e. they have an extended optional infinitive stage, Rice et al., 1995). To test the theory, Rice and colleagues examined the speech of five-year-old children with SLI learning English (Rice & Wexler, 1996; Rice et al., 1995). They found that only tense and agreement markers were significantly delayed, as predicted. The relevant markers were third person singular -*s* (*he plays*), past tense -*ed* (*he played*) and different forms of auxiliary BE (*he is playing*) and auxiliary DO (*does he play?*). Importantly, they compared these to another set of markers, equally short and hard to hear but not related to tense and agreement: present progressive -*ing* (*he is playing*), plural -*s* (*the dogs*) and the prepositions *in* (*in the box*) and *on* (*on the table*). They found that these markers did not show the same delay. Rice and colleagues concluded that the best way to characterise SLI was in terms of an extended optional infinitive stage in which children with SLI treat tense and agreement marking as if they are optional in the language.

Results like these have been replicated across different languages. For example, there is evidence of a similar deficit in both German and Swedish (Leonard, Hansson, Nettelbladt & Deevy, 2005; Rice, Ruff Noll & Grimm, 1997). However, as always, the theory is not without its problems. First, there are effects within English that the theory cannot explain. In particular, Rice and colleagues concluded that children with SLI do not omit markers that are not related to tense and agreement but Leonard found that children with SLI do, in fact, omit these markers (Leonard et al., 1997). They tested 27 children with SLI aged between 3 and 5 years using a similar procedure to that used by Rice. Like Rice, Leonard reported that the SLI children omitted tense-related markers. However, unlike Rice, Leonard also reported that the children omitted other morphemes such as infinitival *to* (*I want to play*), noun plurals (*the dogs*) and possessive -*'s* (e.g. *the girl's shoes*). In other words, the children made the very errors that Rice predicted should not occur. In addition, we must not forget that children with SLI are delayed in other aspects of language, not just morphology. For example, they tend to produce their first word much later than typically developing children and develop vocabulary much more slowly. Thus, some researchers think that the extended optional infinitive theory can only be a part of the story explaining why children develop SLI.

Second, it is not clear whether the predictions hold cross-linguistically. Only some languages are predicted to have an optional infinitive stage – languages like Dutch, German and English. Other languages are not predicted to have an optional infinitive stage – so-called null-subject languages like Spanish and Italian.[2] This means that it is not clear how the theory explains the existence of SLI in such languages. For example, Bedore and Leonard reported that Spanish children with SLI produce "a surprisingly high number of infinitive forms for finite verb items" (Bedore & Leonard, 2001, p. 913), despite the fact that the theory predicts that they will not produce them at all.

In addition, in some languages, children with SLI make other errors that are not predicted by the extended OI account. For example, although Spanish children with SLI do not omit third person verb markers, which is in accordance with the theory's predictions, they do use them incorrectly, in the place of first person forms. They also use singular verb markers when they should use plural verb markers (Bedore & Leonard, 2001). Similarly, Norwegian children use the present tense verb markers instead of the past tense markers (Meyer Bjerkan, 1999) and French children use participles instead of past tense forms (Paradis & Crago, 2001). In fact the cross-linguistic evidence that children are equally likely to use the wrong finite form as the infinitive form in their early speech is strong. It leads Paradis and Crago to suggest that the extended OI account must broaden the definition of what constitutes an error to include "most 'basic' verb forms (i.e. the most minimally inflected form, often phonologically closest to the verb root)" (Paradis & Crago, 2001, p. 278). Without this modification, they argue, the theory cannot explain the profile of SLI across languages.

In sum, the extended OI hypothesis suggests that SLI results from a deficit in the dedicated, innate language-specific mechanism responsible for obligatory tense and agreement marking. If correct, this theory would constitute strong evidence in favour of an innate language-specific mechanism in the brain and thus strong evidence for a dissociation between language and cognition. However, as we have seen there are many who argue that the theory, as it stands, cannot explain all the data.

8.4.2.2 *A processing deficit? I: the surface account*

Leonard and his colleagues have proposed a processing explanation of SLI called *the surface account* (see Leonard, 1998). They suggest that children with SLI find it difficult to process information quickly (a speed of processing deficit) and may have problems storing information in working memory (a capacity deficit). The processing deficit affects certain inflectional markers more than other aspects of language because these markers are short, hard to hear and easy to miss.

More specifically, the theory attributes the problem to the fact that three steps are needed to learn morphology. We need to a) hear the marker, b) process it in order to hypothesise its function and then c) store in memory. For example, in order to

---

2   Null subject languages are those in which it is grammatical to omit the sentence subject under certain circumstances (e.g. in Spanish one says *llueve*, 'is raining'). The reason why these languages are not predicted to have an OI stage is complex and is to do with the agreement category taking on the grammatical subject in null subject languages. Wexler (1998) provides a fuller explanation.

learn to use an -*ed* marker when talking about events in the past, we have to notice that the ending is there, hypothesise that it is there to mark past tense, and then store it as a past tense marker. All this processing has to be done as quickly as possible because the rest of the sentence is coming up fast. Children who are unable to process information quickly are, thus, going to be poor at processing the inflections fully and will take longer to learn them. Leonard suggested that while they are still learning the inflections, they are likely to use the bare stem or uninflected forms instead: "it is reasonable to expect that if an inflected word is incompletely processed, only the bare stem will be retained" (Leonard, 1998, p. 251). In other words, children who have a processing deficit are less likely to use inflected forms.

This processing deficit is not specific to language so this theory does not posit a dissociation between language and cognition. The processing deficit does, however, have a substantial effect on language because so much of language relies on us perceiving and interpreting sounds that are of very short duration. In other words, this theory proposes that SLI results from a general processing deficit that has particularly severe consequences for language and for morphology, in particular.

A robust body of evidence supports the surface account. Across languages, shorter, less salient markers are often more severely affected than longer, more salient ones. In other words, those markers that are harder to hear are omitted. In English, for example, children with SLI are likely to omit the present tense marker -*s* (Leonard, 1989). In Italian, however, where the equivalent inflectional marker is more frequent and easier to hear, children with SLI have far less difficulty (Leonard & Bortolini, 1998).

An interesting piece of evidence comes from work on Hebrew. According to the surface account, remember, the problem stems from having to identify a marker and work out its function within a short space of time. As a result, it predicts that children with SLI have more problems when it is difficult to work out a marker's function. We can test this with Hebrew. Hebrew past tense verbs are arguably more complicated than Hebrew present tense verbs. Present tense verbs only have to agree with the subject in gender and number. However, in the past tense, listeners also have to pay attention to person marking, which makes their function more complicated. As the surface account predicts, Hebrew children with SLI make more errors with the more complex past tense morphology than with the simpler present tense morphology (Dromi, Leonard, Adam & Zadunaisky-Ehrlich, 1999).

As always happens, however, the evidence is not all favourable. First, it is difficult to explain why, in some languages, certain errors are less frequent than the account would predict. For example, the account predicts that Spanish children with SLI should have particular problems with definite articles (e.g. *el*, *la*) but this has proven not to be the case; Spanish children with SLI produced them at the same rate as language-matched control children (Bedore & Leonard, 2001). Similarly, the theory has problems explaining why bilingual children with SLI are not more delayed. The surface account predicts that children with SLI need more exposure to learn morphology than non-delayed children. This means that bilingual children with SLI, who hear two languages and are exposed to even less input from each language, should be even slower at learning morphology than monolingual children, who are learning only one language. However, Paradis and colleagues have reported that bilingual children with SLI do not have significantly more problems with morphology than monolingual children (Paradis, Crago & Genesee, 2005/6).

8.4.2.3 *A processing deficit? II: the temporal processing deficit account*

The third account suggests a temporal processing deficit as the cause of SLI. This account has its roots in the 1970s, when Tallal and Piercy discovered that children with SLI could only discriminate between two brief musical tones when they were presented slowly and distinctly, separated by hundreds of milliseconds. If the two tones were presented rapidly in succession, separated only by tens of milliseconds, the children could not distinguish between them (Tallal & Piercy, 1973a, 1973b). Tallal proposed that children with SLI have a temporal processing deficit that means that they cannot process brief, rapidly presented successive acoustic stimuli. This has a huge effect on language because, of course, language is made up of brief, rapidly presented, successive acoustic stimuli.

Tallal's account is similar to Leonard's surface account in some ways. However, it is different in that it suggests that the problem stems from perceiving the markers themselves, whereas Leonard suggests the problem stems from trying to process the function of the markers. Thus, Tallal's account can be seen as the one that posits the most *cognitively general* factor as a cause of SLI. In fact, the theory predicts that children should have a range of difficulties in processing short-lived acoustic stimuli, not just language sounds.

Some studies show that children with SLI have problems processing these types of short acoustic cue as Tallal predicts, and even that children's ability to process these cues predicts how quickly they will develop language (Benasich & Tallal, 1996). For example, in one enormous study, Tallal and colleagues tested over 160 possible causal factors of SLI including perceptual, motor, neurodevelopmental, speech and demographic variables. They identified six effective predictors of whether children were language impaired or not and all six of these related to temporal processing in some way (Tallal, Stark & Mellits, 1985). In other words, it was possible to discriminate between language impaired and non-impaired children simply by looking at their temporal processing abilities. Tallal even devised a successful intervention programme based on the theory, with the aim of improving language by speeding up the children's processing abilities using a series of training exercises. The 'training speech' was acoustically modified so that the all-important brief, rapidly presented cues were amplified and lengthened. As the children went through the training, the speech slowly become more rapid and less amplified, forcing them to process it more quickly. At the end of the intervention programme the gains were substantial. After intensive training for four weeks (two hours a day for five days a week) the children were significantly better at a number of language skills including grammatical understanding (Tallal et al., 1996).

However, there have also been a number of criticisms of the temporal processing account. First, there is evidence that children with SLI may have both a temporal deficit and a deficit in grammar, as predicted, but that the two deficits have separate origins and are independent. For example, in one study, English children with SLI did have some problems distinguishing between short vowel sounds that were embedded in longer strings (e.g. distinguishing *dabiba* from *dabuba*) but their ability to do this task did not correlate with their ability to produce morphology (Evans, Viele & Kass, 2002). In other words, the children who struggled with the speech perception task were not necessarily those who also had severe problems with morphology. This suggests that the difficulties with morphology and with speech perception may in fact be two separate problems.

Second, although the account might work well for English, there are findings in other languages that it cannot explain. Clahsen and colleagues tested German speaking children with SLI, comparing them with typically developing children matched for overall language ability (language matched controls; Clahsen et al., 1992). The children with SLI produced errors with agreement markers but not preterite tense markers, despite the fact that both are of short duration and should, therefore, have been delayed according to the account.

Third, there have been criticisms of Tallal's methodologies. Mody and colleagues have argued that Tallal and associates did not use the appropriate non-speech control stimuli (musical tones) in their studies (Mody, Studdert-Kennedy & Brady, 1997). This means that we cannot tell if the problem is in processing rapid acoustic information in general, as Tallal predicts, or in processing rapid <u>speech</u> sounds in particular. Mody and colleagues studied skilled and poor readers and found that while the children's ability to discriminate speech sounds was impaired, this was not the case for musical tones. They concluded that the deficit could not be attributed to temporal processing in general, but to a problem processing speech sounds in particular.

8.4.3   Evidence from genetics: a gene for language?

So far we have discussed three theories that take a different view about the origins of SLI and thus about the evidence for a dissociation between language and cognition. However, of course, the ultimate evidence for a dissociation between language and cognition would be finding a gene that affected language development while leaving other cognitive abilities unimpaired. We know that SLI has a strong genetic component because of evidence from twin studies showing co-morbidity. Co-morbidity refers to the fact that one of a pair of twins is significantly more likely to have problems with language if the other twin has a diagnosed language disorder. A large number of studies have demonstrated this genetic link (for a review, see Stromswold, 2001). However, this does not mean that there is a gene for language. As we have seen above, SLI could result from general processing deficits that just happen to be particularly problematic for language.

In the 1990s substantial media coverage was given to the apparent discovery of a language gene. The claim stemmed from research on a family in London, known as the KE family. Many members of this family have a mutation affecting the DNA on a gene on chromosome 7, which results in severe speech and language impairments. The discovery of this gene was hailed as providing strong evidence that language and cognition may be controlled by separate genetically encoded mechanisms. For example, the *New York Times* reported the discovery as a "Language gene" (Wade, 2002).

However, subsequent research has robustly debunked this claim. The gene (FOXP2) is actually a gene that regulates the behaviour of many other genes. It has an effect on the development of many organs, including the lung and the gut, not just those important for language development (see Fisher & Marcus, 2006; Marcus & Fisher, 2003). In fact, affected members of the KE family have problems with oral facial movements more generally, not just those associated with speech (e.g. following commands such as "first open your mouth wide, then close your lips tightly together, then make an 'ah' sound"; Alcock, Passingham, Watkins & Vargha-Khadem, 2000). In addition, most children with SLI in other families do not have abnormalities in the FOXP2 gene (see Watson, 2002).

The KE family is extremely unusual. Most of the time, it is not possible to isolate a single gene as the locus of a language disorder. In fact, many researchers are now starting to argue that it is fruitless to look for a single factor as the cause of SLI and that instead we should just acknowledge that SLI is caused by multiple deficits. Bishop is one such researcher. Her reasoning is this. Language acquisition is such a robust skill that it always tries to find a way to develop. If one route is blocked, another can usually be found. This means that identifiable impairments only occur when there are multiple deficits: "development is compromised precisely because more than one cognitive process is disrupted" (Bishop, 2006, p. 220). This might explain why we find such a wide range of different impairments across children classified as having SLI; the children have different combinations of deficits. It might also explain why different studies sometimes come to different or even contradictory conclusions; some researchers are studying children who have impairments that affect grammar more than other aspects of language (van der Lely, Rosen & McClelland, 1998) whereas others are studying children whose deficits affect language across the board. If Bishop is correct, it becomes meaningless to search for a single cause of SLI, either among language-specific or general cognitive mechanisms.

8.5 CHAPTER SUMMARY

In this wide ranging chapter we have looked at research on individual variation to address three key questions. First we addressed the following key question:

What factors influence how quickly and easily children learn their language under normal circumstances?

We looked at whether individual differences are due to a) our genetic inheritance, b) environmental influences (especially the quality of the language input) or c) the child's own language and cognitive mechanisms. It is probably safe to conclude that all three factors are important though how they interact remains to be discovered.

We also looked at language under extraordinary circumstances, examining evidence from neglected and feral children and from deaf children. Here we asked the key question:

How robust is language learning under extraordinary circumstances?

as well as a subsidiary one:

Is there a critical/sensitive period in language development?

We concluded that language acquisition requires exposure to a language to develop and that there probably is some sort of sensitive period. However, the question of why there is a sensitive period remains outstanding.

Finally we looked at children with specific language impairment, examining the key question:

Is there a dissociation between language and cognition?

We were unable to isolate one single underlying factor as the locus of SLI and thus cannot come to a firm conclusion about this. Perhaps, if Bishop is right, there is no one underlying factor – it might take multiple deficits to disrupt the process.

The over-arching conclusion is that the evidence suggests that language learning is extremely robust; we learn language despite all sorts of difficult circumstances. Only severe social and communicative deprivation and (perhaps multiple) cognitive impairments are capable of disrupting the process. However, as always, there are many questions left outstanding. What kind of input is optimum for language learning? What causes some of us to process our language more quickly? What types of cognitive deficit disrupt language acquisition? And, finally, how do our genetic inheritance and our environments interact to cause individual variation in language acquisition?

8.6 SUGGESTED READING

Bates, E., Dale, P. S. and Thal, D. (1995). Individual differences and their implications for theories of language development. In P. Fletcher and B. MacWhinney (Eds), *The handbook of child language* (pp. 96–151). Blackwell, Oxford. A great investigation of individual differences in typically developing children.

Curtiss, S. (1977). *Genie: A psycholinguistic study of a modern-day 'wild child'*. Boston, MA: Academic Press. A detailed look at Genie's development.

Leonard, L. (1998). *Children with specific language impairment*. Cambridge, MA: MIT Press. Chapters 11, 12 and 13. A readable review of theories of SLI.

Mayberry, R. I. & Squires, B. (2006). Sign language acquisition. In Brown, K. (Ed.), *Encyclopaedia of language and linguistics* (2nd ed.) (Vol. 11, pp. 291–296). Oxford: Elsevier. A good summary of recent research.

8.7 SUGGESTED READING (ADVANCED LEVEL)

Bates, E., Bretherton, I. & Snyder, L. (1988). *From first words to grammar: Individual differences and dissociable mechanisms.* Cambridge: Cambridge University Press. An in-depth look at individual differences within typically developing populations.

Bishop, D. & Leonard, L. (Eds) (2000). *Speech and language impairments in children: Causes, characteristics, intervention, and outcome.* Hove, UK: Psychology Press. A comprehensive coverage of the topic area.

Lieven, E. (1994). Crosslinguistic and crosscultural aspects of language addressed to children. In C. Gallaway & B. J. Richards (Eds), *Input and interaction in language acquisition* (pp. 57–73). Cambridge: Cambridge University Press. A readable discussion of language development across different cultures.

Schick, B., Marschark, M. & Spencer, P. E. (2005). *Advances in the sign language development of deaf children.* Oxford: Oxford University Press. A collection of informative papers on sign language development.

Stromswold, K. (2001). The heritability of language: A review and metaanalysis of twin, adoption and linkage studies. *Language, 77*(4), 647–723. Stromswold's meta-analysis, referenced in the chapter.

8.8 USEFUL WEBSITES

- The British Deaf association website: http://bda.org.uk/

- http://www.ethnologue.com/web.asp. An encyclopedic reference work cataloguing all of the world's 6909 known living languages that cites 130 different deaf sign languages and the relationships between them.

- The TEDs study: http://www.teds.ac.uk/

- The MacArthur-Bates CDI: http://www.sci.sdsu.edu/cdi/

8.9 COMPREHENSION CHECK

1. At the beginning of the chapter we posed the question 'what factors influence how quickly and easily children learn their language under normal circumstances?' What three factors did we discuss?

2. What is behavioural genetics?

3. After a long history of research, two clear findings emerge about the effect of the environment on individual variation in language development. What are these?

4. Give three ways in which sign language is similar to spoken language.

5. Define specific language impairment.

6. In SLI, which area of language tends to be most affected across languages?

7. Which gene is abnormal in the KE family in London? What effect does it have?

The search for language universals

9.1 THE ISSUE

It is generally assumed that three statements can be applied to all languages across all cultures. The first is that all languages are learnable by the human brain. The second is that all healthy infants are capable of processing and learning any language, thus language is universal. The third is that, although language is universal among humans, only they, and not other animals, learn it under normal circumstances. A plausible corollary of these statements is that there must be some biological component that is both unique to humans and universal across all humans that enables us to learn language. The aim of this chapter is to look at the implications of universality for language acquisition. We will consider two different topics: a) the debate about whether languages all share some common universal features that make them learnable and b) the debates about what learning mechanisms might be unique to language or to the human brain.

9.2 LANGUAGE VARIATION AND LANGUAGE UNIVERSALS

All healthy, typically developing babies are capable of learning any language. If, in a totally unethical, illegal and immoral experiment, we removed a British newborn baby from his mother without her consent and gave him to an Inuit mother to raise in the North American arctic, he would grow up speaking Inuktitut as fluently as any other Inuit child. If we were completely without scruples we could repeat this experiment with any child from any culture with the same results. In fact, we know this is true from studies of international adoptees; that is children from one country who are adopted (with the consent of their parents) into families that live in a different country. These studies show that any typically developing newborn child is capable of learning any language (Glennen & Masters, 2002).

However, the more we learn about the world's languages the more surprising this fact becomes. Languages differ on every conceivable level. Apart from the obvious differences in vocabulary, languages differ in the inventory of speech sounds they use (see chapter 2) and in the syntactic and morphological devices they use to convey meaning (see chapters 4 and 5). Some languages like English are heavily reliant on word order to express meaning, which means that changing the order of the words conveys a completely different meaning (compare *man bites dog* with *dog bites man*). However, other languages like Turkish convey meaning with case markers added to the end of words. Still other languages show neither fixed word order nor case marking (Riau Indonesian). Many languages have no morphemes for marking tense (Chinese), others have no auxiliaries (Bininj Gun-wok) and still others have no adjectives (Lao). Some languages express meanings that seem remarkable to English ears. For example, in Kwak'wala, a native American language, words have to be marked for whether their referents are visible or not. In Central Pomo, a language of California, sentences have to be marked for how speakers gained the information they express, for example, whether they saw, heard, touched it, were told about it, inferred it or know it to be true (for all examples, and references to the original studies, see Evans & Levinson, 2009).

How is it possible that any child can learn any one of these infinitely varied languages? One plausible solution is to propose that, despite their differences, languages all share some common, underlying features, which is what makes them learnable. This idea has been vigorously debated for nearly half a century, in one of the most high profile and, at times, acrimonious arguments in the linguistics literature. In the next sections we debate one of the most influential proposals for such universals, and then discuss the evidence for and against this proposal. The focus of the discussion is our key question:

Key question: do languages all share some common, underlying universal features that make them learnable?

It is important to note that there is a subfield of linguistics (language typology) that aims to document and explain the similarities and differences across the languages of the world (see the Konstanz archive at http://typo.uni-konstanz.de/archive/intro/). We will not focus on this research, fascinating though it is. We focus instead on the theories that aim to explain language acquisition by proposing that languages share certain underlying universal features and that humans are born with the knowledge needed to access these features.

9.3 CHOMSKY'S UNIVERSAL GRAMMAR

Chomsky has long argued that humans could not learn languages without access to innate knowledge of universal linguistic principles (Universal Grammar or UG; Chomsky, 1971). UG was initially proposed to solve the problem of the *poverty of the stimulus*. The poverty of the stimulus was introduced in chapter 4 and is a logical argument that can be summarised thus:

> Language comprises a system of rules for combining words. There are only two
> ways to learn these rules. Either the child's environment or the child's genes
> (genetic inheritance) must provide the information necessary to learn the rules.
> Unfortunately, the child's experience does not provide her with the information

necessary to learn the rules. It is not possible for the child to figure out the rules just by listening to people talking around her. As a result, since the rules of language cannot be learned from the environment, the knowledge necessary to learn the rules of language must be specified in the child's genes.

On this argument, language is unlearnable from the environment alone. It is simply impossible to learn the rules of language simply by listening to other people talk (see chapter 4, section 4.1.1 for a more detailed explanation). Chomsky's solution was to propose that we are born with some form of innate knowledge that makes language learnable. He called this knowledge Universal Grammar (UG). According to this view, children are born with knowledge of UG, which constrains the learning process and, thus, makes the task of learning language possible.

9.3.1 What is in Universal Grammar?

Chomsky's description of UG has changed over the years. The Standard Theory proposed in the 1960s morphed into Government and Binding theory in the 1980s, and finally, into the Minimalist program in the 1990s. All these theories have different implications for variation across languages and for language universals. However, one of these theories has stimulated much more research on language acquisition than others, so this theory is the focus of the present chapter: Government and Binding theory (Chomsky, 1981).

Government and Binding theory characterised UG in terms of a set of principles and parameters (see chapter 4). First, UG was said to contain a set of grammatical *principles* that are shared by all languages universally. For example, if all languages have major lexical categories such as noun and verb, UG might contain knowledge of this fact. Second, UG was said to contain a set of *parameters*, which specify which aspects of grammar can be set to different values depending on the specific language being learnt. Each language has its own unique set of parameter settings and children set the parameters to the correct value in response to hearing *trigger phrases* in their input. These are certain key phrases whose grammar provides unequivocal evidence about how to set the parameters.

The principles of UG mean that, although languages may be superficially different, underneath they follow similar underlying principles. Baker (2003) has provided a very clear example of how superficial differences between languages like Japanese and English hide underlying similarities. On the surface, the word order of Japanese translated literally into English comes across as "gibberish" (Baker, 2003, pp. 350, box 351):

Taroo-ga	*Hiro-ga*	*Hanako-ni*	*zibun-no*	*syasin-o*	*miseta*	*to*	*omotte*	*iru*
Taro	Hiro	Hanako-to	self-of	picture	shows	that	thinking	is

'Taro is thinking that Hiro showed pictures of himself to Hanako'

However, the underlying system governing how words are combined is surprisingly similar in the two languages. Both languages contain nouns, verbs and other word classes, and both languages combine these into phrases in similar ways. The difference is that Japanese builds phrases by adding words to the beginning of the phrase whereas English builds phrases by adding words to the end. For example, in English we put the preposition before the noun (*of himself*) whereas in Japanese we put the equivalent postposition after the noun (*himself of*). English then adds a noun before its preposition (*pictures of himself*) whereas Japanese adds the noun after its postposition (*himself-of picture*). In fact, the difference between the two languages can be explained very simply in terms of Chomsky's *head-direction parameter*, which is a part of UG. Children learning English have to set the head parameter to 'head-initial', which means that the head of the phrase usually comes first, with additional words added on to the end. Children learning Japanese set the parameter to 'head-final', which means that the head of the phrase comes last, with ancillary words like postpositions added to the beginning.

The publication of Chomsky's ideas sparked a world-wide search to discover the universal principles and parameters of language. Below we discuss some of the evidence that has come to light in the search for language universals.

9.3.2 The evidence for universals I: cross-language comparisons

Work on a number of languages supports the idea that superficial differences between languages can hide identical underlying principles. It is difficult to think of a language that does not distinguish between nouns and verbs, for example, even if the way in which nouns and verbs behave in sentences differs across languages. Parameters also seemed to be successful at capturing differences across languages. In fact, Baker argues that the major syntactic differences across languages can be explained using only about 10 to 20 parameters (Baker, 2001).

For example, the head-direction parameter described above seems to capture the difference between the ordering of words in English and Japanese. Parameters also seem to explain why certain syntactic features seemed to cluster together in languages. For example, Rizzi (1982) has suggested that there is a *null subject parameter* that affects a number of syntactic features of a language including:

- whether the language allows sentence subjects to be omitted. This is grammatical in Italian but not in English (e.g. *arriviamo* is translated literally as 'arrive', and means *we arrive*).

- whether free subject inversion is allowed in simple sentences, which allows the subject to appear after the verb. This is grammatical in Italian but not English (*arriva Gianni*, literally translates as 'arrives Gianni', meaning *Gianni arrives*).

According to Rizzi (1982), depending on how the null subject parameter is set, languages can either allow both subject omission and subject inversion or they can prohibit both subject omission and subject inversion. However, they cannot allow one and prohibit the other. This generalisation seemed to capture parametric variation across languages quite nicely. For example, Spanish and Italian allow both subject inversion and subject omission, whereas English prohibits both.

However, a universal should, by definition, be true of all languages, not just some languages. This has caused difficulties because languages are so varied on every level that it is difficult to find universal principles that are true of all of them. Every now and again, a new analysis of a new language pops up that breaks the mould. For example, Greenberg (1966) proposed that all languages will mark negatives by adding an extra morpheme, but this is not the case: Classical Tamil marks the negative by deleting a positive tense morpheme (Pederson, 1993). Similarly, Laudau and Jackendoff (1993) claimed that languages should universally distinguish between nouns, which encode features of objects, and spatial prepositions, which encode spatial relations, because these distinctions correspond to the so-called 'what' and 'where' neural pathways in the brain. However, this predicts that no languages will use prepositions to encode the features of objects, which is immediately contradicted by the existence of precisely such a word in the Native American language Karuk. This word means 'in through a tubular space', thus encoding both the spatial relationship (IN) and the feature of the object (tube-shaped; Mithun, 1999, p. 142). Even the universal classification of words into the big four word class categories of noun, verb, adverb and adjective have been challenged (Evans & Levinson, 2009, p. 434). Hengeveld (1992) suggests that there are languages with no open adverb class and Enfield (2004) reports on a language with no adjective class (Lao, the national language of Laos). There are even those who claim there is no universal distinction between noun and verb classes (Croft, 2001).

It has also proven difficult to devise a set of parameters that can explain diversity across all languages. Above we saw that the null subject parameter proposed by Rizzi predicted that languages can either allow or prohibit both subject omission and subject inversion but they cannot allow one and prohibit another (Rizzi, 1982). However, this is exactly what Brazilian Portuguese and Chinese do; they both allow subject omission but prohibit subject inversion (see Chao, 1981, for work on Brazilian Portuguese; and Huang, 1982, 1984, for work on Chinese). In fact, Newmeyer (2004) has even suggested that parameters have problems explaining variation within a single language. English is said to have SUBJECT-VERB-OBJECT word order (SVO) because the basic sentence type places the subject role first, followed by the verb and then the object (e.g. *the dog chased the man*). The explanation within the principles and parameters framework is that this occurs because the head-direction parameter has been set to 'head-first'. However, there are many examples of English sentences which do not have this word order (e.g. VS: *away ran Alec*; VOS: *drink the whole bottle, Alec never would!*; OSV: *that last lecture Alec really hated*). In order to capture this variation we would need to find a way to explain why these sentences are grammatical; perhaps they are governed by another parameter or by a separate rule? But, Newmeyer asks, how many parameters would we need to capture this variation and is it plausible to propose this number:

> if the number of parameters needed to handle the different grammars of the world's languages, dialects, and (possible) idiolects is in the thousands (or worse, millions) then ascribing them to an innate UG to my mind loses all semblance of plausibility. True, we are not yet at the point of being able to 'prove' that the child is

not innately equipped with 7,846 (or 7,846,938) parameters, each of whose settings is fixed by some relevant triggering experience. I would put my money, however, on the fact that evolution has not endowed human beings in such an exuberant fashion.

(Newmeyer, 2004, p. 196)

In summary, it has been extremely difficult to agree on a list of universal principles and parameters that we could then build into children's Universal Grammar. However, it is important to note that this is not the same as stating that there are no universal tendencies at all. There are a number of patterns that seem to repeat across most, if not all, of the world's languages, which do need to be explained (see Comrie, 1981).

For example, there are six possible ways to order subject (S), verb (V) and object (O) in a basic-level sentence: a) SOV, b) SVO, c) VSO, d) VOS, e) OVS and f) OSV. However, most of the world's languages belong to the first three types, which all place the subject before the object in the basic sentence type. Very few of the world's languages belong to the latter three types, which all place the object before the subject in basic-level sentences. In fact, Comrie suggests that fewer than one per cent of the world's languages belong to these three types (Comrie, 1981). Thus there is a very strong tendency for languages to order subjects before objects in the simplest, most basic-level sentences.

These tendencies can be explained if we see UG not as "an absolute constraint excluding all possibility of violation" (Comrie, 1981, p. 20) but as a default constraint, that applies unless the grammar contains a specific instruction that the constraint should not apply. For example, there could be a default assumption in UG that all languages must place the subject before the object in the sentence type. This constraint would apply to most languages. However, there may also be some languages whose grammar contains an instruction that the object should come before the subject. These languages would have object-subject word order. Since this instruction is unlikely to be very widespread across languages, it would mean that very few (in this case, less than one per cent) of the world's languages would have object-subject word order.

The problem comes when we consider whether this is the most plausible explanation for such universal tendencies. Many have suggested that there are alternative explanations for universal tendencies, which would mean that their existence could be explained without the need to posit UG. For example, universal tendencies may emerge in languages because they make languages easier to comprehend, process or produce. We will explore this idea in a little more detail in section 9.3.3 below. At the moment, we will simply conclude that there are a number of repeating patterns across languages that do need to be explained.

9.3.3 The evidence for universals II: pidgins and Creoles

An alternative way to search for universals is to investigate the creation of pidgins and Creoles. At first sight, this work seems to provide strong evidence for the existence of

UG. Pidgin and Creole languages develop when communities of people, all of whom speak different languages, work and live together and have to develop a system of communication. These conditions arose in Hawai'i in the late nineteenth century, when thousands of Chinese, Portuguese, German, Japanese speakers were shipped there to work on the plantations. These communities developed a basic pidgin in order to communicate. Pidgins are rudimentary communication systems, created by adult speakers who do not share a common language. Pidgins have no recognisable syntactic devices and have an unstable vocabulary made up of words borrowed from the speakers' own native languages. Below are some examples of Hawai'i pidgin from Bickerton (1984, pp. 174–175):

Mi	*kape*	*bai,*	*mi*	*chaek*	*meik*
Me	coffee	buy,	me	check	make

'He bought my coffee; he made me out a check'

(Japanese speaker, 1907)

baimbai	*wi*	*bai*	*eka*	*yo,*	*2,500*	*bai,*	*foa*	*eka*	*bai,*	*laend*
Later	we	buy	acre	EMPHASIS	2,500	buy	four	acre	buy,	land

'Later we bought four acres of land for $2,500'

(Japanese speaker, 1907)

However, the children of these pidgin speakers, who had heard this pidgin language all around them as they were growing up, learnt something different. The language they acquired used the pidgin as the raw material but turned it into a rich and systematically grammatical language. It looked like the children had taken the agrammatical, impoverished pidgin communication system and transformed it into a fully fledged language of their own, with all the features of a natural language (syntax, morphology etc.). We call these new languages Creoles. Bickerton argued that this could only have happened if the children had innate linguistic knowledge – a Universal Grammar – from which to construct the Creole language. Bickerton called his theory the Language Bioprogram Hypothesis, referring to the idea that children are innately biologically programmed to construct a language from whatever raw materials they are given (Bickerton, 1981, 1984). Some examples of Creole sentences are presented below:

dei	*wen*	*go*	*ap*	*dea,*	*in*	*da*	*mawning*	*go*	*plaen*
They	went	go	up	there	in	the	morning	to	plant

'They went up there in the morning to plant [things]'

(1896)

pipl	*no*	*laik*	*tekam*	*fo,*	*go*	*wok*
People	no	like	take-him	for	go	work

'People don't want to have him go to work [for them]'

(1902)

Bickerton pointed out that many of the grammatical features in Creole were absent in the children's input pidgin, including the use of markers for tense and aspect, the use of movement rules for focussing (changing the word order of a sentence to emphasise certain words) and the systematic use of determiners. Many of these grammatical features could not be traced back to the parents' original native languages either (these languages are called the *substrate languages*). For example, immigrant pidgin speakers of Japanese origin used SUBJECT-OBJECT-VERB ordering in their pidgin, reflecting the word order of Japanese. Pidgin speakers from a Filipino background used VERB-SUBJECT-OBJECT ordering, reflecting the Filipino language. Both groups, however, had Creole-speaking children who used SUBJECT-VERB-OBJECT word order in their Creole language. This would not have happened if the children were creating their Creole out of their parents' native languages. Thus, Bickerton argued, the children must be creating Creole out of their innate knowledge of linguistic principles.

However, many have disputed Bickerton's interpretation. Bickerton's evidence came from conversations with pidgin and Creole speakers aged 70 years and above, which he took as proxy evidence for how these speakers first learnt the language between 1900 and 1920. However, this means that he did not have first-hand knowledge of the input that Hawai'i Creole and pidgin speakers were exposed to. In particular, he assumed that the first Creole speakers only had the impoverished pidgin as their input, but this assumption may be unwarranted. For example, Siegel (2008) has argued that the first Creole speakers were exposed to a more stable and developed form of the pidgin language than Bickerton assumed. In other words, the children were not creating the Creole grammar from scratch but were adapting and extending grammatical features already present in their input, albeit in a primitive form. Siegel has also argued that the parents' native languages had a greater influence on the creation of the Creole than Bickerton suggested. Bickerton compared the Creole with Filipino and Japanese, concluding that there were very few if any similarities between them. However, the most important substrate languages at the time were, arguably, Cantonese and Portuguese, which are much more similar to Hawai'i Creole than Filipino and Japanese. In particular, like Hawai'i Creole, Cantonese and Portuguese have SUBJECT-VERB-OBJECT word order.

Bickerton has produced cogent, sometimes passionate, replies to his critics (e.g. Bickerton, 2006). However, the basic methodological issue remains: in the study of the origin of Creole languages, it is crucial to pin down exactly what languages children are exposed to. Unless we can do this, it is difficult to determine if Creole languages are truly created from scratch or are based around regularities in the ambient language.

One final aside. In the 1970s Bickerton applied for money for an experiment to maroon six couples speaking six different languages on an island, together with children too young to have learnt their parents' language. The US National Science Foundation approved the project at first. However, they then pulled out, after a panel of experts raised concerns about the long-term social and emotional effects on the children. As recently as 2008, Bickerton still maintained that this would be the only way to provide definitive answers to the question of language creation. He appealed to billionaires to consider funding such a study: "the sum needed is chump change for all the billionaires floating around nowadays. For any who want to be remembered, it's a great deal" (Bickerton, 2008, p. 245).

9.3.4 The evidence for universals III: home-sign

One way to side-step the problem of exposure in the search for UG is to study the language produced by deaf children who have been exposed neither to spoken language nor to conventional sign language. Goldin-Meadow has done exactly this. She has spent many years analysing the spontaneous signs produced by deaf children whose parents chose to use the oral method of deaf education, using spoken language only, not sign language (e.g. Goldin-Meadow & Mylander, 1984, 1990; Goldin-Meadow, Mylander & Butcher, 1995). The children, perhaps unsurprisingly, made little use of this spoken language, paying attention only to the gestures that accompanied their parents' speech. From these basic gestures, the children developed their own sign-based communication system.

The crucial finding for our purposes is that these sign systems, termed *home-sign*, showed "striking evidence for a prespecified skeleton for language" (Jackendoff, 2002, p. 99). In other words, they were very similar in content and structure to the properties of conventional languages, albeit in a limited way. Four facets of home-sign are particularly significant. First, the children tended to concatenate single gestures into gesture sentences. For example, a gesture for *mouse* might be combined with a gesture for *eat* to convey *mouse eats*. Second, the children's gesture combinations followed a consistent word order pattern, akin to a rudimentary syntactic structure. For example, gestures for actors tended to come before gestures for acts (*mouse-go* not *go-mouse*). Gestures for objects also preceded gestures for actions (*cheese-eat* not *eat-cheese*). Third, the children's signs seemed to have a rudimentary morphology in the sense that handshape forms were combined with motion forms to create different signs. For example, a *Revolve* motion form would be combined with a *OTouch* handform to signal 'rotate an small object'.[1] Fourth, the children produced complex sentences. For example, one child produced the following sequence:

clap gesture – point at himself – *twist* gesture – *blow* gesture – point at mother.

This indicated that he wanted his mother to twist open the jar (proposition 1) and blow a bubble (proposition 2) so that he could clap it (proposition 3; see

---

1 Goldin-Meadow and colleagues used a detailed system to classify the different signs by their shapes. *Revolve* means that the wrist or fingers revolved, *OTouch* refers to the handshape form created when the thumb was close to or touching the fingers.

Goldin-Meadow & Mylander, 1998). This final feature of home-sign is particularly important because it was taken by the authors as evidence of recursion. Recursion is the ability to embed one proposition inside another recursively within a single sentence and it is considered to be the feature that makes language generative and productive (e.g. we can embed the clause *that is brown* inside the phrase *the dog is barking* to give *the dog that is brown is barking*).

Two other aspects of the data are particularly interesting. First, the different home-sign systems developed by different children were extremely similar in their structure, despite the fact that the children came from different language backgrounds. For example, four of the children reported in one of Goldin-Meadow and Mylander's studies came from the USA and four from Taiwan (Goldin-Meadow & Mylander, 1998). Thus, the children were not learning and copying the structure of their ambient languages but were creating basic structures from scratch. Second, although the children's mothers used gestures as well, their gestures did not show the same systematicity as those of their children. In other words, the children were not simply copying the structure of their mothers' signs. As a result, Goldin-Meadow suggested that the features found in home-sign are resilient, in the sense that they develop in the absence of any meaningful input, and "ought to be part of anyone's characterisation of Universal Grammar" (Goldin-Meadow, 2005, p. 217). The features she suggested be included in UG were: the use of discrete symbols combined into primitive sentences, the use of consistent word ordering, the use of morphology, and the use of recursion to create complex sign sentences.

However, as always, critics have taken issue with some of these claims. Particularly controversial is the claim that these children are creating these signs from scratch because they hear no spoken language at all. Many deaf children do have some residual hearing, which may be enough for them to "put together cues from lip-reading, facial expression, sound, gesture and context to extract a coherent and even a reasonably complex meaning structure" (Bates & Volterra, 1984, p. 132). This knowledge could then be put to good use in their sign creation. Similarly, we have to be careful not to over-interpret the data. For example, de Villiers noted that only four of the ten children included in Goldin-Meadow and Mylander's first study (1984) showed a statistically significant consistent object-action ordering in their signs (de Villiers, 1984). This suggests that consistent word order is not a robust feature of all children's home-signs after all. Finally, we also have to be careful not to over-interpret the complexity of the children's signs. For example, Goldin-Meadow and Mylander interpreted sequences such as *Susan/WAVE/Susan/CLOSE* as if they were complex sentences with two propositions, meaning something like *you (Susan) wave (then) you (Susan) close the door*. They argued that "The demonstrated capacity of these children to produce two-proposition complex sentences derived from two single-proposition simple sentences reveals their ability to develop a recursive communication system" (1984, p. 39). However, Bates and Volterra argue that these signs may not be complex sentences but two separate simple sign sentences that are signed quickly one after the other (e.g. the phrase Susan/WAVE followed closely by the phrase Susan/CLOSE; Bates & Volterra, 1984). This would not be a recursive utterance because recursion requires that clauses be embedded within other clauses within the same sentence. Thus, although all agree that these children are creating interesting regularities in their home-sign, not all researchers are convinced that we should attribute these regularities to innate knowledge of language within the child's UG.

Finally, as Morgan points out, it is important not to confuse these home-sign systems with fully fledged languages (Morgan, 2005). Unless they are exposed to sign language from an early age, most deaf children do not learn a language. In fact, many deaf children experience very poor language and cognitive development (Peterson & Siegal, 1995). So it is important not to confuse the ability to create language-like gesture patterns with the ability to create a whole language from scratch. Whatever universal properties children bring to language, this knowledge does not allow them to learn a fully fledged language unless they have continued, extensive interaction with native speakers.

9.3.5 The evidence for universals IV: Nicaraguan Sign Language

Home-sign systems are not fully fledged languages. However, when home-sign users come in contact with other home-sign users their signs can develop into a fully fledged language system. The study of such systems provides an interesting new perspective on our search for UG. The most famous example of one of these languages is Nicaraguan Sign Language.

In 1977 a school for deaf children was opened in Nicaragua in Central America, followed by a school for deaf adolescents in 1980, creating a community of hundreds of deaf students. Until then, most deaf children in Nicaragua had lived in isolated communities with very little contact with other deaf children. At school, however, the deaf pupils mingled and interacted with each other.

The school's aim was to teach the children to speak Spanish and to lip-read, at which tasks it failed spectacularly, since many of the children found it very difficult to learn. However, in order to communicate with each other, the children collaboratively adapted their individual home-sign systems into a communal sign-pidgin, just like the Hawai'i immigrants did a century before them. Since the staff at the school were not involved in the creation of the pidgin (which occurred mainly during the children's lunch breaks and on the bus), they could not communicate with the children; it was the ultimate secret code. So the Nicaraguan Ministry of Education asked Judy Kegl, an American Sign Language expert, to help. After studying the children's communication systems, Kegl and colleagues realised that not only had the first cohort of children at the school created their own pidgin sign language, but the second cohort were busy turning this pidgin into a Creole, with all the characteristics of a mature complex sign language. In fact, this language is now recognised as a fully fledged sign language known as *Idioma de Señas de Nicaragua* (ISN; or Nicaraguan Sign Language, see figure 9.1 for an example).

Because ISN emerged so recently, studying the environment in which it was created has been easier than for other Creoles. These studies reveal that the children really did seem to be creating a new grammatical language out of their rudimentary pidgin home-sign systems. For example, Senghas and Coppola (2001) studied the

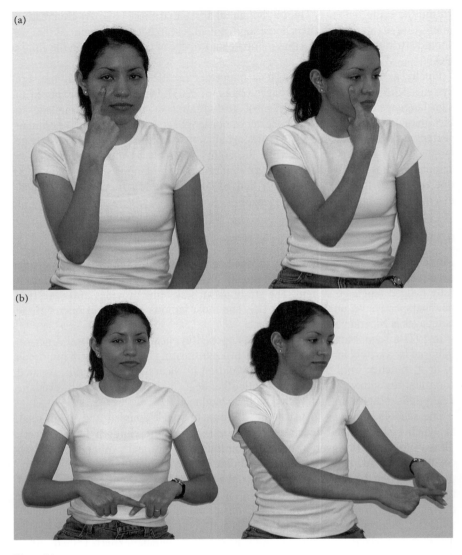

Figure 9.1
The Nicaraguan Sign Language signs (a) 'see' and (b) 'pay' produced in a neutral direction and spatially modulated to the signer's left. Reproduced from Senghas and Coppola (2001, p. 324, Figure 1).

development of spatial modulations in ISN. Spatial modulations refer to the direction of motion in which a sign is produced in sign languages. Most signs are produced centrally, in front of the signer's chest, but by modulating the sign to the right or left, the signer can add a nuanced additional meaning to the relationship between signs. For example, signing *pay* and *see* to the left might indicate that the same man did both the 'seeing' and the 'paying'. Signing *pay* to the left and *see* to the right would convey that one man did the 'seeing' and another did the 'paying'. Similarly, signing *tall* and *cup* in the same location might indicate that the signer is referring to a single 'tall cup'. Senghas and Coppola demonstrated that the first cohort of ISN users did not use spatial modulations in this way. However, the second cohort of ISN users did, despite the fact that the input that they had received had come from the first cohort of signers. In other words, the second cohort had created a consistent, reliable system of spatial modulations in their sign language even though they had not been exposed to such a system in their input.

The creation of ISN among a community of users who had very little exposure to any language has been interpreted as robust evidence that children have access to innate language principles (UG). In addition, it is always the youngest, not the oldest, language users of a community who add complexity to an emerging language, lending support to the idea that childhood is a critical or sensitive period for language acquisition (see chapter 8). However, we must exercise some caution in how we interpret this evidence. It has sometimes been claimed that languages like ISN are created in their full complexity and richness by just one generation of children. If this were the case, it might be strong evidence that children possess powerful innate universal principles. However, this interpretation of the data is considered too strong by some researchers. They argue that interaction with other signers is crucial in the creation of a new language, which suggests a larger role for learning and for the environment than for innate universal principles. Senghas, in particular, has repeatedly emphasised the importance of intergenerational contact for the development of the language, with each new community of users adapting and refining the language of their predecessors (e.g. Senghas, 2003). For example, the spatial modulations that emerged in the second cohort of signers studied by Senghas did not just appear out of nothing but piggybacked off signs that were already being used by the first cohort, albeit in an undifferentiated way. First generation signers were already signing in different locations in space, although they did not use these locations to assign different meanings to their signs as the second cohort did. Thus, according to Senghas, the children are not so much creating a new grammar from scratch as they are modifying and adapting previously meaningless variations in form. This view that language creation occurs when "new functions are first expressed by old forms" (Slobin, 1973, p. 184) is compatible with constructivist ideas about what children universally bring to the language learning task, which we will discuss in section 9.4.

9.4 THE NATURE OF THE LANGUAGE LEARNING MECHANISM

In the previous section we outlined Chomsky's argument that children must be born with innate linguistic principles. As well as disputing the evidence for this statement, as we have seen above, many have disputed the logic behind Chomsky's argument (e.g. Pullum & Scholz, 2002). However, very few have disputed that something needs to be built into the brain to allow us to learn language. On a very simple level this is trivially true, something must be innately built in, otherwise any animal could learn language. So the question is not really whether anything is built in but what is built in? What does the language learning mechanism look like?

Chomsky's answer to the question was to build universal innate linguistic principles into the genetic code. However, there are some prominent alternative ideas about what children bring to the language learning task, which focus on the nature of the language learning mechanism, rather than on searching for universal principles of language. In this section we discuss three of the most influential of these suggestions in an attempt to answer the following key question:

Key question: what mechanisms are required to acquire language, and which of these might be unique to language or to humans?

9.4.1 A specialised linguistic 'toolkit'

Pinker and Jackendoff's (2005) proposal is the closest in kind to Chomsky's original ideas about Universal Grammar. Many of the mechanisms they propose incorporate the type of linguistic universal principles suggested by Chomsky. In fact, Jackendoff has described UG as a linguistic "toolkit" which provides us with a selection of tools with which to build our language (Jackendoff, 2002, p. 75).

What characterises Pinker and Jackendoff's theory is the idea that many of the mechanisms needed to learn language are a) uniquely human, having evolved in our species and no others, and b) specific to language, having evolved for the purpose of communication and no other. According to them, many of the language mechanisms have evolved in humans specifically for the "communication of complex propositions" (Pinker & Jackendoff, 2005, p. 204).

However, it would be a mistake to confuse this with the idea that all the mechanisms involved in language are unique to humans and to language. In fact, Pinker and Jackendoff discuss three different types of language mechanism. The first type are those mechanisms that have multiple functions; those that are used in other tasks as well as language. For example, they suggest that humans must have a mechanism for communicating about concepts such as time, space and causality (*conceptual structure*). This conceptual structure is co-opted for other cognitive tasks as well, such as non-linguistic reasoning, so it is not specific to language. The second type of mechanism refers to those mechanisms that are present in other animals as well as humans, at least in a rudimentary form. For example, much of our speech perception system is shared with other species, including chinchillas (small furry rodents), who can discriminate between pairs of phonemes such as /b/ and /p/ just as human babies can (Kuhl & Miller, 1975, see chapter 2). These mechanisms are not unique to humans.

The third types of mechanism are those that are unique to humans and specific to language. These are the controversial mechanisms because some researchers argue they are not necessary at all (see sections below). According to Pinker and Jackendoff, however, they are essential. In their view, for example, the mechanism that allows us to combine speech sounds in a number of different ways to produce thousands of different words seems to be something only humans can do. In addition, combinations of speech sounds have certain rhythmic properties that seem to be unique to language (and perhaps music).

The mechanisms that learn syntax are also considered to be unique to language and to humans. There are four of these. The *word order* mechanism orders words within phrases and sentences, ensuring that each occupies the correct position. The agreement system ensures that words are marked for functions such as person, tense and number (see chapter 5). The case-marking system ensures that words are marked for their grammatical role (nominative, accusative etc.; see chapter 5). Finally, the recursion mechanism gives language its productivity because it allows us to embed one phrase within another. For example, take the phrase *The TV show that I watched last night was great*, which contains the relative clause *[that I watched last night]*. It is possible to embed another relative clause inside this phrase to produce *The TV show that was directed by Danny Boyle that I watched last night was great*. In fact, it is possible to embed a third relative clause (*The TV show that opened the Olympics that was directed by Danny Boyle that I watched last night was great*) and a fourth, and a fifth ad infinitum. Different languages rely on these four syntactic devices to a greater or lesser extent but they are all considered to be specific to language and to humans.

To summarise, Pinker and Jackendoff conceded that many of the mechanisms involved in language are shared with other animals and with other cognitive functions. However, they hold fast to the idea that some mechanisms, especially those governing phonology and syntax, are unique to humans and have evolved specifically to process language. In numerous articles, published separately and together, Pinker and Jackendoff cite many studies as evidence for their view (see Jackendoff, 1992, 1994, 2002; Pinker, 1994; Pinker & Bloom, 1990; Pinker & Jackendoff, 2005). We have already discussed many similar arguments throughout this book. In fact, one could see the whole of this book as a discussion of evidence for and against the view that humans possess mechanisms that have evolved especially for language. For example, in chapter 2 we discussed the evidence for and against a species-specific mechanism for the production of phonemes (Jakobson's distinctive features, 1941/68). In chapter 3 we discussed evidence for innate constraints on word learning. In chapters 4 and 5 we discussed nativist theories of morphological and syntactic development, all of which propose innate syntax-specific learning mechanisms. Since Pinker and Jackendoff's views effectively build on and synthesise all these debates, it is difficult to decide which arguments to reproduce here. Braving criticisms of misrepresentation and over-simplification, we will not attempt to summarise everything but will focus on some of the arguments that seem to be centrally important.

Pivotal to the theory is the poverty of the stimulus argument. Essentially, the argument is that the speech that children hear is far too impoverished to teach them the grammatical rules necessary to acquire a language. For example, English seems to be governed by something that linguists call *binding principles* in its use of pronouns. These principles govern what pronouns can and cannot refer to. Thus, the pronoun *him* in the sentence *John loves him* cannot refer back to John. If we want to talk about John's narcissism, we have to use a reflexive pronoun: *John loves himself.* Binding principles are highly abstract and seemingly arbitrary so it is difficult to see how they could have been learnt from simply listening to the input (why can't we use *him* in this way?). Yet, children acquire these rules. This is taken as evidence that children have access to innate knowledge that helps them translate the impoverished, unreliable input into a system of structured, systematic rules and, thus, learn their language's grammar.

The evidence for the uniqueness and universality of syntax and morphology is also important for Pinker and Jackendoff's argument (see section 9.2). In their words:

> Languages are full of devices like pronouns and articles, which help signal which information the speaker expects to be old or new to the hearer; quantifiers, tense and aspect markers, complementizers, and auxiliaries, which express temporal and logical relations; restrictive and appositive modification (as in relative clauses); and grammatical distinctions among questions, imperatives, statements, and other kinds of illocutionary force, signaled by phrase order, morphology, or intonation ... Is all this specific to language? It seems likely, given that it is specialized machinery for regulating the relation of sound and meaning. What other human or non-human ability could it serve?
>
> (Pinker & Jackendoff, 2005, pp. 215–216)

In other words, it would seem plausible to assume that such systems derive from a language-specific mechanism that does not serve any other cognitive function. The fact that children create structured, grammatical Creoles out of primitive pidgins also lends weight to the view that children possess a distinct syntax-specific learning mechanism.

However, both the poverty of the stimulus argument and the claims of uniqueness and universality have been challenged. Alternative non-nativist explanations have been provided for a range of phenomena that Pinker and Jackendoff argue can only have emerged from UG. For example, there are challenges to the claim that syntactic principles like binding principles cannot be learnt (van Hoek, 1997). There are also challenges to the claim that the mechanisms underlying syntactic principles are necessarily unique to language. Fitch and colleagues, for example, argue that at least some syntactic principles can be attributed to the conceptual system which even Pinker and Jackendoff acknowledge involves general cognitive mechanisms (Fitch, Hauser & Chomsky, 2005). The universality of certain syntactic features has also been questioned. Tomasello, in particular, tackles head on Pinker's claims about the universality of certain features (Tomasello, 1994). It is worth reproducing his arguments here in full, as they clearly illustrate how difficult it is to find unequivocal evidence for universals:

a) Pinker claims that X-bar version of phrase structure syntax is universal in human languages. However, there are certain types of languages that do not fit well with X-bar syntax. For example, non-configurational languages such as Dyirbal ... stretch the rules considerably (Dixon, 1972) and the language

Lakhota (a native American language) has no coherent verb phrase at all (Van Valin, 1993).

b) Pinker claims that the grammatical relations of subject and object are universal. But there are some languages that show no evidence of these grammatical relations, for example, Acehnese (an Indonesian language, Durie, 1985) and Tagalog (a Philippine language: Maratsos, 1989). If the evidence is viewed in a nondoctrinaire fashion, these languages seem to operate with very concrete linguistic categories such as 'agent', 'topic', and 'actor'.

c) Pinker claims that various phenomena of long-range 'movement' are universal. But for most of the world's languages the whole concept of movement is decidedly inappropriate because when its speakers do such things as form questions they simply substitute a question word for the questioned element, leaving all else in the utterance essentially unchanged (e.g., Mandarin Chinese and Lakhota).

d) It is true, as Pinker claims, that many of the world's languages have grammatical morphemes expressing such things as tense, aspect, modality, case and negation. But which one of these notions particular languages grammaticalize, and how they do so, shows much cross-linguistic variability.

(Tomasello, 1994, pp. 138–139)

Tomasello also takes issue with Pinker's interpretation of the evidence from Creoles. Creoles and sign languages, as we have seen above, may not emerge fully formed from the children's innate syntactic knowledge, but may evolve over generations, as children modify and build on systematic, albeit primitive, regularities in the input that they hear (Senghas, 2003). We also know that language creation requires children to be interacting with a community of like-minded language users. So although the ability to create a new language is clearly unique to humans, the hypothesis that it requires dedicated, language-specific learning mechanisms has not yet been proven.

There is one final, important strand of evidence relevant for Pinker and Jackendoff's theory: the evidence from the profile of certain language disorders. For example, children with Williams syndrome seem to have impaired cognitive functioning but excellent language abilities. Williams syndrome is a genetic disorder that leaves people with, often severe, learning disabilities. However, children with Williams syndrome can have excellent conversational skills. For example, Pinker (1994) cites Bellugi's work with a girl called Crystal who had a very low IQ (50) but seemed to have normal levels of language use. An example of Crystal's conversation is given below:

This is a story about chocolates. Once upon a time, in Chocolate World there used to be a Chocolate Princess. She was such a yummy princess. She was on her chocolate throne and then some chocolate man came to see her. And the man bowed to her and he said these words to her. The man said to her, "Please, Princess Chocolate. I want you to see how I do my work. And it's hot outside in Chocolate World, and you might melt to the ground like melted butter. And if the sun changes to a different color, then the Chocolate World and you – won't melt. You can be saved if the sun changes to a different color. And if it doesn't change to a different color, you and Chocolate World are doomed.

(Pinker, 1994, p. 53)

On the face of it, it looks like Crystal has a successful career as a children's author ahead of her. But she would need a very patient editor because Crystal's learning disability meant that she had a reading age of six years old. Profiles like Crystal's of severe cognitive deficit combined with unimpaired, creative and original language seem to support Pinker and Jackendoff's view that language is governed by at least some mechanisms that are separable and distinct from the mechanisms governing other cognitive functions.

However, this claim is also disputed. When we look closer, the evidence of a dissociation between language and cognition in children with Williams syndrome is less clear. For example, Tomasello has suggested that the language of children with Williams syndrome only appears unimpaired when they are compared with children with Down syndrome, whose language is lower than we would expect given their IQ (Tomasello, 1994). When compared with typically developing children, their language seems far from unimpaired. In addition, the onset of language development seems to be delayed in young children with Williams syndrome, so it would be inaccurate to claim that their language develops according to a typical timescale (for a summary of developmental differences, see Karmiloff-Smith, 2008). This suggests that the dissociation between language and cognition may not be as well defined as first assumed.

In fact, there is now a large body of evidence that questions the assumption that language skills are intact in children and adults with Williams syndrome. Karmiloff-Smith (2008) cites at least eight studies demonstrating that children and adults with Williams syndrome have an atypical profile in language skills, including phonology, vocabulary, morphology, syntax and communicative ability. For example, Mervis and colleagues found that children with Williams syndrome did not acquire a 10-word vocabulary until about 28 months of age, much later than typically developing children, who acquire a 10-word vocabulary at about 12–13 months (Mervis, Robinson, Rowe, Becerra & Klein-Tasman, 2003). It is important to be cautious here because many of the studies with children with Williams syndrome report conflicting results (see Brock, 2007, for a summary). In essence, we need to know a lot more about how cognitive impairments like Williams syndrome affect the brain before we can draw strong conclusions about the dissociation between language and other cognitive mechanisms.

9.4.2 The Language Faculty Broad and Narrow

In 2002, Hauser, Chomsky and Fitch published a paper that was a radical departure from Chomsky's earlier, long-held position that "there is good reason to suppose that the functioning of the language faculty is guided by special principles specific to this domain" (Chomsky, 1980, p. 44). In the new paper, Hauser and colleagues argued that every language mechanism bar one could be seen in other animals or could be used for other cognitive functions (Hauser, Chomsky & Fitch, 2002). Only one language mechanism – recursion – could be considered unique to language and to humans.

Central to this theory was the distinction between what the authors called the *Language Faculty Broad* (LFB) and the *Language Faculty Narrow* (LFN). The Language Faculty Broad was said to contain two systems: the 'sensory-motor' system and the 'conceptual-intentional' system. Importantly, all the mechanisms in the LFB could be found in other animals and/or other cognitive functions. These included the ability to discriminate speech sounds, the ability to imitate speech sounds and the ability to acquire basic words. None of these mechanisms was, thus, unique to language or unique to humans. The Language Faculty Narrow contained all aspects of the language mechanism that were unique both to humans and to language. Surprisingly, given Chomsky's previous position, only one mechanism was proposed to occur in the Language Faculty Narrow: recursion.

Recursion was introduced above. It is the ability to embed one proposition inside another recursively within a single sentence (e.g. we can embed the phrase *that is brown* inside the phrase *the dog is barking* to give *the dog that is brown is barking*). It is considered to be the feature that gives language its combinatorial power because it allows us to produce sentences of indefinite length, simply by embedding short phrases within each other. According to Hauser and colleagues, recursion remains the only language device that cannot be governed by a general cognitive mechanism. It is also the only device that is unique to humans. Similar recursive abilities have not yet been demonstrated in any other primate species despite the creation of some clever experimental techniques to test the recursive abilities of cotton-top tamarins (a species of tiny monkey; Fitch & Hauser, 2004).

Hauser and colleagues have been attacked from both sides, with criticisms coming from nativists and constructivists alike. On the one hand, nativists such as Pinker and Jackendoff have taken issue with the claim that only recursion is specific to language and to humans. As we saw above, Pinker and Jackendoff have strenuously defended the view that many aspects of language cannot be attributed to mechanisms shared with other animals or other cognitive functions (2005). They cite the lexicon, phonology, word order, case marking and agreement, among others, as features of language that must join recursion in the Language Faculty Narrow. On the constructivist side, there have been challenges to the idea that anything at all is specific to language and unique to humans. Constructivists argue that even recursion is not unique to humans.

For example, although recursion may not have been reported in non-human primates, there is some evidence that songbirds can learn recursive syntactic patterns. Gentner and colleagues discovered this by testing the song recognition abilities of starlings. Starling songs consist of long sequences of sound composed of distinct song sequences (motifs) combined in different ways (Gentner, Fenn, Margoliash & Nusbaum, 2006). Using eight 'rattle' and eight 'warble' motifs as the basic vocabulary of song, the researchers created different song 'languages' that followed different grammatical rules. They found that the starlings had no difficulty distinguishing between the different song languages, including those that had two, three or four motifs embedded recursively in the song. In other words, the songbirds were capable of interpreting simple recursive patterns, contrary to the prediction of Hauser, Chomsky and Fitch.

Everett has also challenged the idea that recursion is necessarily universal to all human languages (Everett, 2005). Everett is a field linguist who has been studying the language of a tribe of Amazonian Indians (the Pirahã) for over 30 years. He has reported that the Pirahã language has no number terms or quantifiers (*all, few, every*), no fixed colour terms and, most importantly for our purposes, no evidence at all for recursion (Everett, 2005). What this means is that it is impossible to embed one clause inside another in Pirahã. For example, because the language has no recursion, the sentence *When I finish eating I want to speak to you* has to be translated as two separate clauses with a clear pause between them (effectively *I finish eating … I speak to you*):

kohoai	*-kabáob*	*-áo*	*ti*	*gí*	*ahoia*	*-soog*	*-abagaí*
Eat	-finish	-temporal	I	you	speak	-desiderative	-frustrated initiation

'When [I] finish eating, I want to speak to you'

(Everett, 2005, p. 630)

In other words, because the language lacks recursion, it is impossible to embed one clause within another to produce *When I finish eating I want to speak to you*. Given that Hauser, Chomsky and Fitch had recently claimed that recursion was the only syntactic device that was universal and unique to language, this claim sparked strong criticism (see Nevins, Pesetsky & Rodrigues, 2009a), a robust rebuttal (Everett, 2009) and a reply to the rebuttal (Nevins et al., 2009b). The question of whether recursion really is universal remains controversial to this day.

9.4.3 'A new machine built out of old parts'

The third and final proposal about the nature of the language mechanism goes even further than Hauser, Chomsky and Fitch by removing everything from the Language Faculty Narrow. This is not the same as claiming that nothing about language is unique to humans. Something about the language faculty must be unique to humans, since humans are the only animals to acquire a language. But that 'something' could be a special combination of mechanisms rather than a special mechanism itself. In other words, perhaps what is unique about humans is not a particular language learning mechanism, but the way in which pre-existing mechanisms interact. Individually and separately, all these mechanisms are found in other species or used in other non-linguistic cognitive tasks. In other words, language is "a new machine built out of old parts" (Bates, Thal & Marchman, 1991, p. 35).

The 'new machine' view is held by a number of researchers, some of whom call themselves constructivists, some of whom are cognitive or functional linguists, and some of whom would be happier with the term "anti-nativist" (Scholz & Pullum, 2002, p. 188). Although these researchers differ in their emphasis, all suggest that general cognitive mechanisms are all that is required to learn language. For example, Tomasello (2003) has suggested the following general cognitive abilities could be enough to explain language acquisition, none of which is unique to language:

1. Socio-cognitive skills such as *intention reading* and *cultural learning*. Intention reading refers to the ability to pay attention to what message (verbal or non-verbal) the speaker intends to convey. Cultural learning refers to the fact that some types of information can be transmitted from one generation to the next in a culture or society via, for example, explicit teaching, social interaction or observational learning. These abilities may be unique to humans but they are not unique to language.

2. Pattern-finding and recognition skills such as *categorisation* and *distributional analysis*. These are all-purpose general cognitive abilities, many of which we share with other animals. These allow us to extract meaningful patterns from our input and to link together words that share form or meaning. Categorisation refers to the ability to group referents, ideas or propositions together on the basis of commonalities (e.g. of meaning). Distributional learning refers to the ability to analyse the distribution of referents, ideas or propositions (e.g. the distribution of words in a sentence) and using this information to link those that behave in similar ways and extract the patterns that govern this behaviour. For example, by linking words that occur in similar positions in sentences, children can build grammatical categories such as noun and verb.

3. Speech perception and production abilities, shared with other animals such as chinchillas. These allow us to process the auditory and visual information necessary to learn a spoken or sign language. For example, our ability to do *categorical perception* allows us to accurately identify phoneme boundaries, paying attention to differences that change one phoneme into another (differences that cross a phoneme boundary) and ignoring any others.

Again, much of the evidence for and against the 'new machine' view has been addressed in detail in other chapters. Once more, we risk the criticism of over-simplification by addressing only a few areas of interest, focussing first on the evidence for language universals.

Although the search for language universals has proved difficult, some devices do seem to occur over and over again in different languages (see section 9.2 above and Comrie, 1981). According to the 'new machine' view, these statistical tendencies are explicable in terms of the constraints of human cognitive abilities (e.g. Bybee, 2010). In other words, languages share the features that make language easier for the human brain to process (see also Christiansen & Chater, 2008).

For example, one robust finding is that most languages have subject before object word orders. Thus, the translation equivalents of *John*~SUBJECT~ *kicked the dog*~OBJECT~ and

*John*_{SUBJECT} *the dog*_{OBJECT} *kicked* are both more common across languages than *the dog*_{OBJECT} *John*_{SUBJECT} *kicked* (Dryer, 2011). Hawkins (1994, 2004) has suggested that this is because we can recognise and produce words in subject-object order more rapidly and easily. This pattern then repeats itself across the world's languages not because it is an inbuilt linguistic principle but because this makes it easier for humans to plan their sentences and to understand the sentences of others. In this, Hawkins seems to be right. Even speakers of languages which allow both word orders seem to interpret and produce sentences with subject-object word order faster than sentences with object-subject word order (Hawkins, 1994). Importantly, this could also explain why children create structured, regular Creoles out of impoverished pidgin input – regular, structured systems are easier to understand and produce.

Almost counter-intuitively, the 'new machine' theory is also compatible with the amount of diversity that we see across languages. If the only constraints on languages come from human cognition, then different populations of language users are free to find different solutions to the problem of communication, within the limits of human cognition. Thus, meaning can be expressed by word order, case marking or any other syntactic device. As long as the cognitive mechanism is capable of linking the syntactic structure to its meaning, the sky's the limit.

Finally, Kirby has provided some startling evidence that universal tendencies may evolve to ease language processing (Kirby, Cornish & Smith, 2008). Rather than waiting centuries to observe language evolution in its natural habitat, Kirby reproduced it in an Edinburgh lab, by teaching participants a simple language, recording the participants' own inaccurate attempts at the language, and then training the next participant on this inaccurate language as input. He then analysed how the language changed as a result of its transmission through 10 successive generations.

The first generation of participants were taught an 'alien' language in which pictures of moving objects were associated with strings of letters. For example, a picture of a spiralling red triangle might be associated with the word *tupim*. This alien language was totally random in the sense that the pairing between the words and the pictures to which the word referred was completely arbitrary. After this training session, the participants were presented with a new set of pictures, and asked to recall the word associated with that picture. In a cunning move, the researchers ensured that some of the pictures had never been seen before. Thus, even if the participants managed to reproduce the training set accurately (most did not), some of their responses had to be created because they could not be remembered. The participants' responses were then used as the training set for the next set of participants, who were trained and tested in the same way. At each stage, the output of the previous generation was used as the input for the next generation. In this way, the researchers could see how the language evolved through succeeding generations.

Kirby and colleagues reported that these artificial languages developed more systematic mappings between the words and the pictures as they evolved. In particular, after a few generations, people started to use the same word to refer to a set of related pictures rather than a single picture. For example, by generation 8, one of the languages developed such that all objects that moved horizontally were called *tuge*, all spiralling objects were *poi* and all bouncing objects were labelled according to shape. Importantly, this made each successive generation of languages easier to learn, so that the later generations reproduced the familiar word-picture mappings more accurately than the earlier generations. In other words, the language became more structured simply because this made it easier to learn. In fact, some of the languages were so easy to learn that they were transmitted perfectly towards the end of the experiment. Participants at the end of the evolutionary strings were able to produce exactly the same word–object mappings as the preceding generation even if they had never seen the object in the training phase. For example, by generation 8 in one of the languages, any spiralling object, even one previously unseen, could be accurately labelled *poi*. Kirby's conclusions are strikingly similar to Senghas's remarks about the creation of Nicaraguan Sign Language: languages develop systematic patterns (grammar) because these make them easier for our human brains to learn (Senghas & Coppola, 2001). In Christiansen and Chater's words, "Language has adapted to our brains" (Christiansen & Chater, 2008, p. 490), just as the 'new machine' theorists predicted.

The difficulty for 'new machine' theorists, however, is proving that general cognitive mechanisms can explain how all features of language are acquired. Languages often contain many complex, seemingly arbitrary devices and it is difficult to see why these make languages easier to process or easier to learn. For example, why does English have constraints such that the question *Who did Isla see Rona with?* is grammatical but the question *Who did Isla see Rona and?* is not? Similarly, what is the functional explanation behind the English binding principle, which allows a co-referring interpretation of *George said he won* (*he* can refer back to *George*) but prevents a co-referring interpretation of *George saw him* (*him* cannot refer back to *George*)? There are some functional explanations of these phenomena that attribute them to processing or pragmatic constraints (e.g. O'Grady, 2005; van Hoek, 1997). However, these have not yet provided conclusive answers to silence the critics.

It is also difficult for 'new machine' theorists to pin down exactly what mechanisms are involved in language processing and to specify how they interact. For example, Tomasello's approach has been to highlight the social skills that children bring to language (Tomasello, 2003). A lot of his work has focussed on showing that children can use skills such as intention reading to learn the meaning of words and sentences. Connectionists like Elman have, however, highlighted the statistical learning skills of infants. A lot of Elman's work has focussed on showing that statistical learning mechanisms – pattern recognisers – can extract meaningful over-arching patterns from the speech stream (e.g. Elman, 1993). Neither of these proposals contradicts the other. In fact, most constructivists would agree that children need both mechanisms and more. However, critics argue that such theories invoke too many different mechanisms, with little attempt to weld them all together into a coherent whole (see Newmeyer, 1998). In some cases, theorists only give examples of the types of mechanism that might be involved, allowing themselves wriggle room to add additional mechanisms if the current ones prove inadequate to explain the data. These problems have prompted some to claim that the theories are unfalsifiable.

Another difficulty for the 'new machine' theorists is defining exactly what it is that allows humans, alone of all species, to learn language. Although general cognitive mechanisms may be enough to learn language, no one is claiming that such mechanisms are identical in humans and other animals. The challenge is explaining how they differ. For example, although chinchillas can be taught categorical perception, they do not tune this ability to perceive only the contrasts present in a particular language, as human infants do (Werker & Tees, 1984). Although chimpanzees may understand the difference between intentional and accidental actions (Call & Tomasello, 1998), only humans have evolved the capacity to predict the more complex intentions, beliefs and desires of others. Similarly, although starlings may be able to master simple recursive songs there is no evidence that their recursive ability is as extensive as that of humans (Gentner et al., 2006). Identifying why and how human cognition differs from that of our evolutionary cousins is central to the success of the 'new machine' approach.

9.5 CHAPTER SUMMARY

This chapter began with three relatively uncontroversial statements about language. First, all languages are learnable by the human brain. Second, all healthy infant brains are capable of processing and learning any language. Third, although language is universal, only humans, not other animals, learn language under normal circumstances.

Finding a coherent explanation for why, and to what extent, these three statements are true has proven to be a revealing enterprise. First, we investigated the search for Universal Grammar (UG) in an attempt to answer the following key question:

Do languages all share some common, underlying universal features that make them learnable?

Although it is difficult to pin down what features may be true of all languages (i.e. present in UG), we cannot conclude just yet that these features do not exist. The debate is still live and the existence of UG remains highly disputed. Some argue that it is premature to conclude that UG does not exist just because we have not hit on the right universal features yet (Nevins, 2009; Rizzi, 2009). It is difficult to dispute the logic of this argument, although it may be possible to argue that people are looking in the wrong place. For example, Tomasello strongly urges researchers to look for universals in the "universal processes of human cognition, communication and vocal-auditory processing" rather than searching for innate linguistic principles (Tomasello, 2005, p. 189).

Second, in our investigation of the mechanisms behind language acquisition, we assessed three answers to the following key question:

What mechanisms are required to acquire language, and which of these might be unique to language or to humans?

Pinker and Jackendoff (2005) have argued that many of the mechanisms required for language must have evolved in humans specifically for this purpose. Hauser, Chomsky and Fitch (2002) disagree. They suggest that only recursion is unique to humans and to language, with elements of all other mechanisms shared with other species or other cognitive functions. Finally, 'new machine' theorists argue that nothing need be unique to humans or to language. What is unique is simply the way in which a number of substrate mechanisms have evolved to interact. The language mechanisms make up a "new machine built out of old parts" (Bates et al., 1991, p. 35).

The debate about the nature of the language mechanism is unlikely to be resolved in the near future. However, this is partly because it is central to everything that language acquisition researchers do. Learning a language is the most complex, difficult task we will ever master in our lives. Yet children find it easier and more effortless than learning to ride a bike. If we ever do, finally, discover the mechanisms responsible for this incredible accomplishment, it will be time to go home, sit down and put our feet up, in the knowledge of a job well done.

9.6 SUGGESTED READING

Collins, J. (2008). *Chomsky: A guide for the perplexed*. Continuum: London. A very readable introduction to Chomsky's ideas.

Comrie, B. (1981). *Language universals and linguistic typology*. Oxford: Blackwell. The second edition of Comrie's classic introductory text on language universals.

Everett, Daniel L. (2008) *Don't sleep, there are snakes: Life and language in the Amazonian jungle*. London: Profile. Details Everett's life with the Pirahã and his discovery of their language.

Tomasello, M. (2008). *Origins of human communication*. Cambridge, MA: MIT Press. Read about Tomasello's 'new machine' view of the origin of the language mechanism.

9.7 SUGGESTED READING (ADVANCED LEVEL)

Christiansen, M. H., Collins, C. & Edelman, S. (Eds). (2009). *Language universals*. New York: Oxford University Press. Some neat ideas about language universals by some very influential thinkers.

Comrie, B. (2008). *The world's major languages*. London: Routledge. Full of fascinating detail about the world's 50 major languages.

We focussed here on Nicaraguan Sign Language but there is a lot of work on language creation among deaf communities. Here is a reference to Sandler's work on Al-Sayyid Bedouin Sign Language, for example:

Sandler, W., Meir, I., Padden, C. & Aronoff, M. (2005). The emergence of grammar: *Systematic structure in a new language. Proceedings of the National Academy of Sciences, 102*(7), 2661–2665.

Follow the debate: Pinker and Jackendoff vs. Hauser, Chomsky and Fitch:

1. Original article: Hauser, M. D., Chomsky, N. & Fitch, W. T. (2002). The faculty of language: What is it, who has it, and how did it evolve? *Science, 298*(5598), 1569–1579.
2. P&J's critique: Pinker, S. & Jackendoff, R. (2005). What's special about the human language faculty? *Cognition, 95*(2), 201–226.
3. The reply to the critique. Fitch, W. T., Hauser, M. D. & Chomsky, N. (2005). The evolution of the language faculty: Clarifications and implications. *Cognition, 97*(2): 179–210.
4. The reply to the reply: Jackendoff, R. & Pinker, S. (2005). The nature of the language faculty and its implications for evolution of language (Reply to Fitch, Hauser & Chomsky), *Cognition, 97*(2), 211–225.

9.8 USEFUL WEBSITES

- www.omniglot.com: An online encyclopaedia of different languages to browse through.

- http://typo.uni-konstanz.de/archive/intro/index.php: Browse through the list of over 2000 possible language universals that have been suggested by researchers, including some which we know now to be false. Or click on Rara to browse through a collection of some language idiosyncrasies that only exist in a very few languages.

- http://wals.info/ *The World Atlas of Language Structures* (*WALS*): A large database containing details of the properties of the world's languages, including maps which show the distribution of different properties across languages. It has been compiled by some of the leading linguists in the field.

9.9 COMPREHENSION CHECK

1. According to Chomsky, why do we need Universal Grammar to explain how children learn language?

2. What is the difference between principles and parameters in Chomsky's Government and Binding theory (Chomsky, 1981)?

3. Explain briefly why some researchers think that the existence of Creoles, home-sign and Nicaraguan Sign Language support the claim that we have a Universal Grammar.

4. Describe the key difference between the following three views of the language mechanism:

   a. Pinker and Jackendoff's (2005) linguistic 'toolkit'
   b. Hauser, Chomsky and Fitch's (2002) Language Faculty Broad and Narrow
   c. 'A new machine built out of old parts'

5. Why do some researchers suggest that Williams syndrome provides evidence for a language mechanism that is separate and distinct from the mechanisms governing other cognitive functions?

6. Explain why Kirby and colleagues' (2008) study on language evolution in the lab provides evidence for the 'new machine out of old parts' theory.

References

Abbot-Smith, K., Lieven, E. & Tomasello, M. (2008). Graded representations in the acquisition of English and German transitive constructions. *Cognitive Development, 23*(1), 48–66.

Abe, K. & Watanabe, D. (2011). Songbirds possess the spontaneous ability to discriminate syntactic rules. *Nature Neuroscience, 14*, 1067–1074.

Abrahamsson, N. & Hyltenstam, K. (2009). Age of onset and nativelikeness in a second language: Listener perception versus linguistic scrutiny. *Language Learning, 59*(2), 249–306.

Akhtar, N. (1999). Acquiring basic word order: Evidence for data-driven learning of syntactic structure. *Journal of Child Language, 26*(2), 339–356.

Akhtar, N. & Tomasello, M. (2000). The social nature of words and word learning. In R. Golinkoff & K. Hirsh-Pasek (Eds), *Becoming a word learner: A debate on lexical acquisition* (pp. 115–135). Oxford: Oxford University Press.

Akhtar, N., Carpenter, M. & Tomasello, M. (1996). The role of discourse novelty in early word learning. *Child Development, 67*(2), 635–645.

Akhtar, N., Jipson, J. & Callanan, M. A. (2001). Learning words through overhearing. *Child Development, 72*(2), 416–430.

Aksu-Koç, A. & Slobin, D. (1985). The aquisition of Turkish. In D. Slobin (Ed.), *The cross-linguistic study of language acquisition* (Vol. 1, pp. 839–878). Hillsdale, NJ: Lawrence Erlbaum Associates.

Alba, R., Logan, J., Lutz, A. & Stults, B. (2002). Only English by the third generation? Loss and preservation of the mother tongue among the grandchildren of contemporary immigrants. *Demography, 39*(3), 467–484.

Albright, A. & Hayes, B. (2003). Rules vs. analogy in English past tenses: A computational/experimental study. *Cognition, 90*(2), 119–161.

Alcock, K. J., Passingham, R. E., Watkins, K. E. & Vargha-Khadem, F. (2000). Oral dyspraxia in inherited speech and language impairment and acquired dysphasia. *Brain and Language, 75*(1), 17–33.

Alegre, M. & Gordon, P. (1999). Rule-based versus associative processes in derivational morphology. *Brain and Language, 68*, 347–354.

Allen, S. E. M. (2000). A discourse-pragmatic explanation for argument representation in child Inuktitut. *Linguistics, 38*, 483–521.

Allen, S. E. M. (2007). Interacting pragmatic influences on children's argument realization. In M. Bowerman & P. Brown (Eds), *Crosslinguistic perspectives on argument structure: Implications for learnability* (pp. 191–210). Mahwah, NJ: Erlbaum.

Ambridge, B. & Lieven, E. V. M. (2011). *Child language acquisition: Contrasting theoretical approaches.* Cambridge: Cambridge University Press.

Ambridge, B., Pine, J. M., Rowland, C. F. & Young, C. R. (2008). The effect of verb semantic class and verb frequency (entrenchment) on children's and adults' graded judgements of argument-structure overgeneralization errors. *Cognition, 106*(1), 87–129.

Ambridge, B., Pine, J. M., Rowland, C. F., Freudenthal, D. & Chang, F. (2012). Avoiding dative overgeneralization errors: Semantics, statistics or both? *Language & Cognitive Processes.*

American Psychiatric Association (APA). (2000). *Diagnostic and Statistical Manual of Mental Disorders* (4th edition). Washington, DC: APA.

Aslin, R. N. & Pisoni, D. B. (1980). Some developmental processes in speech perception. In G. H. Yeni-Komshian, J. F. Kavanagh & C. A. Ferguson (Eds), *Child phonology: Perception* (Vol. 2, pp. 67–96). New York: Academic Press.

Aslin, R. N., Werker, J. F. & Morgan, J. L. (2002). Innate phonetic boundaries revisited. *Journal of the Acoustical Society of America, 112*(4), 1257–1260.

Avila, L., Riesgo, R., Pedroso, F., Goldani, M., Danesi, M., Ranzan, J. & Sleifer, P. (2010). Language and focal brain lesion in childhood. *Journal of Child Neurology, 25*(7), 829–833.

Baker, C. L. (1979). Syntactic theory and the projection problem. *Linguistic Inquiry, 10*(4), 533–581.

Baker, M. C. (2001). *The atoms of language: The mind's hidden rules of grammar.* New York: Basic Books.

Baker, M. C. (2003). Linguistic differences and language design. *Trends in Cognitive Sciences, 7*(8), 349–351.

Baldwin, D. A. (1991). Infants' contribution to the achievement of joint reference. *Child Development, 62*(5), 875–890.

Baldwin, D. A. (1992). Clarifying the role of shape in children's taxonomic assumption. *Journal of Experimental Child Psychology, 54*(3), 392–416.

Baldwin, D. A. (1993a). Early referential understanding: Infants' ability to recognize referential acts for what they are. *Developmental Psychology, 29*(5), 832–843.

Baldwin, D. A. (1993b). Infants' ability to consult the speaker for clues to word reference. *Journal of Child Language, 20*(2), 395–418.

Baldwin, D. A. & Moses, L. J. (2001). Links between social understanding and early word learning: Challenges to current accounts. *Social Development, 10*(3), 309–329.

Bannard, C. & Matthews, D. (2008). Stored word sequences in language learning – The effect of familiarity on children's repetition of four-word combinations. *Psychological Science, 19*(3), 241–248.

Barner, D., Brooks, N. & Bale, A. (2011). Accessing the unsaid: The role of scalar alternatives in children's pragmatic inference. *Cognition, 118*(1), 84–93.

Barnes, S. B., Gutfreund, M., Satterly, D. & Wells, G. (1983). Characteristics of adult speech which predict children's language development. *Journal of Child Language, 10*(1), 65–84.

Baron-Cohen, S. (1989). Perceptual role taking and protodeclarative pointing in autism. *British Journal of Developmental Psychology, 7*(2), 113–127.

Baron-Cohen, S. (2000). Theory of mind and autism: A fifteen year review. In S. Baron-Cohen, H. Tager-Flusberg & D. J. Cohen (Eds), *Understanding other minds: Perspectives from autism and developmental cognitive neuroscience* (2nd ed.) (pp. 3–20). Oxford: Oxford University Press.

Bartak, L., Rutter, M. & Cox, A. (1975). A comparative study of infantile autism and specific developmental receptive language disorders. I. The children. *The British Journal of Psychiatry, 126*, 127–145.

Bates, E. & Devescovi, A. (1989). A cross-linguistic approach to sentence production. In B. MacWhinney & E. Bates (Eds), *The crosslinguistic study of sentence processing* (pp. 225–256). New York: Cambridge University Press.

Bates, E. & MacWhinney, B. (1987). Competition, variation, and language learning. In

B. MacWhinney (Ed.), *Mechanisms of language acquisition* (pp. 157–194). Hillsdale, NJ: Lawrence Erlbaum Associates.

Bates, E. & Volterra, V. (1984). On the invention of language: An alternative view. Response to S. Goldin-Meadow & C. Mylander, Gestural communication in deaf children: The effects and noneffects of parental input on early language development. *Monographs of the Society for Research in Child Development, 49* (207, Nos. 3–4), 130–143.

Bates, E., Bretherton, I. & Snyder, L. (1988). *From first words to grammar: Individual differences and dissociable mechanisms.* New York: Cambridge University Press.

Bates, E., Camaioni, L. & Volterra, V. (1975). The acquisition of performatives prior to speech. *Merrill-Palmer Quarterly, 21*(3), 205–226.

Bates, E. Dale, P. S. & Thal, D. (1995). Individual differences and their implications for theories of language development. In P. Fletcher and B. MacWhinney (Eds), *The handbook of child language* (pp. 96–151). Blackwell, Oxford.

Bates, E., Thal, D. & Marchman, V. (1991). Symbols and syntax: A Darwinian approach to language development. In N. Krasnegor, D. Rumbaugh, R. Schiefelbusch & M. Studdert-Kennedy (Eds), *Biological and behavioral determinants of language development* (pp. 29–65). Hillsdale, NJ: Lawrence Erlbaum Associates.

Bates, E., MacWhinney, B., Caselli, C., Devescovi, A., Natale, F. & Venza, V. (1984). A crosslinguistic study of the development of sentence interpretation strategies. *Child Development, 55*(2), 341–354.

Bates, E., Marchman, V., Thal, D., Fenson, L., Dale, P., Reznick, J. S., Reilly, J. & Hartung, J. (1994). Developmental and stylistic variation in the composition of early vocabulary. *Journal of Child Language, 21*(1), 85–124.

Bates, E., Thal, D., Trauner, D., Fenson, J., Aram, D., Eisele, J. & Nass, R. (1997). From first words to grammar in children with focal brain injury. *Developmental Neuropsychology, 13*(3), 447–476.

Bedore, L. M. & Leonard, L. (2001). Grammatical morphology deficits in Spanish-speaking children with specific language impairment. *Journal of Speech Language and Hearing Research, 44*, 906–924.

Bellugi, U. (1967). *The acquisition of negation.* Unpublished doctoral dissertation. Harvard University.

Benasich, A. A. & Tallal, P. (1996). Auditory temporal processing thresholds, habituation, and recognition memory over the first year. *Infant Behavior and Development, 19*(3), 339–357.

Bencini, G. M. L. & Valian, V. V. (2008). Abstract sentence representations in 3-year-olds: Evidence from language production and comprehension. *Journal of Memory and Language, 59*(1), 97–113.

Ben-Zeev, S. (1977). The influence of bilingualism on cognitive strategy and cognitive development. *Child Development, 48*(3), 1009–1018.

Bergelson, E. & Swingley, D. (2012). At 6 to 9 months, human infants know the meanings of many common nouns. *Proceedings of the National Academy of Sciences of the USA, 109*, 3253–3258.

Berko, J. (1958). The child's learning of English morphology. *Word, 14*, 150–177.

Berko, J. & Brown, R. (1960). Psycholinguistic research methods. In P. Mussen (Ed.), *Handbook of research methods in child development* (pp. 517–557). New York: John Wiley.

Berko Gleason, J. (1975). Fathers and other strangers: Men's speech to young children. In D. P. Dato (Ed.), *Developmental psycholinguistics: Theory and applications* (pp. 289–297). Washington, DC: Georgetown University Press.

Berman, R. (1977). Natural phonological processes at the one-word stage. *Lingua, 43*, 1–12.

Berman, R. (1985). The acquisition of Hebrew. In D. Slobin (Ed.), *The cross-linguistic study of language acquisition* (Vol. 1, pp. 255–371). Hillsdale, NJ: Lawrence Erlbaum Associates.

Berman, R. & Sagi, I. (1981). On word formation and word innovations in early age. *Balshanut Ivrit Xofshit, 18.*

Berument, S. K., Rutter, M., Lord, C., Pickles, A. & Bailey, A. (1999). Autism screening questionnaire: Diagnostic validity. *British Journal of Psychiatry, 175,* 444–451.

Best, C. T. (1994). The emergence of native-language phonological influences in infants: A perceptual assimilation model. In C. Goodman & H. Nusbaum (Eds), *The development of speech perception* (pp. 167–224). Cambridge, MA: MIT Press.

Best, C. T. (1995). A direct realist view of cross-language speech. In W. Strange (Ed.), *Speech perception and linguistic experience: Issues in cross-language research* (pp. 171–204). Baltimore, MD: York Press.

Best, C. T., McRoberts, G. W. & Sithole, N. M. (1988). Examination of perceptual reorganization for nonnative speech contrasts: Zulu click discrimination by English-speaking adults and infants. *Journal of Experimental Psychology: Human Perception and Performance, 4,* 45–60.

Bialystok, E. (1986a). Children's concept of word. *Journal of Psycholinguistic Research, 15*(1), 13–32.

Bialystok, E. (1986b). Factors in the growth of linguistic awareness. *Child Development, 57*(2), 498–510.

Bialystok, E. (2001). *Bilingualism in development: Language, literacy, and cognition.* Cambridge: Cambridge University Press.

Bialystok, E. (2006). Effect of bilingualism and computer video game experience on the Simon task. *Canadian Journal of Experimental Psychology, 60*(1), 68–79.

Bialystok, E. (2009). Bilingualism: The good, the bad and the indifferent. *Bilingualism: Language and Cognition, 12*(1), 3–11.

Bialystok, E., Majumder, S. & Martin, M. M. (2003). Developing phonological awareness: Is there a bilingual advantage? *Applied Psycholinguistics, 24*(1), 27–44.

Bialystok, E., Craik, F. I. M., Klein, R. & Viswanathan, M. (2004). Bilingualism, aging, and cognitive control: Evidence from the Simon task. *Psychology and Aging, 19*(2), 290–303.

Bickerton, D. (1981). *The roots of language.* Ann Arbor, MI: Karoma Press.

Bickerton, D. (1984). The language bioprogram hypothesis. *Behavioral and Brain Sciences, 7,* 173–221.

Bickerton, D. (2006). On Siegel on the bioprogram. *Language, 82*(2), 230–232.

Bickerton, D. (2008). *Bastard tongues.* New York: Hill & Wang.

Bishop, D. V. M. (1997). *Uncommon understanding: Development and disorders of language comprehension in children.* Hove, UK: Psychology Press.

Bishop, D. V. M. (1998). Development of the Children's Communication Checklist (CCC): A method for assessing qualitative aspects of communicative impairment in children. *Journal of Child Psychology and Psychiatry, 39*(6), 879–891.

Bishop, D. V. M. (2000). Pragmatic language impairment: A correlate of SLI, a distinct subgroup, or part of the autistic continuum? In D. V. M. Bishop & L. B. Leonard (Eds), *Speech and language impairments in children: Causes, characteristics, intervention and outcome* (pp. 99–113). Hove, UK: Psychology Press.

Bishop, D. V. M. (2003). Autism and specific language impairment: Categorical distinction or continuum? *Novartis Foundation Symposium, 251,* 213–226.

Bishop, D. V. M. (2006). What causes specific language impairment? *Current Directions in Psychological Science, 15*(5), 217–221.

Bishop, D. V. M. & Leonard, L. (Eds). (2000). *Speech and language impairments in children: Causes, characteristics, intervention, and outcome.* Hove, UK: Psychology Press.

Bishop, D. V. M. & Norbury, C. F. (2002). Exploring the borderlands of autistic disorder and specific language impairment: A study using standardised diagnostic instruments. *Journal of Child Psychology and Psychiatry, 43*(7), 917–929.

Bishop, D. V. M. & Rosenbloom, L. (1987). Childhood language disorders: Classification and overview. In W. Yule & M. Rutter (Eds), *Language development and disorders. Clinics in developmental medicine* (pp. 16–41). London: MacKeith Press.

Bleses, D., Vach, W., Slott, M., Wehberg, S., Thomsen, P., Madsen, T. O. & Basboll, H. (2008). The Danish Communicative Developmental Inventories: Validity and main developmental trends. *Journal of Child Language, 35*(3), 651–669.

Bloom, L. (2000). Pushing the limits on theories of word learning. Commentary on Hollich, G., Hirsh-Pasek, K. & Golinkoff, R., Breaking the word learning barrier: An emergentist coalition model for the origins of word learning. *Monographs of the Society for Research in Child Development, 65*(162, No. 3.), 124–135.

Bloom, P. (1990). Subjectless sentences in child language. *Linguistic Inquiry, 21*, 491–504.

Bloom, P. (2000). *How children learn the meanings of words.* Cambridge, MA: MIT Press.

Bloom, P. (2004). Can a dog learn a word? *Science, 304*(5677), 1605–1606.

Boloh, Y. & Ibernon, L. (2010). Gender attribution and gender agreement in 4- to 10-year-old French children. *Cognitive Development, 25*(1), 1–25.

Booth, A. E. & Waxman, S. R. (2002). Word learning is 'smart': Evidence that conceptual information affects preschoolers' extension of novel words. *Cognition, 84*(1), B11–B22.

Booth, A. E. & Waxman, S. R. (2003). Bringing theories of word learning in line with the evidence. *Cognition, 87*(3), 215–218.

Bosch, L. & Sebastián-Gallés, N. (1997). Native-language recognition abilities in 4-month-old infants from monolingual and bilingual environments. *Cognition, 65*(1), 33–69.

Botting, N. & Conti-Ramsden, G. (1999). Pragmatic language impairment without autism: The children in question. *Autism 3*(4), 371–396.

Bouchard, C., Trudeau, N., Sutton, A., Boudreault, M-C. & Deneault, J. (2009). Gender differences in language development in French Canadian children between 8 and 30 months of age. *Applied Psycholinguistics, 30*(4), 685–707.

Bowerman, M. (1973). *Early syntactic development: A cross-linguistic study with special reference to Finnish.* Cambridge: Cambridge University Press.

Bowerman, M. (1978). Systematizing semantic knowledge: Changes over time in the child's organization of word meaning. *Child Development, 49*(4), 977–987.

Bowerman, M. (1988). The 'no negative evidence' problem: How do children avoid constructing an overly general grammar? In J. A. Hawkins (Ed.), *Explaining language universals* (pp. 73–101). Oxford: Blackwell.

Bowerman, M. & Choi, S. (2001). Shaping meanings for language: Universal and language specific in the acquisition of spatial semantic categories. In M. Bowerman & S. L. Levinson (Eds), *Language acquisition and conceptual development* (pp. 475–511). Cambridge: Cambridge University Press.

Bowerman, M. & Brown, P. (2008). *Crosslinguistic perspectives on argument structure: Implications for learnability.* Hillsdale, NJ: Erlbaum.

Bowerman, M., de León, L. & Choi, S. (1995). Verbs, particles, and spatial semantics: Learning to talk about spatial actions in typologically different languages. In E. V. Clark (Ed.). *Proceedings of the 27th annual Child Language Research Forum* (pp. 101–110). Stanford, CA: Center for the Study of Language and Information.

Braine, M. D. S. (1963). The ontogeny of English phrase structure: The 1st phase. *Language, 39*(1), 1–13.

Braine, M. D. S. & Brooks, P. (1995). Verb argument structure and the problem of avoiding an overgeneral grammar. In M. Tomasello & W. E. Merriman (Eds), *Beyond names for things: Young children's acquisition of verbs* (pp. 352–376). Hillsdale, NJ: Lawrence Erlbaum Associates.

Brent, M. R. & Cartwright, T. A. (1996). Distributional regularity and phonotactic constraints are useful for segmentation. *Cognition, 61*(1–2), 93–125.

Brent, M. R. & Siskind, J. (2001). The role of exposure to isolated words in early vocabulary development. *Cognition, 81*(2), B33–B44.

Brock, J. (2007). Language abilities in Williams syndrome: A critical review. *Development and Psychopathology, 19*, 97–127.

Brooks, P. J. & Tomasello, M. (1999). How children constrain their argument structure constructions. *Language, 75*(4), 720–738.

Brooks, P. J., Tomasello, M., Dodson, K. & Lewis, L. B. (1999). Young children's overgeneralizations with fixed transitivity verbs. *Child Development, 70*(6), 1325–1337.

Brooks, R. & Meltzoff, A. N. (2005). The development of gaze following and its relation to language. *Developmental Science, 8*(6), 535–543.

Brown, R. (1973). *A first language: The early stages.* Cambridge, MA: Harvard University Press.

Brown, R. & Hanlon, C. (1970). Derivational complexity and order of acquisition in child speech. In J. R. Hayes (Ed.), *Cognition and the development of language* (pp. 11–53). New York: Wiley.

Bruck, M. & Genesee, F. (1995). Phonological awareness in young second language learners. *Journal of Child Language, 22*(2), 307–324.

Bruner, J. (1978). The role of dialogue in language acquisition. In A. Sinclair, R. Jarvella & W. J. M. Levelt (Eds), *The child's conception of language* (pp. 241–256). Berlin: Springer-Verlag.

Brysbaert, M. (1998). Word recognition in bilinguals: Evidence against the existence of two separate lexicons. *Psychologica Belgica, 38*, 163–175.

Butterworth, G. & Jarrett, N. (1991). What minds have in common is space: Spatial mechanisms serving joint visual attention in infancy. *British Journal of Developmental Psychology, 9*(1), 55–72.

Bybee, J. L. (1995). Regular morphology and the lexicon. *Language and Cognitive Processes, 10*(5), 425–455.

Bybee, J. L. (2010). *Language, usage and cognition.* Cambridge: Cambridge University Press.

Bybee, J. L. & Slobin, D. I. (1982). Rules and schemas in the development and use of the English past tense. *Language, 58*(2), 265–289.

Byers-Heinlein, K., Burns, T. F. & Werker, J. F. (2010). The roots of bilingualism in newborns. *Psychological Science, 21*(3), 343–348.

Cabeza, R. & Nyberg, L. (2000). Imaging cognition ii: An empirical review of 275 PET and fMRI studies. *Journal of Cognitive Neuroscience, 12*, 1–47.

Call, J. & Tomasello, M. (1998). Distinguishing intentional from accidental actions in orangutans (*Pongo pygmaeus*), chimpanzees (*Pan troglodytes*), and human children (*Homo sapiens*). *Journal of Comparative Psychology, 112*(2), 192–206.

Call, J. & Tomasello, M. (2007). *The gestural communication of apes and monkeys.* Mahwah, NJ: Lawrence Erlbaum Associates.

Callaghan, T., Moll, H., Rakoczy, H., Behne, T., Liszkowski, U. & Tomasello, M. (2011). Early social cognition in three cultural contexts. *Monographs of the Society for Research in Child Development, 76*(2), 1–142.

Camaioni, L. (1993). The development of intentional communication: A re-analysis. In J. Nadel & L. Camaioni (Eds), *New perspectives in early communicative development* (pp. 82–96). London: Routledge.

Cameron-Faulkner, T., Lieven, E. V. M. & Theakston, A. (2007). What part of no do children not understand? A usage-based account of multiword negation. *Journal of Child Language, 34*(2), 251–282.

Camus, A. (1942/1946). *The stranger (L'Etranger)* (S. Gilbert, Trans.). New York: Random House.

Carey, S. & Bartlett, E. (1978). Acquiring a single new word. *Papers and Reports on Child Language Development, 15*, 17–29.

Carpenter, M., Nagell, K. & Tomasello, M. (1998). Social cognition, joint attention, and communicative competence from 9 to 15 months of age. *Monographs of the Society for Research in Child Development, 63*(4), 1–143.

Carroll, L. (1871). *Through the looking-glass and what Alice found there.* London: Macmillan.

Cartwright, T. A. & Brent, M. R. (1997). Syntactic categorization in early language acquisition: Formalizing the role of distributional analysis. *Cognition, 63*(2), 121–170.

Casasola, M., Wilbourn, M. K. & Yang, S. (2006). Can English-learning toddlers acquire and generalize a novel spatial word? *First Language, 26*(2), 187–205.

Caselli, C., Casadio, P. & Bates, E. (1999). A comparison of the transition from first words to grammar in English and Italian. *Journal of Child Language, 26*(1), 69–111.

Cazden, C. B. (1968). The acquisition of noun and verb inflections. *Child Development, 39*(2), 433–448.

Chang, F., Dell, G. S. & Bock, K. (2006). Becoming syntactic. *Psychological Review, 113*(2), 234–272.

Chao, W. (1981). Pro-drop languages and nonobligatory control. *University of Massachusetts Occasional Papers in Linguistics, 7*, 46–74.

Chee, M. W. L., Weekes, B., Lee, K. M., Soon, C. S., Schreiber, A., Hoon, J. J. & Chee, M. (2000). Overlap and dissociation of semantic processing of Chinese characters, English words, and pictures: Evidence from fMRI. *Neuroimage, 12*(4), 392–403.

Childers, J. B., Vaughan, J. & Burquest, D. A. (2007). Joint attention and word learning in Ngas-speaking toddlers in Nigeria. *Journal of Child Language, 34*(2), 199–225.

Choi, S. & Gopnik, A. (1995). Early acquisition of verbs in Korean: A crosslinguistic study. *Journal of Child Language, 22*(3), 497–529.

Choi, S., McDonough, L., Bowerman, M. & Mandler, J. M. (1999). Early sensitivity to language-specific spatial categories in English and Korean. *Cognitive Development, 14*, 241–268.

Chomsky, C. (1969). *The acquisition of syntax in children from 5 to 10.* Cambridge, MA: MIT Press.

Chomsky, N. (1957). *Syntactic structures.* The Hague: Mouton.

Chomsky, N. (1959). A review of B. F. Skinner's *Verbal Behavior. Language, 35*, 26–58.

Chomsky, N. (1971). *Problems of knowledge and freedom.* London: Fontana.

Chomsky, N. (1980). *Rules and representations.* New York: Columbia University Press.

Chomsky, N. (1981). *Lectures on government and binding.* Dordrecht: Foris Publications.

Chomsky, N. (1986). *Knowledge of language: Its nature, origin and use.* New York: Praeger.

Chomsky, N. (1995). *The minimalist program.* Cambridge, MA: MIT Press.

Chouinard, M. M. & Clark, E. V. (2003). Adult reformulations of child errors as negative evidence. *Journal of Child Language, 30*(3), 637–669.

Christiansen, M. H. & Chater, N. (2008). Language as shaped by the brain. *Behavioral and Brain Sciences, 31*(5), 489–509.

Christiansen, M. H., Collins, C. & Edelman, S. (Eds). (2009). *Language universals.* New York: Oxford University Press.

Christophe, A., Millotte, S., Bernal, S. & Lidz, J. (2008). Bootstrapping lexical and syntactic acquisition. *Language & Speech, 51*, 61–75.

Christophe, A., Guasti, M. T., Nespor, M., Dupoux, E. & van Ooyen, B. (1997). Reflections on prosodic bootstrapping: Its role for lexical and syntactic acquisition. *Language and Cognitive Processes, 12*(5–6), 585–612.

Clahsen, H., Rothweiler, M., Woest, A. & Marcus, G. F. (1992). Regular and irregular inflection in the acquisition of German noun plurals. *Cognition 45*(3), 225–255.

Clancy, P. M. (2003). The lexicon in interaction: Developmental origins of preferred argument structure in Korean. In J. W. D. Bois, L. E. Kumpf & W. J. Ashby (Eds), *Preferred argument structure: Grammar as architecture for function* (pp. 81–108). Amsterdam: John Benjamins.

Clark, E. V. (1987). The principle of contrast: A constraint on language acquisition. In B. MacWhinney (Ed.), *Mechanisms of language acquisition* (pp. 1–34). Hillsdale, NJ: Lawrence Erlbaum Associates

Clark, E. V. (1990). On the pragmatics of contrast. *Journal of Child Language, 17*(2), 417–431.

Clark, E. V. (1993). *The lexicon in acquisition.* Cambridge: Cambridge University Press.

Clark, E. V. (2003). *First language acquisition.* Cambridge: Cambridge University Press. (2nd edition 2009.)

Clark, E. V. & Amaral, P. M. (2010). Children build on pragmatic information in language. *Language and Linguistic Compass, 4*(7), 445–457.

Clark, E. V. & Clark, H. H. (1979). When nouns surface as verbs. *Language, 55*(4), 767–811.

Clark, E. V. & Estigarribia, B. (2011). Using speech and gesture to inform young children about unfamiliar word meanings. *Gesture 11*(1), 1–23.

Clark, E. V. & Wong, A. D-W. (2002). Pragmatic directions about language use: Offers of words and relations. *Language in Society, 31*(2), 181–212.

Clark, H. H. & Fox Tree, J. E. (2002). Using uh and um in spontaneous speaking. *Cognition 84*, 73–111.

Cole, R. & Jakimik, J. (1980). A model of speech perception. In R. A. Cole (Ed.), *Perception and production of fluent speech.* Hillsdale, NJ: Lawrence Erlbaum Associates.

Collins, J. (2008). *Chomsky: A guide for the perplexed.* Continuum: London.

Colonnesi, C., Stams, G. J. J. M., Koster, I. & Noomb, M. (2010). The relation between pointing and language development: A meta-analysis. *Developmental Review, 30*, 352–366.

Comrie, B. (1981). *Language universals and linguistic typology: Syntax and morphology.* Oxford: Blackwell.

Comrie, B. (2008). *The world's major languages.* London: Routledge.

Comrie, B. (2011). Alignment of case marking. In M. S. Dryer & M. Haspelmath (Eds), *The World Atlas of Language Structures Online.* Munich: Max Planck Digital Library. Retrieved from http://wals.info.

Condry, K. F. & Spelke, E. S. (2008). The development of language and abstract concepts: The case of natural number. *Journal of Experimental Psychology: General, 137*(1), 22–38.

Conti-Ramsden, G. & Botting, N. (1999). Classification of children with specific language impairment. *Journal of Speech, Language and Hearing Research, 42*(5), 1195–1204.

Cooper, R. P. & Aslin, R. N. (1990). Preference for infant-directed speech in the first month after birth. *Child Development, 61*(5), 1584–1595.

Corkum, V. & Moore, C. (1995). Development of joint visual attention in infants. In C. Moore & P. J. Dunham (Eds), *Joint attention: Its origins and role in development* (pp. 61–83). Hillsdale, NJ: Lawrence Erlbaum Associates.

Corvette, G. (1991). *Gender.* Cambridge: Cambridge University Press.

Corvette, G. (2000). *Number.* Cambridge: Cambridge University Press.

Corvette, G. (2006). *Agreement.* Cambridge: Cambridge University Press.

Croft, W. (2001). *Radical construction grammar. Syntactic theory in typological perspectives.* Oxford: Oxford University Press.

Crozier, S., Sirigu, A., Lehaericy, S., van de Moortele, P. F., Pillon, B., Grafman, J., Agid Y., Dubois, B. & LeBihan, D. (1999). Distinct prefrontal activations in processing sequence at the sentence and script level: An fMRI study. *Neuropsychologia, 37*(13), 1469–1476.

Curtin, S. & Werker, J. F. (2007). Perceptual foundations of phonological development. In M. G. Gaskell, G. T. M. Altmann, P. Bloom, A. Caramazza & P. Levelt (Eds), *Oxford handbook of psycholinguistics* (pp. 575–599). Oxford: Oxford University Press.

Curtiss, S. (1977). *Genie: A psycholinguistic study of a modern day 'wild child'.* New York: Academic Press.

Curtiss, S., Fromkin, V., Krashen, S., Rigler, D. & Rigler, M. (1974). The linguistic development of Genie. *Language, 50,* 528–554.

Cutler, A. (1994). Segmentation problems, rhythmic solutions. *Lingua, 92,* 81–104.

Cutler, A. & Carter, D. M. (1987). The predominance of strong initial syllables in the English vocabulary. *Computer Speech & Language, 2,* 133–142.

Cutler, A. & Norris, D. (1988). The role of strong syllables in segmentation for lexical access. *Journal of Experimental Psychology: Human Perception and Performance, 14*(1), 113–121.

Dąbrowska, E. (2001). Learning a morphological system without a default: The Polish genitive. *Journal of Child Language, 28*(3), 545–574.

Dąbrowska, E. (2004). Rules or schemas? Evidence from Polish. *Language and Cognitive Processes, 19*(2), 225–271.

Dąbrowska, E. & Szczerbiński, M. (2006). Polish children's productivity with case marking: The role of regularity, type frequency, and phonological diversity. *Journal of Child Language, 33,* 559–597.

Dale, P. & Goodman, J. C. (2005). Commonality and individual differences in vocabulary growth. In M. Tomasello & D. Slobin (Eds), *Beyond nature-nurture: Essays in honor of Elizabeth Bates* (pp. 41–81). Mahwah, NJ: Lawrence Erlbaum Associates.

Dale, P. S., Dionne, G., Eley, T. C. & Plomin, R. (2000). Lexical and grammatical development: A behavioural genetic perspective. *Journal of Child Language, 27*(3), 619–642.

Davis, K. (1947). Final note on a case of extreme isolation. *American Journal of Sociology, 45,* 554–565.

de Boer, B. (2000). Self organization in vowel systems. *Journal of Phonetics, 28*(4), 441–465.

de Boysson-Bardies, B. (1999). *How language comes to children.* Cambridge, MA: MIT Press.

de Boysson-Bardies, B. & Vihman, M. M. (1991). Adaptation to language: Evidence from babbling and first words in four languages. *Language, 67,* 297–319.

de Boysson-Bardies, B., Hallé, P., Sagart, L. & Durand, C. (1989). A crosslinguistic investigation of vowel formants in babbling. *Journal of Child Language, 6,* 1–17.

De Geer, B. (1992). *Internationally adopted children in communication: A developmental study.* Unpublished doctoral dissertation. Lund University.

De Houwer, A. (1990). *The acquisition of two languages from birth: A case study.* Cambridge: Cambridge University Press.

De Houwer, A. (2007). Parental language input patterns and children's bilingual use. *Applied Psycholinguistics, 28*(3), 411–424.

De Houwer, A. (2009). *Bilingual first language acquisition.* Clevedon, UK: Multilingual Matters.

de Villiers, J. G. (1984). Limited input? Limited structure: Response to S. Goldin-Meadow & C. Mylander, Gestural communication in deaf children: The effects and noneffects of parental input on early language development. *Monographs of the Society for Research in Child Development, 49*(3), 122–130.

de Villiers, J. G. & de Villiers, P. A. (1985). The acquisition of English. In D. Slobin (Ed.), *The cross-linguistic study of language acquisition* (Vol. 1, pp. 27–139). Hillsdale, NJ: Lawrence Erlbaum Associates.

DeCasper, A. J. & Fifer, W. P. (1980). Of human bonding: Newborns prefer their mother's voice. *Science, 208*(4448), 1174–1176.

DeCasper, A. J. & Spence, M. J. (1986). Prenatal maternal speech influences newborns' perception of speech sounds. *Infant Behavior and Development, 9*, 133–150.

Dehaene, S., Dupoux, E., Mehler, J., Cohen, L., Paulesu, E., Perani, D., van de Moortele, P. F., Lehéricy, S. & Le Bihan, D. (1997). Anatomical variability in the cortical representation of first and second languages. *Neuroreport 8*(17), 3809–3815.

Demuth, K. (1988). Noun classes and agreement in Sesotho acquisition. In M. Barlow & C. A. Ferguson (Eds), *Agreement in natural languages: Theories and descriptions* (pp. 305–321). Stanford, CA: CSLI.

Demuth, K. (1989). Maturation and the acquisition of the Sesotho passive. *Language, 65*(1), 56–80.

Demuth, K. (1990). Subject, topic and Sesotho passive. *Journal of Child Language, 17*(1), 67–84.

DePaolis, R. A., Vihman, M. M. & Keren-Portnoy, T. (2011). Do production patterns influence the processing of speech in prelinguistic infants? *Infant Behavior and Development, 34*(4), 590–601.

Deuchar, M. & Quay, S. (1998). One vs. two systems in early bilingual syntax: Two versions of the question. *Bilingualism: Language and Cognition, 1*(3), 231–243.

Deuchar, M. & Quay, S. (2000). *Bilingual acquisition: Theoretical implications of a case study.* New York: Oxford University Press.

Diesendruck, G., Markson, L., Akhtar, N. & Reudor, A. (2004). Two-year-olds' sensitivity to speakers' intent: An alternative account of Samuelson and Smith. *Developmental Science, 7*(1), 33–41.

Dittmar, M., Abbot-Smith, K., Lieven, E. & Tomasello, M. (2008). Young German children's early syntactic competence: A preferential looking study. *Developmental Science, 11*(4), 575–582.

Dixon, R. M. W. (1972). *The Dyirbal language of North Queensland.* Cambridge: Cambridge University Press.

Dobrich, W. & Scarborough, H. S. (1984). Form and function in early communication: Language and pointing gestures. *Journal of Experimental Child Psychology, 38*(3), 475–490.

Dockrell, J., Braisby, N. & Best, R. (2007). Children's acquisition of science terms: Simple exposure is insufficient. *Learning and Instruction, 17*(6), 577–594.

Döpke, S. (2000). *Cross linguistic structures in simultaneous bilingualism.* Amsterdam: John Benjamins.

Dromi, E., Leonard, L. B., Adam, G. & Zadunaisky-Ehrlich, S. (1999). Verb agreement morphology in Hebrew speaking children with specific language impairment. *Journal of Speech, Language and Hearing Research, 42*(6), 1414–1431.

Dryer, M. S. (2011). Order of subject, object, and verb. In M. S. Dryer & M. Haspelmath (Eds), *The world atlas of language structures online.* Munich: Max Planck Digital Library. Retrieved from http://wals.info/.

Dudzinski, K. M., Thomas, J. & Gregg, J. D. (2008). Communication. In W. F. Perrin, B. Würsig & H. C. M. Thewissen (Eds), *Encyclopedia of marine mammals* (2nd ed.). New York: Academic Press.

Dunn, J. & Shatz, M. (1989). Becoming a conversationalist despite (or because of) having an older sibling. *Child Development, 60*(2), 399–410.

Durie, M. (1985). *A grammar of Acehenese.* Dordrecht: Foris.

Durrell, G. (1956). *My family and other animals.* London: Rupert Hart-Davies.

Echols, C. & Newport, E. (1992). The role of stress and position in determining first words. *Language Acquisition, 2,* 189–220.

Eilers, R., Wilson, W. & Moore, J. (1979). Speech discrimination in the language-innocent and the language-wise: A study in the perception of voice onset time. *Journal of Child Language, 6,* 1–18.

Eimas, P. D. (1974). Auditory and linguistic processing of cues for place of articulation by infants. *Perception and Psychophysics, 16*(3), 513–521.

Eimas, P. D. (1975). Auditory and phonetic coding of the cues for speech: Discrimination of the [r–l] distinction by young infants. *Perception & Psychophysics, 18*(5), 341–347.

Eimas, P. D. & Miller, J. L. (1980). Discrimination of the information for manner of articulation. *Infant Behavior & Development, 3*(4), 367–375.

Eimas, P. D., Siqueland, E. R., Jusczyk, P. & Vigorito, J. (1971). Speech perception in infants. *Science, 171*(3968), 303–306.

Elman, J. L. (1993). Learning and development in neural networks: The importance of starting small. *Cognition, 48*(1), 71–99.

Elman, J. L., Bates, E. A., Johnson, M. H., Karmiloff-Smith, A., Parisi, D. & Plunkett, K. (1996). *Rethinking innateness: A connectionist perspective on development.* Cambridge, MA: MIT Press.

Enfield, N. J. (2004). Adjectives in Lao. In R. M. W. Dixon & A. Y. Aikhenvald (Eds), *Adjective classes: A cross-linguistic typology* (pp. 323–347). Oxford: Oxford University Press.

Evans, J. L., Viele, K. & Kass, R. E. (2002). Grammatical morphology and perception of synthetic and natural speech in children with specific language impairments. *Journal of Speech, Language and Hearing Research, 45*(3), 494–504.

Evans, N. & Levinson, S. C. (2009). The myth of language universals: Language diversity and its importance for cognitive science. *Behavioral and Brain Sciences, 32*(5), 429–492.

Everett, D. (2005). Cultural constraints on grammar and cognition in Pirahã: Another look at the design features of human language. *Cultural Anthropology, 46*(4), 621–646.

Everett, D. (2008) *Don't sleep, there are snakes: Life and language in the Amazonian jungle.* London: Profile.

Everett, D. (2009). Pirahã culture and grammar: A response to some criticisms. *Language, 85*(2), 405–442.

Fennell, C. T., Byers-Heinlein, K. & Werker, J. F. (2007). Using speech sounds to guide word learning: The case of bilingual infants. *Child Development, 78*(5), 1510–1525.

Fenson, L., Dale, P., Reznick, J., Bates, E., Thal, D. & Pethick, S. (1994). Variability in early communicative development. *Monographs of the Society for Research in Child Development, 59*(5). Serial No. 242.

Fenson, L., Marchman, V. A., Thal, D. J., Dale, P. S., Reznick, J. S. & Bates, E. (2007). *MacArthur-Bates communicative development inventories: User's guide and technical manual.* Baltimore, MD: Brookes.

Ferdinand, A. (1996). *The acquisition of the subject in French.* Unpublished doctoral dissertation. Leiden University.

Ferguson, C. A. (1964). Baby talk in six languages. *American Anthropologist, 66*(2), 103–113.

Fernald, A. & Hurtado, N. (2006). Names in frames: Infants interpret words in sentence frames faster than words in isolation. *Developmental Science, 9*(3), F33–F40.

Fernald, A. & McRoberts, G. W. (1996). Prosodic bootstrapping: A critical analysis of the argument and the evidence. In J. L. Morgan & K. Demuth (Eds), *Signal to syntax:*

Bootstrapping from speech to syntax in early acquisition (pp. 365–388). Hillsdale, NJ: Erlbaum.

Fernald, A. & Morikawa, H. (1993). Common themes and cultural variations in Japanese and American mothers' speech to infants. *Child Development, 64*(3), 637–656.

Fernald, A., Perfors, A. & Marchman, V. A. (2006). Picking up speed in understanding: Speech processing efficiency and vocabulary growth across the second year. *Developmental Psychology, 42*(1), 98–116.

Fernald, A., Pinto, J. P., Swingley, D., Weinberg, A. & McRoberts, G. W. (1998). Rapid gains in speed of verbal processing by infants in the second year. *Psychological Science, 9*(3), 72–75.

Fernald, A., Taeschner, T., Dunn, J., Papousek, M., de Boysson-Bardies, B. & Fukui, I. (1989). A cross-language study of prosodic modifications in mothers' and fathers' speech to preverbal infants. *Journal of Child Language, 16*(3), 477–501.

Fikkert, P. & Levelt, C. C. (2008). How does place fall into place? The lexicon and emergent constraints in the developing phonological grammar. In P. Avery, B. Elan Dresher & K. Rice (Eds), *Contrast in phonology: Perception and acquisition* (pp. 219–256.). Berlin: Mouton de Gruyter

Fisher, C. (1996). Structural limits on verb mapping: The role of analogy in children's interpretations of sentences. *Cognitive Psychology, 31*(1), 41–81.

Fisher, C. (2001). Partial sentence structure as an early constraint on language acquisition. In B. Landau, J. Sabini, J. Jonides & E. L. Newport (Eds), *Perception, cognition, and language: Essays in honor of Henry and Lila Gleitman* (pp. 275–290). Cambridge, MA: MIT Press.

Fisher, C. (2002). The role of abstract syntactic knowledge in language acquisition: A reply to Tomasello (2000). *Cognition, 82*(3), 259–278.

Fisher, S. E. & Marcus, G. (2006). The eloquent ape: Genes, brains and the evolution of language. *Nature Reviews: Genetics, 7,* 9–20.

Fitch, W. T. & Hauser, M. D. (2004). Computational constraints on syntactic processing in a nonhuman primate. *Science 303*(5656), 377–338.

Fitch, W. T., Hauser, M. D. & Chomsky, N. (2005). The evolution of the language faculty: Clarifications and implications. *Cognition, 97*(2), 179–210.

Flege, J., Takagi, N. & Mann, V. (1995). Japanese adults can learn to produce English /r/ and /l/ accurately. *Language & Speech, 38*(1), 25–55.

Fodor, J. A. (1983). *Modularity of mind: An essay on faculty psychology*. Cambridge, MA: MIT Press.

Francis, W. S. (1999). Cognitive integration of language and memory in bilinguals: Semantic representation. *Psychological Bulletin, 125*(2), 193–222.

Freudenthal, D., Pine, J. M. & Gobet, F. (2007). Understanding the developmental dynamics of subject omission: The role of processing limitations in learning. *Journal of Child Language 34*(1), 83–110.

Freudenthal, D., Pine, J. M. & Gobet, F. (2010). Explaining quantitative variation in the rate of optional infinite errors across languages: A comparison of MOSAIC and the Variational Learning Model. *Journal of Child Language, 36*(3), 643–669.

Freudenthal, D., Pine, J. M., Aguado-Orea, J. & Gobet, F. (2007). Modelling the developmental pattern of finiteness marking in English, Dutch, German and Spanish using MOSAIC. *Cognitive Science, 31*(2), 311–341.

Friederici, A. D., Ruschemeyer, S. A., Hahne, A. & Fiebach, C. J. (2003). The role of left inferior frontal and superior temporal cortex in sentence comprehension: Localizing syntactic and semantic processes. *Cerebral Cortex, 13*(2), 170–177.

Frith, U. (1989). *Autism: Explaining the enigma*. Oxford: Blackwell.

Furrow, D., Nelson, K. & Benedict, H. (1979). Mothers' speech to children and syntactic development: Some simple relationships. *Journal of Child Language, 6*(3), 423–443.

Gagnon, L., Mottron, L. & Joanette, Y. (1997). Questioning the validity of the semantic pragmatic syndrome diagnosis. *Autism, 1*(1), 37–55.

Galambos, S. J. & Goldin-Meadow, S. (1990). The effect of learning two languages on levels of metalinguistic awareness. *Cognition, 34*(1), 1–56.

Galambos, S. J. & Hakuta, K. (1988). Subject-specific and task-specific characteristics of metalinguistic awareness in bilingual children. *Applied Psycholinguistics, 9*(2), 141–162.

Galang, R. (1988). The language situation of Filipino Americans. In S. L. Mackay & S. C. Wong (Eds), *Language diversity: Problem or resource?* (pp. 229–251). New York: Newbury House Publishers.

Gambell, T. & Yang, C. (2003). *Scope and limits of statistical learning in word segmentation.* Paper presented at the 34th North Eastern Linguistic Society (NELS) Meeting, Stony Brook, New York.

Gambell, T. & Yang, C. (2004). *Statistical learning and universal grammar: Modelling word segmentation.* Paper presented at the 20th International Conference on Computational Linguistics, Geneva, Switzerland.

Ganger, J. B., Pinker, S., Chawla, S. & Baker, A. (1999). *A twin study of early vocabulary and syntactic development.* Unpublished manuscript. Pittsburg, PA.

Garcia, G. N., McCardle, P. & Nixon, S. M. (2007). Development of English literacy in Spanish-speaking children: Transforming research into practice. *Language, Speech, and Hearing Services in Schools, 38*(3), 213–215.

Gardner, R. A., Gardner, B. T. & Van Cantfort, T. E. (1989). *Teaching sign language to chimpanzees.* Albany, NY: SUNY Press.

Garnica, O. (1977). Some prosodic and paralinguistic features of speech to young children. In C. E. Snow & C. A. Ferguson (Eds), *Talking to children: Language input and acquisition* (pp. 63–88). Cambridge: Cambridge University Press.

Gathercole, S. & Badderley, A. (1990). Phonological memory deficits in language disordered children: Is there a causal connection? *Journal of Memory & Language, 29*(3), 336–360.

Gathercole, V. C. M. & Thomas, E. M. (2009). Bilingual first-language development: Dominant language takeover, threatened minority language take-up. *Bilingualism: Language and Cognition, 12*(2), 213–237.

Gathercole, V. C. M., Sebastián, E. & Soto, P. (1999). The early acquisition of Spanish verbal morphology: Across-the-board or piecemeal knowledge? *International Journal of Bilingualism 3*(2&3), 133–182.

Gauthier, K., Genesee, F. & Kasparian, K. (2012). Acquisition of complement clitics and tense morphology in internationally adopted children acquiring French. *Bilingualism: Language and Cognition, 15*(2), 304–319.

Gawlitzek-Maiwald, I. & Tracy, R. (1996). Bilingual bootstrapping. *Linguistics 34*(1), 901–926.

Geissmann, T. & Orgeldinger, M. (2000). The relationship between duet songs and pair bonds in siamangs, *Hylobates syndactylus. Animal Behaviour, 60*(6), 805–809.

Gelman, S. A., Coley, J. D., Rosengren, K. S., Hartman, E. & Pappas, A. (1998). Beyond labeling: The role of maternal input in the acquisition of richly structured categories. *Monographs of the Society for Research in Child Development, 63*(1), Serial No. 253.

Genesee, F. (1989). Early bilingual development: One language or two? *Journal of Child Language, 16*(1), 161–179.

Genesee, F. & Nicoladis, E. (2006). Bilingual acquisition. In E. Hoff & M. Shatz (Eds), *Handbook of language development* (pp. 324–342). Oxford: Blackwell.

Genesee, F., Boivin, I. & Nicoladis, E. (1996). Talking with strangers: A study of bilingual children's communicative competence. *Applied Psycholinguistics, 17*(4), 427–442.

Genesee, F., Nicoladis, E. & Paradis, J. (1995). Language differentiation in early bilingual development. *Journal of Child Language, 22*(3), 611–631.

Genesee, F., Paradis, J. & Wolf, L. (1995). *The nature of the bilingual child's lexicon.* Unpublished manuscript. McGill University: Montreal, Quebec.

Gentner, D. (1982). Why nouns are learned before verbs: Linguistic relativity versus natural partitioning. In S. Kuczaj (Ed.), *Language development: Language, cognition, and culture* (pp. 301–334). Hillsdale, NJ: Erlbaum.

Gentner, T. Q., Fenn, K. M., Margoliash, D. & Nusbaum, H. C. (2006). Recursive syntactic pattern learning by songbirds. *Nature Communications, 440*(7088), 1204–1207.

Gergely, G., Bekkering, H. & Király, I. (2002). Rational imitation in preverbal infants. *Nature, 415*(6873), 755.

Gertner, Y., Fisher, C. & Eisengart, J. (2006). Learning words and rules: Abstract knowledge of word order in early sentence comprehension. *Psychological Science, 17*(8), 684–691.

Gillette, J., Gleitman, L. R., Gleitman, H. & Lederer, A. (1999). Human simulations of vocabulary learning. *Cognition, 73*(2), 135–176.

Gleitman, L. R. (1990). The structural sources of verb meanings. *Language Acquisition, 1*(1), 3–55.

Glennen, S. & Masters, M. G. (2002). Typical and atypical language development in infants and toddlers adopted from Eastern Europe. *American Journal of Speech-Language Pathology, 11*, 417–433.

Goldberg, A. E. (1995). *Constructions: A construction grammar approach to argument structure.* Chicago: University of Chicago Press.

Goldberg, A. E. (2004). But do we need universal grammar? Comment on Lidz et al. (2003). *Cognition, 94*(1), 77–84.

Goldberg, A. E. (2006). *Constructions at work. The nature of generalization in language.* Oxford: Oxford University Press.

Goldin-Meadow, S. (2005). What language creation in the manual modality tells us about the foundations of language. *Linguistic Review, 22*, 199–225.

Goldin-Meadow, S. & Mylander, C. (1984). Gestural communication in deaf children: The effects and non-effects of parental input on early language development. *Monographs of the Society for Research in Child Development, 49*(3), 1–121.

Goldin-Meadow, S. & Mylander, C. (1990). Beyond the input given: The child's role in the acquisition of language. *Language, 66*(2), 323–355.

Goldin-Meadow, S. & Mylander, C. (1998). Spontaneous sign systems created by deaf children in two cultures. *Nature, 391*(6664), 279–281.

Goldin-Meadow, S., Mylander, C. & Butcher, C. (1995). The resilience of combinatorial structure at the word level: Morphology in self-styled gesture systems. *Cognition, 56*(3), 195–262.

Golinkoff, R. M., Mervis, C. B. & Hirsh-Pasek, K. (1994). Early object labels: The case for a developmental lexical principles framework. *Journal of Child Language, 21*(1), 125–155.

Golinkoff, R. M., Hirsh-Pasek, K., Bloom, L., Smith, L. B., Woodward, A. L., Akhtar, N., Tomasello, M. & Hollich, G. (2000). *Becoming a word learner: A debate on lexical acquisition.* New York: Oxford University Press.

Gollan, T. H. & Kroll, J. F. (2001). The cognitive neuropsychology of bilingualism. In B. Rapp (Ed.), *What deficits reveal about the human mind/brain: A handbook of cognitive neuropsychology* (pp. 321–345). Philadelphia, PA: Psychology Press.

Gollan, T. H. & Silverberg, N. B. (2001). Tip-of-the-tongue states in Hebrew–English bilinguals. *Bilingualism: Language and Cognition, 4*(1), 63–83.

Gollan, T. H., Montoya, R. I. & Werner, G. A. (2002). Semantic and letter fluency in Spanish–English bilinguals. *Neuropsychology, 16*(4), 562–576.

Gomez, R. L. & Gerken, L. (1999). Artificial grammar learning by 1-year-olds leads to specific and abstract knowledge. *Cognition, 70*(2), 109–135.

Goodluck, H. (1981). Children's grammar of complement-subject interpretation. In S. L. Tavakolian (Ed.), *Language acquisition and linguistic theory* (pp. 139–166). Cambridge, MA: MIT Press.

Goodz, N. S. (1989). Parental language mixing in bilingual families. *Journal of Infant Mental Health, 10*(1), 25–44.

Gopnik, A. & Choi, S. (1995). Names, relational words, and cognitive development in English and Korean speakers: Nouns are not always learned before verbs. In M. Tomasello & W. E. Merriman (Eds), *Beyond names for things: Young children's acquisition of verbs* (pp. 63–80). Hillsdale, NJ: Erlbaum.

Gopnik, M. (1990). Feature-blind grammar and dysphasia. *Nature, 344,* 715.

Graf, E. & Davies, C. (2013). The production and comprehension of referring expressions. In D. Matthews (Ed.), *Pragmatic development in first language acquisition.* Amsterdam: John Benjamins.

Greenberg, J. H. (1966). *Universals of language* (2nd ed.). Cambridge, MA: MIT Press.

Greenfield, P. M. & Savage-Rumbaugh, S. (1990). Grammatical combination in *Pan paniscus*: Process of learning and invention in the evolution and development of language. In S. T. Parker & K. R. Gibson (Eds), *Language and intelligence in monkeys and apes* (pp. 540–579). Cambridge: Cambridge University Press.

Grèzes, J., Costes, N. & Decety, J. (1998). Top-down effect of strategy on the perception of human biological motion: A PET investigation. *Cognitive Neuropsychology, 15,* 553–582.

Grice, H. P. (1989). *Studies in the way of words.* Cambridge, MA: Harvard University Press.

Grodinsky, Y. (2000). The neurology of syntax: Language use without Broca's area. *Behavioral and Brain Sciences, 23*(1), 1–71.

Gropen, J., Pinker, S., Hollander, M. & Goldberg, R. (1991). Affectedness and direct objects: The role of lexical semantics in the acquisition of verb argument structure. *Cognition, 41*(1–3), 153–195.

Grosjean, F. (1982). *Life with two languages: An introduction to bilingualism.* Cambridge, MA: Harvard University Press.

Guasti, M. T., Chierchia, G., Crain, S., Foppolo, F., Gualmini, A. & Meroni, L. (2005). Why children and adults sometimes (but not always) compute implicatures. *Language and Cognitive Processes, 20*(5), 667–696.

Guo, L-Y., Owen, A. J. & Tomblin, J. B. (2010). Effect of subject types on the production of auxiliary *is* in young English-speaking children. *Journal of Speech, Language and Hearing Research, 53*(6), 1720–1741.

Gvozdev, A. (1949). *Formirovanije u rebenka grammaticheskogo stroja russkogo jazyka. [The construction of the grammatical system of Russian by the child].* Moscow: Izdatel'stvo Academii Pedagogicheskikh Nauk.

Hadley, P. A., Rispoli, M., Fitzgerald, C. & Bahnsen, A. (2011). Predictors of morphosyntactic growth in typically developing toddlers: Contributions of parent input and child sex. *Journal of Speech Language and Hearing Research, 54*(2), 549–566.

Hahn, U. & Nakisa, R. (2000). German inflection: Single route or dual route? *Cognitive Psychology, 41,* 313–360.

Hall, D. G. & Waxman, S. R. (Eds) (2004). *Weaving a lexicon.* Cambridge, MA: MIT Press.

Hamburger, H. & Crain, S. (1982). Relative acquisition. In S. Kuczaj (Ed.), *Language development: Syntax and semantics* (pp. 245–274). Hillsdale, NJ: Erlbaum.

Hancock, J. T., Dunham, P. J. & Purdy, K. (2000). Children's comprehension of critical and complimentary forms of verbal irony. *Journal of Cognition and Development, 1*(2), 227–248.

Happé, F. G. E. (1993). Communicative competence and theory of mind in autism: A test of Relevance Theory. *Cognition, 48*(2), 101–119.

Happé, F. G. E. (1997). Central coherence and theory of mind in autism: Reading homographs in context. *British Journal of Developmental Psychology, 15*(1), 1–12.

Hart, B. & Risley, T. (1995). *Meaningful differences in the everyday experience of young American children*. Baltimore, MD: Paul H. Brookes Publishing.

Hartshorne, J. K. & Ullman, M. T. (2006). Why girls say 'holded' more than boys. *Developmental Psychology, 9*(1), 21–32.

Haspelmath, M. & Sims, A. (2010). *Understanding morphology* (2nd ed.). London: Hodder Education.

Hauser, M. D., Chomsky, N. & Fitch, W. T. (2002). The faculty of language: What is it, who has it, and how did it evolve? *Science, 298*(5598), 1569–1579.

Hawkins, J. A. (1994). *A performance theory of order and constituency*. Cambridge: Cambridge University Press.

Hawkins, J. A. (2004). *Efficiency and complexity in grammars*. Oxford: Oxford University Press.

Heath, S. B. (1982). What no bedtime story means: Narrative skill at home and school. *Language and Society, 11*(2), 49–76.

Heath, S. B. (1983). *Ways with words: Language, life and work in communities and classrooms.* Cambridge: Cambridge University Press.

Hengeveld, K. (1992). *Non-verbal predication: Theory, typology, diachrony* (Vol. 15). Berlin: Mouton de Gruyter.

Henning, A., Strianoa, T. & Lieven, E. V. M. (2005). Maternal speech to infants at 1 and 3 months of age. *Infant Behavior and Development, 28*(4), 519–536.

Hespos, S. J. & Spelke, E. S. (2004). Conceptual precursors to language. *Nature, 430*(6998), 453–456.

Hickman, M. & Hendriks, H. (1999). Cohesion and anaphora in children's narratives: A comparison of English, French, German, and Mandarin Chinese. *Journal of Child Language, 26*(2), 419–452.

Hillenbrand, J., Getty, L. A., Clark, M. J. & Wheeler, K. (1995). Acoustic characteristics of American English vowels. *Journal of the Acoustical Society of America, 97*(5), 3099–3111.

Hirsh-Pasek, K. & Golinkoff, R. (Eds) (2006). *Action meets word: How children learn verbs.* New York: Oxford University Press.

Hockett, C. F. (1963). The problem of universals in language. In J. H. Greenberg (Ed.), *Universals of language* (pp. 1–29). Cambridge, MA: MIT Press.

Hockett, C. F. (1982). The origin of speech. In William S-Y. Wang (Ed.) *Human Communication: Language and its psychobiological bases: Readings from Scientific American* (pp. 4–12). San Francisco: W. H. Freeman. (Originally published 1960, *Scientific American, 203*(3), 88–111.)

Hockett, C. F. & Altmann, S. (1968). A note on design features. In T. A. Seboek (Ed.), *Animal Communication: Techniques of study and results of research* (pp. 61–72). Bloomington: Indiana University Press.

Hoekstra, T. & Hyams, N. (1998). Aspects of root infinitives. *Lingua 106*(1), 81–112.

Hoff, E. (2003). Causes and consequences of SES-related differences in parent-to-child speech. In M. H. Bornstein & R. H. Bradle (Eds), *Socioeconomic status, parenting, and child development* (pp. 147–160). Mahwah, NJ: Lawrence Erlbaum Associates.

Hoff, E. & Place, S. (2012). Bilingual language learners. In S. Odom, E. Pungello & N. Gardner-Neblett (Eds), *Re-visioning the beginning: Developmental and health science contributions to infant/toddler programs for children and families living in poverty* (pp. 77–101). New York: Guilford Press.

Hoff, E., Core, C., Place, S., Rumiche, R., Señor, M. & Parra, M. (2011). Dual language exposure and early bilingual development. *Journal of Child Language, 39*(1), 1–27.

Hoff-Ginsberg, E. (1985). Some contributions of mothers' speech to their children's syntax growth. *Journal of Child Language, 12*(2), 367–385.

Hoff-Ginsberg, E. (1998). The relation of birth order and socioeconomic status to children's language experience and language development. *Applied Psycholinguistics, 19*(4), 603–629.

Hohne, E. A. & Jusczyk, P. W. (1994). Two-month-old infants' sensitivity to allophonic differences. *Perception & Psychophysics, 56*(60), 613–623.

Hollich, G., Hirsh-Pasek, K. & Golinkoff, R. (2000). Breaking the language barrier: An emergentist coalition model of word learning. *Monographs of the Society for Research in Child Development, 65*(3), Serial No. 262.

Holmberg, T. L., Morgan, K. A. & Kuhl, P. K. (1977). *Speech perception in early infancy: Discrimination of fricative consonants.* Paper presented at the 94th Meeting of the Acoustical Society of America, Miami, Florida.

Homae, F., Hashimoto, R., Nakajima, K., Miyashita, Y. & Sakai, K. L. (2002). From perception to sentence comprehension: The convergence of auditory and visual information of language in the left inferior frontal cortex. *Neuroimage, 16*(4), 883–900.

Horgan, D. (1978). Development of full passive. *Journal of Child Language, 5*(1), 65–80.

Horgan, D. (1981). Rate of language acquisition and noun emphasis. *Journal of Psycholinguistic Research, 10*(6), 629–640.

Horst, J. A. & Samuelson, L. K. (2008). Fast mapping but poor retention in 24-month-old infants. *Infancy, 13*(2), 128–157.

Huang, C.-T. J. (1982). *Logical relations in Chinese and the theory of grammar.* Unpublished doctoral dissertation. MIT, Cambridge, MA.

Huang, C.-T. J. (1984). On the distribution and reference of empty pronouns. *Linguistic Inquiry, 15*, 531–574.

Hudson Kam, C. L. & Edwards, N. A. (2008). The use of uh and um by 3- and 4-year-old native English-speaking children: Not quite right, but not completely wrong. *First Language, 28*(3), 313–327.

Hulk, A. & Müller, M. (2000). Bilingual first language acquisition at the interface between syntax and pragmatics. *Bilingualism: Language and Cognition, 3*(3), 227–244.

Huttenlocher, J., Vasilyeva, M., Cymerman, E. & Levine, S. (2002). Language input at home and at school: Relation to child syntax. *Cognitive Psychology, 45*(3), 337–374.

Huttenlocher, J., Waterfall, H., Vasilyeva, M., Vevea, J. & Hedges, L. (2010). Sources of variability in children's language growth. *Cognitive Psychology, 61*(4), 343–365.

Huttenlocher, J., Haight, W., Bryk, A., Seltzer, M. & Lyons, T. (1991). Early vocabulary growth: Relation to language input and gender. *Developmental Psychology, 27*(2), 236–248.

Hyams, N. (1986). *Language acquisition and the theory of parameters.* Dordrecht: Reidel.

Imai, M., Li, L. J., Haryu, E., Okada, H., Hirsh-Pasek, K., Golinkoff, R. M. & Shigematsu, J. (2008). Novel noun and verb learning in Chinese-, English-, and Japanese-speaking children. *Child Development, 79*(4), 979–1000.

Indefrey, P., Hagoort, P., Herzog, H., Seitz, R. J. & Brown, C. M. (2001). Syntactic processing in left prefrontal cortex is independent of lexical meaning. *Neuroimage, 14*(3), 546–555.

Ingram, D. (1992). Early phonological acquisition: A cross-linguistic perspective. In C. Ferguson, L. Menn & C. Stoel-Gammon (Eds), *Phonological development: Models, research, implications* (pp. 423–425). Timonium, MD: York Press.

Ingram, D. & Thompson, W. (1996). Early syntactic acquisition in German: Evidence for the modal hypothesis. *Language, 72*(1), 97–120.

Itard, J. (1802). *An historical account of the discovery and education of a savage man: Or the first developments, physical and moral of the young savage caught in the woods near Aveyron, in 1798.* London: printed for Richard Philippo.

Jackendoff, R. (1992). *Languages of the mind.* Cambridge, MA: Bradford/MIT Press.

Jackendoff, R. (1994). *Patterns in the mind: Language and human nature.* New York: Basic Books.

Jackendoff, R. (2002). *Foundations of language: Brain, meaning, grammar, evolution.* New York: Oxford University Press.

Jackendoff, R. & Pinker, S. (2005). The nature of the language faculty and its implications for evolution of language (Reply to Fitch, Hauser & Chomsky), *Cognition, 97*(2), 211–225.

Jakobson, R. (1941/68). *Child language, aphasia and phonological universals.* The Hague & Paris: Mouton.

Jakubowicz, C., Muèller, N., Riemer, B. & Rigaut, C. (1997). The case of subject and object omissions in French and German. In E. Hughes, M. Hughes & A. Greenhill (Eds), *Proceedings of the 21st annual Boston University Conference on Language Development* (pp. 331–342). Somerville, MA: Cascadilla.

James, W. (1890). *Principles of psychology.* New York: Holt.

Johnston, T. (2002). BSL, Auslan and NZSL: Three signed languages or one? In A. Baker, B. van den Bogaerde & O. Crasborn (Eds), *Cross-linguistic perspectives in sign language research: Selected papers from TISLR 2000* (pp. 47–69). Hamburg: Signum Verlag.

Johnstone, J. C., Durieux-Smith, A. & Bloom, K. (2005). Teaching gestural signs to infants to advance child development: A review of the evidence. *First Language, 25*(2), 235–251.

Jones, S. S., Smith, L. B. & Landau, B. (1991). Object properties and knowledge in early lexical learning. *Child Development, 62*(3), 499–516.

Jusczyk, P. W. (2000). *The discovery of spoken language.* Cambridge, MA: MIT Press.

Jusczyk, P. W., Hohne, E. & Bauman, A. (1999). Infants' sensitivity to allophonic cues for word segmentation. *Perception & Psychophysics, 61*(8), 1465–1476.

Jusczyk, P. W., Houston, D. M. & Newsome, M. (1999). The beginnings of word segmentation in English-learning infants. *Cognitive Psychology, 39*(3–4), 159–207.

Kaminski, J., Call, J. & Fischer, M. (2004). Word learning in a domestic dog: Evidence for 'fast mapping'. *Science, 304*(5677), 1682–1683.

Karmiloff-Smith, A. (1998). Development itself is the key to understanding developmental disorders. *Trends in Cognitive Sciences, 2*(10), 389–398.

Karmiloff-Smith, A. (2008). Research into Williams Syndrome: The state of the art. In C. A. Nelson & M. Luciana (Eds), *Handbook of developmental cognitive neuroscience* (2nd ed.). Cambridge, MA: MIT Press.

Katsos, N. & Bishop, D. V. M. (2011). Pragmatic tolerance: Implications for the acquisition of informativeness and implicature. *Cognition, 120*(1), 67–81.

Kemler Nelson, D. G. (1999). Attention to functional properties in toddlers' naming and problem-solving. *Cognitive Development, 14*(1), 77–100.

Keuleers, E., Sandra, D., Daelemans, W., Gillis, S., Durieux, G. & Martens, E. (2007). Dutch plural inflection: The exception that proves the analogy. *Cognitive Psychology, 54*(4), 283–318.

Kidd, E. (2012). Individual differences in syntactic priming in language acquisition. *Applied Psycholinguistics, 33*(2), 393–418.

Kidd, E. & Kirjavainen, E. (2011). Investigating the contribution of procedural and declarative memory to the acquisition of past tense morphology: Evidence from Finnish. *Language and Cognitive Processes 26*, 794–829.

Kidd, E., Bavin, E. L. & Rhodes, B. (2001). 2-year-olds' knowledge of verbs and argument structures. In B. M. Almgren, A. Barreña, M-J. Ezeizabarrena, I. Idiazabal & B. MacWhinney (Eds), *Research on child language acquisition* (pp. 1368–1382). Boston, MA: Cascadilla Press.

Kidd, E., Lieven, E. & Tomasello, M. (2006). Examining the role of lexical frequency in the acquisition and processing of sentential complements. *Cognitive Development, 21*(2), 93–107.

Kiparsky, P. & Menn, L. (1977). On the acquisition of phonology. In J. Macnamara (Ed.), *Language and thought* (pp. 47–78). New York: Academic Press.

Kirby, S., Cornish, H. & Smith, K. (2008). Cumulative cultural evolution in the laboratory: An experimental approach to the origins of structure in human language. *Proceedings of the National Academy of Sciences, 105*(31), 10681–10686.

Kishimoto, T., Shizawa, Y., Yasuda, J., Hinobayashi, T. & Minami, T. (2007). Do pointing gestures by infants provoke comments from adults? *Infant Behavior & Development, 30*(4), 562–567.

Kita, S. (Ed.). (2003). *Pointing. Where language, culture, and cognition meet.* Hillsdale, NJ: Erlbaum.

Kjelgaard, M. M. & Tager-Flusberg, H. (2001). An investigation of language impairment in autism: Implications for genetic subgroups. *Language and Cognitive Processes, 16*(2–3), 287–308.

Kolb, B. & Whishaw, I. Q. (2003). *Fundamentals of human neuropsychology.* New York: Worth Publishers.

Kovas, Y., Hayiou-Thomas, M. E., Oliver, B., Dale, P. S., Bishop, D. V. M. & Plomin, R. (2005). Genetic influences in different aspects of language development: The etiology of language skills in 4.5-year-old twins. *Child Development, 76*(3), 632–651.

Kuhl, P. K. (1991). Human adults and human infants show a 'perceptual magnet effect' for the prototypes of speech categories, monkeys do not. *Perception & Psychophysics, 50*(2), 93–107.

Kuhl, P. K. (2004). Early language acquisition: Cracking the speech code. *Nature Reviews Neuroscience, 5*, 841–843.

Kuhl, P. K. & Miller, J. D. (1975). Speech perception by the chinchilla: Voiced-voiceless distinction in alveolar plosive consonants. *Science, 190*(4209), 69–72.

Kuhl, P. K. & Padden, D. M. (1982). Enhanced discriminability at the phonetic boundaries for the voicing feature in macaques. *Perception & Psychophysics, 32*(6), 542–550.

Kuhl, P. K. & Padden, D. M. (1983). Enhanced discriminability at the phonetic boundaries for the place feature in macaques. *Journal of the Acoustical Society of America, 73*, 1003–1010.

Kuhl, P. K. & Rivera-Gaxiola, M. (2008). Neural substrates of language acquisition. *Annual Review of Neuroscience, 31*, 511–534.

Kuhl, P. K., Conboy, B. T., Coffey-Corina, S., Padden, D., Rivera-Gaxiola, M. & Nelson, T. (2008). Phonetic learning as a pathway to language: New data and native language magnet theory expanded (NLM-e). *Philosophical Transactions of the Royal Society B, 363*, 979–1000.

Küntay, A. & Slobin, D. I. (1996). Listening to a Turkish mother: Some puzzles for acquisition. In D. I. Slobin, J. Gerhardt, A. Kyratzis & J. Guo (Eds), *Social interaction, social context, and language: Essays in honor of Susan Ervin-Tripp* (pp. 265–286). Mahwah, NJ: Lawrence Erlbaum Associates.

Kyle, J., Ackerman, J. & Woll, B. (1987). *Early mother infant interactions: Language and prelanguage in deaf families.* Paper presented at the Child Language Seminar, University of York, UK.

Ladefoged, P. (2004). *Vowels and consonants. An introduction to the sounds of languages.* (2nd ed.). Oxford: Blackwell.

Ladefoged, P. & Maddieson, I. (1996). *The sounds of the world's languages.* Oxford: Blackwell.

Laine, M., Rinne, J. O., Krause, B. J., Tereas, M. & Sipilea, H. (1999). Left hemisphere activation during processing of morphologically complex word forms in adults. *Neuroscience Letters, 271*(2), 85–88.

Landau, B. & Gleitman, L. R. (1985). *Language and experience: Evidence from the blind child.* Cambridge, MA: Harvard University Press.

Landau, B. & Jackendoff, R. (1993). 'What' and 'where' in spatial language and spatial cognition. *Behavioral and Brain Sciences, 16*(2), 217–265.

Landau, B., Smith, L. B. & Jones, S. S. (1988). The importance of shape in early lexical learning. *Cognitive Development, 3*(3), 299–321.

Lane, H. (1976). *The wild boy of Aveyron.* Cambridge, MA: Harvard University Press.

LaSasso, C. & Davey, B. (1987). The relationship between lexical knowledge and reading comprehension for prelingually, profoundly hearing-impaired students. *Volta Review, 89*(4), 211–220.

Lasky, R. E., Syrdal-Lasky, A. & Klein, R. E. (1975). VOT discrimination by four to six and a half months old infants from Spanish environments. *Journal of Experimental Child Psychology, 20*(20), 215–225.

Lee, A., Hobson, R. P. & Chiat, S. (1994). You, me and autism: An experimental study. *Journal of Autism and Developmental Disorders, 24*(2), 155–176.

Lee, J. N. & Naigles, L. R. (2008). Mandarin learners use syntactic bootstrapping in verb acquisition. *Cognition, 106*(2), 1028–1037.

Legate, J. A. & Yang, C. (2007). Morphosyntactic learning and the development of tense. *Language Acquisition, 14*(3), 315–344.

Legerstee, M., Pomerleau, A., Malcuit, G. & Feider, H. (1987). The development of infants' responses to people and a doll: Implications for research in communication. *Infant Behaviour and Development, 10*(1), 81–95.

Lenneberg, E. H. (1967). *Biological foundations of language.* New York: Wiley.

Leonard, L. (1989). Language learnability and specific language impairment in children. *Applied Psycholinguistics, 10*(2), 179–202.

Leonard, L. (1998). *Children with Specific Language Impairment.* Cambridge, MA: MIT Press.

Leonard, L. (2000). Specific language impairment across languages. In D. V. M. Bishop & L. Leonard (Eds), *Speech and language impairments in children: Causes, characteristics, intervention, and outcome* (pp. 115–129). Hove, UK: Psychology Press.

Leonard, L. & Bortolini, U. (1998). Grammatical morphology and the role of weak syllables in the speech of Italian-speaking children with specific language impairment. *Journal of Speech, Language, and Hearing Research, 41*, 1363–1374.

Leonard, L., Eyer, J., Bedore, L. & Grela, B. (1997). Three accounts of the grammatical morpheme difficulties of English-speaking children with specific language impairment. *Journal of Speech and Hearing Research, 40*(4), 741–753.

Leonard, L., Hansson, K., Nettelbladt, U. & Deevy, P. (2005). Specific language impairment in children: A comparison of English and Swedish. *Language Acquisition, 12*(3/4), 219–246.

Liberman, A. M., Harris, K. S., Hoffman, H. S. & Griffith, B. C. (1957). The discrimination of speech sounds within and across phoneme boundaries. *Journal of Experimental Psychology, General, 54*, 358–368.

Lieberman, A. F. & Garvey, C. (1977). *Interpersonal pauses in preschoolers' verbal exchanges.* Paper presented at the Biennial Meeting of the Society for Research in Child Development, New Orleans, USA.

Lieven, E. V. M. (1994). Crosslinguistic and crosscultural aspects of language addressed to children. In C. Gallaway & B. J. Richards (Eds), *Input and interaction in language acquisition* (pp. 57–73). Cambridge: Cambridge University Press.

Lieven, E. V. M. & Tomasello, M. (2008). Children's first language acquisition from a usage-based perspective. In P. Robinson & N. Ellis (Eds), *Handbook of cognitive linguistics and second language acquisition* (pp. 168–196). Abingdon, UK: Routledge.

Linneaus, C. (1758). *Systema naturæ per regna tria naturæ, secundum classes, ordines, genera, species, cum characteribus, differentiis, synonymis, locis. Tomus I.* Editio decima, reformata. Holmiæ. (Salvius).

Liszkowski, U., Brown, P., Callaghan, T., Takada, A. & De Vos, C. (2012). A prelinguistic gestural universal of human communication. *Cognitive Science, 36*(4), 698–713.

Liszkowski, U., Carpenter, M., Henning, A., Striano, T. & Tomasello, M. (2004). Twelve-month-olds point to share attention and interest. *Developmental Science, 7*(3), 297–307.

Loban, W. (1976). *Language development: Kindergarten through grade twelve.* Urbana, IL: National Council of Teachers of English.

Loew, R. (1984). *Roles and reference in American Sign Language: A developmental perspective.* Minneapolis: University of Minnesota.

Lord, C. & Paul, R. (1997). Language and communication in autism. In D. J. Cohen & F. R. Volkmar (Eds), *Handbook of autism and pervasive development disorders* (2nd ed.) (pp. 631–649). New York: John Wiley & Sons.

Lord, C., Rutter, M. & Le Couteur, A. (1994). Autism Diagnostic Interview – Revised: A revised version of a diagnostic interview for caregivers of individuals with possible pervasive developmental disorders. *Journal of Autism and Developmental Disorders, 24*(5), 659–685.

Lord, C., Risi, S., Lambrecht, L., Cook, E. H., Leventhal, B. L., DiLavore, P. C., ... Rutter, M. (2000). The Autism Diagnostic Observations Schedule-Generic: A standard measure of social and communication deficits associated with the spectrum of autism. *Journal of Autism and Developmental Disorders, 30*(3), 205–223.

Lust, B. (2006). *Child language: Acquisition and growth.* Cambridge: Cambridge University Press.

Lyn, H. & Savage-Rumbaugh, E. S. (2000). Observational word learning by two bonobos: Ostensive and non-ostensive contexts. *Language and Communication, 20*(3), 255–273.

Macken, M. (1978). Permitted complexity in phonological development: One child's acquisition of Spanish consonants. *Lingua 44*, 219–253.

Macken, M. (1995). *Phonological acquisition.* Cambridge, MA: Blackwell.

Macnamara, J. (1982). *Names for things: A study of child language.* Cambridge, MA: Bradford Books/MIT Press.

MacSweeney, M., Capek, C. M., Campbell, R. & Woll, B. (2008). The signing brain: The neurobiology of sign language processing. *Trends in Cognitive Sciences, 12*(11), 432–440.

MacWhinney, B. (1975). Rules, rote, and analogy in morphological formations by Hungarian children. *Journal of Child Language, 2*, 65–77.

MacWhinney, B. (2000). *The CHILDES project: Tools for analyzing talk.* Mahwah, NJ: Lawrence Erlbaum Associates.

MacWhinney, B. (2004). A multiple process solution to the logical problem of language acquisition. *Journal of Child Language, 31*(4), 883–914.

MacWhinney, B. & Bates, E. (Eds). (1989). *The crosslinguistic study of sentence processing.* New York: Cambridge University Press.

MacWhinney, B. & Leinbach, J. (1991). Implementations are not conceptualizations: Revising the verb learning model. *Cognition, 40*(1–2), 121–157.

Maital, S. L., Dromi, E., Sagi, A. & Bornstein, M. H. (2000). The Hebrew Communicative Development Inventory: Language specific properties and cross-linguistic generalizations. *Journal of Child Language, 27*(1), 43–67.

Mannle, S. & Tomasello, M. (1987). Fathers, siblings, and the bridge hypothesis. In K. E. Nelson & A. V. Kleeck (Eds), *Children's language* (Vol. 6, pp. 23–42). Hillside, NJ: Erlbaum.

Marantz, A. (1982). On the acquisition of grammatical relations. *Linguistische Berichte: Linguistik als Kognitive Wissenschaft, 80/82,* 32–69.

Maratsos, M. (1989). Innateness and plasticity in language acquisition. In M. Rice & R. Schiefelbusch (Eds), *The teachability of language* (pp. 105–125). Baltimore, MD: Paul Brooks.

Maratsos, M. (2000). More overregularizations after all: New data and discussion on Marcus, Pinker, Ullman, Hollander, Rosen & Xu. *Journal of Child Language, 27*(1), 183–212

Maratsos, M. (2001). How fast does a child learn a word? *Behavioral and Brain Sciences, 24*(6), 1111–1112.

Maratsos, M. & Chalkley, M. A. (1980). The internal language of children's syntax: The ontogenesis and representation of syntactic categories. In K. Nelson (Ed.), *Children's language* (Vol. 2, pp. 127–151). New York: Gardner Press.

Maratsos, M., Fox, D. E. C., Becker, J. A. & Chalkley, M. A. (1985). Semantic restrictions on children's passives. *Cognition, 19*(2), 167–191.

Marchman, V. A. (1997). Children's productivity in the English past tense: The role of frequency, phonology, and neighborhood structure. *Cognitive Science, 21*(3), 283–304.

Marchman, V. A. & Bates, E. (1994). Continuity in lexical and morphological development: A test of the critical mass hypothesis. *Journal of Child Language, 21*(2), 339–366.

Marchman, V. A. & Fernald, A. (2008). Speed of word recognition and vocabulary knowledge in infancy predict cognitive and language outcomes in later childhood. *Developmental Science, 11*(3), F9–F16.

Marcus, G. F. & Fisher, S. E. (2003). FOXP2 in focus: What can genes tell us about speech and language? *Trends in Cognitive Sciences, 7*(8), 257–262.

Marcus, G. F., Brinkmann, U., Clahsen, H., Wiese, R. & Pinker, S. (1995). German inflection: The exception that proves the rule. *Cognitive Psychology, 29*(3), 189–256.

Marcus, G. F., Pinker, S., Ullman, M., Hollander, M., Rosen, T. J. & Xu, F. (1992). Overregularization in language acquisition. *Monographs of the Society for Research in Child Development, 57*(4), 1–165.

Margetts, A. (2008). Learning verbs without boots and straps? The problem of 'Give' in Saliba. In M. Bowerman & P. Brown (Eds), *Cross-linguistic perspectives on argument structure: Implications for learnability* (pp. 111–137). New York: Lawrence Erlbaum.

Markman, E. M. & Hutchinson, J. E. (1984). Children's sensitivity to constraints on word meaning: Taxonomic vs thematic relations. *Cognitive Psychology, 16*(1), 1–27.

Markman, E. M. & Wachtel, G. F. (1988). Children's use of mutual exclusivity to constrain the meaning of words. *Cognitive Psychology, 20*(2), 121–157.

Markman, E. M., Wasow, J. L. & Hansen, M. B. (2003). Use of the mutual exclusivity assumption by young word learners. *Cognitive Psychology, 47*(3), 241–275.

Markova, G. & Legerstee, M. (2006). Contingency, imitation, and affect sharing: Foundations of infants' social awareness. *Developmental Psychology, 42*(1), 132–141.

Martin-Rhee, M. M. & Bialystok, E. (2008). The development of two types of inhibitory control in monolingual and bilingual children. *Bilingualism: Language and Cognition, 11*(1), 81–93.

Mastin, J. D. & Vogt, P. (2011). *Joint attention & vocabulary development: An observational study of Mozambican infants*. Paper presented at the 12th International Congress for the Study of Child Language, Montreal, Canada.

Matthews, D. (2013). *Pragmatic development in first language acquisition*. Amsterdam: John Benjamins.

Matthews, D., Butcher, J., Lieven, E. V. M. & Tomasello, M. (2012). Two- and four-year-olds learn to adapt referring expressions to context: Effects of distracters and feedback on referential communication. *Topics in Cognitive Science, 4*(2), 184–210.

Matthews, D., Lieven, E. V. M., Theakston, A. L. & Tomasello, M. (2006). The effect of perceptual availability and prior discourse on young children's use of referring expressions. *Applied Psycholinguistics, 27*(3), 403–422.

Matthews, D., Lieven, E., Theakston, A. & Tomasello, M. (2007). French children's use and correction of weird word orders: A constructivist account. *Journal of Child Language, 34*(2), 381–409.

Mattys, S. L., Jusczyk, P. W., Luce, P. A. & Morgan, J. L. (1999). Phonotactic and prosodic effects on word segmentation in infants. *Cognitive Psychology, 38*(4), 465–494.

Mawhood, L. & Howlin, L. (2000). Autism and developmental receptive language disorder – a comparative follow-up in early adult life. I: Cognitive and language outcomes. *Journal of Child Psychology and Psychiatry, 41*(5), 547–559.

Mayberry, R. I. & Squires, B. (2006). Sign language: Acquisition. In K. Brown (Ed.), *Encyclopedia of language and linguistics* (2nd ed.) (Vol. 11, pp. 291–296). Oxford: Elsevier.

Maye, J., Werker, J. F. & Gerken, L. (2002). Infant sensitivity to distributional information can affect phonetic perception. *Cognition, 82*, B101–B111.

McCardle, P. D. & Hoff, E. (2006). *Childhood bilingualism: Research on infancy through school age*. Clevedon, UK: Multilingual Matters.

McClelland, J. L. & Patterson, K. (2002) Rules or connections in past-tense inflections: What does the evidence rule out? *Trends in Cognitive Science, 6*(11), 465–472.

McDonough, L. (2002). Basic-level nouns: First learned but misunderstood. *Journal of Child Language, 29*(2), 357–377.

McLaughlin, B. (1978). *Second language acquisition in childhood*. Hillsdale, NJ: Lawrence Ellbaum Associates.

Mehler, J., Dubpoux, E., Nazzi, T. & Dehaene-Lamertz, G. (1996). Coping with linguistic diversity: The infant's viewpoint. In J. L. Morgan & K. Demuth (Eds), *Signal to syntax: Bootstrapping from speech to grammar in early acquisition* (pp. 101–116). Mahwah, NJ: Erlbaum.

Mehler, J., Jusczyk, P., Lambertz, G., Halsted, N., Bertoncini, J. & Amiel-Tison, C. (1988). A precursor of language acquisition in young infants. *Cognition, 29*(2), 143–178.

Meisel, J. M. (2001). The simultaneous acquisition of two first languages: Early differentiation and subsequent development of grammars. In J. Cenoz & F. Genesee (Eds), *Trends in bilingual acquisition* (pp. 11–41). Amsterdam: John Benjamins.

Meltzoff, A. N. (1995). Understanding the intentions of others: Re-enactment of intended acts by 18 month-old-children. *Developmental Psychology, 31*(5), 838–850.

Menn, L. (1978). Phonological units in beginning speech. In A. Bell & J. B. Hooper (Eds), *Syllables and segments* (pp. 157–172). New York: Elsevier.

Mervis, C. B., Robinson, B. F., Rowe, M. L., Becerra, A. M. & Klein-Tasman, B. P. (2003). Language abilities of individuals with Williams syndrome. *International Review of Research in Mental Retardation, 27*, 35–81.

Meyer Bjerkan, K. (1999). *Do SLI children have an optional infinitive stage?* Paper presented at the Congress of the International Association for the Study of Child Language, San Sebastian, Spain.

Miller, G. (1981). *Comments on the symposium papers: The development of language and of language researchers: Whatever happened to linguistic theory?* Paper presented at the Biennial Meeting of the Society for Research in Child Development, Boston.

Mills, A. E. (1985). Speech acquisition in childhood – a study on the development of syntax in small children – German. *Journal of Child Language, 12*(1), 239–244.

Mills, D. L., Coffey-Corina, S. & Neville, H. J. (1997). Language comprehension and cerebral specialization from 13 to 20 months. *Developmental Neuropsychology, 13*(3), 397–445.

Mintz, T. H. (2003). Frequent frames as a cue for grammatical categories in child directed speech. *Cognition, 90*(1), 91–117.

Mithun, M. (1999). *The languages of native North America.* Cambridge: Cambridge University Press.

Mody, M., Studdert-Kennedy, M. & Brady, S. (1997). Speech perception deficits in poor readers: Auditory processing or phonological coding? *Journal of Experimental Child Psychology, 64*(2), 199–231.

Moll, H. & Tomasello, M. (2007). How 14- and 18-month-olds know what others have experienced. *Developmental Psychology, 43*(2), 309–317.

Moon, C., Cooper, R. P. & Fifer, W. P. (1993). Two-day-olds prefer their native language. *Infant Behavior and Development 16*(4), 495–500.

Moore, C. & Corkum, V. (1994). Social understanding at the end of the first year of life. *Developmental Review, 14*(4), 19–40.

Moore, C. & D'Entremont, B. (2001). Developmental changes in pointing as a function of parent's attentional focus. *Journal of Cognition and Development, 2*(2), 109–129.

Moore, R. (2013). Using child language to inform theories of human communication. In D. Matthews (Ed.), *Pragmatic development in first language acquisition.* Amsterdam: John Benjamins.

Morgan, G. (2005). What is homesign? Review of S. Goldin-Meadow (2003) *The resilience of language.* Psychology Press. *Journal of Child Language, 32*(4), 925–928.

Moro, A., Tettamanti, M., Perani, D., Donati, C., Cappa, S. F. & Fazio, F. (2001). Syntax and the brain: Disentangling grammar by selective anomalies. *Neuroimage, 13*(1), 110–118.

Müller, N. & Hulk., A. (2001). Crosslinguistic influence in bilingual language acquisition: Italian and French as recipient languages. *Bilingualism: Language and Cognition, 4*(1), 1–53.

Naigles, L. R. (1990). Children use syntax to learn verb meanings. *Journal of Child Language, 17*(2), 357–374.

Naigles, L. & Hoff-Ginsberg, E. (1998). Why are some verbs learned before other verbs? Effects of input frequency and structure on children's early verb use. *Journal of Child Language, 25*(1), 95–120.

Nazzi, T., Bertoncini, J. & Mehler, J. (1998). Language discrimination by newborns: Towards an understanding of the role of rhythm. *Journal of Experimental Psychology: Human Perception and Performance, 24*(3), 756–766.

Nazzi, T., Iakimova, G., Bertoncini, J., Frédonie, S. & Alcantara, C. (2006). Early segmentation of fluent speech by infants acquiring French: Emerging evidence for cross-linguistic differences. *Journal of Memory and Language, 54*(3), 283–299.

Nelson, K. (1973). Structure and strategy in learning to talk. *Monographs of the Society for Research in Child Development, 38*(1–2), 1–135.

Nelson, K. (1985). *Making sense: The acquisition of shared meaning.* New York: Academic Press.

Nevins, A. (2009). On formal universals in phonology. *Behavioral and Brain Sciences, 32*(5), 461–462.

Nevins, A., Pesetsky, D. & Rodrigues, C. (2009a). Pirahã exceptionality: A reassessment. *Language, 85*(2), 355–404.

Nevins, A., Pesetsky, D. & Rodrigues, C. (2009b). Evidence and argumentation: A reply to Everett (2009). *Language, 85*(3), 671–681.

Newman, A., Bavelier, D., Corina, D. P., Jezzard, P. & Neville, H. (2002). A critical period for right hemisphere recruitment in American Sign Language processing. *Nature Neuroscience, 5*(1), 76–80.

Newmeyer, F. J. (1998). *Language form and language function.* Cambridge, MA: MIT Press.

Newmeyer, F. J. (2004). Against a parameter-setting approach to language variation. In P. Pica, J. Rooryck & J. van Craenenbroek (Eds), *Language variation yearbook* (pp. 181–234). Amsterdam: John Benjamins.

Newport, E. L. (1988). Constraints on learning and their role in language acquisition: Studies of the acquisition of American Sign Language. *Language Sciences, 10*(1), 147–172.

Newport, E. L. (1990). Maturational constraints on language learning. *Cognitive Science, 14*, 11–28.

Newport, E. L., Gleitman, H. & Gleitman, L. R. (1977). Mother, I'd rather do it myself: Some effects and noneffects of maternal speech style. In C. E. Snow & C. A. Ferguson (Eds), *Talking to children: Language input and acquisition* (pp. 109–150). Cambridge: Cambridge University Press.

Nicoladis, E. & Genesee, F. (1996). A longitudinal study of pragmatic differentiation in young bilingual children. *Language Learning, 46*(3), 439–464.

Ninio, A. (1979). The naive theory of the infant and other maternal attitudes in two subgroups in Israel. *Child Development, 50*(4), 976–980.

Ninio, A. (1980). Picture-book reading in mother–infant dyads belonging to two subgroups in Israel. *Child Development, 51*(2), 587–590.

Ninio, A. (2006). *Language and the learning curve: A new theory of syntactic development.* Oxford: Oxford University Press.

Ninio, A. (2011). *Syntactic development, its input and output.* Oxford: Oxford University Press.

Ninio, A. & Snow, C. E. (1996). *Pragmatic development.* Boulder, CO: Westview.

Nittrouer, S. (2001). Challenging the notion of innate phonetic boundaries. *Journal of the Acoustical Society of America, 110*(3), 1598–1605.

Noble, C. H., Rowland, C. F. & Pine, J. M. (2011). Comprehension of argument structure and semantic roles: Evidence from infants and the forced-choice pointing paradigm. *Cognitive Science, 35*(5), 963–982.

Norbury, C. F. (2005). Barking up the wrong tree? Lexical ambiguity resolution in children with language impairments and autistic spectrum disorders. *Journal of Experimental Child Psychology, 90*(2), 142–171.

Norbury, C. (2013). Atypical pragmatic development. In D. Matthews (Ed.), *Pragmatic development in first language acquisition.* Amsterdam: John Benjamins.

Norbury, C. F., Nash, M., Baird, G. & Bishop, D. V. M. (2004). Using a parental checklist to identify diagnostic groups in children with communication impairment: A validation of the Children's Communication Checklist – 2. *International Journal of Language and Communication Disorders, 39*(3), 345–364.

Noveck, I. A. (2001). When children are more logical than adults: Experimental investigations of scalar implicature. *Cognition, 78*(2), 165–188.

Ochs, E. & Schieffelin, B. (1984). Language acquisition and socialization: Three developmental stories and their implications. In R. LeVine & R. Shweder (Eds), *Culture theory: Essays on mind, self, and emotion* (pp. 276–320). Cambridge: Cambridge University Press.

Office of National Statistics (2002). *America's children: Key national indicators of well-being.* Washington, DC: US Government Printing Office.

O'Grady, W. (2005). *Syntactic carpentry: An emergentist approach to syntax.* Mahwah, NJ: Lawrence Erlbaum Associates.

Ogura, T., Dale, P., Yamashita, Y., Murase, T. & Mahieu, A. (2006). The use of nouns and verbs by Japanese children and their caregivers in book-reading and toy-playing contexts. *Journal of Child Language, 33*(1), 1–29.

Oller, D. K. & Eilers, R. (2002). *Language and literacy in bilingual children.* Clevedon, UK: Multilingual Matters.

Ortega, L. (2009). *Understanding second language acquisition.* London: Hodder Arnold.

Osterhout, L., Poliakov, A., Inoue, K., McLaughlin, J., Valentine, G., Pitkanen, I., Frenck-Mestre, C. & Hirschensohn, J. (2008). Second-language learning and changes in the brain. *Journal of Neurolinguistics, 21*(6), 509–521.

Pallier, C., Dehaene, S., Poline, J-B., LeBihan, D., Argenti, A-M., Dupoux, E. & Mehler, J. (2003). Brain imaging of language plasticity in adopted adults: Can a second language replace the first? *Cerebral Cortex, 13*(2), 155–161.

Papafragou, A. & Musolino, J. (2003). Scalar implicatures: Experiments at the semantics/pragmatics interface. *Cognition, 86*(3), 253–282.

Paradis, J. & Crago, M. (2001). The morphosyntax of Specific Language Impairment in French: Evidence for an extended optional default account. *Language Acquisition, 9*(4), 269–300.

Paradis, J. & Genesee, F. (1996). Syntactic acquisition in bilingual children: Autonomous or interdependent? *Studies in Second Language Acquisition, 18*(1), 1–25.

Paradis, J. & Navarro, S. (2003). Subject realization and crosslinguistic interference in the bilingual acquisition of Spanish and English: What is the role of input? *Journal of Child Language, 30*, 371–339.

Paradis, J., Crago, M. & Genesee, F. (2005/6). Domain-general versus domain-specific accounts of specific language impairment: Evidence from bilingual children's acquisition of object pronouns. *Language Acquisition, 13*(1), 33–62.

Parish-Morris, J., Hennon, E. A., Hirsh-Pasek, K., Golinkoff, R. M. & Tager-Flusberg, H. (2007). Children with autism illuminate the role of social intention in word learning. *Child Development, 78*(4), 1265–1287.

Pearson, B. Z., Fernández, S. C., Lewedeg, V. & Oller, D. K. (1997). The relation of input factors to lexical learning by bilingual infants. *Applied Psycholinguistics, 18*(1), 41–58.

Pederson, E. (1993). *Zero negation in South Dravidia.* Paper presented at the CLS 27: The parasession on negation, Chicago, USA.

Pepperberg, I. M. (1991) *The Alex Studies: Cognitive and communicative abilities of grey parrots.* Cambridge, MA: Harvard University Press.

Peters, A. M. (1977). Language learning strategies: Does the whole equal the sum of the parts? *Language, 53*(3), 560–573.

Peters, A. M. (1983). *The units of language acquisition.* Cambridge: Cambridge University Press.

Peters, A. M. (1994). The interdependence of social, cognitive, and linguistic development: Evidence from a visually impaired child. In H. Tager-Flusberg (Ed.), *Constraints on language acquisition: Studies of atypical children* (pp. 195–220). Hillsdale, NJ: Lawrence Erlbaum Associates.

Peterson, C. C. & Siegal, M. (1995). Deafness, conversation, and theory of mind. *Journal of Child Psychology and Psychiatry, 36*(3), 459–474.

Petitto, L. A. (1988). Language in the prelinguistic child. In F. Kessel (Ed.), *Development of language and language researchers: Essays in honor of Roger Brown* (pp. 187–222). Hillsdale, NJ: Lawrence Erlbaum Associates.

Petitto, L. A. & Kovelman, I. (2003). The bilingual paradox: How signing–speaking bilingual children help us resolve bilingual issues and teach us about the brain's mechanism underlying all language acquisition. *Learning Languages, 8*(3), 5–18.

Petitto, L. A., Katerelos, M., Levy, B. G., Gauna, K., Tetrealt, K. & Ferraroi, V. (2001). Bilingual signed and spoken language acquisition from birth: Implications for the mechanisms underlying early bilingual language acquisition. *Journal of Child Language, 28*(2), 453–496.

Phillips, C. (1995). Syntax at age two: Cross-linguistic differences. In C. Schütze, J. Ganger & K. Broihier (Eds), *Papers on language processing and acquisition. MIT Working Papers in Linguistics* (Vol. 26, pp. 325–382).

Phillips, J. R. (1973). Syntax and vocabulary of mothers' speech to young children: Age and sex comparisons. *Child Development, 44*(1), 182–185.

Pierrehumbert, J. (2003). Phonetic diversity, statistical learning, and acquisition of phonology. *Language and Speech, 46*(2–3), 115–154.

Pine, J. M. (1994). The language of primary caregivers. In C. Gallaway & B. J. Richards (Eds), *Input and interaction in language acquisition* (pp. 38–55). Cambridge: Cambridge University Press.

Pine, J. M. & Lieven, E. V. M. (1993). Reanalyzing rote-learned phrases: Individual differences in the transition to multi-word speech. *Journal of Child Language, 20*(3), 551–571.

Pine, J. M. & Martindale, H. (1996). Syntactic categories in the speech of young children: The case of the determiner. *Journal of Child Language, 23*(2), 369–395.

Pine, J. M., Lieven, E. V. M. & Rowland, C. F. (1998). Comparing different models of the development of the English verb category. *Linguistics, 36*(4), 807–830.

Pine, J. M., Freudenthal, D., Krajewski, G. & Gobet, F. (2013). Do young children have adult-like syntactic categories? Zipf's law and the case of the determiner. *Cognition, 127*(3), 345–361.

Pine, J. M., Conti-Ramsden, G., Joseph, K. L., Lieven, E. V. M. & Serratrice, L. (2008). Tense over time: Testing the Agreement/Tense Omission model as an account of the pattern of tense-marking provision in early child English. *Journal of Child Language, 35*(1), 55–75.

Pinker, S. (1979). Formal models of language learning. *Cognition, 7*(3), 217–283.

Pinker, S. (1984). *Language learnability and language development.* Cambridge, MA: Harvard University Press.

Pinker, S. (1989). *Learnability and cognition: The acquisition of argument structure.* Cambridge, MA: MIT Press.

Pinker, S. (1994). *The language instinct: How the mind creates language.* New York: Morrow.

Pinker, S. (1999) *Words and rules: The ingredients of language.* New York: HarperCollins.

Pinker, S. & Bloom, P. (1990). Natural language and natural selection. *Behavioral and Brain Sciences, 13*(4), 707–784.

Pinker, S. & Jackendoff, R. (2005). What's special about the human language faculty? *Cognition, 95*(2), 201–236.

Pinker, S. & Prince, A. (1988). On language and connectionism: Analysis of a parallel distributed processing model of language acquisition. *Cognition, 28*(1–2), 73–193.

Pinker, S. & Ullman, M. (2002a) The past and future of the past tense. *Trends in Cognitive Science, 6*(11), 456–463.

Pinker, S. & Ullman, M. (2002b) Structure and combination, not gradedness, is the issue (Reply to McClelland and Patterson). *Trends in Cognitive Science, 6*(11), 472–474.

Pisoni, D. B. (1977). Identification and discrimination of the relative onset of two component tones: Implications for voicing perception in stop consonants. *Journal of the Acoustical Society of America, 61*(5), 1352–1361.

Pizzuto, E. & Caselli, M. (1992). The acquisition of Italian morphology: Implications for models of language development. *Journal of Child Language, 19*(3), 491–557.

Plomin, R., DeFries, J. C., McClearn, G. E. & McGuffin, P. (2001). *Behavioral genetics* (4th ed.). New York: Worth Publishers.

Plunkett, K. & Marchman, V. M. (1991). U-shaped learning and frequency effects in a multi-layered perceptron: Implications for child language acquisition. *Cognition, 38*(1), 43–102.

Poizner, H., Klima, E. S. & Bellugi, U. (1987). *What the hands reveal about the brain.* Cambridge, MA: Bradford Books / MIT Press.

Polka, L., Sundara, M. & Blue, S. (2002). *The role of language experience in word segmentation: A comparison of English, French, and bilingual infants.* Paper presented at the 143rd meeting of the Acoustical Society of America, Pittsburgh.

Pouscoulous, N., Noveck, I. A., Politzer, G. & Bastide, A. (2007). A developmental investigation of processing costs in implicature production. *Language Acquisition, 14*(4), 347–376.

Prince, A. & Smolensky, P. (1997). Optimality: From neural networks to universal grammar. *Science, 275,* 1604–1610.

Pruden, S. M., Hirsh-Pasek, K., Golinkoff, R. M. & Hennon, E. A. (2006). The birth of words: Ten-month-olds learn words through perceptual salience. *Child Development, 77*(2), 266–280.

Pullum, G. K. & Scholz, B. C. (2002). Empirical assessment of stimulus poverty arguments. *The Linguistic Review, 19*(1–2), 9–50.

Pulverman, R., Golinkoff, R. M., Hirsh-Pasek, K. & Buresh, J. S. (2008). Infants discriminate manners and paths in non-linguistic dynamic events. *Cognition, 108*(3), 825–830.

Pye, C. (1990). The acquisition of ergative languages. *Linguistics, 28*(6), 1291–1330.

Pye, C. (1991). The Acquisition of K'iche' (Maya) In D. Slobin (Ed.), *The crosslinguistic study of language acquisition* (Vol. 3, pp. 221–308). Hillsdale, NJ: Lawrence Erlbaum Associates.

Pye, C. (1992). Language loss among the Chilcotin. *International Journal of the Sociology of Language, 93*(1), 75–86.

Pye, C., Pfeiler, B. & Mateo Pedro, P. (2013). The acquisition of extended ergativity in Mam, Q'anjob'al and Yucatec. In E. L. Bavin & S. Stoll (Eds), *The acquisition of ergativity.* Amsterdam: John Benjamins.

Quine, W. V. O. (1960). *Word and object.* Cambridge, MA: MIT Press.

Radford, A. (1990). *Syntactic theory and the acquisition of English syntax: The nature of early child grammars of English.* Oxford: Blackwell.

Ramscar, M. J. A. (2002). The role of meaning in inflection: Why the past tense doesn't require a rule. *Cognitive Psychology, 45*(2), 45–94.

Rapin, I. & Allen, D. A. (1983). Developmental language disorders: Nosological considerations. In U. Kirk (Ed.), *Neuropsychology of language, reading and spelling* (pp. 155–180). New York: Academic Press.

Rapin, I. & Allen, D. A. (1987). Developmental dysphasia and autism in preschool children: Characteristics and subtypes. In J. Martin, P. Fletcher, R. Grunwell & D. Hall (Eds), *Proceedings of the first international symposium on specific speech and language disorders in children.* London: Afasic.

Rapin, I. & Dunn, M. (2003). Update on the language disorders of individuals on the autistic spectrum. *Brain and Development, 25*(3), 166–172.

Räsänen, S. H. M., Ambridge, B. and Pine, J. M. (in press). Infinitives or bare stems? Are English-speaking children defaulting to the highest frequency form? *Journal of Child Language.*

Redlinger, W. E. & Park, T. (1980). Language mixing in young bilinguals. *Journal of Child Language, 7*(2), 337–352.

Rice, M. L. & Wexler, K. (1996). Toward tense as a clinical marker of specific language impairment in English-speaking children. *Journal of Speech and Hearing Research, 39*(6), 1239–1257.

Rice, M. L., Ruff Noll, K. & Grimm, H. (1997). An extended optional infinitive stage in German-speaking children. *Language Acquisition, 6*(4), 255–296.

Rice, M. L., Wexler, K. & Cleave, P. (1995). Specific language impairment as a period of extended optional infinitive. *Journal of Speech and Hearing Research, 38*(4), 850–863.

Rice, M. L., Oetting, J. B., Marquis, J., Bode, J. & Pae, S. (1994). Frequency of input effects on word comprehension of children with specific language impairment. *Journal of Speech and Hearing Research, 37*, 106–122.

Richards, B. J. (1990). *Language development and individual differences: A study of auxiliary verb learning.* Cambridge: Cambridge University Press.

Rispoli, M. (1998). Patterns of pronoun case error. *Journal of Child Language, 25*, 533–554.

Rivera-Gaxiola, M., Silva-Pereyra, J. & Kuhl, P. K. (2005). Brain potentials to native and non-native speech contrasts in 7- and 11-month-old American infants. *Developmental Science, 8*, 162–172.

Rizzi, L. (1982). *Issues in Italian syntax.* Dordrecht: Foris.

Rizzi, L. (1993). Some notes on linguistic theory and language development. *Language Acquisition, 3*(4), 371–394.

Rizzi, L. (2009). The discovery of language invariance and variation, and its relevance for the cognitive sciences. *Brain and Behavioral Sciences, 32*(5), 467–468.

Rizzolatti, G. & Arbib, M. A. (1998). Language within our grasp. *Trends in Neurosciences, 21*(5), 188–194.

Roberts, J., Krakow, R. & Pollock, K. (2003). Language outcomes for preschool children adopted from China as infants and toddlers. *Journal of Multilingual Communication Disorders, 1*(3), 177–183.

Rohde, D. L. T. & Plaut, D. C. (1999). Language acquisition in the absence of explicit negative evidence: How important is starting small? *Cognition, 72*(1), 67–109.

Rourke, B. P. & Tsatsanis, K. D. (1996). Syndrome of nonverbal learning disabilities: Psycholinguistic assets and deficits. *Topics in Language Disorders, 16*(2), 30–44.

Rowe, M. L. (2008). Child-directed speech: Relation to socioeconomic status, knowledge of child development, and child vocabulary skill. *Journal of Child Language, 35*(1), 95–120.

Rowland, C. F. (2007). Explaining errors in children's questions. *Cognition, 104*(1), 106–134.

Rubino, R. & Pine, J. M. (1998). Subject–verb agreement in Brazilian Portuguese: What low error rates hide. *Journal of Child Language, 25*, 35–60.

Rumelhart, D. E. & McClelland, J. L. (1986). On learning the past tenses of English verbs. In J. L. McClelland, D. E. Rumelhart & the PDP Research Group (Eds), *Parallel distributed processing: Explorations in the microstructure of cognition* (Vol. 2, pp. 216–227). Cambridge, MA: MIT Press.

Rymer, R. (1993). *Genie: An abused child's flight from silence.* New York: HarperCollins.

Saer, O. J. (1923). The effect of bilingualism on intelligence. *British Journal of Psychology, 14*(1), 25–28.

Saffran, J. R., Aslin, R. N. & Newport, E. L. (1996). Statistical learning by 8-month-old infants. *Science, 274*(5294), 1926–1928.

Salomo, D., Graf, E., Lieven, E. V. M. & Tomasello, M. (2011). The role of perceptual availability and discourse context in young children's question answering. *Journal of Child Language, 38*(4), 918–931.

Sampson, T. (1987). A turning point in linguistics. *Times Literary Supplement,* 643.

Samuelson, L. K. & Smith, L. B. (1998). Memory and attention make smart word learning: An alternative account of Akhtar, Carpenter, and Tomasello. *Child Development, 69*(1), 94–104.

Sandler, W., Meir, I., Padden, C. & Aronoff, M. (2005). The emergence of grammar: Systematic structure in a new language. *Proceedings of the National Academy of Sciences, 102*(7), 2661–2665.

Savage-Rumbaugh, E. S. (1996). *Kanzi. The ape at the brink of the human mind.* New York: Wiley.

Savage-Rumbaugh, E. S. (1999). Ape language: Between a rock and a hard place. In B. J. King (Ed.), *The origins of language: What nonhuman primates can tell us* (pp. 115–189). Santa Fe, NM: School of American Research Press.

Savage-Rumbaugh, E. S., Rumbaugh, D. M. & Fields, W. M. (2009). Empirical Kanzi: The ape language controversy revisited. *Skeptic, 15*(1), 25–33.

Savage-Rumbaugh, E. S., MacDonald, K., Sevcik, R. A., Hopkins, W. D. & Rubert, E. (1986). Spontaneous symbol acquisition and communication use by pygmy chimpanzees (*Pan paniscus*). *Journal of Experimental Psychology: General, 115*(3), 211–235.

Savage-Rumbaugh, E. S., Murphy, J., Sevcik, R., Brakke, K. E., Williams, S. L. & Rumbaugh, D. M. (1993). Language comprehension in ape and child. *Monographs of the Society for Research in Child Development 58*, (2–4), 1–220.

Saxton, M. (2000). Negative evidence and negative feedback: Immediate effects on the grammaticality of child speech. *First Language, 20*(2), 221–252.

Saxton, M. (2010). *Child language: Acquisition and development.* London: Sage.

Scarborough, H. & Wyckoff, J. (1986). Mother, I'd still rather do it myself: Some further non-effects of 'motherese'. *Journal of Child Language, 13*(2), 431–437.

Schauwers, K., Govaerts, P. & Gillis, S. (2002). *Language acquisition in very young children with a cochlear implant.* Antwerp: University of Antwerp.

Schick, B., Marschark, M. & Spencer, P. E. (2005). *Advances in the sign language development of deaf children.* Oxford: Oxford University Press.

Schirmer, B. R. (2001). *Psychological, social, and educational dimensions of deafness.* Boston, MA: Allyn and Bacon.

Scholz, B. C. & Pullum, G. K. (2002). Searching for arguments to support linguistic nativism. *The Linguistic Review, 19*(1–2), 185–223.

Schütze, C. T. & Wexler, K. (1996). *Subject case licensing and English root infinitives.* Paper presented at the 20th Boston University Conference on Language Development, Boston, USA.

Scott, C. M. (1984). Adverbial connectivity in conversations of children 6 to 12. *Journal of Child Language, 11*(2), 423–452.

Sebastián-Gallés, N., Echeverría, S. & Bosch, L. (2005). The influence of initial exposure on lexical representation: Comparing early and simultaneous bilinguals. *Journal of Memory and Language, 52*(2), 240–255.

Seidenberg, M. S. (1992). Connectionism without tears. In S. Davis. (Ed.), *Connectionism: Theory and practice* (pp. 84–122). New York: Oxford University Press.

Seidenberg, M. S. & Petitto, L. A. (1987). Communication, symbolic communication and language in child and chimpanzee: Comment on Savage-Rumbaugh, McDonald, Sevcik, Hopkins, and Rupert (1986). *Journal of Experimental Psychology, General, 116*(3), 279–287.

Senghas, A. (2003). Intergenerational influence and ontogenetic development in the emergence of spatial grammar in Nicaraguan Sign Language. *Cognitive Development, 18*(4), 511–531.

Senghas, A. & Coppola, M. (2001). Children creating language: How Nicaraguan Sign Language acquired a spatial grammar. *Psychological Sciences, 12*(4), 323–328.

Serratrice, L. (2002). *Syntax and pragmatics in the acquisition of Italian subjects.* Paper presented at the 9th International Congress for the Study of Child Language, Madison, USA.

Serratrice, L. (2012). The bilingual child. In T. K. Bhatia & W. C. Ritchie (Eds), *Handbook of bilingualism* (pp. 87–108). Oxford: Blackwell Publishing.

Serratrice, L. (2013). Cross-linguistic influence in bilingual development: Determinants and mechanisms. *Linguistic Approaches to Bilingualism, 3*(1), 5–27.

Serratrice, L., Sorace, A. & Paoli, S. (2004). Crosslinguistic influence at the syntax–pragmatics interface: Subjects and objects in English–Italian bilingual and monolingual acquisition. *Bilingualism: Language and Cognition, 7*(3), 183–206.

Sethuraman, N., Goldberg, A. & Goodman, J. (1997). *Using the semantics associated with syntactic frames for interpretation without the aid of non-linguistic context.* Paper presented at the Proceedings of the 27th Annual Child Language Research Forum.

Seyfarth, R. M., Cheney, D. L. & Marler, P. (1980). Vervet monkey alarm calls: Semantic communication in a free-ranging primate. *Animal Behaviour, 28*(4), 1070–1094.

Shields, J., Varley, R., Broks, P. & Simpson, A. (1996). Social cognition in developmental language disorders and high-level autism. *Developmental Medicine and Child Neurology, 38*(6), 487–495.

Shin, S. J. (2002). Birth order and the language experience of bilingual children. *TESOL Quarterly, 36*(1), 103–113.

Shneidman, L. & Goldin-Meadow, S. (2012). Language input and acquisition in a Mayan village: How important is directed speech? *Developmental Science, 15*(5), 659–673.

Siegel, J. (2008). *The emergence of Pidgin and Creole languages.* Oxford: Oxford University Press.

Siegel, L. (2000). *Ergativity and semantic bootstrapping.* Paper presented at the LSA Annual Meeting, Chicago.

Simon, J. R. (1969). Reactions toward the source of stimulation. *Journal of Experimental Psychology, 81*(1), 174–176.

Sinnott, J. M. (1998). Comparative phoneme boundaries. *Current Topics in Acoustical Research, 2*, 135–138.

Skarabela, B. (2007). Signs of early social cognition in children's syntax: The case of joint attention in argument realization in child Inuktitut. *Lingua, 117*(11), 1837–1857.

Skinner, B. F. (1957). *Verbal behavior.* New York: Appleton-Century-Crofts.

Slobin, D. (1973). Cognitive prerequisites for the development of grammar. In C. A. Ferguson & D. I. Slobin (Eds), *Studies of child language development* (pp. 175–208). New York: Holt, Rinehart and Winston.

Slobin, D. (1985). *The cross linguistic study of language acquisition.* Hillsdale, NJ: Lawrence Erlbaum Associates.

Slobin, D. (2006). Issues of linguistic typology in the study of sign language development of deaf children. In B. Schick, M. Marschark & P. E. Spencer (Eds), *Advances in the sign language development of deaf children* (pp. 20–45). Oxford: Oxford University Press.

Smiley, P. & Huttenlocher, J. (1994). Beyond names for things: Young children's acquisition of verbs. In M. Tomasello & W. Merriman (Eds), *Conceptual development and the child's early words for events, objects and persons* (pp. 21–61). Hillsdale, NJ: Lawrence Erlbaum Associates.

Smith, L. B. (2000). Avoiding associations when it's behaviorism you really hate. In R. Golinkoff & K. Hirsh-Pasek (Eds), *Becoming a word learner: A debate on lexical acquisition* (pp. 169–172). Oxford: Oxford University Press.

Smith, L. B. & Yu, C. (2008). Infants rapidly learn word-referent mappings via cross-situational statistics. *Cognition, 106*(3), 1558–1568.

Smith, L. B., Jones, S. S., Yoshida, H. & Colunga, E. (2003). Whose DAM account? Attentional learning explains Booth and Waxman. *Cognition, 87*(3), 209–213.

Smith, M. C. (1997). How do bilinguals access lexical information? In A. M. B. de Groot & J. F. Kroll (Eds), *Tutorials in bilingualism: Psycholinguistic perspectives* (pp. 145–168). Mahwah, NJ: Lawrence Erlbaum Associates.

Smith, N. V. (1973). *The acquisition of phonology: A case study.* Cambridge: Cambridge University Press.

Smith-Hefner, B. (1988). The linguistics socialization of Javanese children. *Anthropological Linguistics, 30*(2), 166–198.

Smoczyńska, M. (1986). The acquisition of Polish. In D. Slobin (Ed.), *The crosslinguistic study of language acquisition* (Vol. 1, pp. 595–686). Hillsdale, NJ: Lawrence Erlbaum Associates.

Snow, C. E. (1972). Mothers' speech to children learning language. *Child Development, 43*(2), 549–565.

Snow, C. E. (1977). The development of conversation between mothers and babies. *Journal of Child Language, 4*(1), 1–22.

Snow, C. E. & Ferguson, C. A. (1977). *Talking to children: Language input and acquisition.* Cambridge: Cambridge University Press.

Sorace, A. (2006). The more, the merrier: Facts and beliefs about the bilingual mind. In S. Della Sala (Ed.), *Tall tales about the mind and brain: Separating fact from fiction* (pp. 193–203). Oxford: Oxford University Press.

Spence, M. J. & Freeman, M. S. (1996). Newborn infants prefer the maternal low-pass filtered voice, but not the maternal whispered voice. *Infant Behavior and Development, 19*(2), 199–212.

Spolsky, B. (2004). *Language policy.* Cambridge: Cambridge University Press.

Sridhar, S. N. & Sridhar, K. K. (1980). The syntax and psycholinguistics of bilingual code mixing. *Studies in the Linguistic Sciences, 10*(1), 203–215.

St Clair, M. C., Monaghan, P. & Christiansen, M. H. (2010). Learning grammatical categories from distributional cues: Flexible frames for language acquisition. *Cognition, 116*(3), 341–360.

Stager, C. L. & Werker, J. F. (1997). Infants listen for more phonetic detail in speech perception than in word learning tasks. *Nature, 388*(6640), 381–382.

Steels, L. & de Boer, B. (2007). Embodiment and self-organization of human categories. A case study for speech. In J. Zlatev, T. Ziemke, R. Frank & R. Dirven (Eds), *Body, language, and mind* (Vol. 1, pp. 241–259). Berlin: Mouton de Gruyter.

Stefanowitsch, A. (2011). Constructional preemption by contextual mismatch: A corpus-linguistic investigation. *Cognitive Linguistics, 22*(1), 107–129.

Stephens, G. & Matthews, D. (2013). Pragmatic development in infancy. In D. Matthews (Ed.), *Pragmatic development in first language acquisition.* Amsterdam: John Benjamins.

Stivers, T., Enfield, N. J., Brown, P., Englert, C., Hayashi, M., Heinemann, T., ... Levinson, S. C. (2009). Universals and cultural variation in turn-taking in conversation. *Proceedings of the National Academy of Sciences, 106*, 10587–10592.

Street, J. A. & Dabrowska, E. (2010). More individual differences in language attainment: How much do adult native speakers of English know about passives and quantifiers? *Lingua, 120*(8), 2080–2094.

Stromswold, K. (2001). The heritability of language: A review and metaanalysis of twin, adoption, and linkage studies. *Language, 77*(4), 647–723.

Swain, M. (1972). *Bilingualism as a first language.* Irvine: University of California.

Swain, M. (1977). Bilingualism, monolingualism and code acquisition In W. Mackey & T. Andersson (Eds), *Bilingualism in early childhood* (pp. 28–35). Rowley, MA: Newbury House.

Swingley, D. (2005). Statistical clustering and the contents of the infant vocabulary. *Cognitive Psychology, 50*(1), 86–132.

Szagun, G., Stumper, B., Sondag, N. & Franik, M. (2007). The acquisition of gender marking by young German speaking children: Evidence for learning guided by phonological regularities. *Journal of Child Language, 34*(3), 445–471.

Tager-Flusberg, H. (1992). Autistic children's talk about psychological states: Deficits in the early acquisition of a theory of mind. *Child Development, 63*(1), 161–172.

Tager-Flusberg, H. (2000). Language and understanding minds: Connections in autism. In S. Baron-Cohen, H. Tager-Flusberg & D. J. Cohen (Eds), *Understanding other minds: Perspectives from autism and developmental cognitive neuroscience* (2nd ed.; pp. 1–45). Oxford: Oxford University Press.

Tager-Flusberg, H. (2007). Evaluating the theory-of-mind theory of autism. *Current Directions in Psychological Science, 16*(6), 311–315.

Tager-Flusberg, H. & Anderson, M. (1991). The development of contingent discourse ability in autistic children. *Journal of Child Psychology and Psychiatry, 32*(7), 1123–1134.

Tallal, P. & Piercy, M. (1973a). Defects of non-verbal auditory perception in children with developmental aphasia. *Nature, 241*, 468–469.

Tallal, P. & Piercy, M. (1973b). Developmental aphasia: Impaired rate of non-verbal processing as a function of sensory modality. *Neuropsychologia, 11*(4), 389–398.

Tallal, P., Stark, R. & Mellits, E. (1985). Identification of language-impaired children on the basis of rapid perception and production skills. *Brain and Language, 25*(2), 314–322.

Tallal, P., Miller, S. L., Bedi, G., Byma, G., Wang, X., Nagarajan, S. S., Schreiner, C., Jenkins, W. M. & Merzenich, M. M. (1996). Language comprehension in language-learning impaired children improved with acoustically modified speech. *Science, 271*(5245), 81–84.

Tardif, T. (1996). Nouns are not always learned before verbs: Evidence from Mandarin speakers' early vocabularies. *Developmental Psychology, 32*(3), 492–504.

Tavakolian, S. (1981). The conjoined clause analysis of relative clauses. In S. Tavakolian (Ed.), *Language acquisition and linguistic theory* (pp. 167–187). Cambridge, MA: MIT Press.

Terrace, H. S. (1979). *Nim.* New York: Knopf.

Theakston, A. L. (2004). The role of entrenchment in constraining children's verb argument structure overgeneralisations: A grammaticality judgment study. *Cognitive Development, 19*, 15–34.

Theakston, A. L., Lieven, E. V. M. & Tomasello, M. (2003). The role of input in the acquisition of third-person singular verbs in English. *Journal of Speech Language and Hearing Research, 46*(4), 863–877.

Theakston, A. L., Lieven, E. V. M., Pine, J. M. & Rowland, C. F. (2001). The role of performance limitations in the acquisition of verb-argument structure: An alternative account. *Journal of Child Language, 28*(1), 127-152.

Theakston, A. L., Lieven, E. V. M., Pine, J. M. & Rowland, C. F. (2005). The acquisition of auxiliary syntax: BE and HAVE. *Cognitive Linguistics, 16*(1), 247-277.

Thiessen, E. D. & Saffran, J. R. (2003). When cues collide: Statistical and stress cues in infant word segmentation. *Developmental Psychology, 39*(4), 706–716.

Tomasello, M. (1992). *First verbs: A case study of early lexical development*. Cambridge: Cambridge University Press.

Tomasello, M. (1994). Language is not an instinct. Review of Pinker's (1994) *The language instinct: How the mind creates language*. New York: William Morrow. *Cognitive Development, 10*(1), 131–156.

Tomasello, M. (2000). Do young children have adult syntactic competence? *Cognition, 74*(3), 209–253.

Tomasello, M. (2003). *Constructing a language: A usage-based theory of language acquisition*. Cambridge, MA: Harvard University Press.

Tomasello, M. (2005). Beyond formalities: The case of language acquisition. *The Linguistic Review, 22*(2–4), 183–197.

Tomasello, M. (2008). *Origins of human communication*. Cambridge, MA: MIT Press.

Tomasello, M. & Abbot-Smith, K. (2002). A tale of two theories: Response to Fisher. *Cognition, 83*(2), 207–214.

Tomasello, M. & Akhtar, N. (1995). Two-year-olds use pragmatic cues to differentiate reference to objects and actions. *Cognitive Development, 10*(2), 201–224.

Tomasello, M. & Barton, M. (1994). Learning words in nonostensive contexts. *Developmental Psychology, 30*(5), 639–650.

Tomasello, M. & Kruger, A. C. (1992). Joint attention on actions: Acquiring verbs in ostensive and non-ostensive contexts. *Journal of Child Language, 19*(2), 311–333.

Tomasello, M., Carpenter, M. & Liszkowski, U. (2007). A new look at infant pointing. *Child Development, 78*, 705–722.

Trauner, D., Wulfeck, B., Tallal, P. & Hesselink, J. (1995). Neurologic and MRI profiles of language impaired children. Technical Report CND-9513. Center for Research in Language: University of California at San Diego.

Trehub, S. E. (1976). The discrimination of foreign speech contrasts by infants and adults. *Child Development, 47*(2), 466–472.

Tuominen, A. (1999). Who decides the home language: A look at multilingual families. *International Journal of the Sociology of Language 140*(1), 49–76.

Valian, V. (1986). Syntactic categories in the speech of young children. *Developmental Psychology, 22*(4), 562–579.

Valian, V., Solt, S. & Stewart, J. (2009). Abstract categories or limited-scope formulae: The case of children's determiners. *Journal of Child Language, 36*(4), 749–778.

van der Lely, H. K. J. (1994). Canonical linking rules: Forward vs reverse linking in normally developing and specificially language impaired children. *Cognition, 51*(1), 29–72.

van der Lely, H. K. J., Rosen, S. & McClelland, A. (1998). Evidence for a grammar-specific deficit in children. *Current Biology, 8*(23), 1253–1258.

van Gelderen, V. & Van der Meulen, I. (1998). *Root infinitives in Russian: Evidence from acquisition*. Unpublished manuscript. Leiden University.

van Hoek, K. (1997). *Anaphora and conceptual structure*. Chicago: Chicago University Press.

Van Valin, R. (1993). A synopsis of role and reference grammar. In R. Van Valin (Ed.), *Advances in role and reference grammar* (pp. 1–164). Amsterdam: John Benjamins.

Vihman, M. M. (1976). From prespeech to speech: On early phonology. *Stanford Papers and Reports on Child Language Development, 12*, 230–244.

Vihman, M. M. (1978). Consonant harmony: Its scope and function in child language. In J. H. Greenberg (Ed.), *Universals of human language* (pp. 281–334). Palo Alto, CA: Stanford University Press.

Vihman, M. M. (1993). Variable paths to early word production. *Journal of Phonetics, 21*, 61–82.

Vihman, M. M. (1996). *Phonological development: The origins of language in the child*. Oxford: Basil Blackwell.

Vihman, M. M. & Croft, W. (2007). Phonological development: Toward a 'radical' templatic phonology. *Linguistics, 45*(4), 683–725.

Vihman, M. M. & Velleman, S. L. (2000). Phonetics and the origins of phonology. In N. Noël Burton-Roberts, P. Philip Carr & G. Docherty (Eds), *Phonological knowledge* (pp. 305–339). Oxford: Oxford University Press.

Vihman, M. M., Macken, M. A., Miller, R., Simmons, H. & Miller, J. (1985). From babbling to speech: A re-assessment of the continuity issue. *Language, 61*(20), 397–445.

Volterra, V. & Taeschner, T. (1978). The acquisition and development of language by bilingual children. *Journal of Child Language, 5*(2), 311–326.

von Frisch, K. (1954). *The dancing bees: An account of the life and senses of the honeybee* (D. Ilse, Trans.). London: Methuen & Co Ltd.

Wade, N. (2002, 15 August). Language gene is traced to emergence of humans, *The New York Times*.

Waterson, N. (1971). Child phonology. *Journal of Linguistics, 7*, 179–211.

Watson, J. (2002). A genomewide scan identifies two novel loci involved in specific language impairment. *American Journal of Human Genetics, 70*(2), 384–398.

Weber-Fox, C. & Neville, H. J. (1996). Maturational constraints on functional specializations for language processing: ERP and behavioral evidence in bilingual speakers. *Journal of Cognitive Neuroscience, 8*, 231–256.

Werker, J. F. & Curtin, S. (2005). PRIMIR: A developmental framework of infant speech processing. *Language Learning and Development, 1*(2), 197–234.

Werker, J. F. & Tees, R. C. (1984). Cross-language speech perception: Evidence for perceptual reorganization during the first year of life. *Infant Behavior and Development, 7*, 49–63.

Werker, J. F., Fennell, C. T., Corcoran, K. & Stager, C. L. (2002). Infants' ability to learn phonetically similar words: Effects of age and vocabulary size. *Infancy, 3*(1), 1–30.

Wexler, K. (1998). Very early parameter setting and the unique checking constraint: A new explanation of the optional infinitive stage. *Lingua, 106*(1–4), 23–79.

Wijnen, F. (1996). Temporal reference and eventivity in root infinitives. *MIT Occasional Papers in Linguistics, 12*, 1–5.

Wilson, S. (2003). Lexically specific constructions in the acquisition of inflection in English. *Journal of Child Language, 30*(1), 75–115.

Wolk, S. & Schildroth, A. N. (1986). Deaf children and speech intelligibility: A national study. In A. N. Schildroth & M. A. Karchmer (Eds), *Deaf children in America* (pp. 139–159). Boston, MA: College-Hill Press.

Woll, B. & Kyle, J. G. (1989). Communication and language development in children of deaf parents. In S. Tetzchner, L. S. Siegel & L. Smith (Eds), *Social and cognitive aspects of normal and atypical language development* (pp. 129–145). New York: Springer Verlag.

Wonnacott, E., Newport, E. L. & Tanenhaus, M. K. (2008). Acquiring and processing verb argument structure: Distributional learning in a miniature language. *Cognitive Psychology, 56*(3), 165–209.

Woodward, A. L. & Markman, E. M. (1998). Early word learning. In W. Damon, D. Kuhn & R. Siegler (Eds), *Handbook of child psychology, Volume 2: Cognition, perception and language* (pp. 371–420). New York: John Wiley and Sons.

Woolfe, T., Herman, R., Roy, P. & Woll, B. (2010). Early vocabulary development in deaf native signers: A British Sign Language adaptation of the communicative development inventories. *Journal of Child Psychology and Psychiatry, 51*(3), 322–331.

Wuillemin, D., Richardson, B. & Lynch, J. (1994). Right hemisphere involvement in processing later-learned languages in multilinguals. *Brain and Language, 46*(4), 620–636.

Xu, F. & Tenenbaum, J. B. (Eds). (2005). *Word learning as Bayesian inference: Evidence from preschoolers.* Proceedings of the 27th Annual Conference of the Cognitive Science Society.

Yang, C. (2002). *Knowledge and learning in natural language.* Oxford: Oxford University Press.

Yip, V. & Matthews, S. (2000). Syntactic transfer in a Cantonese–English bilingual child. *Bilingualism: Language and Cognition, 3*(3), 193–208.

Yip, V. & Matthews, S. (2007). *The bilingual child: Early development and language contact.* Cambridge: Cambridge University Press.

Zentella, A. C. (1997). *Growing up bilingual: Puerto Rican children in New York.* Oxford: Blackwell.

Zwanziger, E. E., Allen, S. E. M. & Genesee, F. (2005). Crosslinguistic influence in bilingual acquisition: Subject omission in learners of Inuktitut and English. *Journal of Child Language, 32*(4), 893–909.

Index

Only first authors of references are indexed

www.routledge.com/linguistics

Understanding Pragmatics

By Gunter Senft

Understanding Pragmatics takes an interdisciplinary approach to provide an accessible introduction to language use.

This book discusses how the meaning of utterances can only be understood in relation to overall cultural, social and interpersonal contexts as well as culture specific conventions and the speech events in which they are embedded. Discussed from a cross-linguistic and cross-cultural perspective, this book debates a selection of core issues within pragmatics such as speech act theory, conversational implicature, linguistic ideologies, gesture conversation analysis and interaction strategies. The insights into the complex field of the study of language use are illustrated with examples from a broad variety of different languages and cultures.

Written by an experienced teacher and researcher, this introductory textbook is essential reading for all students studying pragmatics.

2014 | 224 Pages | HB: 978-0-415-84056-9| PB: 978-1-44-418030-5
Learn more at: www.routledge.com/9781444122435

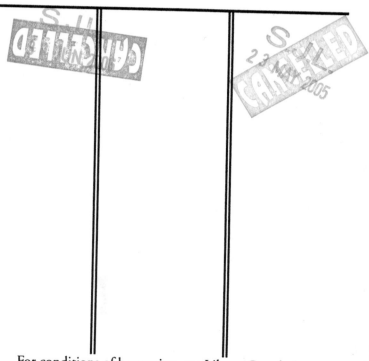

EDINBURGH TEXTBOOKS IN EMPIRICAL LINGUISTICS

CORPUS LINGUISTICS
by Tony McEnery and Andrew Wilson

LANGUAGE AND COMPUTERS
A PRACTICAL INTRODUCTION TO THE COMPUTER ANALYSIS OF LANGUAGE
by Geoff Barnbrook

If you would like information on forthcoming titles in this series, please contact
Edinburgh University Press, 22 George Square, Edinburgh EH8 9LF